Executive
Corporate Finance

FT Prentice Hall
FINANCIAL TIMES

In an increasingly competitive world, we believe it's quality of thinking that will give you the edge – an idea that opens new doors, a technique that solves a problem, or an insight that simply makes sense of it all. The more you know, the smarter and faster you can go.

That's why we work with the best minds in business and finance to bring cutting-edge thinking and best learning practice to a global market.

Under a range of leading imprints, including *Financial Times Prentice Hall*, we create world-class print publications and electronic products bringing our readers knowledge, skills and understanding which can be applied whether studying or at work.

To find out more about Pearson Education publications, or tell us about the books you'd like to find, you can visit us at www.pearsoned.co.uk

PEARSON
Education

Executive Corporate Finance

The business of enhancing shareholder value

SAMIR ASAF

FT Prentice Hall
FINANCIAL TIMES

An imprint of **Pearson Education**

London • New York • Toronto • Sydney • Tokyo • Singapore
Hong Kong • Cape Town • Madrid • Paris • Amsterdam • Munich • Milan

PEARSON EDUCATION LIMITED

Edinburgh Gate
Harlow CM20 2JE
Tel: +44 (0)1279 623623
Fax: +44 (0)1279 431059
Website: www.pearsoned.co.uk

First published in Great Britain in 2004
© Pearson Education Limited 2004

The right of Samir Asaf to be identified as author of this work has been
asserted by him in accordance with the Copyright, Designs and Patents Act 1988.

ISBN 0 273 67547 4

British Library Cataloguing-in-Publication Data
A catalogue record for this book is available from the British Library

Library of Congress Cataloging-in-Publication Data
Asaf, Samir, 1970-
    Executive corporate finance : the business of enhancing shareholder value / Samir Asaf.
        p. cm.
    Includes bibliographical references and index.
    ISBN 0-273-67549-4 (alk. paper)
     1. Corporations--Finance. 2. Corporations--Valuation. I. Title.

 HG4026.A83 2004
 658.15--dc22

                                                                    2004043636

This publication is designed to provide accurate and authoritative information in regard to
the subject matter covered. It is sold with the understanding that neither the authors nor
the publisher is engaged in rendering legal, investing, or any other professional service. If
legal advice or other expert assistance is required, the service of a competent professional
person should be sought.

The publisher and contributors make no representation, express or implied, with regard to the
accuracy of the information contained in this book and cannot accept any responsibility or liability
for any errors or omissions that it may contain.

10 9 8 7 6 5 4 3 2
08 07 06 05 04

Typeset in ITC Garamond light 10/14pt by 30
Printed and bound in Great Britain by Ashford Colour Press, Hampshire

The publisher's policy is to use paper manufactured from sustainable forests.

To Abbu & Amma…
the reason for all my reasons,

To Ammi, Barapu, Chotapu & Apu…
for all your affections.

Contents

Preface   viii

Acknowledgements   x

Chapter executive summaries   xii

1 Optimizing the corporate finance function   1

Introduction   1

The external business environment and corporate financial strategy   10

The strategic logic of high growth   15

2 Shareholder value maximization   24

Introduction   24

Corporate valuation   28

Valuation models: public company   30

Valuation models: closely held company   33

Corporate performance measurement: economic value added (EVA)   37

3 Financial policy   50

Introduction   50

Capital structure   51

Operating leverage   70

Dividend policy   71

Pricing strategy   78

Tax planning   87

Optimal capital budgeting with real options   100

Mergers and acquisitions   108

Asset-liability management: optimizing the balance sheet   118

4 Risk management   123

Introduction   123

Identifying and estimating risk exposure   126

Off-balance-sheet (OBS) risks 134
Financial risk management 146
Operational risk management 165
Enterprise wide risk management (EWRM) 187
Risk hedging strategies 220

5 Financial reporting, planning, and control 250

Introduction 250
Financial reporting: GAAP convergence 251
Business and financial planning 253
Treasury management 269
Financial control and audit 301
Optimize amid changing operating conditions 308

6 Corporate performance management: the balancing act? 311

Introduction 311
The execution problem 317
The balanced scorecard 319
Real-time financial systems: corporate performance management (CPM) 324
Integrated financial management 337

Appendix: Applied financial optimization modeling 340

Value maximization: analytical techniques 340
Company size, asset utilization, and financial leverage 341

Acronyms 343
Bibliography 346
Index 354

Preface

Today's fast-paced business environment demands effective implementation of corporate growth strategies through sophisticated financial management. There is a pressing need for clear strategies, and for adaptive and innovative implementation that can deliver on the objectives set out. Leading multinationals like AT&T, Citigroup, Daimler Chrysler, Exxon-Mobil, General Electric, GlaxoSmithKline, Hewlett-Packard, IBM, Intel, Merrill Lynch, Microsoft, Procter & Gamble, Royal Dutch/Shell, Siemens, and Toyota are employing corporate financial innovations as a source of gaining competitive advantage.

These firms have consistently demonstrated the ability to satisfy customers with compelling value propositions. They embody superior business and financial strategies, responsive leadership, in consort with operational integrity. They anticipate and prepare for critical events, and craft successful strategies to prosper amidst different scenarios. What these firms specifically do to build shareholder value is a matter we shall return to in the following pages. But companies around the globe are now facing a broad set of business challenges, including dramatically shortened business cycles and heightened competition. Increased uncertainty has placed a premium on effective execution of business strategies. In response, they are improving their strategic capabilities to out-maneuver the competition.

As these best-of-breed corporations follow the continuous improvement philosophy both in operational and financial management, the stakes get higher. Most companies have spent the last decade reengineering their operations for improved efficiencies. They are now applying real-time information systems and advanced financial management techniques enabling them to "sense-and-respond" optimally to changing business conditions.

This improvement is necessary just to stay in the game. Slow adopters in contrast find themselves failing to deliver on their financial objectives. The finance function plays a critical role here. However, constant and intense focus on running a business leaves little time for corporate executives like yourselves, to learn about the latest techniques and solutions. This book, therefore, presents an executive-level review of "best-in-class" corporate finance practice and insights, as we focus on the relationships among principal business functions and strategic finance.

Topics covered include shareholder value maximization, the balanced scorecard, economic value added, value at risk, enterprise-wide risk management, earnings at risk, tax planning, Monte Carlo simulation financial optimization, mergers and acquisitions, real options, treasury management, pricing strategy, and business planning. In this book, you will experience first-hand, how high-performance finance organizations across a broad spectrum of industries go about their business of creating and sustaining shareholder value, and can selectively apply best practices to your corporation's unique circumstances.

Samir Asaf
New Jersey, USA

Acknowledgements

I would like to thank the following individuals for their helpful comments on various drafts of the manuscript:

Syed Ali, CPA
Adriana Adjiashvili, MBA
Savant Ahmad, PhD
Mehreen Asaf, MBA
Jeofrey Bean, MBA
Professor Marc Bertoneche (Harvard/Bordeaux)
Yunhui Chen, PhD
Pradeep Crasto, MBA CFA
Arif Dowla, PhD
Fahim Dowla, MBA
Professor Michael Earl (Oxford)
Nitin Gupta, MBA
Kenneth Hannan, MBA
Julia Homer
Alexander Kaganovich, PhD
Michael Keenan, MBA CPA
Dilshad Khawaja, PhD
Bernd Klink, MBA
Michael Mahoney, MBA
Gregory Marsh, MBA CPA
Debra McCann, MBA
Professor John Mulvey (Princeton)
Youssef Nasr, MBA
Professor Richard Nolan (Harvard)
Gary Noyes, MSc
Montgomery Pereira, PhD
Professor Danny Quah (London School of Economics)

Douglas Ranck, MBA CPA
Jurgan Usman, MSc MBA
Robert Weiner, MBA
Christopher Womack, MBA
Zahide Yildirmaz, PhD

I would like to thank Holly Menino Bailey of Palisade Software for providing financial simulation optimization and decision analysis software. I would also like to thank Laurie Donaldson, formerly with Pearson Education, now with University of London's Imperial College Press, for his excellent support during the publication process. Lisa Reading of Pearson Education, Financial Times Prentice Hall, provided remarkable support. Thank you Lisa. I would like to thank Linda Dhondy for the thorough editing of the entire manuscript, and for many suggestions for improvement. Thanks Linda. Kate Salkilld provided superb support throughout the publication process. Thanks Kate. Julie Knight, Managing Editor of Higher & Professional Education Division at Pearson Education Ltd. provided outstanding support in the final phase of the editing work. Thanks Julie. Finally, a special thanks to Tamanna Rabbani for her encouragement and support.

Chapter executive summaries

1 Optimizing the corporate finance function

Each business is unique in terms of product, market, size, industry, management, culture, and financial strength. Companies need to tailor any generic corporate finance strategy or technique to their own unique needs and circumstances. The corporate finance function supports shareholder wealth creation by managing corporate growth objectives within a disciplined financial foundation. It ensures that return and risk objectives are balanced, and the financing, investing, and operating decisions are internally consistent.

Corporate financial management includes financial strategy alignment with the overall corporate strategy. Financial operations include financial reporting, risk management, treasury and investment management, capital planning, tax planning, financial planning, and performance assessment. In this chapter, we discuss different aspects of the finance function, and present a conceptual model that views these different finance functions in an integrated planning context. It uses the 'balanced scorecard' as the business performance assessment tool. We discuss the impact of the external business environment on corporate financial strategy, and the strategic logic of high growth.

2 Shareholder value maximization

Shareholder value is maximized when a company maximizes its growth opportunities by making superior financing and investing decisions, while optimally managing the operational risks of the business. In this chapter, we discuss the corporate shareholder valuation models, and analytical techniques for value maximization.

This includes minimization of earnings and cash flow volatility. It also includes minimization and optimization of the cost of capital through alternative financing vehicles. We discuss aspects of borrowing costs and define the effective borrowing rate for a company. We focus on the economic valuation aspects or economic value added (EVA) valuation techniques in addition to accounting-based valuations, and cover both publicly listed as well as privately held companies. We present a numerical calculation of a cash flow based valuation model using a detailed pro forma five-year business plan. We also calculate minority and controlling interest valuation of the intrinsic fair market value of a hypothetical privately held company. Finally, we discuss some general issues around maximizing shareholder value over time and use GlaxoSmithKline and DaimlerChrysler as examples of best practice. We also discuss value drivers and how these have an impact on value creation.

3 Financial policy

Corporations usually have some guidelines they use for financial management, such as dividend payout amounts or payout ratios, debt-to-equity ratios, accounts receivable-to-revenue ratios, and so on. As competition gets harder, simple rules-of-thumb or directionally right benchmarks are increasingly sub-optimal for corporate management purposes. Beyond the analytical techniques, however, optimal financial policy making involves superior insights into financial market dynamics, so that anticipated losses can be averted with appropriate risk management initiatives, and new market opportunities capitalized upon.

In this chapter, we discuss and demonstrate advanced quantitative techniques that are used to reach optimal financial policy decisions, and how they can be modified over time for dynamic optimization. We review issues around capital structure and show a quantitative model of how a theoretically optimal capital structure can be derived. Contingent convertibles are discussed as an example of recent innovations in derivatives used for leverage optimization. We review various asset- and liability-linked structured financing vehicles that are applied in practice, including alternative financing vehicles such as revolving lines of credit, banker's acceptances, commercial paper, reverse repurchase agreements, revolving credit agreements, capital and operating leases, and mezzanine financing. We review operating leverage optimization through outsourcing. We discuss issues around dividend policy optimization. For example, the impact of share buybacks as an effective means of correcting under-pricing, and other dividend policy optimization issues. We discuss the issue of optimal pricing strategy, and how it differs from strategic pricing. We review absorption cost versus variable cost pricing models, and present a systems context for price response estimation.

Next, tax planning issues are discussed, including tax arbitrage methods, the SAVANT tax planning model, and other issues around global tax policy optimization. We look at effective tax rates of IBM, DaimlerChrysler, Procter & Gamble and Toyota, and discuss Nestlé's tax planning including treatment of deferred taxation. We also review some of GlaxoSmithKline's tax planning issues. We review capital investment policy, and take a look at how "real options" methodology is applied to a numerical example of a capital investment. We review the traditional discounted cash flow model of net present value (NPV), and how that is modified with the value of an expansion option, a contraction option, and a real option to choose. Real options analysis extends the traditional NPV estimate to an expanded NPV (ENPV).

We conclude this chapter with a review of merger and acquisition (M&A) policy, and discuss why such a large portion of M&A deals do not deliver the anticipated "synergies." We look at IBM's acquisition of PricewaterhouseCoopers, Glaxo Wellcome's merger with SmithKline Beecham, and Exxon's merger with Mobil.

4 Risk management

This is a difficult topic, since risk, in general, is poorly understood and poorly estimated. Leading companies have integrated risk management systems in place that allow them to dynamically evaluate various financial risks such as exchange rate risk, interest rate risk, commodity price risk, and operational risks. By calling attention to potential fault lines in the corporate financial stability, risk management programs seek to play a major role in preventing crises before they erupt, thereby contributing to sustained stability in corporate financial results.

In this chapter, we look at asset-liability management and balance sheet optimization issues, and present Merrill Lynch as an example of best practice. After discussing some issues under the general theme of corporate risk management for both financial institutions and non-financial corporates, we review off-balance-sheet risks. We look at the content and context of Statement Financial Accounting Standards (SFAS) 133 for US GAAP and the International Accounting Standards (IAS) 39 accounting pronouncements for European corporates. Citigroup, IBM, General Electric, Ericsson, and Toyota's off-balance-sheet activities are reviewed.

We review issues around corporate financial risk management and present a calculation of the value at risk (VAR) of a two-asset portfolio. We look at how Citigroup, Siemens, Hong Kong Shanghai Banking Corporation (HSBC), AT&T, General Electric, Procter & Gamble, DaimlerChrysler, Toyota, Intel, Nestlé, and GlaxoSmithKline conduct their financial risk management practices. Next we discuss operational risk management, and discuss the delta-EVT method of operational risk estimation. Risk-adjusted performance measures are presented. We review operational risk management practices at HSBC, Citigroup, Ericsson, Merrill Lynch, DaimlerChrysler, Toyota, Intel, and Shell.

Enterprise-wide risk management (EWRM), where the different risk dimensions come together, are reviewed. We take a look at how alternative risk transfer (ART) instruments are increasingly being adopted by companies. Microsoft, Chase, DuPont, Citigroup, Siemens, Merrill Lynch, Ericsson, DaimlerChrysler, HSBC, Procter & Gamble, and DuPont's EWRM practices are reviewed. We calculate quarterly earnings at risk (EAR) for DaimlerChrysler and Microsoft, and cash flow at risk (CFAR) for Shell.

Specifically applicable for financial institutions, we review the revised Basel II accord for capital adequacy requirements and the three pillars of the new accord.

Finally, we review corporate risk hedging strategies using derivatives, and discuss hedging, synthetic asset exposure, speculation, and arbitrage. We present conceptual models of the risk management cycle, and discuss risk retention, risk transfer, and risk financing. We review the motivations for utilizing Credit Default Swaps. We review how Gillette, Toyota, Nestlé, IBM, Ericsson, Shell, GlaxoSmithKline, and Exxon-Mobil apply risk hedging strategies to their different risk exposures.

5 Financial reporting, planning, and control

In this chapter, we discuss general issues around financial planning and control, and issues around GAAP convergence. We present a conceptual model of financial reporting called Value-reporting™ developed by PricewaterhouseCoopers. We discuss issues around improving corporate financial planning, and present a detailed financial planning model for a hypothetical company linking its balance sheet, income statement, and cash flow. Finally, we discuss some issues on financial forecasting methods.

Next, we discuss the treasury function, and the linkage between financing, cash management, risk management, and tax planning. We review a company's operating cycle, cash conversion cycle, and cash flow timeline with detailed schematic representations. Cash conversion efficiency is defined along with a discussion of the different types of float. We also review latest best practices in liquidity management such as regional pooling, cash concentration structures, and straight through processing (STP). We look at how Coca-Cola, HSBC, Citigroup, Merrill Lynch, General Electric, Ericsson, Marks & Spencer, Toyota, Shell, Nestlé, Cisco, GlaxoSmithKline, and Hewlett-Packard optimise treasury operations.

We conclude this chapter with a review of best practices in financial control and audit. Strategic, tactical , and operational aspects are discussed. We review control structures in Citigroup, Marks & Spencer, Shell, Exxon-Mobil, and Merrill Lynch.

6 Performance management

In this chapter, we discuss corporate performance measurement and management issues. We look at some recent research around best practices, and find that good execution of strategy has been the principal difficulty for most corporations. Real-time performance management systems offer the most effective means of improving quality, execution and responsiveness.

We discuss the limitations of accrual-based accounting metrics, and review the "balanced scorecard" and how it is being used my many leading companies to better understand actual corporate performance. In the balanced scorecard, the financial perspective is complemented with the customer perspective, internal process perspective, and learning and growth perspective.

We conclude with a discussion of real-time financial systems, and how companies are using this tool to improve operational and financial performance.

Appendix: Applied optimization modeling

In this section, we briefly discuss how corporations can use advanced analytical techniques to help them make better decisions. We also point to the limitations of analytical techniques. We discuss how a financial planning model can be optimized using stochastic programing, incorporating uncertainty into the model, and how Monte Carlo simulations can be performed on the financial planning model to generate probabilistic estimates.

Financial data: annual revenue, asset utilization, and financial leverage

In this book, we review different aspects of financial management best practices of several global multinationals. In order to get an idea of size, here we present their annual revenues for 2002, revenues as a share of total book value of assets, and total debt in the capital structure as a share of total assets.

CHAPTER 1

Optimizing the corporate finance function

Introduction

In any corporation, the chief financial officer (CFO) plays a pivotal role – aligning business strategies with the financial capabilities of the company, and shareholders' demands for value creation with the chief executive officer's (CEO's) leadership of the business.

PricewaterhouseCoopers' recent global survey of 1,000 CEOs from 43 countries from Europe, North America, South and Central America, Africa, and Asia-Pacific shows that corporate finance plays the quintessential role in corporate strategy and leadership.[1]

In addition, a renewed focus on corporate sustainability indicates the vital importance of strategy, execution, and risk management to the continued profitability of the company. Seventy-one percent of CEOs said that they would sacrifice short-term profitability in exchange for long-term shareholder value when implementing a sustainability program.

CFOs are spending a growing proportion of their time with the CEO and business unit executives. They lead many enterprise-wide improvement initiatives, and participate in many others. This is partly because CFOs hold the financial key to all critical decisions.

To optimize financial, investment, and operating decision making, the corporate finance function provides essential decision support in business planning and financial control. World-class companies recognize that optimizing their finance functions is critical to success. Strategic financial planning involves managing the operating, investment, and financing policies of the firm (see Figure 1.1).

Ericsson needed to manage its expansion into an explosive growth market for mobile phones in the late 1990s. Shaping Ericsson's strategy in this market, where demand was rising over 30 percent a year, president Johan Siberg asked new CFO, Lars Lindquist, to continue improving the business control function. Lindquist saw finance as uniquely positioned to pool knowledge and information to create value for the business.[2]

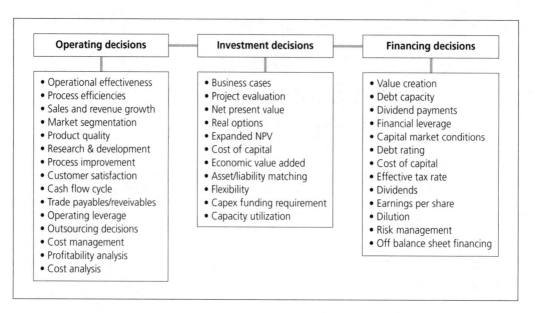

FIGURE 1.1 ■ Strategic financial planing

"Global competition and dynamically evolving business conditions are forcing companies to rethink many long-standing corporate practices. Corporations, particularly those that are highly leveraged or have significant international activity, are finding that the traditional activities and structures of their finance departments are inadequate to meet today's challenges."[3]

Both financial and non-financial corporations are simultaneously managing several aspects of the business: developing and executing corporate strategy in the light of competitive and macroeconomic dynamics, and optimizing marketing and sales initiatives. In addition, end-to-end product management, financial management, customer relationship management, operational effectiveness, human resources management, investor relations, and internal management leadership are areas that top executives spend a lot of time on.

When shareholder value maximization is the prime objective, optimal financial policy making and clever financial management become the key drivers of value creation. The financial function includes the sets of inter-connected responsibilities, shown in Figure 1.2.

More and more companies are adopting a business process approach.

To design internal responses to marketplace change, executives are implementing change as part of a process view: structural, people, and technological changes all tend to follow implementation of newly designed business processes. So, more and more companies are adopting a business process approach.

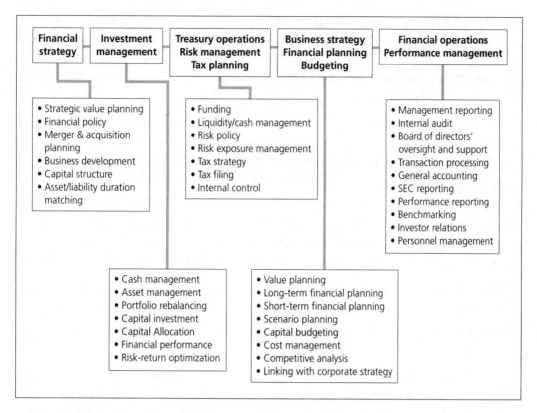

FIGURE 1.2 ■ The finance function

The changing external environment presents new risks as well as new opportunities to the business enterprise. In order to identify and capitalize on opportunities, it is necessary to develop a deep understanding of the industry and competitive dynamics affecting the business, and the company's competitive position within it. This is where insightful corporate strategy guides the company into new growth areas. But often, the main problem businesses face is not lack of growth opportunities, but a failure to optimally capitalize on existing ones. It is not a lack of good strategy, but poor execution, that has been the Achilles' heel for many otherwise successful companies.

Risk exposures are often not managed optimally because integrated corporate risk management has not been part of top management's agenda; corporate value is not being maximized because the companies are concerned only with revenue and accounting earnings, not economic value creation; and the business lacks key data on economic product margins or profits at a product, unit, or division level.

Without a balanced scorecard in place, corporate performance monitoring is often inadequate, resulting in sub-optimal utilization of resources; tax planning, pricing policy, and asset-liability management are not optimized as part of the financial planning process; and advanced analytical techniques are not used for financial optimization and real-time decision support. The corporate finance function is not optimized unless it addresses and resolves these issues, and supports corporate management in dynamically positioning the company for sustainable wealth creation.

> "Firms need to clearly define and communicate the roles and responsibilities of the board of directors, CEO, and CFO, in implementing sound corporate governance. As firms rethink their organisational structure, they will need to empower the CFO to balance two essential roles: as a financial steward and as a corporate strategist."[4]

A survey by Deloitte Consulting and *BusinessWeek* of 519 senior executives (members of boards of directors, CEOs, and CFOs) of US and Canadian firms with more than 1,000 employees, attempted to find out how corporations are responding to the new corporate governance environment and its effects on the role of the CFO. Key findings are as follows:[5]

- There appears to be considerable confusion over whether the CEO or the CFO leads the firm's efforts to respond to the new corporate governance rules and requirements.

- A large proportion of CEOs and CFOs disagree about the independence of the finance function.

- Executives are sharply divided on whether the CEO and chairman roles should be split between two individuals. "Although it is common for European firms to separate the roles of CEO and chairman, in the US, three out of four companies in the *Standard & Poor's* 500 have a single individual filling both roles."[6]

- Although the conventional view is that the CFOs have become strategists since the 1990s, more than two-thirds of board members, CFOs, and executive vice presidents (EVPs) said their CFO served primarily as a financial steward or else played a dual role as both a steward and a strategist.

- Only slightly more than half of the CEOs gave high ratings to the performance of their CFO as a strategic planner.

Figure 1.2 presents a view of the separation of power amongst the board, the CEO, and the CFO. In addition to defining roles, corporations need to ensure appropriate checks and balances. A critical question is the relative power of the board of directors and the CEO. When the balance of power tilts toward the CEO – as is almost inevitable when the CEO is also the chairman of the board – the result can be a "tyranny of the executive" with the potential for corporate excesses.

Corporate financial policies can be judiciously optimized in various areas such as capital structure, dividend policy, pricing strategy, market sizing and segmentation, merger and

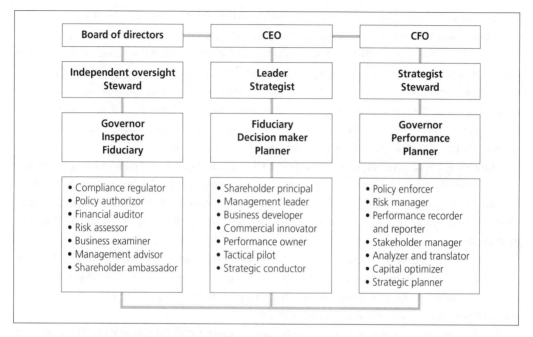

FIGURE 1.3 ■ The corporate governance framework

acquisition planning, investment management, real-time performance reporting, and risk exposure management. However, in the real world, dynamic optimization is difficult to achieve because of the inherent complexity of the business, industry, and markets.

In practice, the treasury performs fund and risk exposure management, but *ad hoc* risk exposure identification results in many unhedged exposures, resulting in turn in earnings volatility. Financial planning teams produce quarterly, annual, and five-year business plans, but rarely apply advanced simulation techniques to identify optimal levels of decision variables that would maximize shareholder value.

Corporate strategy is often unclear to operational managers, poorly communicated to different business units, and poorly integrated with financial planning. This creates the gap in the strategy–planning–execution trio. Furthermore, for public companies, the pressure to deliver upon quarterly earnings guidance causes management to be myopic in terms of strategic initiatives.

In fact, for most companies, it is probably fair to say that the corporate finance function is not fully optimized. Finance theory has fallen short of providing the required guidance for optimal financial management. However, the corporate

> *The pressure to deliver upon quarterly earnings guidance causes management to be myopic.*

finance function has evolved in the last few decades. From what was essentially a bean-counting function, it has now taken center stage as the quintessential strategic function.

In the past, the role of the CFO was to oversee the transactional systems and to report operational performance to creditors, investors and management. That role has evolved dramatically in recent years. Today's CFOs are increasingly seen as true business strategists and partners in developing and managing the business. Being a business partner means that CFOs have to increase the value of the finance department by providing leadership in the areas of strategy, planning, reporting, and analysis (see Figure 1.4).

Industry leading corporations utilize financial management as a tool to gain competitive advantage in the market. Today, e-commerce, globalization, deregulation, and market volatility have increased competition to unprecedented levels, and the market offers a premium to those companies that can manage uncertainties and uniquely position themselves in the marketplace.

Superior value creation results from a superior understanding of the business through powerful analysis, superior strategy and execution, and real-time decision making. Business planning and financial planning provide decision support by applying critical analysis to financial and operational resource allocations.

A company cannot truly increase shareholders' wealth by accelerating its revenue growth without also improving profitability. Internal and external growth need to be distinguished in the financial planning process. Internal organic growth consists of sales increases

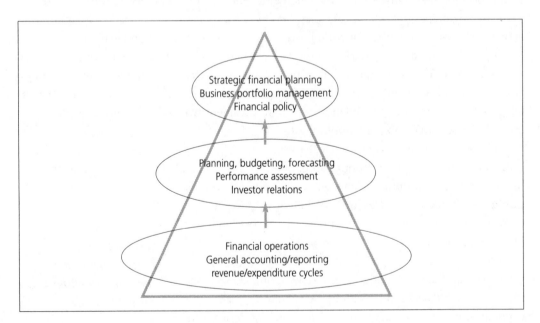

FIGURE 1.4 ■ The finance function pyramid

generated from a company's existing operations, while external growth represents incremental sales brought in through acquisitions.

External growth can increase shareholders' wealth if the merger leads to improvements in profitability through synergies. An integrated financial planning model, as depicted in the simplified schematic shown in Figure 1.5, can be used to optimize corporate financial planning in the context of a balanced scorecard.

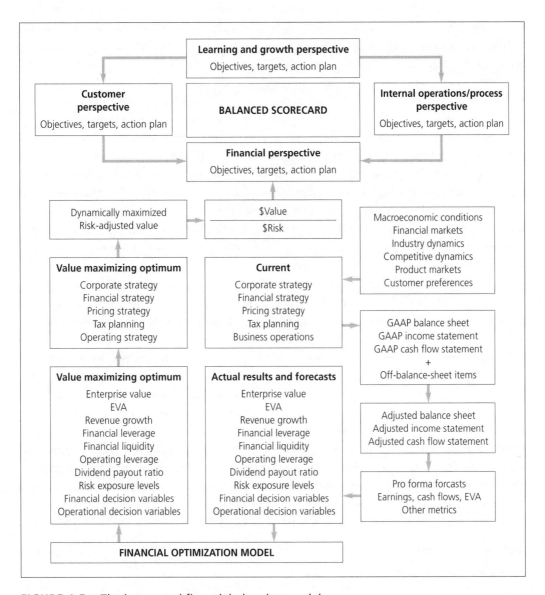

FIGURE 1.5 ■ The integrated financial planning model

Leading corporations formulate their business strategies and operational plans taking into consideration their external economic conditions, industry dynamics, other environmental conditions and future prospects. Their operating and financial performance are summarized in financial statements that are based on a complex set of accounting principles called Generally Accepted Accounting Principles (GAAP).

GAAP accounting has many limitations as it does not represent a true economic picture of corporate profitability, and is amenable to various manipulations by management to represent favorable earnings trends. GAAP accounting rules largely exclude off-balance-sheet assets and liabilities as well. Therefore, in order to get a true picture of financial performance, adjusted financial statements need to be developed that reflect economic realities of actual performance and normalized by excluding one-time events. The "adjusted" financial statements should be used for pro forma financial planning purposes. Financial optimization techniques are to be applied on these adjusted financials, resulting in optimized values for key decision variables such as financial and operating leverage, dividend policy, risk exposures, etc. to maximize the objective function which is the risk adjusted corporate value.

These quantitative optimality numbers are to be used as directionally correct and a great deal of additional management judgment and sophisticated financial wizardry are required to develop operational decisions for value maximization. The financial results represent the financial perspective, which is to be supplemented with the operational perspective, learning and growth perspective, and customer perspective that ultimately result in a "balanced" performance assessment for the company.

The balanced scorecard, as part of an integrated financial planning model, can be derived from real-time financial performance management systems, allowing management to proactively pin-point areas of sub-optimization or under-performance, and take appropriate action to get business results back on course.

Today's finance function fulfills a bigger role in managing the business than just financial reporting. In order to execute oversight responsibility for the financial management process, the CFO must be able to identify key objectives and determine if the assessment and measurement processes for their attainment are adequate.

Today's finance function fulfills a bigger role in managing the business than just financial reporting.

As management shifts to a business process approach, finance professionals, less concerned with vertical command and control, focus on optimal decision support and horizontal process-led change. These are driven by an integrated set of finance functions that include:

- increasing shareholder value

- macroeconomic and industry analysis

- financial strategy and optimal financial policy

- strategic and operational decision support
- pricing strategy
- investment decisions
- mergers and acquisitions analysis
- investment management
- corporate risk management
- funding
- tax planning
- analytical support on pricing strategy
- treasury and liquidity management
- performance management
- financial reporting
- financial operations
- business planning
- budgeting and cost planning
- financial control and audit.

EXAMPLE[7]

A consumer products company with operations in the US and more than 90 subsidiaries worldwide formed a new business strategy aimed at improving profitability and cash generation. The new CFO took a double-barrelled approach to change. Starting with financial strategy, he used shareholder value analysis techniques to benchmark the company against peer group competitors, revealing major opportunities for value creation.

Strategy implementation involved overhauling the capital investment appraisal process, and incorporating new, value-driven targets in medium-term plans and annual budgets. Accountability was sharpened by overturning the performance measurement system company-wide, replacing it with a smaller number of more strategically relevant measures, linked to target shareholder value improvements. Taken down to a personal level, this meant relatively junior front-line managers now had clear goals, harmonized with overall strategy.

After a global review of treasury risk, new hedging policies were introduced, reinforced with systems that provide an up-to-the minute picture of worldwide exposures. A stronger mix of debt-to-equity funding cut the cost of capital.

Clearly, one of the challenges for the CFO is to drive fundamental process-led change to benefit the business. Advanced analytical skills are a *sine qua non* in the CFO's repertoire, as they use specialist knowledge to support optimal decision making.

The external business environment and corporate financial strategy

"The world's financial centres, from New York to Hong Kong, boast stock markets whose stirring rallies and jittery retreats are measured by arithmetic indices, the most readily available means of taking the temperature and pulse of the global financial system."[8] Understanding today's environmental forces and risks faced by the CFO requires more systematic evaluation of a wider variety of influences on the corporate financial position than ever before.

CFOs must focus on the financial, operational, and investment decisions of the corporation – decisions that cannot be made without anticipating developments and minimizing the risks inherent in the economic and political arenas.[9]

Do not lose sight of the global context. The global business environment has grown more connected and more complex for most firms. With that greater complexity, however, comes an opportunity to diversify the consumer base as well as the supplier base, which results in more consistent financial performance results that are less tied to the business cycles of the home market. Of course, firms operate within the context of their own industry structure, competitive conditions, capital market conditions, macroeconomic influences, and other unique attributes or limiting factors that are particular to its own processes, history, and culture. Corporate operational and financial strategies are formulated within this dynamic framework, where technological factors play a critical role in enhancing functional efficiencies.

It is important for corporate financial strategy and planning to be formulated under a broad perspective on the empirical characteristics of financial markets. It is the CFO's responsibility to determine the firm's overall performance including valuation, expected returns required by equity investors in general, the expectations for returns among equity investment alternatives such as convertible bond holders, etc., the magnitude of risk exposures faced by the business, and its management of those risks.

Especially in the case of financial strategy and planning, capital market conditions form an essential reference point in regard to all policy decisions, for example, financial leverage, dividend policy, timing and nature of debt or equity security offerings to the public or private markets, general market trends, institutional versus non-institutional shareholding structure, etc.

In order to identify new opportunities in the marketplace, the external macro-economic, macro-financial, and industry competitive dynamics must be tracked, understood and closely monitored. Superior insights into the nature of changes taking place in the industry and competitive positioning allow top management to identify competitive advantages and disadvantages. For example, the government's fiscal policies will directly affect taxation of profits, and import and export duties, as well as investment tax credit and allowances. A company engaged in global trade needs to keep abreast of not only its domestic fiscal policies, but those of its trading partners as well. On the monetary policy front, the cost of capital is directly affected by the central bank's interest rate determination. Corporate fund sourcing decisions are thus affected by macro-financial conditions. For example, steep yield curves, particularly in the US, have allowed financial institutions to improve their earnings through traditional carry trades and maturity mismatches.[10]

However, when growth prospects improve, and investors shift to higher risk assets, short and long-term interest rates are likely to rise. This interest rate risk can be significant, as these financial institutions have invested substantially in long-term treasury and agency securities, funding these positions with short-term money to benefit from the steep yield curves. Market sources suggest that most of these positions are unhedged, as the cost of hedging would erode much of the interest rate differential benefit.

In order to identify market niches for the company, markets should be segmented to understand the growth drivers in each sub-segment. Tailored product offerings and value propositions to the chosen target segments allow companies to pursue a strategy of focus or differentiation. Market opportunities can be viewed as a portfolio that needs to be optimized.

In addition, the company's expected returns, growth, and risk variables need to be constantly compared to those of the general economy, its particular sector, and key competitors, to determine the attractiveness of investment in the company, and the resulting valuation. Gaps between management's expectations and investors' understanding should be eliminated via the investor relations programs.

The CFO has responsibility to understand the business and the capital markets. The CFO works in tandem with the CEO to understand the pressures for change, and the needs of the organization, to assess how the financial resources can optimally support organizational growth. Trends in the capital market provide essential guidance as to timing and pricing of sources of capital. They provide shareholders' perspectives on how shareholders prefer to be rewarded, and thus affect dividend or share buyback policies.

Funding gaps are likely to exist elsewhere in Europe. Unless equity and corporate bond markets recover, these funding gaps are expected to weigh on corporate profitability and contribute to market uncertainty in estimating future earnings.

Capital market conditions impact corporate profitability. Available data indicate that corporate defined-benefit pensions in the US, the UK, the Netherlands, and Japan are experiencing sizable funding gaps. While precise data are not widely available, such funding gaps are likely to exist elsewhere in Europe. Unless equity and corporate bond markets recover, these funding gaps are expected to weigh on corporate profitability and contribute to market uncertainty in estimating future earnings.[11]

Exchange rates and interest rate movements also impact corporate profitability, and leading companies take pre-emptive action against such possible adverse impacts on the bottom line through hedging activities. Well-developed derivative markets offer efficient instruments for corporate risk management, and experience shows that sound macroeconomic and regulatory policies can mitigate to a large extent their potentially negative effects on financial stability.

A broad understanding of the characteristics of the equity and bond markets is necessary for raising the required capital in a timely fashion. Fund sourcing is often accomplished from global capital markets, and not only limited to the domestic credit and equity markets. However, the market continues to differentiate borrowers by perceived credit quality. This has contributed to tiering by credit quality. For example, the combined impact of the global recession, further effects of the bursting of the telecom bubble, and corporate accounting irregularities pushed US corporate default rates to record levels in 2002.

Twelve-month default rates on speculative US bonds peaked at 11.4 percent in January 2002. In Europe, where the economic cycle, and thus the credit cycle, lags behind that in the US, corporate debt default rates are high compared to traditional levels, especially in the small and medium size enterprise sector.[12]

Characteristics of the US capital markets

At the end of 2000, there were a little over 6,000 firms that were publicly traded non-financial companies. According to a study by Joseph Ogden *et al.*,[13] the composite market values of these firms far exceeded their composite book values, with a market-to-book value of 3.7. This means that the US capital market expects non-financial firms trading in US capital markets to be very efficient in creating value for shareholders.

In terms of broad valuations and returns, the authors found that, in year 2000, these non-financial firms had a composite price-earnings (P/E) ratio of 42.8, composite return on equity (ROE) of 9.6 percent, composite dividend payout ratio of 43.4 percent, and composite dividend yield of 1.0 percent.

Thus, firms have tended to distribute about half of their earnings in dividends. However, the dividend payout ratio, dividend yields, and ROE trended downwards while the P/E ratio trended upwards during the period from 1980 to 2000.

In addition, Ogden *et al.* find that the composition of balance sheet assets in publicly-listed, US non-financial companies have changed dramatically over the last two decades, as property, plant, and equipment declined from 56 percent of total assets in 1980 to only 32 percent in 2000, suggesting that intangibles, equity investments, and non-current assets have gained prominence in the asset structure. The results indicate that financial leverage has, in general, increased over time. Both debt and non-current liabilities have increased in proportion over time with debt increasing from 27 percent in 1980 to 32 percent in 2000.

During this period, the S&P Industrials have internally funded most of their capital requirements, since the greatest net source of funds was cash flow from operations. These companies engaged in a great deal of merger and acquisition activity, as well as debt issuance and retirement.

In the US capital market, although both common dividends and stock repurchases generally increased over time, the growth of composite stock repurchases far outpaced the growth in dividends. In 1997, for example, the composite value of stock repurchases actually exceeded the composite value of cash dividends.

External financial market conditions form a significant part and context of the company's financial policy and planning. Similarly, external economic trends, and dynamics of industry competitive forces should be incorporated in corporate strategy and planning.

Markets in which corporate financial instruments – equities, bonds, credit derivatives – are traded continue to exhibit considerable volatility. Nonetheless, mature capital markets remain resilient and broadly open to funding needs in both the US and European financial centres.

An understanding of the characteristics and trends within domestic and international financial markets helps in understanding how financial comparative advantages can be exploited to create value. As global operations require an international context for financial decision making, it is important to understand that different regions and countries of the world have their unique differences.

Germany and Japan in particular, and less-developed countries in general, are often said to be "bank-oriented" economies in the sense that a high proportion of company financing in these countries is channelled through banks rather than directly from capital market security issuance. In contrast, Britain and the US are referred to as "market-oriented" because public financial markets play a more important role in company financing.[14] As a result, companies in Britain and the US, on average, have relatively higher equity financing in their capital structures compared to their German or Japanese counterparts.[15]

Sluggish economic recovery prospects impact the price-earnings ratios as these expectations are internalized by market participants. Conditions in the corporate bond markets need to be closely monitored to optimize fund sourcing. Global competition requires that companies sell their products or services wherever it makes market and financial sense to do so; and access to capital is an around-the-clock and around-the-world-business.

At the core of this trend is the increasing interaction across borders, both economically and financially. Globalization of markets, coupled with constrained growth in domestic markets, have spurred rapid growth in global trade and investments. At the same time, innovations in financial instruments allow corporates and financial institutions to further optimize on fund and risk exposure management.

Global financial markets have continued their disintermediation: the provision of credit moved from banking systems to markets with many sources of corporate funding resulting in distinct markets for equities, corporate bonds, commercial paper, and bank loans. In the past, pricing in these markets operated largely independently of each other, although each responded to the same broad economic forces.

More recently, the rising use of credit derivatives – particularly credit default swaps – on corporate risks has facilitated a shift away from this "silo" approach to pricing toward a unified method of pricing bank loans, corporate bonds, and equities. The resulting stronger cross-market arbitrage should contribute to more efficient pricing of credit risk.

The corporate bond and loan markets are typically illiquid. When multinational corporates are cautious about making large capital investments, the resulting diminished need to fund capital spending softens demand for bank loans, thus favorable impacting pricing.

Markets are changing faster and are ignoring national borders more than ever before. While sensitivity to local customs and patterns will always be critical, it is increasingly the case that market segments are viewed by product, industry, or demographic trends first, and geography second. This is driven by the all-important need to fulfill, and satisfy customers' demands and expectations on a global basis.[16]

Market segments are viewed by product, industry, or demographic trends first, and geography second.

Mature versus emerging markets offer strategic choices to global companies seeking to expand their product reach through multiple sales channels of distribution. The enlarged global market offers greater opportunities to seek growth through a larger portfolio of environments in which to operate.

However, the ability to spread operations across more markets is often accompanied by greater volatility in many of those markets. The higher average growth rates in many Asian and Latin American economies are accompanied by the increased political risk of policy instability and economic risks of hyperinflation and financial market fluctuations.

The CFO facing a global marketplace must often seek higher returns in emerging and non-traditional markets, and must manage the increased risk often associated with growth expectations. External conditions form the essential platform based on which corporate finance decisions are optimized over time. Increasingly, this external environment must be understood in a global context, as corporate markets, suppliers, and competitors commonly operate within a multinational framework.

Nearly every dimension of corporate financial position can be affected by changes in the business environment. If we look at a typical firm's income statement, for example, both revenue and cost dimensions can be affected by numerous factors that should be anticipated in a planning exercise. Thus corporate profits are critically affected by the inter-play of economics-driven factors affecting both the revenue and expense sides of the income statement on a global basis for larger firms traditionally limited to domestic markets.

To address this complexity, CFOs must approach business management as one would approach an investment portfolio. For any business, there is a portfolio of revenue opportunities and a portfolio of alternative cost strategies encompassing different countries and market segments. This requires a systematic assessment of risk and a careful balancing of potential opportunities against those risks.

The successful firms and CFOs understand the variety of opportunities that exist in the global context, and have a healthy and well-considered respect for the risks that must be balanced to sustain growth and competitive advantage regardless of the upturns and downturns that inevitably occur.

Monitoring and projecting the impact of changes in the economic and business environment on the financial performance of the firm must include the ability to assess risks and alternative financial scenarios (see Chapter 4 for more on this).

The strategic logic of high growth

Among all other influences, the desire to grow has perhaps the most pervasive effect on strategy. Apparent saturation of the target markets lead managers to broaden the position by extending product lines, adding new features, imitating competitors' new services, matching processes, and even making acquisitions. Profitable growth is a tremendous challenge many companies face, especially those that are in a relatively mature stage of the growth cycle.

Growth in revenues and profitability is not only affected by macro-economic conditions and industry competitive dynamics, it's a direct result of the quality of a company's strategy and execution. Strategic planning is thus centre stage. Growth is also a result of how successful a company is in developing and marketing products or services that are in the growing segment of the product life-cycle. Pricing strategy plays a key role in ensuring that the customer's product-price value proposition is attractive. Organic growth is often complemented with external growth through acquisitions.

To manage profitability, the focus is on efficiency. On the expense and operations management side, sophisticated financial corporate performance management (CPM) and enterprise resource planning (ERP) systems allow best-in-class competitors to maintain margins through increasingly efficient business management.

However, some companies are able to sustain high growth in revenues and profits – and others are not. Why is that? To answer this question, W. Chan Kim and Renée Mauborgne of *INSEAD* spent five years studying more than 30 companies around the world.[17] They found that the difference between high-growth companies and their less successful competitors was in each group's assumptions and approach to corporate strategy. Managers of high-growth companies followed what the authors call the "logic of value innovation "

These value innovators do not use rivals as benchmarks. Examples included French hotelier Accor that discarded traditional notions of what a hotel is supposed to be, focussing on a strategy to deliver a good night's sleep at a low price. Virgin Atlantic challenged industry conventions by eliminating first-class service and channelling savings into innovations for business-class passengers. Bert Claeys, a Belgian company that operates movie theatres, similarly introduced the innovative idea of multiplexes, with Kinepolis in Brussels as a first such experiment which captured 50 percent of the market in Brussels in the first year, and revolutionized the movie experience worldwide.

According to Kim and Mauborgne's study, the less successful companies took a conventional approach: their strategic thinking was dominated by the idea of staying ahead of the competition. Sounds familiar? In stark contrast, the high-growth companies paid little attention to matching or beating their rivals. Instead they sought to take customer satisfaction to a different level altogether by non-traditional "out-of-the-box" thinking and innovations that worked.

The World Economic Forum performed a study of global companies for the past five years to identify the top performing enterprises. Beginning with a list of 25,000 companies, 200 were short-listed in terms of shareholder value creation, revenue growth, and job creation.[18] The report concludes that shareholder value and revenue growth are positively correlated. This is known as the value-growth link. It transcends local economies, and applies widely in the Americas, Europe, and Asia-Pacific. It is not a localized phenomenon. For a set of 4,000 North American companies in every size category, as revenue growth increases, investor value grows apace. Data drawn for a group of 350 Australian publicly listed companies corroborates the same results. Similar results were derived for companies in Asia-Pacific.

However, Asia-Pacific companies tend to survive longer periods of low performance. In other words, they have more resilience to survive downturns than companies in the Americas or Europe. For smaller companies, the value-growth linkage is more muted. Smaller companies are more volatile, thus riskier. Companies under $100m revenues have much higher failure rates. Furthermore, the single most important determinant of a company's cost of capital is its size. As revenues increase, the cost of capital declines if unsystematic risk poses no concern. In essence, smaller companies with higher risks are also likely to generate higher returns.

Reengineering processes in order to meet customer needs is no longer enough. Product innovation is essential but insufficient in itself. As efficiency becomes the basis for survival but not necessarily for prosperity, the future will confer its greatest rewards on growth and on those who reinvent the business itself – the model, its scope, and its competencies.

The top shareholder performers in the past decade delivered double-digit revenue growth rates. They were not pledged to growth at any cost, to growth without consideration of asset intensity, and certainly not to growth through acquisitions that increased revenue without creating value.

Total shareholder return (TSR) is the combination of dividends and share price appreciation. Analysis by Dauphinais *et al.* of PricewaterhouseCoopers' concluded that top-line growth is a significant and sustainable engine of shareholder returns.[19] According to this research, double-digit revenue growth rates are associated with strong value creation.

Strong revenue growth stems from innovative product and service offerings that create distinctive value for customers and allow companies to capture higher margins as well as higher growth. These offerings in turn require innovative business systems. Growth is not, however, a stand-alone objective. Leading firms seek to penetrate and manage the costs of growth.

Effective approaches to growth include:

- superior leadership and execution,
- track global best-in-class competitor processes and innovations,
- innovate products to drive differentiation and margins,
- continuous improvement culture,
- optimize price-points for products or services,
- sub-segment markets to exploit the potential of each segment and customer,
- reinvent distribution or service delivery channels,
- exploit global potential,
- reinvest in brands,
- use technology to enable more efficient processes,
- use alliances to advance strategy,
- understand and manage the costs of growth,
- optimize capital investment choices through value-based analysis,
- flexibility to change and adapt business to customer demands,
- attract and invest in highly talented employees,
- link compensation to value-based return metrics,
- encourage innovation without penalizing mistakes.

High-growth firms commit to product innovation to create competitive differentiation and sustain margins. Many firms fuel their growth in a competitive marketplace by redefining their markets and applying customer segmentation. Companies that can identify untapped growth and profit potential in new customer segments and quickly reconfigure their business systems are able to realize the potential growth.

In an increasingly globalizing marketplace, managing growth requires firms to fashion sophisticated mental maps of the dynamics of market development, as well as of patterns for exploiting them. Firms can identify the level of product adaptation to support the individual markets. As firms move to thinking of the world as the marketplace for their product portfolio, the ability to manage costs and complexity against returns are vital to creating and sustaining value. Local customs need to be respected while exploiting the global appeal of the brand. Higher customization in turn needs to be balanced against the efficiency of standardization on product and delivery.

New market entries are expensive, not only in money but also in time and learning, and consistency is key to sustaining long-term growth and value creation. Brands promise the assurance that customers have come to expect from the name and logo. Therefore, the intangible value of brands need to be nurtured and enhanced.

High-growth firms measure the value of technology by its capacity to help them meet specific objectives and enhance implementation of their strategy. It is no coincidence that Procter & Gamble's implementation of an enterprise-wide SAP® system was shortly followed by the move to global product divisions based on enhanced visibility.[20]

Hypergrowth

Hypergrowth is generally defined as consistent and organic annual revenue growth in excess of 30 percent. Companies need sustainable product advantages for this sort of rapid growth. Intel's microprocessors, Phillip Morris' Marlboro brand of cigarettes, and Microsoft's personal computer operating systems are examples of sustainable product advantages. For Dell Computers, the direct customer sales model strengthened customer relationships.

As part of the multi-channel sales distribution strategy, most companies are using the internet for sales, service, or both. Hypergrowth is driven by internal speed and urgency, by the need to pre-empt competitors swiftly and exploit opportunities. Failure to attain growth is often due to poor market fundamentals. Yet statistics show that corporate rates of growth differ dramatically within any industry. This is often a result of leaders able to evaluate, sequence, and prioritize opportunities, and invest in the most promising ones.

Hypergrowth is rare. In any one industry there is typically only one company with hypergrowth. The uniqueness of hypergrowth companies should make them beware of standard benchmarking, since these high-growth companies achieve superior results often by disregarding industry norms. However, the constraints of hypergrowth companies typically include availability of investment capital, working capital, human resources, and strain on current management and control structures.

In any one industry there is typically only one company with hypergrowth.

According to Michael Dell, Chairman and CEO of Dell:

"The roots of our success lie in continually analyzing what we are doing, and drawing out correct inferences and interpretations from the environment, without falling victim to what I call analysis paralysis."[21]

In order to attain higher growth, some firms limit spending to projects with quick payoffs, and concentrate on defending market shares and profit margins. However, a global market implies that as you expand coverage from local to national to regional to global customers, the number of suppliers rises geometrically, while buyers get bids from suppliers from all over the world. This makes pricing, quality, branding, and differentiation of critical importance.

A strategy for sustainable growth requires evaluation of the risks involved, and an understanding of alternatives. Some hypergrowth companies require each of their businesses to achieve a certain earnings growth throughout the business cycle, and generate returns, say, 300 to 500 basis points above the weighted average cost of capital. Those businesses that do not meet these criteria are divested. However, divestitures often penalize sales volumes in the short term, and can negatively affect earnings per share. Similarly, synergistic acquisitions that are financed using discretionary cash often strengthens the acquirer's leadership posture in the industry, and enhances its long-term earnings growth.

Often companies use acquisitions as a substitute for organic growth. Growth leaders use acquisitions to absorb technology, build distribution, and gain access to customers and markets. They have a distinctive ability to exploit the acquired or partnered assets, and a sensible plan to do so. These firms also use mergers and acquisitions to invest in human capital and therefore expand capability. Alliances and partnerships are used to build and expand complementary distribution channels. However, growth carries costs, and in many instances, these costs exceed the benefits that growth generates. Understanding and managing them is vital to avoid the downside of growth.

"There is no single path to growth that produces significant rewards for shareholders, no magic formula. ...different companies, industries, and regions require different solutions. One firm can learn from another, but copying is probably of limited use....vision demands revision. No strategy is sacred. Some are interesting – but often for a limited time. Growth will not come painlessly and effortlessly. Growth requires change – and that is always difficult, and usually expensive."[22]

Use of technology and innovation spurs internal efficiencies and growth. High-growth companies accelerate their growth by adding important functionality to their products and services on almost a continuous basis, where much of it is in fact customer driven.

Financial management considers the stage of maturity of the business and ensuing cash-flow characteristics, includes earnings management, negotiations with banks and financial institutions for credit lines and security issuance, management of financial, operational, and legal risks, the balancing of short-term versus long-term priorities, tax planning, and optimization of cash management in the business cycle. It also includes undertaking and managing strategic financial transactions to manage leverage and optimize capital structure, real-time performance analysis, asset-liability management, and assessment of business cases for investment feasibility.

In practice, optimization of resources is a continuous process. Corporate financial management is dynamic and considers continuous innovations in strategic financial transactions to ensure that business growth is optimally supported.

One-time events

In terms of financial analysis of the health of a firm, a realistic assessment of the economic results of the firm's performance requires an understanding of the underlying financial performance of the business. Non-recurring unusual events are ignored, as the financials are normalized for these one-time events.

These one-time events may include write-offs of receivables and inventories, gains or losses on foreign currency translation, gains or losses on disposal of a segment of a business or sale of assets. In recent years, restructuring charges have become common items in financial reporting. These charges are outside the normal course of business but do not qualify for below-the-line treatment as extraordinary items.

Each year, more than a quarter of all companies filing with the US Securities and Exchange Commission (SEC) take a non-recurring charge. As recently as 1970, only 1 percent of companies did.[23] In the US, the Sarbanes-Oxley Act, for example, requires public companies that report normalized results, to reconcile reported GAAP and normalized figures in their quarterly and annual reports.

Steady earnings growth is highly valued by the capital market and creditors, but rarely occurs naturally. Overstating near-term reported earnings by recognizing sales prematurely is a revenue-related accounting manipulation that appears to be rather prevalent. Sometimes, management delays revenue recognition to understate short-run profits to smooth year-to-year earnings growth that equity investors reward with high price-earnings multiples. GAAP, however, does not give companies discretion to create such artificial reserve funds.

In terms of earnings management, companies can boost sales through alternative accounting recognition techniques or acquisitions. Increase in the rate of revenue growth through mergers and acquisitions is the most common example. A corporation can easily accelerate its sales growth by buying other companies and adding their sales to its own. "With so many discretionary items at its disposal, Coca-Cola's management had absolute control over the earnings it would report through the end of 1998" said Oppenheimer analyst, Roy Burry.[24]

To maximize value in the marketplace, in some instances, large P/E multiples have been reached with rapid earnings per share growth through financial engineering, rather than bona fide synergies. Starting with a modest multiple on its stock, a company can make a few small acquisitions of low-multiple companies to get the earnings acceleration it needs. For financial reporting, as opposed to tax-accounting purposes, publicly listed companies generally seek to maximize reported net income, which investors use as a basis for valuing its shares. Therefore, its incentive in any situation is to minimize expenses, capitalize whatever expenditures it can, and depreciate its fixed assets over as long a period as possible.

In contrast, a privately held company has less obligations in terms of financial reporting to the SEC. A private company typically prepares one set of financial statements, with tax authorities foremost on its mind. Its incentive is not to maximize but minimize the income it reports, thereby minimizing its tax bill as well.

Corporate managers can be creative in minimizing and slowing down the recognition of expenses as they are in maximizing and speeding up the recognition of revenues. Since investors attach little significance to non-recurring profits and losses in valuing stocks, a public company has strong incentives to aggregate cumulative losses into a one-time event, and to break up a unique non-recurring gain into smaller pieces, recognizing it over several periods. A corporation has the power to fire its auditor, and may use that power to influence accounting decisions that are matters of judgment.[25]

Enhancements to reported revenues boost reported earnings without increasing cash flows commensurately. A company might lower the credit standards it applies to customers without simultaneously raising the percentage of reserves it establishes for losses on receivables. The result would be a rise in both revenues and earnings in the current period, with a corresponding increase in credit losses not becoming apparent until a later period.

Alternatively, a manufacturer may institute short-term discounts that encourage its dealers or wholesalers to place orders earlier than they would otherwise. In this case, sales and earnings will be higher in the current quarter than they would be in the absence of the incentives, but the difference represents merely a shifting of revenues from a later to an earlier period.[26]

The sustainable revenue growth rate of the firm is its return on equity multiplied by its retention ratio. As long as a firm limits growth within this rate, the current financial resources of the firm will be sufficient to support that growth. Too much growth can cause the financial system to overheat as a result of high cash requirements for inventory and working capital.

Sustainable growth rate = Return on equity × Retention ratio

Are you optimizing sales and earnings growth? An empirical study of 2,156 companies during the period 1990 through 2000, using Compustat data, found that although corporate profitability measures generally rise with earnings and sales growth, an optimal point exists beyond which further growth adversely affects profitability and destroys shareholder value.[27]

Dynamic value management

How near or how far are you from where you want to be? The business' capability to generate expected returns must be diagnosed, and areas of weaknesses identified. Reviewing the status, effectiveness and alignment of client risk and value management processes against a target vision is called "dynamic value management", according to PricewaterhouseCoopers. This can be facilitated by a benchmarking diagnostic tool, by which companies rate client processes in terms of the extent to which they are value driven, risk focussed, and integrated across businesses, risks and assets. The senior managers agree on the key change priorities in moving towards this vision, and map out a development agenda on this basis.

Under dynamic value management, the full value cycle is detailed, from overall objective setting, through strategy formulation, strategy execution, performance evaluation/compensation, and communication. The infrastructure and resourcing of people and systems, as well as the policy, governance, and control frameworks needed to support and regulate dynamic value management processes need to be assessed. This includes the design of performance management frameworks and internal value accounting procedures, for example, key performance indicators, balanced scorecards, transfer pricing protocols, risk capital attribution procedures, etc.

Consistent with the principle of integrating risk and value management, the formulation of enterprise-wide risk management (EWRM) processes and structures need to support shareholder value objectives. Under EWRM, core processes of objective setting includes the specification of risk appetite, risk identification and prioritization, risk measurement, risk management, risk monitoring, risk-adjusted performance measurement and risk reporting.

Risks, and risk management processes, are fundamentally predicated on how shareholder value may be impacted, and this will differ from company to company. However, recognize that certain risk classes demand highly technical and specialized risk management solutions and quantitative methodologies. These include financial risk management. Market risks, credit risks, liquidity risks, and actuarial model risks are primary risk elements. Other risk elements include operational effectiveness, security and privacy, internal audit, and accounting compliance.

The unifying principle is that the objective at all times is to maximize the value of assets, individually and collectively, by maximizing the net present value of future cash flows. Certain asset classes, however, demand highly technical and specialized value management solutions and quantitative methodologies. These include project or investment value management, including acquisitions, research and development, value management, and intellectual asset management (including brand value management, human resources value management, and customer value management).

Along with high growth, companies embrace risk rather than avoid it. High-growth companies offer their owners, employees, and customers a genuine opportunity for growth. Building on their core strengths, management of the business is often decentralized worldwide so that quick decisions may be made. The growth culture of continuous innovation and entrepreneurial ambience is nurtured within the firm, so that employees can clearly see their contributions to the bottom line.

NOTES

1   PricewaterhouseCoopers (2003a).

2   Dauhinais *et al.* (2000).

3   George, Abraham (1996).

4   Deloitte Research (2003b).

5   Ibid.

6   "The Way We Govern Now", *The Economist*, Jan 11, 2003.

7   Dauhinais *et al.* (2000).

8   Allen, L (2001). *The Global Financial System 1750-2000*

9   Beck and Brinner (1997).

10   International Monetary Fund (2003).

11   Ibid.

12   Ibid.

13   Ogden *et al.* (2003).

14   Higgins (2001).

15   OECD (2002).

16   Beck and Brinner (1997).

17   Kim and Mauborgne (1997).

18   Doorley, T L (2000).

19   Dauphinais *et al.* (2000).

20   Ibid.

21   Michael S. Dell (2000).

22   Dauphinais, W *et al.* (2000).

23   Hanna in Fabozzi *et al.* (2002).

24   Karayan (2002).

25   Ibid.

26   Fridson and Alvarez (2002).

27   Ramezani *et al.*, (2002).

CHAPTER 2

Shareholder value maximization

Introduction

Over the past two decades, the global capital market has experienced revolutionary developments in information technology and the proliferation of information that have intensified global competition, thus increasing pressure on the CEO to strengthen shareholder value. Creating shareholder value depends on bringing about a positive pattern of cash-flows in excess of investor expectations. In order to achieve this, many leading companies have linked corporate strategy directly to value, and changed management compensation to value creation.

"Prosperity requires people to abandon old industries and old ways of doing things, and bet on new ones and new ways." [1]

We can classify management decisions into financing, investing, or operating categories that are interrelated. Shareholder value maximization results from optimal decision making in each of these categories. It is fair to say that the investing decision is of the greatest strategic importance to a company, since it is the basic driving force of business activity.

"While there is uncertainty about the speed of change, there is no question about the direction of change. The shareholder value movement is here to stay, and participation is mandatory" [2]

Investment decisions are a source of growth that supports management's explicit competitive strategies, and are normally based on carefully planned capital budgets for committing funds into working capital, physical assets, or other resource commitments. These investments are to be recovered, over time. Shareholder value creation thus depends on a combination of ongoing successful performance of existing investments, and the addition of successful new investments that require continued reassessment of the company's total portfolio of activities.

Operating decisions focus on effective utilization of funds invested to ensure that their implementation and continued operation meet expectations. Various operating ratios are regularly tracked by businesses. These operating ratios vary greatly by type of business, because they have to be tailored to the specific variables that drive performance.

Activity-based analysis identifies the operational functions or processes followed for particular product lines, for instance. It has become an important technique for supporting the current emphasis on corporate reengineering and value-based management. In addition, benchmarking activities against industry best practices represent another popular way of refining the measures and standards to be applied.[3]

Financing decisions present choices to the senior management in terms of which sources of funding are to be utilized for funding the investments and operations of the business over the long term. The company's capital structure and disposition of profits are key policy areas.

For-profit corporations channel financial resources from creditors and shareholders into economic activities that generate adequate returns to suppliers of its capital. The returns due to shareholders and stakeholders must be commensurate to the levels of risk they are taking by investing in the company.

Debt-holders enjoy seniority over common shareholders in getting their interest payments and principal repayments, while common and preferred shareholders are residual claimants. For both these categories of investors, the more valuable the company becomes, the higher returns they can enjoy from the investment. Therefore, shareholder value maximization has become the primary objective for most companies around the world, although led by US corporate culture. It is less noticeable in Europe and Asia, but is pervading corporate thinking there as well.[4]

Maximizing shareholder value means maximizing the present value of expected cash-flows to the shareholders of the firm after payments on debt obligations. Maximizing the value of the enterprise, on the other hand, looks at the value of the entire cash-flows to the firm, before deductions on debt payments. In order to maximize shareholder value, the focus is on cash flows derived from profitable growth and economic value creation, not just accounting profits. If viewed analytically, the shareholder value function can be maximized subject to corporate financial and operational constraints:

Maximize enterprise value = Maximize present value of expected cash flows

Subject to constraints such as:

■ cost of capital under alternative leverage ratios

■ credit rating status quo

■ financial plan assumptions on sustainable revenue growth

■ financial plan assumptions on assets and liabilities

■ financial plan assumptions on cost structure

- financial plan assumptions on CAPEX and dividends
- risk exposure limits set by management
- other constraints.

Corporate valuation is necessary for purchase or sale, and merger or acquisition activity. It is also important for the incumbent management of public as well as private companies to know how much the business entity is worth, and how that value is changing over time. Economic valuation takes into consideration both explicit costs of debt and implicit costs of equity to determine whether shareholder value is being created or destroyed. However, the key to value creation is not new measurements, but developing appropriate strategies and implementing them properly.

In order to create value, companies must address the following questions:

- what are the business strategies and operating activities that are supporting value creation?
- how is our strategic posture changing?
- is the business delivering a return above its total cost of capital?
- are we measuring ourselves with financial and operational performance metrics?
- do we have the right capital structure that minimizes our cost of capital?
- which business units, products, or services, are adding value and which ones are not?
- what additional investments are required to sustain and enhance our competitive edge in the market?
- are we taking and managing risks optimally?
- what are we doing to enhance customer satisfaction and intimacy?

Figure 2.1 depicts the components of a value-based management framework. Strategy, execution, and performance management are the three dimensions of value creation. Leading companies view these three pillars of value creation in an integrated context. Value management thus becomes the process by which the firm develops an executes strategy, and measures success based on the economic contribution to the business. The three pillars integrate strategic, financial, and operational planning. Strategy is the collective set of corporate choices to gain and hold positions generating returns on invested capital in excess of the cost of capital. As a definition, a company creates shareholder value only if it generates returns on invested capital (ROIC) in excess of its weighted average cost of capital (WACC).[5]

Clearly, corporate strategy is dependent on the financial capabilities of the firm. A wonderful strategy may not be possible to implement because of such limitations. As companies make strategic choices on product markets, the operational execution of those strategies also requires financial commitment. In order to increase the return on invested capital, companies often pull both cost and revenue levers: operational cost minimization is driven by taking

Strategy	Execution	Performance management
• Develop strategies that create value • Benchmark current comparative valuation against peers • Identify value centres • Optimize product/service portfolio based on customer preferences • Evaluate the value impact of alternative growth strategies • Investment strategies • Financial strategies • Align corporate objectives with employee incentives • Awareness of corporate social responsibility	• Communicate mission, vision, and strategies to employees • Develop leadership and a culture of commitment to a greater cause • Establish and prioritize strategic initiatives • Develop value-based business and operational plans for project implementation • Fund projects • Leverage business alliances • Maintain and build brand and customer relationships • Encourage responsiveness, agility and innovation	• Select financial and non-financial performance measures in a 'balanced scorecard' framework • Estimate economic value added (EVA), and return on invested capital (ROIC) versus weighted average cost of capital (WACC) • Estimate total shareholder return (TSR) • Design and implement real-time reporting systems • Track implementation and implement exception reporting • Align performance results with compensation and reward structure

FIGURE 2.1 ■ Shareholder value maximization

unnecessary operating costs out of the business, and financial costs are minimized by structuring the capital base with appropriate debt, equity, and hybrids. On the revenue side, sales are maximized by expanding product lines, customer markets, building multi-channel sales distribution strategies with appropriate partnerships and alliances, and through customer intimacy.

In an analysis of 416 companies over a five-year period, researchers concluded that companies participating in highly attractive industries or that were competitively advantaged in their industry, realized total shareholder returns (TSR) significantly better than their average peers.[6]

> "To realize superior value creation, companies need to be highly analytical and discerning about the strategic choices they make, and place value maximization as the overriding objective that drives decisions."[7]

Successful companies realize that markets exist that may not have a standard industry definition. As a result, these firms extend their analysis from industry or business unit to the true economics and competitive dynamics surrounding specific products and customers. Disaggregating the business into value centers – economic units subject to distinct strategic conditions that can be managed independently for value – allows strategic and financial analysis at this level.

Disaggregating the business into value centres allows strategic and financial analysis.

Companies content to identify attractive market spaces at a more aggregated level, may fail to capture the uniqueness of the respective sub-segments in question, and thus misunderstand the details of a particular market. As a result, value-destroying positions may go unchecked while value-creating spaces remain unexploited. The financial and non-financial results of the business units need to be viewed within a balanced-scorecard perspective. (See more on the balanced-scorecard in Chapter 6)

Leading-edge companies understand that financial measures tend to be preceded by operational results. That is why non-financial metrics such as the customer perspective, learning, and growth perspective, and internal process perspective are necessary. However, value measures are often rather meaningless to business unit managers who operate at the grass-roots operational level, unless value-based metrics are translated to the operational level using value driver trees. These trees decompose shareholder value metrics and targets into meaningful front-line targets, and enable the selection of appropriate operational measures and the establishment of targets at multiple levels where individuals have control. But shareholder value is not only about creating economic wealth, it is also about caring for individuals, the society, and being a good corporate citizen.

"The corporate social responsibility movement continues to gain momentum worldwide. Beyond an intrinsic desire to do the right thing, CEOs seek standards and measures to define better what constitutes a sustainable business practice."[8]

Corporate valuation

The fair market value of a company is the total amount of money a willing buyer will pay to the owner of the company in an arm's length transaction. This fair market value will be applicable on the date of the valuation and may change subsequent to that date as business conditions change. The present value of future cash flows are discounted at the weighted average cost of capital to derive enterprise value or corporate value. By deducting the value of outstanding debt, a fair value estimate of the value of equity or shareholder value can be made.

Enterprise value = Total corporate value = Present value of cash flows

Enterprise value – Value of outstanding debt = shareholder value (or value of common and preferred equity stock)

In practice, forecasts of corporate cash flows can be difficult, especially for new companies without any history, and therefore alternative valuation techniques are used such as multiples-based valuation or residual income based valuation. In all buy–sell transactions, both for controlling and non-controlling interests, an estimate of corporate valuation is called for.

The accounting financial statements that list the assets and liabilities are inadequate for purposes of deriving corporate valuation estimates because they are historical cost-based, and do not capture the present value of growth opportunities. Therefore the cash flow based approach is often applied. There are basically three different approaches to corporate valuation.

In the *income approach,* the future expected free cash flow to the firm (FCFF) is estimated and discounted to present value using the weighted average cost of capital (WACC):[9]

FCFF = EBIT (1– tax rate) + Depreciation – capital expenditures – ΔWorking capital

WACC = Debt share of total capital × After tax cost of debt + common equity share of total capital × Cost of common equity + preferred equity share of total capital × Cost of preferred equity

Value of firm = Present value of expected FCFF

A commonly used definition for free cash flow is as follows:

Net income
+ Interest expense
+ Income taxes
– Interest income
= EBIT
– Cash taxes
= NOPAT
+Depreciation and amortization
= Gross cash flow
– Increase in net working capital
– CAPEX
= Free cash flow

In the *market approach*, the company is valued by using an average market multiple of comparable companies, and applying that multiple to a fundamental variable for the company. For example, the price-to-book multiple takes the average equity market capitalization to equity book value of a set of comparable traded companies, and applies that multiple to the subject company's book equity, thus deriving an implied market capitalization for the non-traded subject company as if it were publicly traded. Applying a price-to-income multiple is not a good way to compare the total enterprise values of companies with dissimilar capital structures.

The *asset-based approach:asset accumulation method* revalues each significant asset and liability of the subject company, and derives a current value equivalent adjusted balance sheet. It then adds off balance sheet (OBS) contingent assets and liabilities to the valuation, since intangible assets and contingent liabilities are not normally recorded on financial statements prepared under GAAP. Those companies that have material pending litigation, tax dues, or environmental claims outstanding against them, may find that these contingent liabilities have a significant effect on the risk and value of the business.[10]

In practice, these three approaches should give different estimates of enterprise value, but not be too divergent. Ideally, at least two of the three methods should be used to value the company or its shares, and perform a reconciliation at the end, often with a weighted average of the individual valuations to get the final valuation estimate.

Figure 2.2 shows the financial valuation of XYZ Corp. The projected five-year pro forma financial statements are used to derive free cash flow. We then value the company by discounting the free cash flow at the weighted average cost of capital at 10.44 percent, assuming that the firms grows at a 4 percent sustainable growth rate.

The detailed derivation of the valuation is presented in Figure 2.3.

Valuation models: public company

In general, it is easier to value publicly listed companies than privately held ones, since share prices provide a real-time barometer of the market value of equity. If debt is also traded publicly, that value can also be derived from the market. The sum of the values of equity and debt provide the total enterprise market value, which is defined to measure the price an acquirer would pay for a company as a whole.

XYZ Corp. ($ Million)	Actual	Forecast				
Free Cash Flow	**2003**	**2004**	**2005**	**2006**	**2007**	**2008**
Net Income	239	274	303	362	465	664
+ Interest expense	12	21	28	45	77	139
+ Income taxes	129	147	163	195	250	357
- Interest income	0	48	86	179	356	711
= EBIT	380	394	408	422	436	449
- Cash taxes	133	138	143	148	152	157
= NOPAT	247	256	265	274	283	292
+Depreciation and amort.	90	104	120	138	158	180
= Gross cash flow	337	360	385	412	441	472
- Increase in net working capital		5	5	5	6	6
- Capex		140	158	178	201	226
= Free cash flow		215	222	229	235	240

XYZ Corp. ($ Million)	Actual	Forecast				
Valuation	**2003**	**2004**	**2005**	**2006**	**2007**	**2008**
Return on equity	47.9%	29.4%	23.5%	17.2%	12.8%	9.9%
Retention rate	90.0%	90.0%	90.0%	90.0%	90.0%	90.0%
Sustainable growth rate	43.1%	26.4%	21.2%	15.4%	11.5%	8.9%
Debt Ratio	24%	24%	24%	24%	24%	24%
Cost of Debt	6.5%					
Cost of Equity	12.4%					
WACC	10.44%					
Corporate Value	$ **3,212**					

FIGURE 2.2 ▦ Financial evaluation

XYZ Corp. ($ Million)	Actual	Forecast				
	2003	2004	2005	2006	2007	2008
Free Cash Flow		215	222	229	235	240
WACC%	10.44%					
Discounted Present Value		195	182	170	158	146
Sustainable growth rate						4%
Terminal Value						3,880
Present Value of Terminal value	$ 2,362					
Corporate Value	**$ 3,212**					

FIGURE 2.3 ■ Detailed derivation of the valuation

Enterprise value = Market value of debt and equity – Value of cash and investments

An example of enterprise valuation for a Japanese company is presented in Figure 2.4.

Net debt is defined here as long-term debt including the current portion net of cash and cash equivalents. If debt is not traded, then book values are used from the balance sheet. Minority interest represents shares of consolidated subsidiaries not owned by the subject company.

The *market approach* can be used for comparability purposes, and a popular multiple is the enterprise value to EBITDA ratio, which normalizes for size. Because the numerator is enterprise value, the EV/EBITDA ratio is a valuation indicator for the overall company, rather than common stock.[11]

Another multiple in popular use is the P/E (price/earnings) ratio. However, EV/EBITDA may be more appropriate than P/E for comparing companies with different financial leverage, because EBITDA is a pre-interest earnings figure, in contrast to EPS, which is post-interest. EBITDA controls for differences in depreciation and amortization across businesses. Often, EBITDA is positive when EPS is negative, allowing a wider application of EV/EBITDA than P/E.

In applying the *income approach*, the discounted cash flow and dividend discount valuation models are often used for fundamental valuation. When the dividends per share are discounted using the capital asset pricing model (CAPM), it provides a per share fundamental equity valuation estimate. The Gordon dividend discount model simply divides the DPS by a rate equal to the CAPM discount rate minus the sustainable long-run perpetual dividend growth rate. The Gordon equity valuation model is as follows:

Enterprise Value (Yen Billion)					
Shares outstanding	Share Price	Equity Market Capitalisation	Net Debt	Minority Interest	Enterprise Value
1,000	20	20,000	5,000	820	**25,820**

FIGURE 2.4 ■ Enterprise valuation example

Value of equity = (Expected value of dividends)/(Cost of equity – Sustainable growth rate)

There are two-stage and three-stage dividend discount models that basically forecast alternative dividend growth trajectories until they converge to the long-run sustainable growth rate. The problem with dividend valuation models is that they cannot be applied to value firms that do not pay dividends. Dividends can also be subject to manipulation by corporate management to smooth payout trends so that dividends are less volatile than earnings. The discounted cash flow valuation is more suitable in these circumstances.

The discounted cash flow valuation model is very similar to the dividend discount model except that it is more flexible and can be applied to companies that do not pay dividends as well as those that do. If enterprise valuation is being estimated, the economic variable to be discounted is the free cash flow to the Firm (FCFF), discounted at the weighted average cost of capital (WACC) rate. FCFF and WACC are defined as:[12]

FCFF = Net income available to common shareholders
+ Net non-cash charges
+ Interest expense (1 – Tax Rate)
– Investment in fixed capital
– Investment in working capital

A firm's cost of capital is the average return it must pay to its investors in order to induce them to hold its securities. The WACC should also be adjusted for any hybrid security issuance.

WACC = (Debt/Total capital) × Cost of debt (1 – Tax rate) + (Equity/Total capital) × Cost of equity

Effective Borrowing Rate (EBR)

Borrowing objectives include adequate credit facilities for ongoing and prospective liquidity needs of the company. Borrowing costs should be minimized, which includes interest costs, fees, and related restrictive bond or loan covenants. This relates to the default risk as well as the need to maximize the company's flexibility in its operations, and keeping it as unencumbered as possible from limitations from creditors. Factors affecting borrowing costs include loan pricing which are comprised of an all-in rate (base rate plus spread). Other issues include fixed versus variable rates, committed versus uncommitted lines of credit, whether or not the line of credit will be a revolving one, secured versus unsecured debt, maturity or tenure, and other enhancements to the structure.

The EBR can be calculated as follows:

$$\text{EBR} = \frac{\text{Interest rate} + \text{Fees}}{\text{Average usable loan}} \times \frac{365}{\text{No. of days loan is outstanding}}$$

On the other hand, equity valuation requires application of the free cash flow to equity (FCFE) as the numerator, and the CAPM cost of equity is used in discounting the expected cash flows to present value. Alternatively, equity value can be stated as:

Value of equity = Enterprise value – Value of debt

Neither the dividend nor the cash flow model use any stochastic or probabilistic modeling of variables or their expectations. The equity value or enterprise value thus obtained is then used as a base value from which additional discount may be subtracted or premium added to account for marketability or non-marketability characteristics of the shares.

In addition, controlling and non-controlling interests require further adjustments to reflect the fact that controlling interests are worth more per share than non-controlling or minority interests. Individual shares traded in the stock exchanges are priced as minority or non-controlling interests.

Share price × No. of shares outstanding = equity market capitalization
+ Net debt to the equity market cap.
+ value of minority interests
+/– Other special items
= Enterprise value.

Valuation models: closely held company

A privately held company, by definition, has no government-mandated standards for information disclosures that will be scrutinized by public investors.

With the absence of outside investors, management does not need to labor over quarterly earnings reporting. Private companies have the luxury of managing their business for longer-term goals and objectives, as it becomes possible sometimes to forgo short-term profit growth in return for improved long-term results. As a result, cash-flow generation and creation of real economic value, instead of pressure to constantly improve reported earnings, is often the mark of a private company. "It is a rare and very strong public company CEO who can sell long-term results to a short-term oriented marketplace".[13]

For companies that are not publicly traded, valuation becomes more difficult because a market proxy for equity value is not readily available. However the income, market, or asset-based approaches can be used to perform the valuation of the company. Under the *income approach,* internal pro forma financial statement projections provide forecasts of cash flows to the firm that need to be discounted at the firm's weighted average cost of capital.

This approach is often difficult to apply for companies that are in new industries or that do not have sufficient history to forecast future cash-flows. Again, for companies that do not pay regular dividends, the dividend discount model cannot be applied. Under these circum-

Closely held companies can be valued using the market-based approach.

stances, closely held companies can be valued using the *market-based approach*, where comparable market multiples for the industry or a selected comparable peer group is used as the analog proxy.

For example, if the publicly traded peer group is trading at a price-earnings multiple of 10, then we multiply the subject company's earnings per share by 10 to derive its implied market price per share as if the shares were publicly traded. Multiplying that share price by the outstanding shares gives us the equity market capitalization.

A non-marketability discount, usually in the 35–50 percent range, is then applied to the equity market capitalization to derive the closely held company equivalent value for minority interest shares.[14] If a majority of the shares or a controlling interest is being valued, then an additional control premium needs to be added to the minority interest value. It matters very much in the corporate valuation process, whether a minority or a controlling interest is being valued in the subject company. As discussed, publicly traded share prices do not represent controlling interest values.

The key is to understand that a pro rata share of the company stock is usually not worth that pro rata share of the company's value, because the controlling shareholder enjoys the benefits of corporate control, which obviously has value. Therefore, controlling shareholders enjoy a disproportionate share of the total value of the company. To be clear, if you own 51 percent of the shares of a company and have effective control over corporate affairs, the value of your shareholding will be more than 51 percent of the value of the total company. Conversely, if you own 1 percent interest in a company's equity, and do not have effective ownership control, the value of your shares will be less than 1 percent of the entire value of the company. This is because you will have no effective control over corporate affairs. In buy–sell transactions or merger and acquisition type deals, applying an appropriate discount for a minority interest or a control premium for a controlling interest is critical to reaching an accurate valuation estimate. The process of determining the right discount or premium rate is critical. However, a minority interest may enjoy a premium if it can influence the balance of power among other shareholders. For example, if two shareholders each have 49 percent holdings, the third shareholder with 2 percent holdings will enjoy such a premium for those minority holdings.

Market data on merger or acquisition transactions provide information on average premiums paid for controlling interests. Therefore, if the enterprise valuation has been performed that provides a minority interest valuation, then the average percentage premium that was paid on similar market transactions needs to be added to this base value to derive a value for the controlling interest, the remainder being allocated to the residual minority interest.

In Figure 2.5, we first derive the intrinsic valuation of a privately held firm, using its normalized projected pro forma financial statements for the next five years.

ABC Private Corp. ($ Million)

Assumptions	2003		2003
Net revenue growth	13%	Current liabilities	70
Current year sales	$200	Equity	25
Interest rate on debt	7%	Beg retained earnings	5
Dividend payout ratio	5%	Current assets	93
Tax rate	35%	Property, plant, and equ	9
Cost of goods sold / net revenue	58%	Accumulated depreciati	1
SG&A / net revenue	13%		
Depreciation rate	10%		
Liquid asset interest rate	9%	Sustainable growth rate	4%
Current assets / net revenue	47%	Target Debt to asset ratio	25%
Current liabilities / net revenue	35%		
Net fixed assets / net revenue	60%		
PP&E / net revenue	61%		

ABC Private Corp. ($ Million)	Actual	Forecast				
Income Statement	**2003**	**2004**	**2005**	**2006**	**2007**	**2008**
Net revenue	200	226	255	289	326	368
- Cost of goods sold	116	131	148	167	189	214
= Gross profit	84	95	107	121	137	155
- Sales, general, and admin	26	29	33	38	42	48
= EBITDA	58	66	74	84	95	107
- Depreciation and amort.	12	15	19	23	28	34
= EBIT	46	50	55	61	66	73
- Interest expense	7	17	22	36	66	127
+Interest Income	-	72	95	172	333	669
= Income before Taxes	39	105	129	197	333	615
- Taxes	13	37	45	69	117	215
= Net Income	25	68	84	128	217	400
Beg. Retained earnings	5	29	94	173	295	501
Dividends	1	3	4	6	11	20
Ending retained earnings	29	94	173	295	501	880
Balance Sheet	**2003**	**2004**	**2005**	**2006**	**2007**	**2008**
Cash and cash equivalents	-	796	1,060	1,913	3,694	7,437
Current assets	93	105	119	134	152	171
Property, plant, and equip.	121	152	188	231	282	342
Accumulated depreciation	1	16	35	58	86	120
Net fixed assets	120	136	153	173	196	221
Total assets	213	1,037	1,332	2,220	4,042	7,829
Current liabilities	70	79	89	101	114	129
Debt	113	259	333	555	1,010	1,957
Stock	25	670	816	1,391	2,622	5,243
Retained earnings	5	29	94	173	295	501
Equity	30	699	909	1,564	2,917	5,743
Total Liabilities and equity	213	1,037	1,332	2,220	4,042	7,829

FIGURE 2.5 ■ Deriving intrinsic value

ABC Private Corp. ($ Million)	Actual	Forecast				
Free Cash Flow	2003	2004	2005	2006	2007	2008
Net Income	25	68	84	128	217	400
+ Interest expense	7	17	22	36	66	127
+ Income taxes	13	37	45	69	117	215
- Interest income	0	72	95	172	333	669
= EBIT	46	50	55	61	66	73
- Cash taxes	16	18	19	21	23	25
= NOPAT	30	33	36	39	43	47
+Depreciation and amort.	12	15	19	23	28	34
= Gross cash flow	42	48	55	62	71	81
- Increase in net working capital		3	3	4	4	5
- Capex		31	36	43	51	60
= Free cash flow		14	15	16	16	17

ABC Private Corp. ($ Million)	Actual	Forecast				
Valuation	2003	2004	2005	2006	2007	2008
Return on equity	83.5%	9.8%	9.2%	8.2%	7.4%	7.0%
Retention rate	95.0%	95.0%	95.0%	95.0%	95.0%	95.0%
Sustainable growth rate	79.4%	9.3%	8.8%	7.8%	7.1%	6.6%
Debt Ratio	53.05%	25%	25%	25%	25%	25%
Cost of Debt	6.5%					
Cost of Equity	12.4%					
WACC	10.36%					
Value before Marketability discount	$ 227.4					
Marketability discount	30%					
Value after Marketability discount	$ 159.2					
Minority discount	45%					
Ownership level	20%					
Value of 20% minority interest	$ 17.5					
Value of 80% controlling interest	$ 141.7					

FIGURE 2.5 ■ Deriving intrinsic value (continued)

The discounted free cash flow model can be used to calculate either a control or a minority value. Generally, if the inputs in the valuation model reflect changes that only a control owner would or could make, for example, changes in the capital structure, then the model would be expected to produce a control value.

In the example in Figure 2.5, we have assumed that the capital structure is changed from a 53 percent leverage to a 25 percent leverage, with equity injections increasing substantially through venture capital funding.

If, however, the cash flow projections merely reflect the continuation of present policies, then the model would be expected to produce a minority value. The argument is often made that, because discount rates are typically developed from minority trades in publicly traded stocks, the discount rate is a minority interest discount rate and the value indicated by discounted free cash flow models that use the capital asset pricing model or the arbitrage pricing theory to derive costs of equity from publicly traded stocks represent a minority value.

However, most of the differences between a minority and a controlling value are derived from differences in cash flows and not from differences in the discount rate. While costs of equity capital are estimated from trades of minority ownership interests, the capital structure of the subject company is clearly influenced by the controlling shareholder.[15]

If valuing a company on a stand-alone basis, the use of that company's own economic income projections and a market derived cost of capital as the discount rate would be expected to estimate the fair market value of the subject business enterprise.

Corporate performance measurement: economic value added (EVA)

The value financial markets assign to a company reflects its prospects for growth and profitability. CEOs naturally seek to enhance shareholder value. CFOs have found a variety of measures useful for different purposes. These include financial as well as non-financial or operational metrics. Each of these measures has its special function for helping management understand a certain dimension of corporate performance or efficiency.

A firm's management creates value when it makes investment decisions that provide benefits exceeding costs. These benefits may be received in the near or distant future, and the costs include the cost of the investment and a less obvious cost, the cost of equity capital.[16]

Commonly used financial performance measures include:

■ revenue growth

■ gross margin

■ EBITDA margin

■ operating margin

■ net income

■ earnings per share (EPS)

■ return on asset (ROA)

■ return on equity (ROE)

■ return on invested capital (ROIC)

■ economic value added (EVA)

■ market value added (MVA)

■ cash flow return on investment (CFROI)

■ enterprise value/EBITDA

■ net debt/EBITDA

- value at risk (VAR)
- cash flow from operations
- free cash flow
- effective tax rate.

Managers are finding that careful development of an array of non-financial measures is a key part of improving performance. (See more on this in Chapter 6 on the balanced scorecard.) Care must be taken in the selection of the non-financial metrics. What gets measured, gets attention. If you measure something that is not vital, managers will waste time on it, and worse yet, make sub-optimal decisions based on it.

General Electric's CFO Dennis Dammerman said:

"We as finance people have to recognize that there are more measurements than machine output per labor hour, or contribution margin on a widget. There's a whole range of things that are becoming more and more important to managing the business. The focus on time, for example. Are we managing our speed of getting something done? If we make tape recorders, how fast do we make them? What are the steps? How do we do it? Are we as good at measuring that and understanding the ramifications of that measurement as we are on cents per light bulb? Similarly, are we as good understanding how we measure customer satisfaction as we are measuring returns in customer concessions?"[17]

The level and scope of non-financial measures will vary with the scope of responsibility of the managers who have influence on the outcomes. A recent Conference Board study showed that key non-financial measures of performance include:[18]

- quality of output
- customer satisfaction/retention
- employee training
- research and development investment
- productivity level
- new product development
- market growth/success
- environmental competitiveness.

The appropriate combination of financial and non-financial measures are most likely to provide the true indication of how business is performing. Non-financial measures often serve as leading indicators of imminent financial problems. A company's value, of course, depends on how efficiently it can earn returns above its cost of capital. Although corporate value is measured largely in financial terms, corporate executives with experience on the operational side know first-hand that it is operational efficiency and effective implementation of growth strategies that are responsible for adding value.

Each of the valuation approaches discussed thus far is applied in practical valuation exercises in the majority of cases. However, there are various limitations in using GAAP accounting-based financial data for deriving free cash flows or dividends for the income approach, or to use book value of assets for the multiples-based market approach to valuation. Accounting earnings data in the income statement do not deduct a charge for the cost of equity when arriving at the net profit figure, and therefore provide an incomplete picture of corporate financial performance, as they over estimate economic profits. A firm may earn a net profit in an accounting sense, but when the cost of equity is deducted from net profits, it may be insufficient and instead show a net operating loss. In these cases, the firm is in fact not creating shareholder value in an economic sense.

Residual income models of equity value have become widely recognized tools in investment practice, corporate finance, and research. Conceptually, residual income is net income less a charge (deduction) for common shareholders' opportunity cost in generating net income.[19]

As an economic concept, residual income has a long history. As far back as the 1920s, General Motors employed the concept in evaluating business segments.[20] More recently, residual income has received renewed attention and interest in the form of economic value added (EVA) or economic profit.

The appeal of residual income models stems from the shortcomings of traditional accounting. The extreme conservative bias in standard accounting in general and the auditing profession in particular, has resulted in limitations in the usefulness of the accounting data. This has in turn necessitated the introduction of alternative economic measures for assessment of corporate performance.

The appeal of residual income models stems from the shortcomings of traditional accounting.

Specifically, although a company's income statement includes a charge for the cost of debt capital in the form of interest expense, it does not include a charge for the cost of equity capital. A company can have positive net income, but may still not be adding value for shareholders if it does not earn more than the cost of equity capital. "The association between accounting data and market values is not only weak, but appears to have been deteriorating over time. Overall, the fragile association between accounting data and capital market values suggests that the usefulness of financial reports … is rather limited". [21]

The first departure from GAAP accounting made by economic profit measures is to recognize the full cost of capital. The resulting net operating profit after taxes estimate of corporate earnings is a much truer picture of the economics of the business.

Value based metrics or economic profit measures directly measure the value that a firm's managers add to the business. Since the accounting income statement ignores the cost of equity capital in its calculation of profits, economic profit estimates correct for and refine this measure, and are designed to provide a formal link between the firm's cash-adjusted operating profit and its economic capital. In principle, the net present value of any firm can be expressed in terms of the present value stream of economic profit generated by both the firm's current and future assets. [22]

EXAMPLES

Economic profit measures were applied early on in the corporate world – as evidenced during the 1980s by Coca Cola's embracing economic profit measure of corporate success. They were then energized during the 1990s by Credit Suisse First Boston, Goldman Sachs, and Salomon Smith Barney, among others. Centura Bank became the first US bank to employ Stern Stewart's economic value added (EVA) measure of corporate success. In Europe, DaimlerChrysler uses EVA as its primary corporate performance measurement metric.

The firm's EVA for any given period is equal to its unlevered net operating profit after tax less the capital charge on the firm's economic capital at the start of the period. Banc One rolled out EVA incentives and a financial management system in 1997, while economic profit concepts have been promoted around the world including Citibank, ANZ bank in Australia, and in South Africa by ABSA bank.[23]

Theoretically, EVA can be expressed as the current adjusted book value of assets in place plus the present value of growth opportunities of the company. EVA is a currency based metric. It makes some adjustments to accounting data to calculate the net operating profit after taxes (NOPAT), and deducts a charge for both debt and equity capital invested in the business using the WACC rate. The result is economic value added, which can be forecasted into the future, based on the pro forma financial projections of the financial plan of the company.

Economic value added (EVA) = NOPAT – Capital charge

EVA = NOPAT – (Total debt + Equity capital) × WACC %

NOPAT = EBIT (1 – Tax rate)

Figure 2.6 calculates EVA for XYZ Corp.

In the example shown in Figure 2.6, XYZ Corp. will be generating positive economic profit until 2006, but destroys value thereafter, as it will be unable to generate sufficient

XYZ Corp.						
EVA	Actual	Forecast				
Valuation	2003	2004	2005	2006	2007	2008
EBIT	380	378	375	371	365	358
Tax rate	35%	35%	35%	35%	35%	35%
NOPAT	247	246	244	241	237	233
WACC%	10.25%	10.25%	10.25%	10.25%	10.25%	10.25%
Total Assets	750	1,328	1,744	2,184	2,650	3,142
Capital Charge	77	136	179	224	272	322
EVA	170	110	65	17	(34)	(89)
Net Income	238	261	277	294	310	327
Return on equity	47.5%	28.3%	22.5%	18.8%	16.2%	14.4%

FIGURE 2.6 ■ Calculating the Economic Value Added (EVA)

returns for both debt and equity holders. It is interesting to see that XYZ Corp. is projected to be making positive and increasing accounting profits throughout 2003–08. Its return on equity is also strong in the 14–16 percent range in the out-years. This result is rather common among many corporations, because accounting earnings show a positive accounting profit, although the company actually generated negative economic profit when the cost of equity capital is explicitly considered.

A more detailed *bottom-up approach* to calculating NOPAT is as follows:[24]

NOPAT

= EBIT

+ Implied interest expense on operating leases

+ Increase in LIFO reserve

+ Goodwill amortization

+ Increase in bad debt reserve

+ Increase in net capitalized R&D

= Adjusted operating profit before taxes

– Cash operating taxes

A detailed *top-down approach* to calculating NOPAT is as follows:

NOPAT = Sales

+ Increase in LIFO reserve

+ Implied interest expense on operating leases

+ Other income

– Cost of goods sold

– Sales, general and administrative (SG&A) expenses

– Depreciation and amortization expenses

= Adjusted operating profit before taxes

– Cash operating taxes

The amount of capital employed within a firm can be estimated by making adjustments to the balance sheet. The calculation of capital using the *asset approach* is as follows:

Total capital = Net short-term operating assets

+ LIFO reserve

+ Net plant and equipment

+ Other assets

+ Goodwill

+ Accumulated goodwill amortization

+ Present value of operating leases

+ Bad debt reserve

+ Capitalized R&D

+ Cumulative write-offs of special items

The calculation of capital using the *source of financing* approach is as follows:

Total capital = Book value of common equity

+ Preferred stock

+ Minority interest

+ Deferred income tax reserve

+ LIFO reserve

+ Accumulated goodwill amortization

+ Interest bearing short-term debt

+ Long-term debt

+ Capitalized lease obligations

+ Present value of non-capitalized leases

Over time, a company must generate positive EVA in order for its market value to increase. A related concept is market value added (MVA), the difference between the market value of the company and the book value of total capital:[25]

MVA = Market value of the company – Book value of debt and equity capital

A company that generates positive EVA should have a market value in excess of the accounting book value of its capital. The economic profit approach to enterprise valuation looks at the firm's aggregate value. The value of debt and equity capitalization is expressed as the sum of its economic book value plus the net present value generated by its existing and anticipated future assets.

Enterprise value = Value of debt + Value of equity
= Economic book value + Net present value of existing and anticipated future assets

Credit Suisse First Boston (CSFB) utilizes EVA concepts in its analyst reports. The generic EVA valuation formula:

Firm's economic value = Value of existing assets + Value of future investments

where,

Value of existing assets = NOPAT/WACC
Value of future investments = Average future annual EVA/WACC

Corporate MVA = Present value of expected EVA stream
(discounted at the weighted average cost of capital)

There are three versions of EVA that a company can estimate depending on how much accuracy it desires.[26]

- *Basic EVA* uses unadjusted GAAP operating profits and GAAP balance sheet.

- *Disclosed EVA* makes about a dozen major adjustments to the financials.

- *True EVA* makes about 160 or so accounting adjustments to the disclosed GAAP financial statements.

The various types of adjustments include the treatment of such things as the timing of revenue and expense recognition, passive investments in marketable securities, securitized assets and other off-balance-sheet financing, restructuring charges, inflation, foreign currency translation, inventory valuation, bookkeeping reserves, bad debt recognition, intangible assets, taxes, pensions, post-retirement expenses, marketing expenses, goodwill and other acquisition issues, and strategic investments.[27]

Some adjustments are necessary to avoid mixing operating and financing decisions. while others provide a long-term perspective. Some adjustments avoid mixing stocks and flows while others convert GAAP accrual items to additions to capital. These adjustments correct deficiencies in GAAP accounting. For example, US GAAP requires companies to immediately expense all outlays for R&D. The EVA treatment is to capitalize R&D investments (add current outlays to the balance sheet as an asset) and amortize them (charge a portion against earnings each year) over an appropriate period. To estimate true economic profits, companies should move all off-balance sheet items such as uncapitalized leases and securitized receivables back onto the balance sheet.

Some companies generate negative economic profit or EVA. They operate predominantly in mature, competitive markets with low-growth prospects, and are perceived to have limited strategic growth alternatives. This group is populated by manufacturing, service, retail, and other trading companies.

A second category of companies generate positive EVA, but its ability to increase its rate of economic profit growth is restricted because of constrained strategic growth opportunities derived from limited product or geographic expansion potential, overall market competitiveness, high capital requirements, or low barriers to entry.

Other companies that generate positive EVA operate in high-growth markets, or have significant strategic assets that provide high economic profit opportunities. These firms' significant strategic potential is the major driving force of positive EVA valuations. Often these companies rely less on physical assets and more on intangible assets as the basis for their competitive advantage. In other circumstances, this reflects dominant market positions, such as Micosoft, Cisco, Oracle, and Dell. [28]

However, there are critics of EVA. It has been shown that the correlation of EVA and share price performance is poor.[29] EVA may not be a good tool to use for day-to-day brokerage and speculation with stocks – but it is used by many Fortune 500 companies as a primary tool to assess value creation. For example, at DaimlerChrysler, EVA is the primary corporate performance management tool. Clearly, those companies that have destroyed shareholder value such as AOL Time Warner,[30] choose to highlight EVA as a useless measure!

The substantive criticisms of EVA can be handled by adjusting the EVA measure to develop more accurate economic value added measures. EVA can be biased against new capital investment projects, since the large capital charge reduces EVA in the initial years of the project. As the investment depreciates, the capital charge reduces proportionally.

As the investment depreciates, the capital charge reduces proportionally.

EVA, unadjusted for this effect, thus encourages managers to "milk the business" by reducing assets faster than earnings. This reduces the capital charge so much that an artificially high and positive EVA can be manufactured. EVA can also be biased in favor of large, low-return businesses, since it represents large incremental earnings above the base level set by the cost of capital employed. The EVA measure does not become useless, however. What is required is to adjust the measure to a cash basis by adding depreciation and amortization back to NOPAT, and accumulated depreciation back to book capital.[31]

Another residual income valuation model is the CFROI (cash flow return on investment) which is similar in concept to EVA since it considers the cost of equity explicitly in the valuation process, but it is a percentage based metric, and is to be compared to a hurdle rate of return such as the after-tax WACC rate. CFROI can be viewed as the after-tax internal rate of return on a firm's existing assets. The firm's NPV is positive if the CFROI exceeds the hurdle rate or cost of capital.

$$CFROI\% = NOPAT/(Total\ debt + Equity\ capital)$$

However, in practice, CFROI is difficult to apply because the inputs to the model are stated in real, not nominal currency terms, and because it is a proprietary model owned by HOLT associates, a US-based financial consulting firm. While EVA has been popular for corporate governance, the CFROI has been the most popular value-based metric amongst institutional investors.

A relatively new metric around this same concept is the economic margin (EM) which is the spread between a firm's operating cash flow return and its cost of invested capital. It combines elements of EVA as well as CFROI in one model, since it encompasses a valuation system that explicitly addresses the four main drivers of enterprise value: profitability, competition, growth, and cost of capital.[32]

Economic margin = (Operating cash flow – Capital charge)/ Total invested capital

EM% = [OCF – (Total debt + Equity capital) x WACC %]/ Total invested capital

where Operating cash flow = Net income
+ Depreciation and amortization
+ After-tax interest expense
+ Rental expense
+ R&D expense
± Non-recurring items

Capital charge = (Debt + Equity capital) × WACC

Invested capital = Total assets
+ Accumulated depreciation
+ Gross plant inflation adjustment
+ Capitalized operating rentals
+ Capitalized R&D
– Non-debt current liabilities

As we can see, many challenges exist when trying to estimate a company's economic profit. The plethora of accounting adjustments that are necessary to calculate EVA, CFROI, or EM makes them somewhat subjective and difficult to apply. However, the goal of measuring economic profit is worth the extra time and effort, as value-based metrics are directly related to the net present value of the firm's present and anticipated future growth opportunities.

The dividend discount model, discounted cash flow model, and the residual income models are in theory mutually consistent. However, the recognition of value in the residual income models typically occurs earlier than in dividend discount or discounted cash flow models, which may be an advantage of the residual income model where there are uncertainties in forecasting future cash flows or dividends. In other words, the majority of the total value is in the form of current book value rather than terminal value calculation which tends to be highly sensitive to model assumptions.

The world's major consulting firms such as PricewaterhouseCoopers, McKinsey, Boston Consulting Group, KPMG, Deloitte & Touche, etc. all have fast-growing value-oriented practices, and shareholder value concepts now receive unprecedented levels of coverage in the business press as well as in capital markets. In general, Europe and Asia are years behind the US in value-based thinking.[33]

Value drivers include the following elements:[34]

- Revenue growth

  - multi-channel sales strategies
  - broaden market coverage
  - higher growth customer segment focus
  - optimal pricing and bundling
  - deliver enhanced customer experience
  - pursue complementary alliances and acquisitions;

- Higher margins

  - internal restructuring
  - improve process efficiencies
  - cost control
  - scale advantages
  - lower working capital
  - higher inventory turns
  - focus on collection processes;

- Optimize asset utilization

  - careful capital planning
  - improve turn-over ratios;

- Optimize financial management

  - minimize effective taxes
  - optimize cost of capital and financial leverage
  - optimize financial policy.

CASE STUDY 2.1 GlaxoSmithKline[35]

GlaxoSmithKline uses sales, trading profit, profit before taxes, adjusted earnings, and adjusted earnings per share as the primary business performance measures. Non-recurring items are excluded and adjusted or normalized results are presented for purposes of assessing underlying business performance for periods presented.

The GlaxoSmithKline group, as a multinational business, operates in many countries, and earns revenues and incurs costs in many currencies. The results of the group, as reported in sterling, are therefore affected by movements in exchange rates between sterling and other overseas currencies. For performance reporting purposes, the GlaxoSmithKline group uses the average exchange rates prevailing during the year to translate the results of overseas companies into sterling. The currencies that most influence these transactions are the US dollar, the euro, and the Japanese yen.

In order to illustrate underlying performance, GlaxoSmithKline's practice is to discuss the results in terms of constant exchange rate (CER) growth. This represents growth calculated as if the exchange rates used to determine the results of overseas operations in sterling had remained unchanged from those used in the previous year.

CASE STUDY 2.2 DaimlerChrysler[36]

Within the control framework, DaimlerChrysler differentiates between the group level and the operating level of the business units and segments. On the group level, economic value added (EVA) is an absolute earnings ratio calculated by subtracting the weighted average cost of capital from net operating income. Economic Value Added (EVA) is the core element of the control system and therefore represents the most important performance standard at DaimlerChrysler.

In the calculation of the corporate profitability ratio, return on net assets (RONA), net operating income is divided by the capital employed within the group. This shows the extent to which the DaimlerChrysler group as a whole generates or exceeds the rate of return required by its investors and creditors. The required rate of return and the weighted average cost of capital for the group are derived from the minimum returns that investors and creditors expect for equity and capital provided by outside sources.

The cost of equity is determined in accordance with the capital asset pricing model (CAPM), using the interest rate for long-term, risk-free securities (e.g. government bonds, fixed-interest bonds) plus a risk premium for investment in shares. The cost of capital from outside sources is derived from the required rate of return for obligations entered into by the company with the outside sources providing the capital.

At the level of the industrial business units and segments, economic value added (EVA) is calculated as operating profit less the weighted average cost of capital. The calculation is based on the result before interest and taxes, since this reflects the area of responsibility of management more accurately than an after-tax figure. The capital base is net assets, i.e. assets less non-interest-bearing liabilities.

The financial services activities usually apply return on equity (ROE) as a controlling benchmark. The objective of an adequate cost of capital rate is to promote value-adding investment projects and exploit corresponding growth opportunities. In this way, the group is continually pursuing the goal of creating sustained value for DaimlerChrysler's shareholders.

In order to create sustained value for the DaimlerChrysler shareholders, the business units and segments are required to considerably exceed this hurdle. The objective is derived from benchmarks with the best comparable companies and exceeds the minimum requirements.

NOTES

1 Reuven Brennar (2002).

2 Dauphinais *et al.* (2000).

3 Helfert (2003).

4 Young in Fabozzi *et al.* (2000).

5 Dauphinais *et al.* (2000).

6 "Highly attractive industries" were defined as those in which average ROIC–WACC spread was 200 basis points over a five-year period, while "competitively advantaged companies" were those with ROIC–WACC spreads greater than 300 basis points compared to industry average. See Dauphinais *et al.* (2000).

7 Dauphinais *et al.* (2000).

8 PricewaterhouseCoopers (2003a).

9 Damodaran (1994).

10 Pratt, *et al.* (2000).

11 Stowe *et al.* (2003)

12 Stowe (2002).

13 Stonich, T W (1997).

14 Pratt *et al.* (2000).

15 Ibid.

16 Peterson and Peterson (1996).

17 "Fast times at General Electric" in *CFO* magazine June, 1995.

18 Brancato, C (1995).

19 Stowe *et al.* (2003).

20 Young in Fabozzi *et al*. (2000).

21 Lev, B in Fabozzi *et al*. (2000).

22 Fabozzi and Grant (2000).

23 Savarese, C (2000).

24 Fabozzi *et al.* (2000).

25 Stowe, J (2003).

26 Ehrbar in Fabozzi *et al.* (2000)

27 Ibid.

28 Savarese, C (2000).

29 Merrill Lynch (1998).

30 According to *CFO Magazine*'s analysis of companies that have destroyed economic value, i.e., have had negative EVA during 1999–2002, AOL Time Warner destroyed the most shareholder value, at $27.5bn, see July 2003 issue.

31 Olsen, E E (1998).

32 Obrycki and Resendes (2000).

33 Young, D in Fabozzi *et al.* (2000).

34 Bertoneche and Knight (2001).

35 GlaxoSmithKline Annual Report (2002).

36 DaimlerChrysler Annual Report (2002).

CHAPTER 3

Financial policy

Introduction

Financial policy considers the near-term and long-term corporate strategy to determine which policy measures optimally support the execution of strategic objectives. The strategic financial operations are guided by a set of high-level and strategic policy directions, often approved at board level. Tactical financial operations are rather mundane, and require adequate and effective processes and controls. For example, the capital structure, and the composition of the debt and equity structures within the capital structure reflect a company's funding needs, its need for flexibility and risk tolerance, debt covenants, credit rating, asset-liability mix, dilutive effects on equity holdings, and utilization of debt capacity, among other issues.

Dividend policy considers investor demands, competitor dividend yields, and internal funding requirements, and is linked to cash-flow projections in the long-term financial plan. It is used as an important indicator to investors regarding management's expectations of cash inflows, outflows, and sustainability. For example, share buybacks may be preferred to special one-time dividends if they are tax-advantageous to investors, and because of their anti-dilutive and generally positive effect on share prices.

Financing, operating, and investing activities are thus guided by strategy, and at the same time limited by prudent guidelines. For example, treasury and risk management follow specific policy directions set by the senior executives and board. Almost all of the best in class companies reviewed have a policy of not actively trading financial derivative instruments for speculative purposes. Most of these firms also have clear risk tolerance limits, and use either the duration-based sensitivity analysis or value at risk (VAR) based measurements of risk exposures estimation.

Financial institutions are subject to more rigorous regulatory compliance requirements than non-financial corporates. For example, the capital adequacy standards set by the Basel II Accord require strict adherence to risk capital requirements. It was interesting to see that, although not required to do so, some European corporates, such as DaimlerChrysler and Siemens, follow the stricter capital adequacy guidelines that are set for financial institutions according to the Basel II Accord.

Financial policy may specify use of EVA as a corporate performance standard, or use of enterprise-wide risk management (EWRM) systems to track real-time risk exposures at a total company level. Financial policy includes requirements and processes for independent internal and external audits of corporate affairs and financials.

Accounting policy is a key area for corporate boards to be especially vigilant on, since corporate controllers, with a green light from the CEO and CFO, and in association with their accounting audit firms, can manipulate the financials "at-will."

Optimizing corporate financial policy is clearly a multi-faceted task. It requires careful assessment of corporate strategy and its implications for financial requirements. Advances in financial analysis and insights can help in decision support, while real-time financial systems help in the timeliness of execution.

Capital structure

Capital structure management addresses this question: assuming the firm's investment strategy is determined, what is the optimal proportion of debt and equity for the firm?

Just as the nature of the asset base impacts its rate of return, the structure of debt and equity impacts the firm's cost of capital. For a wide variety of reasons, every company has its unique financial structure, resulting in financing costs that are very specific to that firm.[1] In its fullest sense, managing the liability side of the balance sheet involves determining not only the aggregate amount of debt to incur, but also the choice of maturities, the mix of fixed and floating rates, the use of options and other derivatives, and, in general, the selection of capital structure from the rich variety of alternatives available in the global capital markets.

Effective capital structure management focuses on the characteristics of the firm's debt in a portfolio context. This can mean, for example, that new debt issues are structured to offset the interest rate risk of existing debt. It can also mean using the techniques of active liability management on outstanding issues to alter the characteristics of the debt portfolio.

Optimal capital structure means having the right balance of debt and equity financing in the business. Debt financing decisions for most corporations involves balancing a series of trade-offs involving cost, liquidity, choice of maturity, and the basis and frequency of interest rate resets.

In this light, the decision process of financing with debt typically represents a very large-scale, multi-variable risk management exercise. Effective planning to optimize these trade-offs requires a debt-financing plan well integrated into the operating and strategic fabric of the firm, that takes into account the drivers of optimal capital structure (see Figure 3.1)

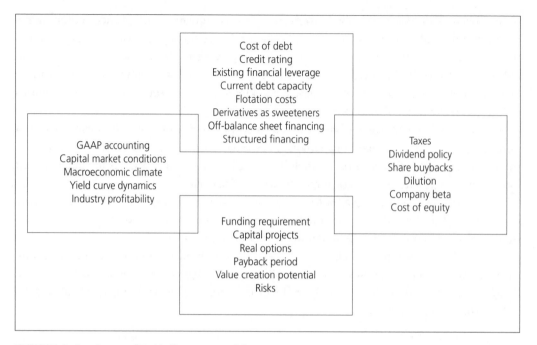

FIGURE 3.1 ▨ Internal capital structure drivers

Maintenance of adequate capital resources to meet diverse, ongoing funding needs and to deal with unforeseen contingencies is among the primary objectives of any CFO.

Some debt instruments have equity-like characteristics such as convertible debt, and some equity instruments have debt-like attributes like preferred stock. The exact level of fixed obligations may be different from traditional long- and short-term debt on the balance sheet. In addition, off-balance-sheet fixed obligations, like operating leases, should be capitalized to get a truer picture of effective debt obligations.

Since interest payments on debt are tax deductible, the effective cost of debt is lower than equity in most cases. Higher debt leverage also improves the return on equity measure of financial performance. Debt thus is an attractive funding source for companies, compared to equity. However, the cost of debt increases as leverage increases and credit ratings consequently deteriorate. Other things remaining equal, the benefits of debt are greater when tax rates are higher. Firms that have substantial non-debt tax shields, such as depreciation, should be less likely to use debt than firms that do not have these tax shields.

The types of debt financing used by a firm impact its overall cost of capital, or the weighted average cost of capital. For example, if a company's suppliers allow a long payment period, its accounts payable at all times would be larger than otherwise, possibly at a low cost. Similarly, if the company has a high proportion of short-term or floating rate debt, it may incur a lower cost of capital than another firm that uses more fixed-rate longer-term debt. However, with changes in market conditions, the relative financing costs would change.

As a firm increases debt relative to equity in its capital structure, the weighted average cost of capital initially decreases until a point, before increasing as a result of higher costs of debt. This is because of the interest tax shield. Eventually, higher cost of capital fully offsets the benefits of tax shields such as interest expenses, accounting depreciation, depletion allowances, investment tax credits, and tax-loss carry-forwards.

The financial leverage ratio that minimizes the weighted average cost of capital is the optimal debt-equity mix for the company since the firm value is maximized at that point, and beyond this point the firm value actually falls.

The actual rate of interest charged on incremental debt will depend, of course, on the credit rating of the company, and on the degree of leverage introduced into the capital structure by the new debt. The specific cost will be affected not only by current market conditions for all long-term debt instruments, but also as a function of the company-specific risk as perceived by lenders, underwriters, and investors.

Other costs implicit in raising long-term debt include legal and underwriting expenses connected with the issue, and the nature of covenants imposed by creditors. At times, a variety of specific provisions can involve implicit costs to the company.

In theory, the first Modigliani-Miller (MM) irrelevance proposition tells us that the value of a company is independent of its capital structure. In other words, financial leverage does not affect the value of the firm. According to the MM propositions, although debt appears to be a cheaper source of financing for a firm, issuing debt increases the risk of holding equity, thereby leading investors to demand a higher expected return on equity. This increase in the cost of equity capital exactly offsets the benefit of the cheaper debt in the firm's capital structure, leaving the overall cost of capital unchanged. However, imperfections in the capital market cause violations of certain MM assumptions. For example, unequal access of participants to the capital markets, taxes, and asymmetric information can all motivate firms to manage risk in a manner that is consistent with value-maximizing behaviour.

Risk management can add value when it reduces the firm's cost of capital or increases its expected future cash-flow. Empirical research suggests that generally, equity increasing transactions result in stock price decreases, while leverage increasing transactions result in stock price increases.[2] In practice, the optimal capital structure in the financial planning process is driven more by the need for external funds than specific attempts to reach an optimal capital structure. This can be explained by the pecking order hierarchy, according to which, debt is the second-best financing alternative after internal financing, and ahead of external equity. It may also be influenced by the transaction costs of issuance of equity versus debt, where the former is often the more expensive of the two.

the optimal capital structure in the financial planning process is driven more by the need for external funds than specific attempts to reach an optimal capital structure.

According to a survey of 176 corporate CFOs, 69 percent of respondents indicated a preference for the *pecking order hypothesis*.[3] In the pecking order theory, there is no well-defined optimal debt ratio. The attraction of interest tax shields and the threat of financial distress are assumed second-order. Debt ratios change when there is an imbalance of internal cash-flow, net of dividends, and real investment opportunities. Highly profitable firms with limited investment opportunities work down to lower debt ratios, while firms whose investment opportunities exceed internally generated funds borrow more.

The life-cycle of the business

Any attempt to reach an optimal financial leverage must take into consideration the life-cycle of the business entity and its industry, and the ensuing business risks. High-risk businesses, for example, should have low-leverage financial strategies that allow sufficient bandwidth to play in times of demand volatility. Lower-risk businesses that have more stable cash-flows can afford to have more aggressive gearing.

If we look at Microsoft's business planning, for example, it is a mature company but sits on a huge cash balance. With an asset base of $79.6bn, Microsoft had literally no debt and $49.0bn of total cash and short-term investments on its books as of June 2003. We would therefore expect Microsoft to get more levered in the future.

The currency composition of debt and equity is crucial to the determination of the cost of capital. Companies have a choice of financing much of their global activity with base or parent's reporting currency debt, or with local currency denominated debt from outside sources.

In most cases, foreign subsidiaries carry only local currency debt to match local currency assets. This is often accomplished by the parent lending in the local currency of the subsidiary, regardless of whether third-party debt is in the base currency. The net result of such financing activity is that the asset, and hence the income, is in the local currency of the subsidiary, while the liability and the net interest expense are in the reporting currency of the firm.

This currency mismatch of revenues and expenses, and assets and liabilities is not clearly visible when each entity is separately analysed. However, the parent's reporting currency rate of return and cost of funds are being impacted by exchange rate movements.

Microsoft is both profitable and cash generative, but has only recently started paying dividends. The company does not have a formal stock repurchase plan. However, since its flotation in 1986, it has frequently bought back shares from its shareholders. The conservation of cash reduces the risk profile of Microsoft's business, thereby increasing its share price.

Capital structure choices of firms in developing countries are affected by the same variables as in developed countries, although the institutional features differ.[4] Both the Anglo-Saxon capital markets model and the Continental–German–Japanese banking models were studied by Booth *et al.* Industry average leverage, however, does not appear to be a significant factor in market valuations for companies. The market does not consider industry averages for leverage as discriminators for firms' financial leverage.[5]

Financial leverage rises with increasing cash-flow requirements of the business, whether for investments, capital expenditures, or working capital needs. Focusing on the cash-flow cuts though many of the accounting issues.

The cash-flow statement provides the best information about a highly leveraged firm's financial health, given the overriding importance of generating cash to retire debt. Business enterprises typically go though phases of development. Accordingly, it is necessary to condition the financial plan of the business based on its stage of maturity.

From negative cash-flow start-ups to heavily positive cash generating mature companies, optimal cash management is key to maintaining appropriate levels of financial liquidity. Consolidation is a typical feature of mature industries, where companies seek to bolster their diminishing profit margins by capturing economies of scale. Declining companies, on the other hand, struggle to generate sufficient cash as a consequence of meagre earnings from deteriorating core businesses.

A careful evaluation of capital structures shows a common pattern in the way highly successful companies have financed themselves. This pattern corresponds to the corporate life-cycle.[6]

When a company first begins, it typically is dealing in a new product market. In this introductory stage, the best companies will generally have very little debt. There is plenty of risk to shareholders in the product market, and hence no reason to add more risk by levering the capital structure. At this stage of the company's life, it has little taxable income, so the tax shield from any meaningful level of debt is irrelevant.

In addition, in this *introductory phase*, a company must often move extremely quickly on new investment opportunities. If its actions are restricted by debt covenants, the most important projects may have to be delayed while the company negotiates with its creditors. On balance, many start-up companies view the expected opportunity losses on foregone projects as far more costly than avoiding tax payments.

Private equity is often sought by a company at the start-up phase of its growth-cycle. The private equity market is one of the fastest growing capital markets for corporate finance. In fact, the amount of capital raised through private equity has competed directly with initial public offerings (IPOs) and gross issuance of public high-yield corporate bonds. Private equity is an important source of funds for new firms, financially distressed firms, private mid-market firms, and public firms in need of buyout capital. The most widely recognized use of private equity is to support the rapid growth of start-up high-tech firms such as Dell Computers and Microsoft. In the 1980s, huge amounts of private equity were used in large mergers and take-overs. Limited Partnerships represent the major intermediary in the private equity market.[7]

In the second stage of the life-cycle, the *growth stage*, the company may add some debt as it expands output significantly. The company is still risky, however, so debt might be kept at very low levels. Again, the company may have little taxable income, so tax shields from interest expense may have very little value.

The third stage is *maturity*. At this point, investment opportunities that promise spectacularly large net present values are relatively scarce. The value of the tax shields on debt financing rises, and the expected cost of having to pass up extraordinary opportunities falls. At maturity, the company should be distributing cash to its shareholders in a reasonably predictable manner. Therefore an increasing proportion of a company's capital structure is in the form of debt, as creditors find the stability of cash-flows attractive. Excess cash is distributed to shareholders typically in the form of dividends and share repurchases.

The fourth stage is *decline*. If it is at all possible, now is the time for the company to incur substantial debt, distribute the proceeds to shareholders, and allow the creditors to bear the very real risk of default. Lenders, of course, recognize this risk and will not lend the company all it wants. Nevertheless, at this stage, debt financing is most ardently sought.

The basic cash-flow, defined as net income plus depreciation plus deferred income tax, is an indicator of financial flexibility. A rise in the cost of debt financing may lead to greater optimal debt levels since higher interest rates generate greater tax benefits, which in turn dictate more debt despite its higher costs.[8]

Usually, highly leveraged firms continuously monitor market conditions for opportunities to reduce debt through strategic financial transactions. This might include sale of non-core and marginally profitable business units or product lines. Leveraged recapitalizations may be optimal for companies that have low stock market valuation. Deleveraging through debt-for-debt or debt-for-equity exchanges can be used to restructure the financial obligations.

However, sudden swings in market capitalization sometimes reveal more about the dynamics of the market than they do about short-run changes in companies' earnings prospects. In the 1980s, for example, when interest rates were high, hybrid debt – combining a conventional debt issue with a derivative such as a forward, swap, or option – was used by riskier firms to reduce their interest costs to manageable levels.[9]

In some cases, companies are using hybrid debt to lower their risk profile and thus avoid the higher funding costs now associated with being a riskier corporate borrower. In other cases, hybrids are providing access to debt capital that would otherwise be denied on any terms.

Leasing is an important financing vehicle for firms in most countries. For example, in the US, equipment under lease accounts for nearly a third of the total annual new equipment investment in recent years.[10]

According to FASB 13 a lease is a *capital lease* if:

- it transfers ownership of the asset to the lessee by the end of the lease term; or
- it contains an option to purchase the leased property at a bargain price; or
- the lease term is equal to or greater than 75 percent of the asset's estimated economic life; or
- the present value of the lease payments equals or exceeds 90 percent of the fair value of the leased asset.

If the lease does not qualify as a capital lease, it is an operating lease. For accounting purposes, a capitalized lease is treated much like any other owned asset. It must be booked as an asset with a corresponding liability, depreciation is taken over time, and the interest portion of each payment is expensed. Payments in operating leases are expensed as incurred, and thus are harder on the earnings. If a firm has limited debt capacity, a lease displaces debt in the firm's capital structure. An exception worth mentioning is the case of the all-equity firm. Some profitable high-growth firms are successful in generating positive economic returns and shareholder wealth, but do not have any meaningful debt in their capital structure.

EXAMPLE

Microsoft is a case in point. Despite its successful business model, it has little or no debt in its capital structure. This is because Microsoft's free cash-flow has consistently exceeded its Capex, suggesting that the firm rarely needed to tap the debt markets for expansion. In addition, Microsoft's capital intensity generally has been very low, indicating that it has a relatively small amount of collateralizable assets.

To the extent that debt is utilized in the capital structure, return on equity is boosted as long as after-tax interest cost does not exceed earnings power. Companies with different degrees of leverage experience different costs of debt as well. Costs of debt will rise as lenders assess the risks of high debt levels. Optimal debt levels can be derived from financial optimization analysis subject to realistic constraints, since no management is completely free to vary the capital structure at will.

Optimal debt levels can be derived from financial optimization analysis.

There are practical as well as legal and contractual constraints on any company to maintain some normalcy on the liability side of the balance sheet. Even though no absolute rules exist as to leverage optimization, lenders will impose upper limits on the amounts of debt capital to be utilized by any potential borrower.

For manufacturing companies, the amount of long-term debt will normally range between 0 and 50 percent of their capitalization, whereas public utilities will range between 30 and 60 percent. Trading companies with highly liquid assets might have even higher debt proportions. At the same time, restructuring and corporate reengineering are shifting both capital requirements and debt levels in many instances. For example, outsourcing as part of corporate strategy might serve to reduce the need for capital, including debt, because part of the asset base is effectively transferred to suppliers.[11]

Impact on market value

The most important issue around the use of financial leverage, however, relates to its impact on the company's overall market value. Financial theory has firmly established that introduction of financial leverage into an unleveraged capital structure will raise the market value of the company because of the change in total return to debt and equity holders – but only up to a point.

The lift in market value is in fact a function of the corporate tax deductibility of the interest cost of debt. As debt levels increase, the value of this favorable tax shield impact increases. The trade-off is simply between the cash-flow implications from the obtainable tax savings and the cash-flow implications from financial stress and even failure. Therefore, the optimal level of leverage will differ greatly among companies, industries, and management styles. This policy decision ought to be as objective as possible, where financial optimization techniques can provide essential guidance to its determination.

Finding the optimal degree of leverage for a business requires a careful assessment of potential financial risks, which are a function of the variability of business performance, the outlook for the markets served, competitive conditions, strategic positioning, and so on. In short, successful application of financial leverage is much more than a numerical exercise.

Empirical studies have shown that fast-growing companies tend to create superior value through a capital structure with a conservative debt level, allowing them to maintain flexibility in accessing financial markets. This is generally accompanied by low dividend payout and emphasis on internal funds sources in financing growth.

Consistent with the pecking order hypothesis, equity is raised only when absolutely necessary to maintain profitable growth, whereas new debt is limited to relatively modest leverage targets. In contrast, slow-growing mature companies that generate sizable cash-flows can create superior value by disposing of the excess cash through share repurchases, reducing the equity base.

The effect of restructuring and the more successful performance achieved by many companies in the first half of the 1990s has led to a shift toward more conservative capital structures for some firms, with the notable exception of complex, partially hidden debt structures in certain companies, of which the failed Enron is a prime example.

Strong cash-flows obtained from disposals of under-performing businesses and leaner ongoing operations have often been applied to reducing the temporarily inflated debt proportions of many companies. This was in part a reaction to the heavy use of leverage during the 1980s. At the same time, imprudent acquisitions at premium prices can seriously impair a company's capital structure through increased leverage.[12]

The drive to create shareholder value in the past decade has included a rethinking of sustainable capital structure proportions in relation to business performance and outlook, not just from the standpoint of minimizing the cost of capital. Ultimately, of course, we must view the optimal capital structure in the broad context of the interrelated investment, operational, and financing aspects of the business.

A typical corporation funds its debt needs through a combination of instruments. Contingent convertibles have gained some popularity in recent years, as a method to lower funding costs of newly issued debt. For example, some companies have issued zero-interest cost debt by attaching a conversion option to the debt issue, but the option is contingent on the price level of the stock. Since contingent options do not need to be accounted for under GAAP, this does not dilute the earnings per share number.[13]

A committed revolving line of credit may provide liquidity directly or indirectly by supporting the issuance of commercial paper. Term debt may have been issued in public capital markets or through a private placement, or it may be provided by the bank or group of banks that provided the revolving credit. Interest rate swaps may have been arranged to hedge the interest rate risk of certain underlying debt. The possibilities are diverse and sometimes complex.

The foundation of a debt financing plan is a cash-flow forecast to determine expected funding needs. Additionally, an assessment of factors that might cause the funding needs to change is necessary. The importance of carefully weighing the amount of flexibility needed in the future depends on the degree of risk of having insufficient funds available, offset by the cost of providing more funds than are necessary.[14]

Providing adequate liquidity

Failure to meet a future payroll due to lack of liquidity represents an obvious and severe problem. However, maintenance of excess liquidity to guard against this risk is not free. The most common means of providing liquidity is a committed line of credit facility with a bank or syndicated among a group of banks. Such an arrangement will specify the term and maximum amount of the commitment. It will contain a negotiated set of financial and other covenants, and it will specify pricing considerations on both a drawn and undrawn basis.

A company's debt rating and financial position determine the interest rates to be charged on outstanding loan balances. The line of credit must be secured by paying a nominal commitment fee. While pricing fluctuates with the level of liquidity and degree of competitiveness in the banking system, it is often a function of the extent of existing and potential overall relationships.

The assessment by a CFO of the appropriate amount of liquidity should include an analysis of the possible extent and likelihood of material deviations from a base cash-flow forecast. A key element of this overall assessment is a judgment regarding the firm's financial flexibility and capacity to fund liquidity needs by internal means as needs arise, or through traditional external sources.

Tighter working capital management often improves the internal cash position. However, on a larger scale, the sale of non-strategic assets, or deferral of planned capital investments provides another recourse. Obviously, consideration of such possible actions naturally includes careful thought regarding the probable effect on the execution of a corporation's overall strategy.

The choice of maturity for a given debt issue balances the likely duration of the need for funds with the relative cost of the various maturities in the context of the weighted average maturity of the existing debt. This context is a very important consideration.

The basic framework for a maturity analysis is a review of the pattern and extent of future cash-flows from operations, net of financing costs (interest expenses and dividends), but before accounting for the effect of debt maturities. On this basis, companies match amounts and timing of debt maturities to the respective projected dates of positive future cash-flows. This process is called "duration-matching." The objective is to match, as closely as possible, the weighted average maturities of the assets and liabilities.

However, in the real world, needs change, creating mismatches. Additionally, moderate intentional mismatches appropriately result from balancing future refinancing risk against current fund availability and cost considerations.

When faced with this series of trade-offs, some CFOs opt for the longest available maturity of debt when the need to borrow arises, on the belief that refinancing risk is minimized by this technique. Refinancing risk is the risk of providing adequate liquidity in the future to refund the excess of a maturing debt obligation over available funds from operations.

This cost is potentially severe. Longer maturities typically carry higher interest rates through a combination of higher-reference treasury yields in a positive-sloping yield-curve environment. Investors demand higher spreads from treasuries for longer-maturity corporate debt.

The interest rate structure is an important consideration with respect to the interest rate risk exposure of the firm. A borrowing is typically priced at a fixed or a floating interest rate that resets periodically based on prevailing market rates.

Fixed rates offer the luxury of certainty.

In a sense, the terms fixed and floating are not precise because a "floating" rate is actually "fixed" for a short time, say one month. Fixed rates offer the luxury of certainty, and cash-flows necessary to service the interest component of fixed-rate borrowings can be forecast with precision.

Floating rates, in contrast, can and do change, sometimes abruptly. Floating rates are often indexed to the London Interbank Offer Rate (LIBOR). Cash-flows necessary to service a liability priced against this floating benchmark is inherently imprecise to predict.

From a borrower's perspective, the attraction of floating rates is that a series of floating rate borrowings sequentially rolled-over will more often than not cost less than fixed-rate borrowing. This is due to yield curve and credit spread issues, and because there is an additional cost to be paid for the certainty of the fixed-rate borrowing as the borrower shifts the price risk to the lender.

The more interest rate risk a firm is willing to assume, the more expected interest savings will accrue to the benefit of the firm. Striking the appropriate balance between fixed and floating rates on the debt portfolio requires an analysis that models the effect of reasonably possible changes in interest rates on hypothetical mixes of fixed and floating rate exposure. One method that is heavily applied in practice is the duration-convexity approach, which assumes parallel shifts in the interest rate structure to determine possible impact on the value of the debt securities and interest rate expenses.

There is evidence that increases in leverage are followed by improvements in operating efficiency.[15] Empirical research shows evidence of modest improvements in operating efficiency at firms involved in leveraged buyouts and leveraged recapitalizations.[16]

In Palepu and Deuis's study of 29 firms that increased debt substantially, they report a median increase in the return on assets of 21.5 percent. Much of this gain seems to arise out of cutbacks in unproductive capital investments. Leveraged recapitalizations – where companies increase their debt ratios by borrowing money to buy back stock or pay dividends – are one form of financial management to get to an optimal capital structure.

In practice, firms often do not use their debt capacity to the fullest. One of the reasons is that they like to preserve some cushion for unexpected future funding or investment needs. Firms that borrow to capacity lose this flexibility and have no fall-back funding if they do get into trouble or suddenly find a very attractive investment opportunity. The value of the firm may be maximized by preserving some flexibility to take on future projects as they arise.

Financial flexibility

Financial flexibility refers to the capacity of firms to meet any unforeseen contingencies that may arise or take advantage of unanticipated opportunities, using the funds they have on hand and any excess debt capacity they might have available. The value of flexibility can be analysed using the option pricing framework. A firm maintains large cash balances and excess debt capacity in order to have the option to take projects that might arise in the future.

The value of the option will depend on the excess return that the firm earns on its projects that provides the value for flexibility. If flexibility is viewed as an option, its value will increase when there is greater uncertainty about future projects.

Firms that have large and unpredictable demands on their cash-flows will value flexibility more and borrow less than firms with stable investment requirements. Thus, even the most successful firms in the high-technology arena such as Intel and Microsoft use very little debt in their capital structure. As firms and industries mature, excess returns on projects drop off and project requirements become more stable. These changes increase the capacity of firms to borrow money.

While theory suggests that firms should pick the mix of debt and equity that maximizes firm value, the most common approach is to set leverage close to that of the peer group to which the firm belongs. If firms in the peer group have similar financial characteristics in terms of tax rates and cash-flow variability, this approach may provide a guideline to arriving at an optimal. However, since individual firms have unique characteristics, this approach is likely to be sub-optimal.

External debt financing reduces a firm's flexibility for future financing because the firm reaches its debt capacity with increasing leverage. Bond covenants also curtail management's freedom to manage the business. Therefore, CFOs and boards prefer retained earnings as a source of capital. The pecking order theory applies very well to actual practice.

There is some empirical evidence to support a pecking order hierarchy. In a survey by Pinegar and Wilbright, CFOs of multinationals ranked their preference for source of funding as follows:[17]

Rank of priority	Funding source
1	Retained earnings
2	Straight debt
3	Convertible debt
4	External common equity
5	Straight preferred stock
6	Convertible preferred

External debt is strongly preferred over external equity as a way of raising funds. Given a choice, firms would much rather use straight debt than convertible debt in spite of lower interest costs of the latter. The primary reason for not issuing external equity seems to be the avoidance of dilution, while the main reason for using debt is the maximization of stock prices.

The costs of securing external funding is also a factor in the optimal leverage decision. Floatation of debt is an expensive business. Equity issuance is even more expensive. And the costs, as a proportion of the issue, become larger the smaller the size of the issue. This suggests that fewer and larger issues are more desirable than numerous smaller ones. In comparison, retained earnings do not carry these fees and costs.

Trade-offs between the costs and benefits of the various forms of debt and debt-like financing instruments form the basic strategic considerations in approaching the topic of optimal capital structure. Formulation of a debt financing plan that considers disparate and often conflicting aspects of funding needs is necessary to judge debt financing risk in an organized and thoughtful manner.

The choice of a target debt-to-capital ratio is only the first step in corporate financial leverage optimization. The structure of a firm's liability portfolio should reflect the nature of its assets and revenues, as well as its near and long-term business plans.

For many mature industrial corporations, debt is viewed as an ongoing component of the capital structure, providing desirable tax benefits without impairing the credit risk of the firm. As debt matures or is called in, it is refinanced at prevailing market rates.

There are, of course, exceptions to this approach. Project financing is an important example. Typically, the funding will be structured to match the operating life of the project and, as closely as possible, the revenues generated by the project.

Asset-liability mismatches can have unfavorable consequences. For example, if funds are raised before actually needed, the issuer suffers "negative arbitrage": interest earned on the deposited cash typically falls far short of the borrower's cost of funds. Other problems arise if the issuer needs to retire debt before the completion of the project.

Financial institutions, for example, practice a continual discipline of asset-liability management in order to limit the interest rate exposure of their financial assets. Since financial institutions typically have high gearing, often exceeding 80 percent, the need to avoid the danger of funding mismatches is exacerbated.

Industrial firms typically have a debt-to-capital ratio between 30 to 40 percent.[18] However, the internal structure of the debt portfolio can be quite varied. If the firm's operating income is particularly vulnerable to interest rate upswings, long-term fixed-rate debt will constitute the bulk of the debt. This may be tempered by a desire to reduce annual interest expense by using investments with shorter maturities, and repaying them with proceeds from fresh issues. For example, the company can roll its short-term commercial paper over and over again.

While reducing interest costs, this strategy exposes the issuer to "roll-over" risk – the uncertainty about the level of the firm's financing rate when outstanding debt matures. The trade-off between cost and risk is often the key criterion by which financing decisions are made.

One way to reduce the effective cost of long-term debt is to introduce refunding provisions into the bond's structure. Other sweeteners such as conversion options or put options can be utilized. Interest rate swaps are also used to restructure interest payments to more desirable terms. In order to increase flexibility, firms often attach a call option to the debt issue in exchange for a slightly higher coupon.

Structured financial vehicles

Structured financing vehicles can be used in various ways to create novel, and sometimes unusual, financial structures. In the area of liability-linked structures, issuers who prefer fixed-rate financing, but can obtain a preferential rate by issuing floating-rate debt often enter into a swap as the fixed-rate payer to effect this conversion.

Issuers who want to obtain fixed-rate debt but want the flexibility to call the bond and reissue at a lower rate if interest rates fall often attach a call option to the original debt issue in exchange for a higher coupon, or issue a straight bond and buy a receiver's swaption in order to convert the bond into a synthetic floating rate liability.[19]

In addition to changing the callability or puttability of an issue, borrowers often use swaps, caps, and floors to alter the interest rate exposure based on the shape of the yield curve. Debt structures can be reengineered in many ways. For example, a fixed-rate structure can be converted into a floating-rate structure by engaging in a receive-fixed swap. Alternatively, a floating-rate debt issue can be converted to a fixed-rate structure by engaging in a pay-fixed swap.

Asset-linked structures include swap-linked notes that are essentially short-term notes with a redemption value linked to swap rates. Deleveraged floating rate notes have coupons that are a fraction of constant maturity treasury yields. Index amortization swaps are designed as a hedge against asset or mortgage-backed securities because the principal is amortized according to a preset formula linked to prevailing interest rates. Differential swaps have also been successfully used by many companies. These are a special variation of a basis swap where both rates are floating, but one is indexed to the LIBOR of a foreign currency, while all payments are made in a single currency.

Although the liability side of the balance sheet may thus be modified over time, most firms opt to have a capital structure that is within the norm of its industry, although their interest rate hedging policies vary considerably. Companies differ widely on the ratio of short-term financing to all debt carried at a time, and the degree to which interest rate risk is hedged through fixed-rate borrowings.

Many companies set interest expense or interest rate ceilings below what they would like their interest costs to remain. Consequently, their hedging policy is influenced by where the current cost of debt is in relation to the ceiling.

Alternative financing vehicles

Alternative financing vehicles include:

- Line of Credit
- Revolving Credit Agreement (RCA)
- Commercial Paper (CP)
- Reverse Repurchase Agreements (RRA)
- Bankers' Acceptances (BA)
- Asset-based Borrowing (securitization)
- Leasing (operating or capital lease)
- Mezzanine Financing (MF)

A *Line of Credit* is an agreement in which the lender gives the borrower access to funds up to a maximum amount over a specific period of time. Lines of credit are generally used to provide short-term financing, to back-up commercial paper, or to provide a liquidity cushion. Lines of credit are usually revolving, meaning the borrower may borrow, repay, and reborrow funds during the commitment period.

A *Revolving Credit Agreement (RCA)*, also known as a revolver, is a facility that allows the borrower to borrow, repay, and reborrow up to a defined amount. RCAs are contractual commitments with loan agreements, including covenants. Usually there is a commitment fee on the unused portion, as well as a facility fee.

Commercial Paper (CP) is an unsecured promissory note issued by a company for a specific amount, generally issued at a discount, with maturities ranging from overnight to 270 days for public issues.

In a *Reverse Repurchase Agreement (RRA)*, a company holding securities in its short-term portfolio sells the securities to a dealer with an agreement to buy them back at a specific price at a specific time. In effect, the company is borrowing cash from the dealer, and using its securities as collateral for the loan.

A *Banker's Acceptance (BA)* is a negotiable short-term instrument used primarily to finance the import, export, or domestic shipment of goods or the storage of readily marketable staples.

Asset-Based Borrowing (ABB) represents a form of secured borrowing based on pledging accounts receivable, inventory, or equipment as collateral for a loan.

Securitization is a financing technique by which a company issues debt securities backed by a pool of its selected receivables such as mortgages, auto loans, credit-card receivables, equipment leases, or other kinds of low-risk receivables. Assets suitable for debt securitization usually have a predictable cash flow stream to retire the issue and a low level of historical loss experience. Securitization is a type of off-balance sheet (OBS) financing. Neither the debt nor the assets securing the financing appear on the company's balance sheet. By removing debt financing from the balance sheet, securitization improves some companies' financial ratios.

Operating and Capital Leases

Leases provide an alternative to long-term loans for financing capital equipment. One motivation for leasing rather than borrowing and buying an asset is to avoid recognition of the debt on the lessee's financial statements. Lease capitalization eliminates this advantage. Leases may be structured to qualify as operating leases to achieve desired financial reporting effects and capital structure benefits. Operating leases allow lessees to avoid recognition of the asset, and report higher profitability ratios and indicators of operating efficiency. Reported leverage is also lower because the related liability for contractual payments are not recognized.

Short-term, or *operating leases* allow the lessee to use leased property for only a portion of its economic life. The lessee accounts for such leases as contracts reporting only the required rental payments as they are made. Because the lessor retains substantially all the risks of ownership of leased property, the leased the asset remains on its balance sheet and are depreciated over their estimated economic lives; rental payments are recognized as revenues over time according to the terms of the lease.

Alternatively, longer-term leases may effectively transfer all, or substantially all the risks and rewards of the leased property to the lessee. Such leases are the economic equivalent of sales with financing arrangements designed to effect the purchase (by the lessee) and sale (by the lessor) of the leased property. Such leases – referred to as finance or *capital leases* – are treated for accounting purposes as sales. The asset and associated debt are carried on the books of the lessee, and the lessor records a gain on 'sale' as the inception of the lease. The lessee depreciates the asset over its life, and treats the lease payments as payments of principal and interest. The financial reporting differences between accounting for a lease as an operating or capital lease are far-reaching, and affect the balance sheet, income statement, cash flow statement, and associated ratios.[20]

Mezzanine Financing

The need for additional financing, whether for expansion, acquisition, or liquidity, is a crucial element for the future growth of a business. Particularly in the senior debt market, *Mezzanine Financing (MF)* is an increasingly important capital option for growing middle market companies. In the venture capital world, MF is a debt instrument that bridges a gap in time between earlier rounds of venture financing and a liquidity event – usually an acquisition, refinancing or an initial public offering (IPO). This financing is generally structured as subordinated debt with warrants with a term of not more than three years. This facility is expected to be deployed very quickly with little due diligence on the part of the lender. It is therefore priced fairly aggressively with the lender seeking a return in the 30–40 percent range. However, the company is offered strong incentives to pay the loan off prior to the end of the term. If the loan is paid off early, the amount of warrants is reduced. Conversely, if the loan is not paid off within the agreed upon term, the amount of warrants is increased.

We can also look at MF in terms of the capital structure rather than elapsed time. Here, MF is used to fill a void that can exist in a company's capital structure between equity and senior secured debt. It is generally structured as subordinated debt with warrants or some other equity feature. MF has been used extensively by private middle market companies and has been particularly useful in financings for buyouts, recapitalizations, acquisitions and growth where there is a capital need beyond what the senior secured lender is willing to provide and more than the equity provider can afford or is willing to invest. MF is typically an unsecured facility with a term of five to eight years, depending upon the term of the senior facility, the needs of the company and the term appetite of the lender.

Transactions are usually structured with no amortization, with principal due at the term of the facility or with principal amortized over the last several years of the facility. A company will generally use MF because it does not have the business assets to borrow sufficient senior debt to complete the contemplated transaction and/or the owners/managers wants to retain control or minimize equity dilution. MF providers generally take minority ownership positions and seek board observation rights rather than actual board representation, though they often reserve the right to gain board representation if things do not go as planned. The combination of the debt and equity features of MF enables both the lender and the borrower to take advantage of the benefits of debt and equity while minimizing the negatives.[21]

In the following example, we analyse the optimal financial leverage ratio for XYZ Corp., which currently has 24 percent debt in its capital structure. Based on the assumption that costs of both debt and equity are likely to rise as a company gets more leveraged, the assumptions shown in Figure 3.2 were made regarding the relative costs of debt and equity capital at alternative leverage ratios.

EXAMPLE

XYZ Corp. ($ Million)

Debt ratio(%)	WACC (%)	Blended cost of debt(%)	Cost of equity (%)	Debt rating
0	12.00	6.5	12.0	AAA
10	11.49	6.5	12.3	AAA
20	10.77	6.5	12.4	A+
30	9.97	6.6	12.4	A−
40	10.28	7.0	14.1	BB
50	10.76	11.4	14.1	B
60	10.89	11.4	16.1	CCC
70	10.88	13.3	16.1	CCC
80	10.88	13.3	19.8	CCC
90	11.05	15.5	19.8	CC
100	11.57	17.8	19.8	CC

FIGURE 3.2 ■ Analyzing the optimal financial leverage ratio

As the company's debt leverage increases, its higher financial risks will result in lower debt ratings, thus leading to higher costs of debt. But since the higher leverage risk also impacts the volatility of earnings of the company, its beta will rise, thus increasing its cost of equity as well.

XYZ Corp.'s current valuation is shown in Figure 3.3.

XYZ Corp.	Actual	Forecast				
Valuation	2003	2004	2005	2006	2007	2008
Return on equity	47.9%	29.4%	23.5%	17.2%	12.8%	9.9%
Retention rate	90.0%	90.0%	90.0%	90.0%	90.0%	90.0%
Sustainable growth rate	43.1%	26.4%	21.2%	15.4%	11.5%	8.9%
Debt ratio	24.00%	24%	24%	24%	24%	24%
Cost of debt	6.5%					
Cost of equity	12.4%					
WACC	10.44%					
Corporate value	$3,212 m					

FIGURE 3.3 ■ Current valuation

At the current 24 percent leverage structure, the value of the company is $3,212m. However, when we use a financial leverage optimization program, we find that, given the graduated cost of capital schedule, the optimal financial leverage ratio is 39 percent, since it maximizes the value of the firm.

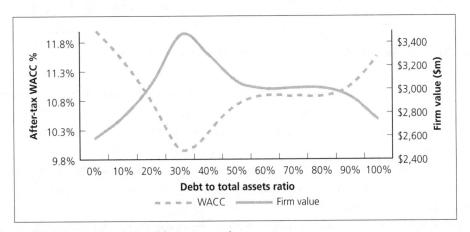

FIGURE 3.4 ■ The optimal leverage ratio

RUN [Restore]	#1: 8/12/2003 12:28:26 AM
Cell to Optimize	'ProForma (Target Debt)'!$G$15
Optimization Goal	Maximum Mean
RESULTS	
Valid Sims	2305
Total Sims	2305
Original Value	3212.494036
+ soft constraint penalties	0
= result	3212.494036
Best Value Found	3944.040741
+ soft constraint penalties	0
= result	3944.040741
Occurred on trial #	1823
Time to find this value	1:45:14
Stopped Because	Optimal Value Found
Optimization Started At	10:21:19 PM
Optimization Finished At	12:28:12 AM
Total Optimization Time	2:06:51
Adjustable Cell	'ProForma (Target Debt)'!$C$15
ORIGINAL	0.24
BEST	0.390158409
CONSTRAINTS	
ADJUSTABLE CELLS	
Description	N/A
Solving Method	Genetic Algorithm: RECIPE
Number of Time Blocks	N/A
Const/Prec Range	N/A
Mutation Rate	0.1
Crossover Rate	0.5
Input Cell/Range Constraint	0<'ProForma (Target Debt)'!$G$15<1
OPTIONS	
Population Size	50
Pause On Error	FALSE
Graph Progress	FALSE
Update Display	Off
Log Simulation Data	TRUE
Random Seed	11253072 (Randomly Chosen)

FIGURE 3.5 ■ RiskOptimizer summary for optimal financial leverage

The type of optimization modeling shown in the example requires simulation optimization, as it has logical multi-nested if-then-else type functions in the model that make the cost of capital a discontinuous function, and not a monotonically increasing function of leverage.

We used *Palisades' RiskOptimizer* software to run the optimization program using Latin Hypercube simulation and genetic algorithm (GA) technology to solve the problem, and the results are shown in Figure 3.5.

The detailed business plan corresponding to the optimal financial leverage is shown in Figure 3.6.

XYZ Corp. ($ Million)

Assumptions	2003		2003
Net revenue growth	6%	Current liabilities	70
Current year sales	$1,000	Equity	400
Interest rate on debt	7%	Beg retained earnings	100
Dividend payout ratio	10%	Current assets	150
Tax rate	35%	Property, plant, and equip.	900
Cost of goods sold / net revenue	41%	Accumulated depreciation	300
SG&A / net revenue	12%		
Depreciation rate	10%		
Liquid asset interest rate	9%	Sustainable growth rate	4%
Current assets / net revenue	15%	Target Debt to asset ratio	39%
Current liabilities / net revenue	7%		
Net fixed assets / net revenue	60%		
PP&E / net revenue	90%		

XYZ Corp. ($ Million)	Actual	Forecast				
Income Statement	2003	2004	2005	2006	2007	2008
Net revenue	1,000	1,060	1,124	1,191	1,262	1,338
- Cost of goods sold	410	435	461	488	518	549
= Gross profit	590	625	663	703	745	790
- Sales, general, and admin	120	127	135	143	151	161
= EBITDA	470	498	528	560	593	629
- Depreciation and amort.	90	104	120	138	158	180
= EBIT	380	394	408	422	436	449
- Interest expense	12	34	46	74	125	228
+Interest Income	-	48	85	177	353	705
= Income before Taxes	368	408	448	526	663	926
- Taxes	129	143	157	184	232	324
= Net Income	239	265	291	342	431	602
Beg. Retained earnings	100	315	554	816	1,123	1,511
Dividends	24	27	29	34	43	60
Ending retained earnings	315	554	816	1,123	1,511	2,053
Balance Sheet	2003	2004	2005	2006	2007	2008
Cash and cash equivalents	-	529	949	1,969	3,923	7,837
Current assets	150	159	169	179	189	201
Property, plant, and equip.	900	1,040	1,198	1,376	1,577	1,802
Accumulated depreciation	300	404	524	661	819	999
Net fixed assets	600	636	674	715	757	803
Total assets	750	1,324	1,792	2,863	4,870	8,840
Current liabilities	70	74	79	83	88	94
Debt	180	516	699	1,116	1,899	3,448
Stock	400	418	461	847	1,759	3,788
Retained earnings	100	315	554	816	1,123	1,511
Equity	500	733	1,014	1,663	2,882	5,299
Total Liabilities and equity	750	1,324	1,792	2,863	4,870	8,840

FIGURE 3.6 ■ Detailed business plan

XYZ Corp. ($ Million)	Actual	Forecast					
Free Cash Flow	**2003**	**2004**	**2005**	**2006**	**2007**	**2008**	
Net Income	239	265	291	342	431	602	
+ Interest expense	12	34	46	74	125	228	
+ Income taxes	129	143	157	184	232	324	
- Interest income	0	48	85	177	353	705	
= EBIT	380	394	408	422	436	449	
- Cash taxes	133	138	143	148	152	157	
= NOPAT	247	256	265	274	283	292	
+Depreciation and amort.	90	104	120	138	158	180	
= Gross cash flow	337	360	385	412	441	472	
- Increase in net working capital		5	5	5	6	6	
- Capex		140	158	178	201	226	
= Free cash flow		215	222	229	235	240	

XYZ Corp. ($ Million)	Actual	Forecast					
Valuation	**2003**	**2004**	**2005**	**2006**	**2007**	**2008**	
Return on equity	47.9%	36.1%	28.7%	20.6%	15.0%	11.4%	
Retention rate	90.0%	90.0%	90.0%	90.0%	90.0%	90.0%	
Sustainable growth rate	43.1%	32.5%	25.8%	18.5%	13.5%	10.2%	
Debt Ratio	24%	39%	39%	39%	39%	39%	
Cost of Debt	6.6%						
Cost of Equity	12.4%						
WACC	9.24%						
Corporate Value	$ 3,944						

FIGURE 3.6 ■ Detailed business plan (continued)

The fact that costs of debt and equity actually increase as a firm's leverage increases reflects that firms with high financial leverage are riskier as they have a higher probability of facing financial difficulty in down-time.

When we perform an analysis of financial leverage optimality, we find that the company's optimal leverage ratio is 39 percent, because that is where the corporate value is maximized, and after-tax WACC minimized.

Pro forma financial models do not incorporate any risk or uncertainty factors.

Typically pro forma financial models do not incorporate any risk or uncertainty factors. In other words, these models see a static view of the world. All variables and their projections in the model are deterministic – they are assumed to be point estimates and not have any variability.

Financial projections made under this methodology are unrealistic since, in reality, the future cannot be forecasted with certainty, and some element of randomness is always present. There are three methods to refine our static view of pro forma financials:

■ sensitivity analysis

■ scenario analysis

■ simulation analysis.

Sensitivity analysis is the crudest of the three methods. It takes the base case financial model and creates an upside and a downside to the forecasts based on optimiztic or pessimistic assumptions of the future state-of-nature of key variables.

Scenario analysis is similar to sensitivity analysis, but is more sophisticated because it incorporates changes in multiple variables at the same time as it creates the optimiztic and pessimistic scenarios.

The most sophisticated method for incorporating risk into the pro forma financial plan is to specifically address the variables that are uncertain and assign appropriate probability distributions to them, so that the entire model now becomes a stochastic programing model – *simulation analysis*. The cash-flows and valuations are now not point estimates, but actually represent empirical probability distributions, with mean, standard deviation, and higher moments.

Since the pro forma financial models and future projections of cash-flow, sales and interest rates, among other variables, are fairly uncertain, a static view of the future is clearly inappropriate. In simulation analysis, uncertainty and risk are incorporated into the financial model by assigning appropriate probability distributions to the uncertain variables.

In our model predicted in Figures 3.2–3.6, we have assumed that revenue growth, interest rate on debt, interest rate on cash balances, SG&A/revenue ratio, and cost of goods sold/revenue ratio follow a normal probability distribution with appropriate variances. This makes the model stochastic, and the financial leverage optimization problem more realistic.

Operating leverage

Operating leverage refers to the rate at which net income escalates as sales volume rises over the beak-even sales volume. In terms of costs, it can also be defined as the relative proportion of fixed costs in the total operating cost structure. Capital-intensive companies usually have more fixed costs compared to labor-intensive companies.

Since product demand is a function of the business cycle which follows periodic patterns of high and low growth, the resulting fluctuation in demand presents challenges in optimally managing the supply of products or services. In particular, down-turns in demand cause profit margins to come under greater pressure the more operating leverage a firm has, since the high fixed costs cannot be cut down immediately but rather must continue to be incurred even though revenue growth has fallen.

High operating leverage thus causes more earnings volatility in the business cycle, and limits management flexibility in terms of real options. Earnings volatility is in turn related to cash-flow volatility. The best single predictor of bankruptcy is a declining trend of cash-flow to total debt.[22]

Similar companies with similar net incomes can have substantially different enterprise values. Likewise, companies with similar interest coverage can have substantially different default risk.

Operating leverage = percentage change in operating income/percentage change in sales

As a practical matter, operating leverage is largely determined by the nature and line of business that has industry-specific average capital intensities. The capital investment plan in the business and financial planning process takes into consideration the need to maintain adequate levels of fixed capital investments to run the business. However, operating risks can become unduly high with excessively high fixed costs in the business.

Therefore, operating leverage optimization should be attained by considering alternative methods of production or service delivery that use more variable costs in the operating cost structure, or outsourcing certain functions that allow reduced operating leverage.

A company with relatively large fixed costs has a high break-even sales level. Even a modest economic downturn will reduce its capacity utilization below the rate required to keep the company profitable. Such a cost structure poses a substantial risk of earnings falling below the level needed to cover the company's interest expense. A predominantly variable cost structure, on the other hand, aids financial flexibility. The analytical value of understanding the company's cost structure dynamics is thus enormous for planning purposes.

Dividend policy

Dividends form an important part of total shareholder return in the form of current income. The other part is composed of capital gains which remain unrealized until the shares are sold. Long-term investors such as institutional shareholders and pension funds that do not speculate in the market find dividend-paying stocks particularly attractive since they provide current income. However, dividends are less important to investors that seek capital gains as the main source of cash returns. The composition and nature of the shareholding structure thus impacts dividend policy.

Dividends are distributions of profits to owners of the business, and an effective market-signaling mechanism regarding future cash generation expectations of the business. Empirical research shows that dividend changes provide information about future company profitability, and are positively related to earnings changes in each of the two years after the dividend change.[23]

For corporate management, the optimal dividend policy must be a function of the ongoing cash requirements of the business, and the existing shareholding structure, among other factors. If institutional shareholding is an insignificant fraction of the shareholder structure, share buybacks may well present a more attractive avenue of residual income distribution since its anti-dilutive effects reduce outstanding shares thus increasing prices. Share buybacks also increase earnings per share, and reduce future cash dividend payouts as a result of net reduction in outstanding shares.

If cash dividends are paid, investors look at the comparative dividend yields across companies in the same industry, and therefore the level of dividends paid ought to consider the relative attractiveness of the shares to the investor community, given average share prices.

In addition, the sustainable growth rate (SGR) of the company – the rate of organic revenue growth which can be supported by the existing capital structure without draining the financial resources – is higher the lower the dividend payout.

SGR% = Return on equity × (1 – Dividend payout ratio)

If the company wished to grow at a rate higher than the SGR, additional funds will have to be raised from new debt or new equity, thus changing one or more financial policy constraints. If the company grows at a lower rate than the SGR, some of the funding potential could be used to pay increased dividends, buy back outstanding shares, or retire debt instead of providing an expanded asset base.

Assuming stable corporate financial policy conditions, as a growing company experiences increasing sales revenues, it will require proportional increases in working capital, as well as proportional investments in fixed assets and other assets supporting operations. Funding of these requirements comes from debt, equity, or internal sources.

Dividend policy, insofar as it directly affects retained earnings and therefore the level of internal funding capacity, is an important determinant of capital structure policy. Given stable policies and performance, the rate of increase in shareholders' equity will represent the rate of expansion of the balance sheet necessary to support the growth.

The financial planning model can be used to determine the optimal level of dividend payout which would enable the company to meet its revenue and earnings growth projections, in keeping with the traditional requirement that fluctuations in dividends are not well received by the market.

Empirical evidence corroborates that, in the US, fluctuation in corporate earnings are much higher than corporate dividends, attesting to the fact that dividend smoothing is a real market phenomenon, practiced by major corporations.[24] Firms are typically reluctant to change dividends, making for sticky dividend policies. They also remain concerned about their capability to maintain higher dividends in future periods. Finally, they need to consider the negative market view of dividend decreases and the consequent drop in the stock price.

Notwithstanding the levels to which corporations go to preserve them, dividends must be viewed as a potential source of financial flexibility in a period of depressed earnings. Despite the benefits that financial flexibility confers, maintaining a funds cushion such as a large cash balance or retained earnings is not universally regarded as a wise corporate policy.

According to this argument, management should dividend all excess cash-flows to shareholders, where excess cash-flows are defined as cash-flows in excess of that required to fund all of a firm's projects that have positive net present value when discounted at the relevant cost of capital. Clearly, financial flexibility can translate directly into operating flexibility when tight credit conditions make it difficult to finance working capital needs.

Several factors influence the dividend policy of a firm. In many countries, dividends are not tax-deductible at the corporate level, and are fully taxable for recipient investors. This may explain the increase in share or stock repurchases in recent years. The flexibility of the stock repurchase plan allows management to fine-tune its leverage over time. A stock repurchase would be a more effective means of taking advantage of, and eventually correcting, the under-pricing of the firm's stock in the market. Since selling shares rather than collecting dividends has a more favorable tax consequence, institutional shareholders will pressure firms to consider the tax consequences of their payout policy to those shareholders.

Recent empirical research suggest that stock repurchases are paid out of temporary increases in free cash-flow, while dividends payments or increases are paid from free cash-flows that are more permanent and reliable. Stock repurchases are pro-cyclical, while dividends increase steadily over time. In addition, market price reaction has been found to be greater for a dividend increase than the announcement of a stock repurchase program, which is rational given that the former implies a more permanent increase in cash-flows.[25] However, some shareholders prefer the share-repurchase alternative since it defers part of the tax liability.[26]

Dividend payments and equity repurchases divide stockholders and bondholders. A firm that has built up a large cash reserve but has very few good projects available needs to make a decision about what to do with the cash balances. Stockholders in this firm may benefit if the cash is paid out as a dividend or used to repurchase stock. Bondholders, on the other hand, will prefer that the firm retain the cash, since it can be used to make payments on debt, thereby reducing default risk.

Effect on bond prices

If increases in dividends are bad news for bondholders, bond prices should react negatively to the announcement of such increases. Empirical evidence supports this hypothesis. Bond prices decrease following the announcement of dividend increases, while they are relatively unaffected by dividend decreases. At the same time, stock prices increase following the announcement of dividend increases.[27]

Bondholders can protect themselves against such loss by restricting dividends in the bond covenants to a certain percentage of earnings or by limiting dividend increases to a specified amount. One of the by-products of the conflict between stockholders and bondholders is the introduction of strict bond covenants that reduce the flexibility of firms to make investment, financing, or dividend decisions.

A firm's dividend policy tends to follow the life-cycle of the firm. High-growth firms with great investment opportunities do not usually pay dividends, whereas stable firms with larger cash-flows and fewer high-return investment projects tend to pay out more of their earnings as dividends.

Not surprisingly, just as high-growth firms tend to pay out less dividends, high-growth countries pay out less dividends in the aggregate than more advanced mature economies. For instance, Japan had much higher expected growth in 1982–84 than the other G7 countries and paid out a much smaller percentage of its earnings as dividends. The dividend payout ratios of companies in emerging markets are much lower than those in the G7 countries.[28]

In the US, corporate dividends are double-taxed, but Germany taxes corporate retained earnings at a higher rate than corporate dividends. In general, publicly listed firms pay lower dividends than closely held firms.

There are two widely used measures of dividend policy. Dividend yield provides a measure of that component of total shareholder return that comes from dividends, with the balance coming from price appreciation.

Dividend yield = Annual dividends per share/ Share price

Expected return on stock = Dividend yield + Price appreciation

Some investors use dividend yield as a measure of risk and as an investment screen, that is, they invest in stocks with high dividend yields. Studies indicate that stocks with high dividend yields earn excess returns, after adjusting for market performance and risk. One rationale as to why dividends are preferred to capital gains is that dividends are certain, whereas capital gains are more uncertain. Risk-averse investors therefore prefer dividends.

An argument against dividends compared to share repurchases has to do with tax treatment: dividends create a tax disadvantage for investors because they are usually taxed much more heavily than capital gains. Consequently, firms will be better off either retaining the money they would have paid out as dividends or repurchasing stock.

Since the stock price tends to drop ex-dividend, investors who receive higher dividends will find themselves losing an equivalent amount in price appreciation, in present value terms.

Some firms pay dividends in years in which their operations generate excess cash. They take their long-term investment and funding needs into consideration, even as they attempt to return excess cash to shareholders. If the excess cash is a temporary phenomenon, resulting from an unusually good year or a non-recurring event, and the firm expects cash shortfalls in future years, firms prefer to retain the cash to cover these shortfalls. Another course followed is to pay "one-time" excess dividends.

Optimal dividend policy considers the composition and nature of shareholders. The dividend clientele effect refers to the tendency of investors to buy stock in firms that have dividend policies that meet their preferences for high, low, or no dividends. The existence of a clientele effect has some important implications. It suggests that firms attract investors partly pursuant to their dividend policies. In addition, firms are likely to have some difficulty changing dividend policies.

> *The existence of a clientele effect has some important implications.*

Changes in dividend policy

Financial markets examine every action a firm takes for implications for future cash-flows and firm value. When firms announce changes in dividend policy, they convey information to markets. By increasing dividends, firms create a cost to themselves, since they commit to paying these dividends in the long-term. The fact that they are willing to make this commitment indicates to investors that they have the capacity to generate higher cash-flows on a sustainable basis.

On the other hand, decreasing dividends operates as a negative signal largely because firms are reluctant to cut dividends. Thus firms that take this action signal to the market that cash-flows are expected to suffer sustained declines. Consequently, such actions lead to a drop in stock prices.

The question of how much to pay in dividends is intimately connected to the financing decisions made by the firm, that is, how much debt the firm should carry. Firms that want to change debt leverage can do so by changing their dividend policy. Increasing dividends increases leverage, and decreasing dividends reduces leverage.

Firms that increase dividends may harm bondholders by increasing their default risk. In response to this threat to their interests, bondholders often write in specific covenants on dividend policy into bond indentures. These covenants effectively restrict the payment of dividends, and often play a role in determining a firm's dividend policy.

Given the pros and cons of paying dividends, and the lack of consensus on the effect of dividends on value, recent research provides evidence that CFOs of multinationals believe that their dividend policies and payout ratios affect firm value and operate as signals of future prospects.

Alternatives to dividends

Dividends represent just one way of returning value to shareholders. There are other approaches that may provide more attractive options to firms, depending on their stockholder characteristics and their objectives. These include equity repurchase, which is anti-dilutive, and forward contracts to buy equity in future periods.

The most widely used alternative to paying dividends is to use cash to repurchase outstanding stock. There are three widely used approaches to buy back equity:

- repurchase tender offers
- open market purchase
- privately negotiated repurchases.

In a *repurchase tender offer*, a firm specifies a price at which it will buy back shares it intends to repurchase, and the period of time for which it will keep the offer open, and invites stockholders to submit their shares for the repurchase. This approach is used primarily for large equity repurchases.

In the case of *open market purchases*, firms buy shares in the market at the prevailing market price. In terms of flexibility, an open market repurchase affords the firm much more freedom in deciding when to buy back shares and how many shares to repurchase.

In *privately negotiated repurchases*, firms buy back shares from a large stockholder in the company at a negotiated price.

In the last decade, an increasing number of US firms have used equity repurchases as an alternative to paying dividends. The rationale for this includes the advantages this method offers:

▪ Equity repurchases are one-time returns of cash to shareholders in the form of capital gains, and do not carry the commitment to continue payment in future periods.

▪ The decision to repurchase stock affords firms more flexibility to reverse themselves and/or spread the repurchases over a longer period than a special one-time dividend.

▪ Equity repurchases may offer tax advantages to stockholders.

▪ Equity repurchases are anti-dilutive and increase earnings per share.

▪ Equity repurchases may be used as a tool to manage the market price of the stock by buying up stock when its prices are declining.

Empirical studies show that stock and bond prices react positively to share buybacks. Furthermore, the increase seems to be permanent rather than transitory.[29]

In many countries, corporate earnings distributed as dividends face both the corporate income tax and the individual income tax. This "double taxation" leads to a combined marginal tax rate of up to 60 percent in many cases. By contrast, interest is deductible to the corporation and thus only faces taxation at the individual level. A review of tax policies in 30 industrial countries finds that nearly all major nations provide partial or full relief of dividend double taxation.

Dividend tax policy for nations in the Organization for Economic Cooperation and Development, based on data from the OECD, Ernst & Young, and various country-specific sources, found that a variety of approaches are used to provide dividend tax relief. A dozen OECD countries give individuals a tax credit that either fully or partially offsets the double-taxation of dividends. Countries offering partial tax credits include Canada, France, and the UK. Countries providing credits that fully offset double-taxation include Australia, Finland, Italy, Mexico, New Zealand and Norway. In Norway, the combined corporate and individual top tax rate on dividends is just 28 percent, less than half the US top rate of 60 percent. The most common form of dividend tax relief is providing a tax rate on dividends that is lower than the top ordinary rate on wages. About half of OECD countries have a lower, often flat, tax rate on dividends, including Austria, Belgium, the Czech Republic, Denmark, Iceland, the Netherlands and Poland.

Some countries, including Finland, Norway, and Sweden, have "dual income tax systems" that impose high rates on wage income, but lower flat rates on capital income, including dividends and capital gains. Two countries, Germany and Luxembourg, offer a 50 percent dividend exclusion to individuals. That means that if a shareholder receives $1,000 in dividends, $500 would be tax-free. Greece fully exempts domestic dividends from individual taxation (a 100 percent exclusion). Dividends can be given parallel treatment to interest by allowing corporations to deduct dividends at the corporate level. The Czech Republic and Iceland allow corporations to partially deduct dividends. Only Ireland and Switzerland do not offer relief from dividend double taxation among the 30 OECD countries. High-dividend tax rates damage the economy by creating numerous distortions. First, high-dividend taxes add to the income tax code's general bias against savings and investment. Second, high-dividend taxes cause corporations to rely too much on debt rather than equity financing because interest is deductible against the corporate income tax but dividends are not. Highly indebted firms are more vulnerable to bankruptcy in economic downturns. Third, high-dividend taxes reduce the incentive to pay out dividends in favor of retained earnings. That may cause corporate executives to invest in wasteful or unprofitable projects. Also, it is harder for investors to accurately value firms when they do not receive a regular hard cash dividend stream. Fourth, high and uneven tax rates on dividends and other types of capital income greatly increase financial engineering efforts to avoid taxes, which ends up wasting resources and confusing investors.[30]

In the US, the recent "Jobs and Growth Tax Relief Reconciliation Act of 2003", signed into law in May 2003, reduces a variety of individual income tax rates, including for equity investors, the rates on dividends and capital gains. Income tax rates on corporate dividends are lowered generally to 15 percent (however, for individuals in the lowest tax brackets, the dividends tax rate will be as low as 5 percent) from previous rates as high as 38.6 percent, the highest ordinary income tax rate. The tax on long-term capital gains (for stocks held at least one year) is lowered to 15 percent from 20 percent for sales incurred after May 5, 2003. The rates are in effect through 2008, and then will return to pre-enactment rates unless extended. Investors during this period will be able to retain 85 percent of dividends and capital gains. The reduced tax rates are generally applicable to US individual investors in US corporations and to a range of non-US equities and American Depository Receipts (ADRs) issued by entities that satisfy the definition of "qualified foreign corporations." The reduced rates are not available for investors who hold share for a limited period. Specifically, the stock must be held for more than 60 days during the 120-day period beginning 60 days before the date on which the stock becomes ex-dividend with respect to the dividend in question. For these purposes, the more than 60-day holding period generally will be tolled for periods where the taxpayer has substantially diminshed risk of loss with respect to the stock through various hedging techniques.[31]

Pricing strategy

"There is always a price that maximizes profit."
– Robert Dolan, Harvard Business School

Companies use product-line pricing as a strategic instrument for revenue and profit maximization. There are alternative pricing strategies employed by companies in order to achieve this goal.

The determination of the optimal price for a product is a complex exercise that needs to factor the following variables into the decision process:

- product/service market positioning/target segment
- customer willingness to pay
- degree of product differentiation/availability of substitutes
- price elasticity of demand and supply
- revenue and profitability impact
- industry competitive structure
- degree of rivalry
- bargaining power of suppliers
- product life-cycle
- government regulations on pricing
- internal cost structure/contribution margins
- capacity utilization
- barriers to capacity adjustment
- buyer and supplier concentration
- product perishability
- demand and supply factors
- efficiency of price shopping
- brand loyalty
- industry growth rate
- consumers affinity to product
- scale economies
- bundling opportunities
- alternative distribution channels.

In the late 1970s, the most prominent strategic thinking of the day focussed on the importance of market revenue shares. In the words of an extremely well known *Harvard Business Review* article "Market Share: A Key to Profitability," the route to long-term profitability was seen to be through building revenue market share – foregoing short-term profit if necessary, and reaping profits from the business as it matured.[32] "Cash cows" for the firm were those businesses that had high market share in low-growth industries.

The environment in the twenty-first century has seen a shift in this thinking. In one industry after another, the aggressive pursuit of revenue market share has led to overcapacity, price-cutting, and profits for nobody. Firms that are enjoying higher margins are following profitable markets, customers, and products.

The focus is shifting from revenue market share to a broader conception of industry profitability. Price impacts not only market share but also the size of the market and the value of a market share point. McKinsey has articulated this point, describing the dimensions of a fundamental transformation that is taking place in competitive dynamics. First among the dimensions of change is a redefinition of objectives from market share to market surplus.

What matters is not share of market, but share of scarce market profits…"market surplus" will replace market share as the measure of success. Companies – and their marketers will take a much wider view of their industry… They will think not just about their own profits, but also about maximizing both the total profits in their industry – the market surplus – and their companies' share of these profits.[33]

Few companies proactively manage their business to create the conditions that foster more profitable pricing. The difference between price setting and strategic pricing is the difference between reacting to market conditions and proactively managing them.[34]

Strategic pricing is the coordination of interrelated marketing, competitive, and financial decisions to set prices profitably. It requires anticipating price levels before beginning product development. The only way to ensure profitable pricing is to reject early those products for which adequate value cannot be captured to justify the cost.

Strategic pricing requires that management take responsibility for establishing a coherent set of pricing policies and procedures, consistent with the strategic goals of the company. Abdicating pricing responsibility to the sales force or to the distribution channel is abdicating responsibility for the strategic direction of the business. Perhaps most important, strategic pricing requires a new relationship between marketing and finance. Strategic pricing is actually the interface between marketing and finance.[35]

However, research shows that few companies apply a coherent and strategic approach to developing optimal pricing for their products, and instead apply simple cost-plus-margin pricing plans.[36] Cost-plus pricing is, historically, the most common pricing procedure because it carries an aura of financial prudence. Financial prudence, according to this view, is achieved by pricing every product or service to yield a fair return over all costs, fully and fairly allocated. In theory, this is a simple guide to profitability; in practice, it is a blueprint for mediocre financial performance.[37]

The problem with cost-driven pricing is fundamental: in most industries, it is impossible to determine a product's unit cost before determining its price, because unit costs change with volume. This cost change occurs because a significant portion of costs are "fixed" and are allocated to a unit level to determine full unit cost. Since these allocations depend on volume, which changes with changes in price, unit cost is a moving target. To solve the problem of determining fully allocated unit cost, cost-based pricers are forced to make the assumption that they can set prices without affecting volume. This failure to account for the dynamic price–volume–cost interactions leads to sub-optimal pricing.

Value-based pricing is becoming more popular than cost-based pricing, since it starts with the customer, and the value proposition to the customer is derived from an understanding of customer willingness to pay.

Cost-based pricing:

Product → Cost → Price → Value → Customers

Value-based pricing:

Customers → Value → Price → Cost → Product

Most companies now recognize the fallacy of cost-based pricing and its adverse effects on profits.[38] They realize the need for pricing to reflect market conditions. As a result, many have taken pricing authority away from financial managers and given it to sales or product managers. In theory, this trend is consistent with value-based pricing since marketing and sales are that part of the organization best positioned to understand value to the customer.

In practice, the misuse of pricing authority to achieve short-term sales objectives often undermines perceived value and depresses profits even further. The optimal solution is therefore to have both marketing and finance functions work as a team to determine pricing strategies for the long-term sustainable value creation for the company.

The purpose of value-based pricing is to price more profitably by capturing more value, not necessarily making more sales. Pricing at whatever customers are willing to pay may not be the optimal strategy, since sophisticated customers will often under-price their willingness to pay. This is not to say that customer willingness to pay should be discounted, only that it need not be taken as the final word. Pricing should instead reflect its true worth, which is a function of both costing and customer willingness to pay. Also note that both the cost side and the customer willingness to pay change over time with new technologies and changing customer preferences.

Finally, consider the policy of letting pricing be dictated by competitive conditions. Managers will often reduce the profitability of each sale simply to achieve the market share goal. Strategically, prices should be lowered only when they are no longer justified by the value offered in comparison to the value offered by the competition. Although price-cutting is probably the quickest, most-effective way to achieve sales objectives, it is usually a poor decision financially, unless forced by competitive conditions. This is because prices, like taxes, are sticky upwards. It is easy to add value to the customer value proposition by lowering prices, but a company needs to explain itself in ten different ways to the customer if it increases prices when competitors have not. Market share can be lost.

The goal of pricing

The goal of pricing should be to find the combination of margin and market share that maximizes profitability over the long term. Often, the most profitable price is one that substantially restricts market share relative to the competition. Godiva Chocolates, BMW cars, Georgio Armani clothing, Cartier Jewelry, Bang & Olufsen audio systems, Chanel perfumery, and other luxury product suppliers would no doubt

The goal of pricing ... to find the combination of margin and market share that maximizes profitability over the long term.

all gain substantial market share if they priced closer to the competition. It is doubtful, however, that the added share would be worth forgoing their profitable and successful positioning as high-priced brands.

Given actual estimates of the likely customer and competitor reactions to a price change, there are different analytical techniques that can be used to derive optimal short- and long-term price points that maximize profits. However, cost allocations are difficult to make at the product-level. Semi-variable costs are typically a mix of multiple components of fixed and variable costs, making product level price optimization in a multi-product firm difficult.

For corporations, pricing strategies can form a basis for competitive advantage. Corporations need to achieve operating margins that provide enough cushion to cover all of the fixed costs as well as the variable costs of the product or services. However, pricing strategy for revenues or market share maximization will be different from that for profit maximization. Goals therefore need to be clarified at the outset.

There are two main concepts in cost-based pricing:[39]

- *Absorption cost pricing* adds a fixed margin to the average total cost per unit of output.

- *Variable cost pricing* only considers variable costs per unit so that the resulting margins contribute to covering fixed costs.

Beyond a certain volume of sales, that is the break-even point, the incremental units contribute to profits. However, these alternative cost-based pricing strategies are inward focused, and present a price to the market that may be out of tune with consumer willingness to pay, and how that willingness changes at different price levels. This is where the price elasticity of demand becomes a very useful tool, which is simply the price coefficient in a log regression of sales volume on price.[40]

However, pricing is much more an art than a science, and successful pricing decisions cannot be based on costs alone, and must consider customer willingness to pay, competitive response, and production capacity utilization. In practice, some degree of product differentiation is a necessary condition for any pricing leverage. Differentiation is achieved by unique attributes of products or services, or by branding. Brand image and marketing play a pivotal role in supporting demand.

It becomes increasing difficult to maintain product differentiation in a commoditizing market. As the product matures, changing prices out of line with inflation trends or industry levels can risk customer dissatisfaction and a large drop in demand for products that have highly elastic demand and many substitutes.

In these cases, corporations often trick consumers by changing the product name – giving it a marketing or packaging spin – to increase or decrease prices for what is essentially the same product. When competitive conditions or falling demand cause margin pressure, margins are often maintained by lowering the quality of the product unbeknownst to the customer.

When a new product is introduced in the market, for example, *price skimming strategy* is rarely feasible when the differentiation is not explicit. In these cases, a lower price penetration strategy becomes the default course of action. However, one specific version of demand-oriented penetration strategy is worth mentioning – *progressive segmentation*, that is, using a penetration strategy for the operational product, and skimming strategy for the associated consumables. Gillette uses this strategy with its razors, which themselves cost very little, but the consumable blades are expensive. Many automobile companies use similar pricing strategies for their parts business in a captive monopoly market.

Pricing strategies

Pricing strategies are also very different for fixed price off-the-shelf consumable products as opposed to negotiated price products that tend to be larger ticket durables, service contracts, or real estate purchases. Financial institutions, for example, employ first-degree price discrimination at the point of sale based on the borrower's credit history and risk profile. The price for its product is the interest rate that can be fixed or variable. Other pricing techniques include bundling, discounting, financing, and utilization of alternative channels.

Integrated simple pricing, flat-rate pricing, incremental-use pricing, and pre-paid pricing are examples of pricing tactics for engineered cash inflow. The web, for example allows producers to cut distribution intermediaries to reach consumers directly. However, the more complex the product, the less the e-channel is likely to be used as an effective distribution channel.

Traditionally, wholesalers and retailers add a mark-up to the price they buy in the product to cover overhead and sales costs and yield a profit. The manufacturer is therefore often unable to dictate the ultimate selling price of products as distributors may manipulate margins. Relationships with channel partners therefore become a key competitive differentiator.

In order to maximize profits, corporations should not attempt to squeeze as much producer surplus as they can when the customer is a repeat purchaser. Market size and growth dynamics during the life-cycle of the product determines the maximum value that producers can generate from each product. When additional sales volume is a viable option, a rational pricing policy will share the surplus so that the customers consistently find superior value in the purchase decision.

Besides, competitive conditions limit management flexibility in any mature product segment. Consumer tastes and preferences, and the availability of complements and substitutes, need to be factored into strategic pricing. Customer willingness to pay can be influenced by adding sweeteners such as financing arrangements, warranties, or superior customer service as a competitive differentiator.

Within the corporation's manufacturing process, transfer pricing should be consistent with the implicit equilibrium market prices of the products consumed internally, so that cross-subsidization is minimal.

Pricing strategists endeavor to develop trade policies so that receivables are a low share of revenues, and days' sales outstanding is a small number. Inventory management and accounting policies such as FIFO versus LIFO will affect pricing economics as well.

Strategic pricing is complex as it touches upon many areas of strategy and market economics. A sound analytical framework coupled with superior market intelligence and customer behavioral insights allow leading firms to develop and successfully implement powerful pricing strategies to support superior value creation.

In practice, it is important to assess the revenue and profitability impact of price changes. To illustrate the profit impact of a specific price and possible changes in price, consider the simple case of product X shown in Figure 3.7.

In this case, at a sales volume of 1m units, average contribution margin from product X is 40 percent. Thus each unit sold contributes $4 to the recovery of fixed costs and to profit. After subtracting $3m of fixed costs, gross profits are $1m or a return on sales of 10 percent.

Assume price is decreased by 20 percent: sales would have to double in order to provide the same profit level, assuming no increase in fixed costs. Now assume a price increase of 20 percent: unit contribution margin increases to 60 percent, thereby requiring only 667,000 units to be sold to generate the same profit. For example, if 750,000 units were sold at this price, profit would increase by a staggering 50 percent to $1.5m.

As we can see in our example, price increases and decreases can have highly leveraged effects. A seemingly small price reduction can have a large negative impact on unit contribution, requiring a tremendous increase in sales volume to generate the same profit. Similarly, a small price increase can have a strong positive effect on unit contribution, creating a large acceptable decrease in sales volume while still retaining the profit level.

Manufacturing firms, being more capital intensive than service firms, typically have lower variable costs as a proportion of the price compared to service firms that are more labor intensive. The underlying economics and drivers of strategic pricing are therefore significantly different based on the sector and product line.

	Original price (€)	20% price decrease (€)	20% price increase (€)	
Annual net sales volume	1,000,000	1,200,000	667,000	750,000
Unit price	10.00	8.00	12.00	12.00
Annual revenue	10,000,000	9,600,000	8,004,000	9,000,000
Variable cost per unit	6.00	6.00	6.00	6.00
Total variable cost	6,000,000	7,200,000	4,002,000	4,500,000
Unit contribution to fixed cost	4.00	2.00	6.00	6.00
Total fixed cost	3,000,000	3,000,000	3,000,000	3,000,000
Total gross profit	1,000,000	−600,000	1,002,000	1,500,000

Figure 3.7 ■ Profitability impact of alternative price-points

The cost structure has a strong impact on the price-profit relationship. The cost structures of service industries such as financial institutions, hotels, airlines, telecommunications, and IT service providers are characterized by relatively high fixed costs, and thus high operating leverage. Similar cost structures characterize industries such as software, and pharmaceuticals, where research and development accounts for the bulk of costs, and unit variable costs tend to be very low.

Break-even analysis is another simple way to look at the interaction of price, costs, and profit. Break-even analysis determines for a given price the sales volume at which profit from that product line becomes zero, where total contribution equal fixed costs. It shows how sensitively the break-even volume reacts to price changes. However, its utility is limited since it does not address the issue of profit-maximizing price.

"There is always a price that maximizes profit," says Harvard Professor Robert J Dolan. Derivation of the optimal price for a product-line requires the application of mathematical programing techniques, as we show with an example. A price-response curve is estimated based on a number of approaches including econometric estimation of price elasticity. Price elasticity is an extremely useful measure of the impact of price changes on sales volume and profitability.

Price elasticity = % change in sales volume/% change in price

For example, if the current price of $100 per unit is increased by 10 percent, so that it becomes $110 per unit, and that causes sales volumes to fall by 20 percent, then the price elasticity is $[(-20\%) / 10\%] = -2.0$. The price elasticity has a negative sign since demand typically falls in response to price increases.

The values of price elasticity vary strongly across products, competitive situations, and individual customers. The price elasticity is also different at different points on the price response curve. In practice, if price elasticity is estimated to be less than 1, a price increase can be recommended, since this means that the percentage of decrease in sales volume will be smaller than the percentage of increase in price.

One of the implicit assumptions we have made is that firms have profit maximization as their objective. Indeed, empirical studies have shown this to be the most common goal. But there are also theories that suggest other goals such as revenue maximization. Japanese companies, for example, are said to often strive for revenue market share rather than direct profit goals.[41]

Many firms have explicit volume or market-share goals. In the auto industry, for example, marketing plans usually prescribe a certain number of cars to be sold. In the computer industry, plant capacity is set according to volume goals, and capacity utilization thresholds exist. In service industries, occupancy rates for hotels and airlines are a critical indicator of success. Given these industry and company norms, profit is hardly ever the only goal being pursued in pricing decisions. A mixture of profit and volume goals is more typical for business practice.

A mixture of profit and volume goals is more typical for business practice.

Profit impact of price change

The structure of variable and fixed costs has a very strong influence on the profit impact of a price change. The higher the variable cost relative to price, the stronger the profit impact of a price change. In order to determine the price which yields the highest profit, both the price response and the costs must be known.

While popular in practice, cost-plus pricing does not optimize profitability, since it does not satisfactorily consider the demand effects of price. Costs can be used to determine long- and short-term price floors, where the long-term price floor is defined by total unit costs, while short-term price floor is equal to variable costs only.

Sophisticated pricing techniques estimate the price response function in a systems context, that is, taking competitor pricing action into consideration. Typically, managers know their internal cost structures pretty well, but are weak on customer and competitor response to changes in price.

The systems context of price response estimation uses historical market data, and places revenue, price, and profit on three different scales to derive optimal price-points for products or services (see Figure 3.8).

According to this analysis, the price–response estimation shows the optimal sales volume is 12.0m units, at a price of 6.8 (currency units), which provides the highest profit index level of 125.

There are four major approaches whose application and careful execution have proven useful in practice:[42]

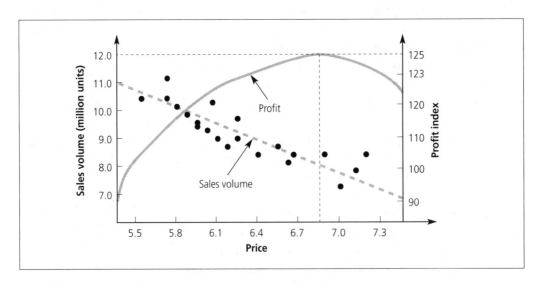

FIGURE 3.8 ▥ The systems context for price response estimation

- econometric estimation of price elasticity (discussed above);
- customer surveys of willingness to pay;
- expert judgment of industry professionals;
- price experiments and beta testing.

No one method is inherently superior to the others, as each has its advantages and disadvantages.

In the literature, we find numerous estimates of price elasticities. In a survey of 367 price elasticity estimates, the mean absolute value found was 1.76.[43] This figure says that a 1 percent price reduction increases sales by 1.76 percent. According to the authors, 2.0 to 2.5 are realistic average values for price elasticities.

Empirical work by Lambin has shown a high degree of pricing inter-dependence among firms. Specifically, for the sample, the author found an average price reaction elasticity of 0.71, meaning that on average a 10 percent price decrease was met by a 7.1 percent decrease in competitors' prices.[44]

Given strong evidence that a sound pricing strategy can create real value, some CFOs are being enticed into this neglected area. When CFOs get involved in pricing, the impact can be significant. According to a recent report by McKinsey, an average 5 percent improvement in return on sales from improved pricing creates $1.5bn of additional value over five years for an average S&P 500 company.[45] Also, according to the research, which included more than 500 case studies over two years, committed leadership on pricing strategy improves a company's operating margin by between 2 percent and 7 percent.

Tax planning

Taxes are among the most important components of any corporate profit and loss statement. Taxes impact corporate valuation, financial planning, and performance assessment because operating decisions are generally based on risk-adjusted net present value of expected after-tax cash-flows.

Income taxes, sales taxes, import-export duties, and property taxes often add up to one of the largest expense items of an organization. In addition, tax payments typically have a high legal priority claim on an organization's cash-flow. Finally, rapid business expansion overseas broadens the scope of tax planning considerations.

For public companies, earnings must be reported to the investor community and the Securities and Exchange Commission on an after-tax basis. Companies that manage to minimize tax expenses increase net cash-flows for the company, and thus create wealth for the shareholders. Tax planning therefore is a key part of the corporate financial planning process.

While corporate financial planning is ultimately concerned with ensuring that the financial objectives of the company are met with optimally managed risk exposures resulting in shareholder value creation, the ultimate goal of tax planning is to reduce taxes, while not excessively intruding on the organization's overall operations. However, not every idea that saves taxes is a good one. Tax strategies are usually based on taking advantage of time value of money (paying taxes later) or differences in tax rates (tax-rate arbitrage). In tax arbitrage, accounting entries are used to shift profits to jurisdictions that impose the lowest net taxes. Tax savings strategies usually fall into four types: creation, conversion, shifting, and splitting.[46]

Creation involves plans that take advantage of tax subsidies, such as moving operations to a jurisdiction that imposes lower taxes.

Conversion entails changing operations so that more tax-favored categories of income or assets are produced.

Shifting involves techniques that move amounts being taxed to more favorable tax-accounting periods, for example, accelerated depreciation which allows more of an asset's cost to be a tax-deductible expense in early years, thus deferring the payment of taxes on that asset until later.

Splitting techniques entail spreading the tax base among two or more tax payers to take advantage of differing tax rates.

The SAVANT tax planning framework recognizes this by striving toward optimizing taxes rather then minimizing them. The strategy, anticipation, value-adding, negotiating, and transforming (SAVANT) framework is a transactions approach to tax management.[47]

Tax management should work to enhance the firm's *strategy*. Tax minimizing transactions should not deter the company from its strategic plan. The presence of net operating loss (NOL) carry-forward has an impact on strategic tax planning.

Tax planning should *anticipate* potential changes in the tax code, and attempt to incorporate tangible changes into tax planning. Tax planning can add value (*value adding*) by deferring or decreasing tax payments using alternative accounting techniques. Effective tax planning involves *negotiating* tax benefits both with tax authorities as well as counter-

Strategy	Enhance the firm's business strategy
Anticipation	Anticipate changes to the tax code
Value-**A**dding	Defer/decrease tax payments by using alternative accounting techniques
Negotiating	Negotiate tax benefits with tax authorities and other counterparties
Transforming	Transform income into gains, expenses into losses, etc. to minimize effective tax rate

FIGURE 3.9 ■ The SAVANT tax planning model

parties. Tax management also includes *transforming* certain types of income into gains, certain types of expenses into losses, and certain types of taxable income into non-taxable income. The components of tax planning are shown in Figure 3.10.

In general, tax management seeks the following transformations: taxable income to tax-exempt income (or gain), ordinary income to capital gain income, non-deductible loss (expense) to tax deductible loss (expense), and capital loss to ordinary loss.

Each country and jurisdiction has its own unique corporate tax code, and therefore a thorough understanding of the tax laws and regulations help develop an optimal tax management strategy and plan. However, some common features apply in most countries, such as special tax benefits for certain kinds of investments, tax credits for operating in certain geographies, use of tax loss carry forwards of acquired companies, taxable versus non-taxable merger transactions, etc. According to tax laws in most countries, stock-for-stock mergers and acquisitions transactions are tax-free exchanges, unlike cash-for-stock transactions.

For example, in the US, the effective corporate tax rate is almost never the statutory rate, because the Securities and Exchange Commission (SEC) and the Internal Revenue Service (IRS) allow companies to maintain two separate accounting books, one for SEC reporting, and the other for tax reporting. Companies therefore report higher expenses and lower earnings to the IRS, and pay lower actual taxes than indicated in published financial statements. In Europe or Asia, only one set of financial statements is allowed.

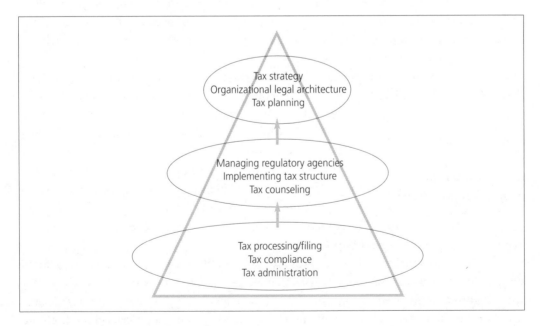

FIGURE 3.10 ■ Components of tax planning

Optimal tax planning of course does not mean that business operations should be allowed to be significantly affected only to be eligible for tax breaks. It does, however, attempt to minimize the tax burden for the corporation, and therefore is integral to the financial planning process.

One key performance indicator for the corporate tax department is the effective corporate tax rate. The effective tax rate is usually lower than the statutory rate. A company's effective tax rate can reflect investment and operating decisions, and prior operating performance, as well as strategic tax planning. Achievement of an effective tax rate below the statutory rate could be the by-product of poor business results as well as a capital investment or expansion program.

Merger and acquisition transactions are often motivated by tax considerations. A loss-making company with tax loss carry-forwards is an attractive candidate to be acquired by a company that desires a lower effective tax rate.

Because certain components of the tax equation can be controlled, reducing the effective tax rate remains a primary goal for most corporate tax departments. A relatively small reduction in the effective tax rate often translates into significant savings for corporations. In recognition of the bottom-line impact of significant tax savings, some companies tie incentive compensation for tax managers and other financial officers to an overall reduction in their cash outlay for taxes.

Effective tax rate is, however, an accounting concept. For many companies, the difference between the tax provision and the actual cash outlay for taxes can be significant. It is therefore important to determine the amount of actual cash savings achieved through the implementation of tax planning strategies.

Wherever possible, planning strategies should attempt to reduce rather than merely postpone taxes. This will reduce both the effective tax rate as well as any current cash outlay for taxes. Examples of permanent reduction strategies are the purchase of tax-free bonds and the utilization of net operating losses by filing consolidated corporate income tax returns.

Planning strategies should attempt to reduce rather than merely postpone taxes.

Permanent reductions in both the effective tax rate and the cash-flow for taxes can increase earnings per share, return on equity, and after-tax return on assets. These factors, in turn, raise the company's perceived value in the marketplace in relation to other investment opportunities.

Reducing the annual cash-flow for taxes also can improve reported earnings. Tax deferral strategies that increase expenses or losses that are deductible for tax purposes before they are recognized in financial income should also be considered. Investment in depreciable assets or depletable resources and intangibles when accelerated depreciation methods are employed is an example of such a deferral strategy.

For US companies, the 'timing difference' between book and tax reporting generated by the use of accelerated depreciation will ultimately turn around for individual assets. However, expanding companies that continue to purchase fixed assets can benefit from the cumulative impact of such investments. The CFO should work with the corporate tax department to ensure that tax strategies blend with overall business strategies in general and investment strategies in particular.

Attempts to increase pre-tax earnings that are enhanced by intelligent tax planning will produce superior after-tax returns. In today's increasingly global economy, a discussion of corporate tax rates must recognize the impact of foreign investments and taxes. The corporate tax department must be concerned with international tax planning strategies.

While industry competitors can act as preliminary benchmarks for measuring performance, it is important to remember that differences in corporate structure, international location, product mix, and investment goals can cause wide variations between companies.

The pressure to reduce costs and better control funds makes liquidity management an important management function. However, corporate treasurers need to weigh up carefully the overall economic benefits of liquidity management strategies against the resulting tax implications.[48]

While it is important to take advantage of the new tax laws, there are three year-end tax strategies which almost always make sense:

- tax reduction
- tax deferral
- income shifting.

Tax reduction occurs when a company takes action that results in payment of less tax than would otherwise have been due. *Tax deferral* is achieved when income is earned now, but tax payments are made in the future. *Income shifting* generally involves transferring income receipts to geographies or other categories that are taxed at a lower rate.

The global perspective

International tax planning involves the reduction of the global effective tax rate of a multinational group by minimizing taxable income in high–tax jurisdictions and maximizing taxable income in low–tax jurisdictions.

According to PricewaterhouseCoopers, a global tax strategy should consider the following components:[49]

- impact of tax planning solutions on world-wide operations,
- focus on achieving either a deferral from home tax or a permanent tax saving,

- flexibility of the business model used by the company,

- holding company structure,

- group funding structure,

- intangible assets,

- royalty structures,

- insurance/re-insurance structures,

- coordination centres,

- tax holidays and incentives,

- double tax relief, treaty interpretation and planning,

- thin capitalization,

- repatriation planning,

- e-business planning.

Tax planning is integrally related to treasury management. The European Economic and Monetary Union (EMU) heralded a new era of more efficient pan-European liquidity management for corporate treasurers. The phasing out of legacy currencies in the 15 EU member states intensified the pace of reform as treasurers looked to leverage the benefits provided by a single pan-European currency.

Yet whilst the technologies underpinning cash management have increased in sophistication, accounting structures remain relatively complex. As long as domestic clearing infrastructures continue to predominate, a single euro account is a noble yet fruitless pursuit for most corporate treasurers. Hence the need for enhanced liquidity management solutions, which have evolved from stand-alone products to form an integral part of more sophisticated cash management offerings such as centralized payment factories and shared service centres.

A significant majority of multinationals have implemented liquidity management structures, either notional pooling or cash concentration, as a means of reducing interest paid on balances and exerting greater control over inter-company finances.

Recent economic pressures have also brought a renewed sense of urgency to the aspect of liquidity management. Pooling or concentration solutions are important treasury management strategies that impact corporate liquidity. Corporations need to have greater insight into how funds are being used across global accounting structures and how to mitigate the risks associated with doing business in an increasingly borderless world.

There are only a handful of banks and tax consultants that have the global reach and expertise to navigate the complex barrage of taxation regulations. With a strong track record as a major settlement and clearing provider in the euro zone, Deutsche Bank offers corporates liquidity management solutions that are flexible enough to absorb the impact of different regulations without compromising the overall objective. Corporate treasurers also benefit from an integrated solution tied into other cash management services such as account reporting and initiation of bulk and treasury transactions.

Leading tax consultants Deliotte & Touche, PricewaterhouseCoopers, Cap Gemini Ernst & Young, and Bearing Point are among the big accounting firms able to combine global reach with strong in-country capabilities. Their specialist teams present an in-depth overview of tax treaties in the various countries and leverage cross-border relationships that encompass the bigger picture.

To help corporate treasurers identify tax implications pertaining to the most common forms of liquidity management techniques, Deutsche Bank and Cap Gemini Ernst & Young jointly produced a report reviewing the key taxation implications of the three most common forms of liquidity management solutions:

- cash concentration
- notional pooling
- reference account structures.

Zero balancing or cash concentration is the physical act of transferring funds from a source to a target account. Interest is calculated and paid on the aggregated net balance held on the target account. It allows treasurers to optimize control of funds and interest positions and to offset fully consolidated balance sheets. One of its drawbacks, however, is that it works largely on a single currency basis.

The transfer of funds between accounts is based on terms defined in a cash pooling contract which can take either of two forms:

- zero balancing, where debit and credit balances are put to zero at the end of each day, or
- conditional balancing where an end-of-day balance is specified.

Within the cash concentration structure, funds are swept or covered between accounts held by different legal entities, which constitutes an inter-company lending and borrowing situation, which has specific tax implications.

Not all corporations, however, are equipped to handle the complexities of inter-company loan management encompassing different legal entities. An alternative to cash concentration is notional pooling. As the term suggests, balances are consolidated on a virtual basis without the transfer of funds between a source and target account. Companies are thus provided with a tool for managing their liquidity needs on a multi-currency basis without the complexities of managing inter-company loans.

Multinational companies with accounts in different currencies that wish to use long balances in some accounts to offset short positions in others but do not wish to generate inter-company loans would implement a notional pooling structure. By offsetting negative and positive balances in a range of currencies the company pays less interest charges on overdrafts while increasing its interest income on credit balances.

Banks, nevertheless, are reluctant to offer full interest compensation due to capital adequacy requirements imposed on debit balances. Therefore, on a cross-border basis banks tend to offer interest optimization notional pooling structures. Reference account notional pooling structures work on a single entity basis and provide full compensation, but this leads to inter-company loans. Therefore, from a tax perspective this is comparable to cash concentration.

Tax implications

The tax implications should be reviewed for each jurisdiction. This is particularly true for inter-company loans generated between different legal entities. So for example, a company looking to transfer liquidity to a target account held by its US subsidiary would need to consider the tax implications in its home country as well as the US.

Taxation issues typically impact companies implementing cash concentration structures. Sweeping and covering funds between accounts held by different legal entities gives rise to inter-company loans, which have a number of tax implications for the participant and target account holder. The bank's relationship with customers is changed to an intercompany loan relationship, which qualifies it for withholding taxes to be levied on related interest payments.

Double-taxation treaties between two countries can also reduce the withholding tax paid on inter-company loans. In the case of an Italian company that uses a long target account in Germany to cover its short positions, the interest paid on inter-company loans would be subject to withholding tax in Italy. However, as a tax treaty exists between Germany and Italy, the rate of withholding tax is reduced from 12.5 percent to 10 percent. Before claiming the reduction, the target account holder needs to prove they are resident in Germany and entitled to the interest.

Interest payments on inter-company loans are tax deductible whereas dividends, which are profits earned and distributed to company shareholders, are non-tax deductible. However, under thin capitalization regulations, interest payments may qualify as dividend payments and be subject to corporation tax in many countries.

Transfer pricing issues arise when income in the form of interest is transferred between companies in different countries or jurisdictions. The tax authorities could view this as an attempt to shift income or expenses from one country to take advantage of variable tax rates in another. The tax implications are moderated if the interest paid on inter-company loans complies with what authorities term an arm's-length transaction.

In some countries, controlled foreign company (CFC) regulations were introduced to prevent companies transferring certain activities to foreign subsidiaries in low-tax jurisdictions. In most countries, income is normally taxed once it is distributed to shareholders. However, in some instances, borrowing or lending by a target account holder may qualify as passive income, which could be taxed in the hands of the shareholder even before a distribution is effected. For example, a French company that holds 10 percent in the form of shares, financial or voting rights in a target account company operating in a lower tax regime, may be liable for corporate tax on interest earned on the target account.

Both notional pooling and cash concentration structures have their tax implications for corporations contemplating a choice between the two. Notional pooling does not result in an inter-company loan situation, so the tax implications may be less complex. However, the structure of the notional pool and the contractual liabilities of participants could raise tax issues similar to those that apply to cash concentration structures.

For example, notional pooling participants that guarantee a loan provided by a third party, such as a bank, to one of its subsidiaries, could be viewed as a substitute for a direct intercompany loan, thus subject to withholding taxes. Structures that entail moving liquidity across borders and between different legal entities typically have more profound tax implications. However, from a commercial perspective with respect to full interest offset, balance sheet offset and control over funds, cash concentration may be the more attractive structure. Therefore, many corporates favor cash concentration.

As the CFO of any multinational business enterprise knows, the complexity of tax laws and corporate decision making grows in proportion to the number of government entities, cultural traditions, and business practices involved. Tax planning can become a patchwork of internal and advisor opinions, past practices, and inconsistent interpretations. This can be particularly problematical when shareholders and management have differing views over the conflict between paying the minimum tax legally possible, and the long-term benefits of paying a fair and equitable share of the tax burden.[50]

E-business offers tremendous opportunities to multinational companies to reengineer the manner in which they interact with customers, suppliers, group members, employees, and other stakeholders. By using tax planning in an integrated way with the e-business change process, companies using the web to do business can achieve significant tax savings and simplification. An important consideration is transfer pricing. By adjusting the price which subsidiaries pay or receive for goods and services, groups of companies can alter where and how much tax they pay. The transformation to e-business can be the catalyst for meaningful transfer pricing planning and enable companies to adjust their tax profiles, and generate tax efficiencies.

To counter the misuse of transfer pricing and ensure that each country receives its fair share of tax, the Organisation for Economic Cooperation and Development (OECD) introduced guidelines on transfer pricing. Globalization and rapid technological innovation are driving companies to embrace fundamental changes to their supply chain structures.

New structures are being put into place to access and compete in an ever-growing number of geographic markets. Companies are building intellectual property for which little value may have been recognized. Those companies will need to establish where and how to locate assets, economic functions, and risks to obtain efficient tax structures.

Under constant pressure to improve net earnings and cash-flow in the evolving global economy, companies are reducing costs and minimizing risk by restructuring supply chains as well as international and domestic operating structures as they globalize. Companies typically create appropriate tax and legal structures to optimize their new configuration. The corporate strategy aligns the company's tax profile with the restructured value chain.

The following items are important in this tax planning process:

- optimize overall structural tax rates;

- create a new and transformed income and cash-flow stream;

- realign structures in a more tax advantagous way;

- establish potential synergies within the supply chain and operating structure;

- provide appropriate documentation for the restructured business process.

To achieve long-term sustainable tax solutions, companies thus need to take a look at their global tax position. Tax outlays reduce net income and cash-flows, and therefore affect shareholder value. It also impacts the effective cost of capital.

The cost of capital has a significant impact on shareholder value. Optimal tax planning can reduce the company's cost of capital by enhancing the use of equity, debt, and surplus funds through the finance and treasury functions.

Companies need to take a look at their global tax position.

Even a minor adjustment in the cost of capital can have major implications for the bottom line and greatly enhance shareholder value. For example, for a $10bn company, even a 0.5 percent cut in a 10 percent cost of capital can add $750m to market capitalization.[51]

Treasury management becomes more important as worldwide financial, accounting, regulatory and tax issues become more complex. Leading-edge companies are using sophisticated tax planning methodologies to manage capital and enhance cash-flow through structured finance, securitizations, and other customized finance and treasury solutions.

Financial products and structured finance help companies structure a variety of transactions, including:

- financing capital assets on a low-cost basis, through cross-border financing;

- reducing foreign tax liabilities through high-quality equity investments;

- designing and implementing inter-company financing to optimize foreign tax credit, reduce worldwide taxes, and enable more cost-effective repatriation of funds;

- designing structured finance portfolios, including the management, growth, and divestiture of assets;

■ designing investment programs that create opportunity in complex capital investment markets;

■ developing and marketing products that maximize tax attributes of profitable corporations.

Securitization focuses on monetizing a variety of assets to reduce a company's cost of capital.

CASE STUDY 3.1 | IBM[52]

A reconciliation of IBM's continuing operations effective tax rate to the statutory US federal tax rate is as shown in Figure 3.11:

Year-end (% points)	2002	2001	2000
Statutory tax rate	35	35	35
Foreign tax differential	–7	–6	–6
State and local	1	1	1
Valuation allowance	0	0	–1
Other	0	–1	2
Effective tax rate	29	29	31

FIGURE 3.11 ■ IBM CORP.: statutory and effective tax rates

For tax return purposes, IBM has available tax credit carry-forwards of approximately $2,234m as of year-end 2002, of which $1,316m have an indefinite carry-forward period and the remainder begin to expire in 2005. The company also has state and local, and foreign tax loss carry-forwards, the tax effect of which is $543m. Most of these carry-forwards are available for five years or have an indefinite carry-forward period.

CASE STUDY 3.2 | Daimler Chrysler[53]

In 2002, the DaimlerChrysler Group recorded income tax expense of €11.2bn, compared with an income tax benefit of €10.8bn in the previous year. The effective tax rate was 19.4 percent in 2002, compared with the previous year's rate of 52.4 percent. The low effective tax rate in 2002 was principally due to the tax-free sale of the investments in T-Systems ITS and Conti Temic microelectronic.

The high tax rate in 2001 was due to the pre-tax loss reported in 2001 combined with the tax-free sales of the remaining Debitel shares, the Rail Systems business unit, and 60 percent of the group's interest in TEMIC. Because of the pre-tax loss reported in 2001, the tax-free gains realized in 2001 had the effect of increasing the effective tax rate.

CASE STUDY 3.3 Toyota[54]

Provision for income taxes decreased by ¥101.1bn during fiscal 2002 compared with the prior year primarily as a result of decrease in income before income taxes and decreased provision for taxes on undistributed earnings of affiliated companies accounted for by the equity method. The effective tax rate for fiscal 2002 decreased to 43.5 percent from 47.3 percent for the prior year due primarily to decreased provision for taxes on undistributed earnings of affiliated companies.

CASE STUDY 3.4 Nestlé[55]

Nestlé's tax planning includes current taxes on profit and other taxes such as taxes on capital. Also included are actual or potential withholding taxes on current and expected transfers of income from group companies and tax adjustments relating to prior years. Income tax is recognized in the income statement, except to the extent that it relates to items directly taken to equity, in which case it is recognized in equity.

Deferred taxation is the tax attributable to the temporary differences that appear when taxation authorities recognize and measure assets and liabilities with rules that differ from those of the consolidated accounts. Deferred taxes are calculated under the liability method at the rates of tax expected to prevail when the temporary differences reverse.

Any changes of the tax rates are recognized in the income statement unless related to items directly recognized in equity. Deferred tax liabilities are recognized on all taxable temporary differences excluding non-deductible goodwill. Deferred tax assets are recognized on all deductible temporary differences provided that it is probable that future taxable income will be available.

CASE STUDY 3.5 Procter & Gamble[56]

Procter & Gamble follows SFAS No. 109, under US GAAP for accounting for income taxes. Income taxes are recognized for the amount of taxes payable for the current year, and for deferred tax liabilities and assets for future tax consequences of events that have been recognized differently in the financial statements than for tax purposes. Deferred tax assets and liabilities are established using the enacted statutory tax rates and adjusted for tax rate changes.

Procter & Gamble's effective income tax rate was 31.1 percent, 31.8 percent and 36.7 percent in 2003, 2002 and 2001, respectively, compared to the US statutory rate of

35.0 percent. The country mix impacts of foreign operations reduced the company's effective tax rate to a larger degree in 2003 and 2002 than in 2001: 3.8 percent in 2003 and 3.1 percent in 2002.

Procter & Gamble's higher tax rate in 2001 reflected the impact of restructuring costs and amortization of goodwill and indefinite-lived intangibles prior to the adoption of SFAS No. 142. Taxes impacted shareholders' equity with credits of $361m and $477m for the years ended June 30, 2003 and 2002, respectively. These primarily relate to the tax effects of net investment hedges and tax benefits from the exercise of stock options.

Procter & Gamble has some undistributed earnings of foreign subsidiaries as of June 30, 2003, for which deferred taxes have not been provided. Such earnings are considered indefinitely invested in the foreign subsidiaries. Realization of certain deferred tax assets is dependent upon generating sufficient taxable income in the appropriate jurisdiction prior to expiration of the carry-forward periods. Although realization is not assured, Procter & Gamble believes it is more likely than not that the deferred tax assets, net of applicable valuation allowances, will be realized.

CASE STUDY 3.6 GlaxoSmithKline[57]

The GlaxoSmithKline Group operates in countries where the tax rate differs to the UK rate. The standard rate of tax for the group has been estimated by aggregating the local standard tax rates and weighting these in proportion to accounting profits. Profits arising from manufacturing operations in Singapore, Puerto Rico and Ireland are taxed at reduced rates. The effect of this reduction in the taxation charge increased earnings per share by 3.6p in 2002, 2.7p in 2001 and by 3.2p in 2000.

The integrated nature of the Group's worldwide operations, involving significant investment in research and strategic manufacture at a limited number of locations, with consequential cross-border supply routes into numerous end-markets, gives rise to complexity and delay in negotiations with revenue authorities as to the profits on which individual group companies are liable to tax.

Disagreements with, and between, revenue authorities as to intra-group transactions, in particular the price at which goods should be transferred between group companies in different tax jurisdictions, can produce conflicting claims from revenue authorities as to the profits that fall to be taxed in individual territories. Resolution of such issues is a continuing fact of life for GlaxoSmithKline.

In the US for a number of years, GlaxoSmithKline has had significant open issues relating to transfer pricing. These issues affect all years from 1989 to the present and concern a number of products, although the most significant relates to the success of Zantac, in

▶

respect of which the claims of the US Internal Revenue Service (IRS) substantially exceed the group's estimation of its taxation liabilities.

The IRS claims, which are not completely quantified, continue to be the subject of discussions between the US and UK tax authorities under the competent authority provisions of the double-tax convention between the two countries. Within these discussions there is a wide variation between the views of the US and UK tax authorities and, exceptionally, they may be unable to reach agreement to settle the dispute.

In the event of the UK and US tax authorities not reaching agreement, the matter may have to be resolved by litigation. GlaxoSmithKline uses the best advice in determining its transfer pricing methodology and in seeking to manage transfer pricing issues to a satisfactory conclusion and, on the basis of external professional advice, continues to believe that it has made adequate provision for the liabilities likely to arise from open assessments.

Income, excise and all other taxes and duties totalled $64.3bn in 2002, a decrease of $2.2bn or 3 percent from 2001. Income tax expense, both current and deferred, was $6.5 bn compared to $9.0bn in 2001, reflecting lower pre-tax income in 2002. The effective tax rate of 39.8 percent in 2002 compared to 39.3 percent in 2001. During 2002, the company continued to benefit from favorable resolution of tax-related issues. Excise and all other taxes and duties were $57.8bn.

Income, excise and all other taxes and duties totalled $66.5bn in 2001, a decrease of $1.9bn or 3 percent from 2000. Income tax expense, both current and deferred, was $9.0bn compared to $11.1bn in 2000, reflecting lower pre-tax income in 2001. The effective tax rate of 39.3 percent in 2001 compared to 42.6 percent in 2000, benefiting from a higher level of favorably resolved tax-related issues. Excise and all other taxes and duties were $57.6bn.

Optimal capital budgeting with real options

Making optimal 'go' or 'no-go' decisions regarding capital investments can be a source of significant competitive advantages for companies. Standard project appraisal techniques are now being complemented with more sophisticated analysis methods that allow managers to assess more accurately the real value of returns from capital projects.

Real options analysis provides a sophisticated tool for evaluating capital investment decisions by incorporating the value of management flexibility during the lifetime of the project.

Capital investments that are required for ongoing maintenance and expansion requirements of business operations are based on a long-term outlook of the cash generation capability of the project vis-à-vis its capital investment requirements. Traditionally, the investment is considered to be viable if the net cash-flows represent a positive net present value (NPV) or an internal rate of return (IRR) which is above the required hurdle rate.

However, traditional capital budgeting is rather unsophisticated since it is a static view of the world, and assumes that management has no flexibility to revise its originally planned project outlays even in the long term.

In reality, however, plans are rarely ever carried out as originally conceived. Changing business assumptions on external or internal conditions, or over- or under-achievement of project goals often necessitate revisions of original plans.

Management often does have a fair amount of flexibility in expanding or contracting subsequent project outlays as project performance comes to fruition. In order to incorporate this management flexibility into the capital budgeting process, real options valuation analysis is used. "Real options are useful for identifying, understanding, valuing, prioritizing, selecting, timing, optimizing, and managing strategic business and capital allocation decisions."[58]

A *Harvard Business Review* article states:[59]

"Unfortunately, the financial tool most widely relied on to estimate the value of a strategy is the discounted cash-flow which assumes that we will follow a predetermined plan regardless of how events unfold.

A better approach to valuation would incorporate both the uncertainty inherent in business and the active decision making required for a strategy to succeed. It would help executives to think strategically on their feet by capturing the value of doing just that – of managing actively rather than passively and real options can deliver that extra insight."

The real options approach incorporates a learning model such that management makes better and more informed strategic decisions when some levels of uncertainty are resolved through the passage of time. The traditional discounted cash-flow analysis assumes a static investment decision, and assumes that strategic investment decisions are made initially with no recourse to choose other pathways or options in the future.

"Business conditions are fraught with uncertainty and risks. These uncertainties hold with them valuable information. When uncertainty becomes resolved through the passage of time, managers can make the appropriate mid-course corrections through a change in business decisions and strategies. Real options incorporates this learning model, akin to having a strategic roadmap, while traditional analyses that neglect this managerial flexibility will grossly undervalue certain projects and strategies."[60]

There are different kinds of options at management's disposal, that can be decided upon over time, based on the type of project being evaluated, and its ongoing success rate:

■ option to abandon,

■ option to expand,

■ option to contract,

- option to choose,

- compound option (and sequential compond option),

- option to switch.

An *abandon option* provides management with the ability to discontinue the project.

An *expansion option* provides management with the right and ability to expand into different markets, products, and strategies, or to expand the capacity of its current operations under the right market conditions.

An *option to contract* means management has the ability to decrease the scale of production according to the demand conditions in the market.

A *chooser option* implies that management has the flexibility to choose among several strategies, including the option to expand, contract, abandon, switch, and so forth.

A *compound option* means that the execution and value of a strategic option depends on another strategic option.

A *sequential compound option* means that the execution and value of future strategic options depends on previous options in the sequence of execution.

A *switching option* provides the right and ability, but not the obligation, to switch among different sets of business operating conditions, including different technologies, markets, or products.

A firm can also create strategic value through setting up contractual agreements with *barrier options.* For example, for the promise of seed financing, a venture capital firm gets the right of first refusal, but not the obligation, to invest in a second or third round should the start-up achieve certain management set goals or barriers. The cost of this barrier option is seed financing, which is akin to the premium on a stock option. Should the option be in-the-money, the option will be executed through second and third round financing.

By obtaining this strategic option, the venture firm has locked itself into a guaranteed favorable position should the start-up be highly successful, similar to the characteristics of a financial call-option which has an unlimited upside potential. At the same time, the venture firm has hedged itself against missing the opportunity with limited down-side proportional to the expenditure of a minimal amount of seed financing.

Fortune 500 firms are embracing this new valuation concept. Companies such as Boeing, Hewlett Packard, AT&T, and General Motors have successfully applied real options as a tool for capital investment valuation.[61]

Traditional discounted cash-flow approaches to capital investments underestimate the value of a project by ignoring the value of managerial flexibility. One of the value-added components of using real options is that it takes into account management's ability to create, execute, and abandon strategic and flexible options.

> **EXAMPLES**
>
> General Motors applies real options to create switching options in producing its new series of automobiles. Hewlett Packard uses real options to evaluate project investments with delay options on building assembly plants in foreign countries. Boeing uses real options in capital investment decisions on aircraft development projects, by using the option to choose, so that parallel development of multiple aircraft designs can occur simultaneously.
>
> Oil and gas companies like Schlumberger spend millions of dollars to refurbish refineries and add new technology to create an option to switch their mix of outputs among heating oil, diesel, and other petrochemicals as a final product. These companies use real options as a means of making capital investment decisions.
>
> In the telecommunication industry, companies like Sprint and AT&T installed more fiber-optic cable and other telecommunications infrastructure than other companies in order to create a growth option in the future by providing a secure and extensive network, and to create a high barrier to entry, providing a first-to-market advantage.

There are several potential problem areas in using traditional discounted cash-flow calculations on strategic optionalities. These problems include:

■ undervaluing assets that currently produce little or no cash-flow;

■ non-constant nature of weighted average cost of capital over time;

■ estimation of an asset's economic life;

■ forecast errors in estimating future cash-flows;

■ insufficient tests for plausibility of final results.

Real options, when applied using an options theoretic framework, can mitigate some of these problem areas. Traditional approaches are more relevant for shorter time-frames that have more certainty. In a longer time-frame, where strategic opportunities arise, a more appropriate approach incorporates new advanced analysis, including real options, Monte Carlo simulations, and portfolio optimization.

EXAMPLE

In this following example, we look at the value of a potential $225m capital project investment. The net present value is $134.06m. Based on simulation analysis the probability of the project delivering between $130m and $140m is only 5.70 percent! See Figures 13.12 and 13.13.

			Present value (Cash Flow)	$323.64
Discount rate (Cash Flow)	12.00%			
Discount rate (Impl. Cost)	5.00%		Present value (Impl. Cost)	$189.58
Tax Rate	30.00%		Net Present Value	$134.06
Cost of revenue as % of revenue	28.00%			
Operating expenses as % of revenue	20.00%			

	Forecast				
	2004	2005	2006	2007	2008
Revenue	$98.00	$163.00	$231.00	$297.00	$364.00
Cost of Revenue	$27.44	$45.64	$64.68	$83.16	$101.92
Gross Profit	$70.56	$117.36	$166.32	$213.84	$262.08
Operating Expenses	$19.60	$32.60	$46.20	$59.40	$72.80
Depreciation Expense	$5.00	$5.00	$5.00	$5.00	$5.00
Interest Expense	$3.00	$3.00	$3.00	$3.00	$3.00
Income Before Taxes	$42.96	$76.76	$112.12	$146.44	$181.28
Taxes	$12.89	$23.03	$33.64	$43.93	$54.38
Income After Taxes	$30.07	$53.73	$78.48	$102.51	$126.90
Non-Cash Expenses	$12.00	$14.00	$17.00	$21.00	$24.00
Cash Flow	$42.07	$67.73	$95.48	$123.51	$150.90
Implementation Cost	$25.00	$25.00	$50.00	$50.00	$75.00

FIGURE 3.12 ■ Traditional NPV of $134.06 million excluding real option valuation

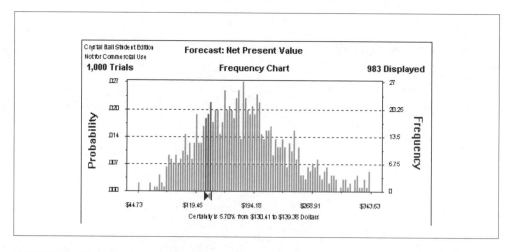

FIGURE 3.13 ■ Monte Carlo Simulation Output. 5.7 percent profitability of NPV between $130 million and $140 million

On the other hand, simulation analysis also tells us that with a 95 percent probability, the project will yield an NPV between $81m and $323m.

Now, let's look at the Expanded Net Present Value (ENPV) of this project taking into consideration the strategic option management has of expanding the scale of this project by 50 percent of its current size, if profitability and market demand really take off.

We will consider an expansion option, which provides management with the right but not the obligation to expand the project. This real option has intrinsic value which is completely ignored in conventional NPV analysis performed above (see Figure 3.12).

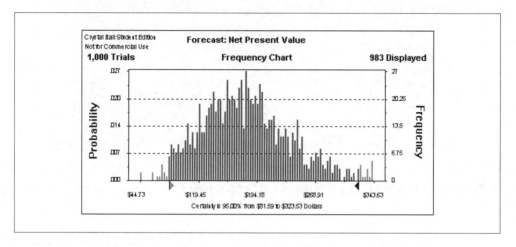

FIGURE 3.14 ■ Monte Carlo Simulation Output. 95.0 percent probability of NPV between $81 million and $323 million

When the expansion option is taken into account, the ENPV (expanded NPV) of the project becomes $149.98m (see Figure 3.15). The ENPV is $15.96m higher that the conventional NPV without real options. Therefore, the value of the expansion option is approximately $16m.

Taking this strategic real option into consideration, we can now see how traditional capital budgeting techniques would have undervalued this business case. Clearly, the project is more attractive with the expansion option.

Alternatively, if management sees that the project is not on track, and profitability is not up to expectations, it may choose to reduce the scale of the production or service delivery capacity, thus reducing overhead and minimizing margin contraction.

We assess the real options value of contracting production capacity by 25 percent anytime over the next five years (see Figure 3.16).

In this case, we have assumed that management has the right but not the obligation to contract the scale of the project downward by 30 percent, which would yield not only a cash savings of $50m, but would in fact increase the ENPV to $145.40m, which is $11.34m higher than the original NPV of $134.06m.

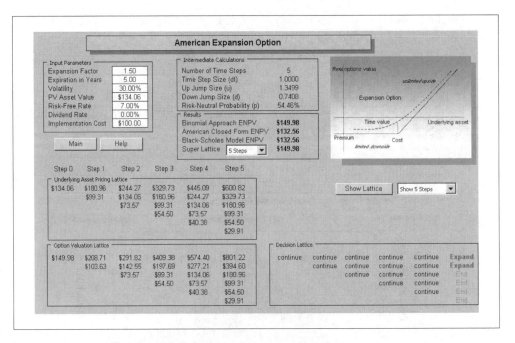

FIGURE 3.15 ■ Expanded NPV (ENPV) of $149.98 million including expansion options

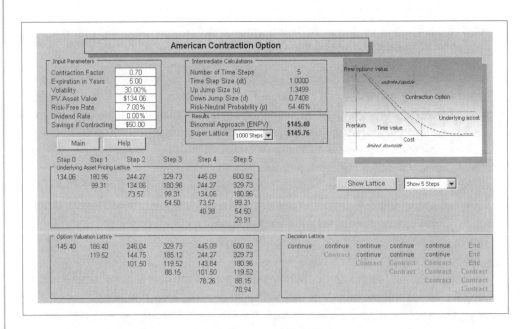

FIGURE 3.16 ■ ENPV of $145.40 million including contraction options

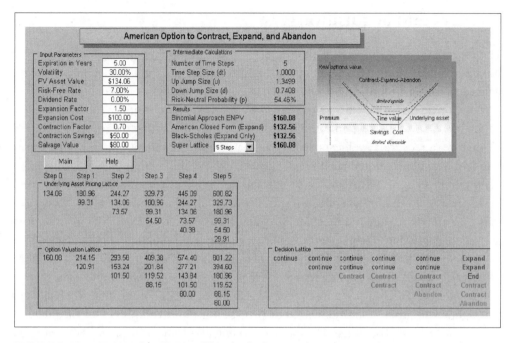

FIGURE 3.17 ■ ENPV of $160.08 million including option to expand, contract, or abandon project

Therefore, the value of the strategic real option to contract is worth approximately $11m.

Now, lets incorporate both the expansion and contraction options into the valuation process. In the real world, management may have the option to either expand or contract the scale of a project as it sees fit. Management may even choose to abandon the project altogether. Therefore, this can be a realistic scenario.

In this case, management has the right to expand the project scale by 50 percent any time over the five years following inception, at a cost of $100m. Management also has the right to contract the scale of the project by 30 percent any time over the five years following inception, at a cash savings of $50m. In addition, we have assumed that management has the right to abandon the project for a residual value of $80m.

We see that the ENPV of the project is now $160.08m, (see Figure 3.17) which is $26.02m higher than the static NPV estimate. Clearly, these real options ought to be considered in the capital budgeting valuation process.

Mergers and acquisitions

The essence of an acquisition is to create a strategic advantage by paying for an existing business and integrating that entity with the firm's strategy. The incentive to acquire exists when acquisition is more cost-effective than organic internal development.

Long-term survival of any corporation depends on its continued ability to develop strength relative to its competitors. Success in achieving this strength depends on the ability to shift resources from well-established, mature business activities to emerging business activities with growth potential.

Within this ongoing process of self-renewal, the company must decide whether, given its basic strategy, it is better off shifting these resources through acquisitions or through redistribution among existing entities. Mergers and aquisitions (M&A) activity is an important avenue through which companies can rebalance their product and market portfolios.

A diversified firm may have a hierarchy of business strategies that develop a set of interrelated businesses which provide reasonable balance and stability within the firm.

Planning for an acquisition involves a search for business entities that will balance and strengthen the firm's overall portfolio or provide for improved processes or efficiencies. Acquisitions may also be dictated by the need to enter new growth markets. However, releasing optimal value from a merger or acquisition has traditionally been difficult. Research shows that a staggering 80 percent of deals fail to deliver the intended shareholder value.[62]

Many acquirers justify their acquisitions and acquisition prices on expected synergies. Examples include a new product line that fits the acquirer's present distribution channels, a raw materials supplier that assures a manufacturer's uninterrupted needs at reasonable prices, or a seasonal business that buys a counter-seasonal business to smooth out the revenue stream.

EXAMPLE

Pfizer Inc., offered a hefty 44 percent premium over the market price for Pharmacia Corp, paying $60bn in stock for Pharmacia, which in June 30, 2002 had a book value of only $12.2bn.[63]

Success in M&A requires the careful identification and valuation of acquisition candidates based on both strategic and financial criteria. For corporate acquirers, the analysis looks at a deal's potential for improving the performance of both the acquired business and the parent. Improvements often depend on merger synergies. Yet, these synergies frequently fall short of expectations, particularly when the economy turns for the worst. Consequently, a forecast of the macro-economic condition is critical to M&A strategy.

Some acquisitions are secured at high premiums because of unrealistic assessments of future returns from the synergies expected to be generated from the performance of the combined entity.

Most M&A valuations are performed by discounted expected future income streams which are based on assumptions of future performance of the company, future economic expectations, and future earnings increases through synergies. In practice, most acquisitions are made at a premium to the intrinsic value calculated through discounted cash-flow valuation.

If the assumptions are too optimiztic, overly generous premiums may never be recouped. The extent of premium to be paid is a key element in the decision to acquire a business. The purchase price is usually higher than the current value of the business, primarily because stockholders of the target company need an incentive to transfer control to another owner. Sophisticated buyers regard the final premium as the outcome of negotiation or bidding, not as a predetermined figure.[64]

Sophisticated buyers regard the final premium as the outcome of negotiation or bidding.

Corporate buyers are usually motivated by strategic objectives – expanding an existing business, improving financial performance, reducing costs in the existing business, enhancing top-line revenues or valuation multiples, improving liquidity, or extending into a new line of business. Such a move can potentially strengthen the firm's internal operations by broadening its product or service spectrum while simultaneously reducing competition.

An acquisition is made on the premise that some estimated gains from the transaction will exceed the premium paid for the acquired company. The post-acquisition problems reside in the exploitation of these estimated gains. Typically, this is a considerable challenge, because interaction between the acquirer and target company's management is very delicate. Winning commitment from the target company's management depends on the modalities of the transaction, i.e. whether it is an unfriendly takeover or merger. The degree of cultural mismatch plays a role in terms of how easy or difficult it will be to integrate one into the other.

The integration of productive assets is also an important dimension of the post-acquisition challenge. A frequent reason for acquisition is the use of shared resources between firms. However, the cost of unbundling the target firm's physical facilities, production plants, and distribution channels, for example, often may exceed pre-acquisition estimates. Alternatively, a subsidiary company may not fit with the future business strategy of the corporate parent, leading the parent to initiate the divestiture of the subsidiary.

The fundamental financial justification for a corporation to make an acquisition is to increase the per share value of the acquirer over the long term. In order for this to happen, the projected incremental cash-flows from the acquisition must be valued higher than the acquisition price. The fundamental reason for a company to agree to be acquired, if the transaction is for cash, is that the selling shareholders have an immediate opportunity to be paid for some of the acquisition's expected benefits.

In a transaction in which the seller receives the acquirer's stock, the seller, as one of the acquirer's shareholders, will also share in the benefits of the merger over time. In determining whether an acquisition will, on balance, create value for the acquirer, several rules are becoming commonly accepted among the experts:[65]

- Pure conglomerate acquisitions do not necessarily create new shareholder value.
- Counter-cyclical acquisitions do not necessarily create value.
- The market does not reward purely acquisition-induced growth.
- Related diversification can be an important means of creating value in acquisitions.
- Acquisitions can be an important means of reaching a critical mass, where size is an important industry factor.
- Acquisitions are tax-efficient means of investing excess corporate funds.

Rising above the statistics and extracting maximum value from a corporate transaction is crucial for both entities. The dangers of mergers and acquisitions have long been known. The reality is that deals are often disruptive and may result in short-term value leakage. Many businesses underperform on budget expectations in the pre-deal process as vital energies are directed towards the transaction.

An aggressive M&A market emerged towards the end of 2000.[66] M&A deals are now a prominent feature in the corporate landscape. For the CFO, a strong M&A presence in the marketplace presents considerable challenges. At no other time is a CFO and their management team under such public scrutiny. The way they respond to this situation is an important driver of shareholder value.

Based on the *CFO 100 Survey*, evidence would suggest pricing premiums in the market have come down considerably in the last decade. One of the drivers of M&A activity for companies is the desire to gain a significant competitive advantage in its product or service category.

Worldwide consolidation pressures in sectors like banking and finance, telecommunications, resources and those with global brands, continue their trend to global consolidation. Low interest rates make funding available at relatively cheap rates for well-capitalized companies looking into M&A as a means of growth.

Shareholder concerns

Shareholders will have one of two concerns, dependent on whether they are shareholders in the acquiring company or target company. Firstly, given the potential for assets to be relatively cheap, shareholders of the target company will be concerned with capturing the maximum possible value from assets. High takeover premiums often indicate disposing shareholders generally do benefit from M&A transactions, providing they are on appropriate terms.

For shareholders of the acquiring company, it is usually hard to extract value from an M&A deal. Empirical evidence suggests 60 percent of mergers and acquisitions are unsuccessful from the shareholders' point of view. Most commonly, this occurs because in a competitive auction, the highest bidder typically pays a premium greater than the expected benefits of the deal to win. This is otherwise known as the "winner's curse."

Therefore, shareholders of acquiring companies will be concerned that management does not pay too much for the target company. Average US and Australian M&A premiums, 41 and 13 percent respectively during the year 2000, indicate it may be easier for US acquirers to create value than for their domestic counterparts to do so. However, the body of academic and commercial research on M&A issues suggests it is more likely that disposing shareholders rather than acquiring shareholders will benefit from the deal.

PricewaterhouseCoopers' research reveals most businesses continue to suffer shortfalls against budget in the post-deal period – necessitating a dramatic increase in revenue to achieve original expectations. Value from a corporate transaction is most often lost because organizations fail to act quickly to capture the synergies available.

If the organization was involved in a competitive bid process, it will have reflected a significant part of that synergistic value in its bid price. If it has not realized all that synergistic value, it has lost value for its shareholders. Companies need to "seize the day" and immediately set about extracting value. Unfortunately, this is the exception rather than the norm.

Acquiring is only half of realizing the value. The other half lies in establishing an implementation process which delivers that value. So, where are organizations falling down? Many fail to devote adequate time to planning and implementation.

A well-thought out planning process ensures you have a solid foundation from which to work. It acts as a map to guide you through the maze of issues you will encounter as you progress through the life-cycle of a deal.

Too many transactions are undertaken without the necessary plans in place – plans crucial to ensuring an optimal result. Knowing your own strengths and weaknesses allows you to identify the most attractive targets for your company. Once you have a target in your sight, you need to keep an eye on your original plan. Evaluate the target carefully. Does it fit in with both your strategic and financial objectives?

People get caught up in future projections and the idea that this makes great strategic sense – and overlook the financial impacts. Any deal constructed under such circumstances is leaching value from the outset. Once you are sure the transaction is in line with your over-all strategy, you need to pull together the right team to take you from the evaluation to integration process. If you want to reap the full benefits of the deal, now is the time to assemble an expert team of both your own people and external advisors.

A multi-disciplinary team should include people with project management skills and pre-vious experience working on corporate transactions. You also need people who know your business – and the business you are looking to acquire. Finally, you need to build a team of tax, finance, legal, human resources and accounting people – either from within your organ-ization or from an external provider.

Bringing in expert advice plays a major role in ensuring the effectiveness of a deal. A dili-gent approach to planning is required. Due diligence presents one of the greatest opportunities to maximize the benefits of the deal. This phase of the transaction has a larger role to play than simply sizing up the financial and market position of the company. For the smart players, due diligence is where the integration planning begins.

Due diligence of a target should include likely post-deal synergies and human resource and information technology issues. The due diligence phase also represents a real opportu-nity to examine the human capital of the organization.

An effective human resources strategy is a vital component to the success of a business restructuring strategy. Although it may seem clichéd, people are usually the company's most important asset. Unfortunately, this is often overlooked in a large financial transaction, as the "traditional" due diligence process focuses largely on the balance sheet and perceived key financial risks.

One of the key risks involved is dealing with employee share and option plans. The due diligence process can also afford opportunity to conduct a cultural audit of the business – allowing you to ascertain how compatible the cultures are and identify areas for immediate attention on day one.

It is crucial you identify the key people in the organization as early as possible. They are the ones who have assisted in creating the company's value – and having them on board places you in the best position to derive maximum value.

Achieving value greater than the sum of the parts: the due diligence process is the time to understand exactly what the value drivers in the business are – and how that value is going to be extracted from day one. You cannot underestimate the importance of the links between upfront planning, due diligence and the post-deal activities undertaken.

The best way to get proper linkage is to ensure that line management and those involved in the everyday business are involved throughout the transaction – and most crucially in due diligence. Many companies lose value on transactions because the deal makers failed to understand the business they were acquiring. People have a grip on the revenue stream, but not the logistics.

You need to ensure you know how the business operates – how things actually get done. What IT is involved in the business? How is it maintained? What licenses are held? These are simple questions but they go to the heart of identifying and capturing the value.

Value is often lost from a transaction because "deal fatigue" sets in once the signatures are on the dotted line. People pour their hearts and souls into this for months – and once the acquisition phase is over, the passion dies. To combat this, especially on complex deals which have taken an age to resolve, form both an acquisition and integration team. The integration team should share some of its members with the acquisition group, but generally the key movers and shakers in the integration team should be people with an intimate knowledge of the businesses. They will bring a degree of energy that would be lacking if you tried to use the entire acquisition team again.

Once you have been through the due diligence process – and have agreed on a deal designed to optimize your tax benefits and deliver greatest value, day one rolls around with frightening speed. This is especially so given the fact that the window between closing the deal and taking ownership will involve as much blood, sweat and tears as the deal itself.

Signing the deal should trigger an intensive planning mindset. Focus should quickly turn to empowering management to build the framework that will allow the business to meet its objectives and value expectations. The integration team should be dedicated to performance improvement; revenue and cost synergies should be estimated and achievements monitored to enable rapid and proactive re-calibration of effort. There should be great focus on projects delivering the greatest value in the shortest time – with the least risk.

Finally, you want the team focussed on capturing all pre-deal identified synergies in the post-deal environment. This means you have got to go back to all the value you recognized in the due diligence phase and extract it – quickly. Speed is critical in ensuring organizations reap the most value from an M&A transaction.

It is vital that benefits flow quickly. Acquirers need to minimize disruption, manage conflict and interdependencies to allow rapid transition to proceed. When it comes to addressing barriers to success, cultural issues are the most significant inhibitors to successful transition.

Communication and change management needs to be handled carefully. Communicating the changes at hand to both internal stakeholders and the market will help manage any perceived drop in value.

Post-transaction, it is important to measure the effectiveness of the transaction. Keeping track of where the business is at and taking steps to plug value leakage is part of the ongoing game plan. The business must be able to produce timely, accurate and useful information, especially in relation to working capital and cash-flows.

Reporting systems should be capable of providing regular updates of current versus historical performance – including coverage of key performance indicators and the efficiency of working capital usage. Most important however, is forecast performance, particularly in respect of cash-flows and debt headroom. When done correctly, the benefits of investing heavily in your new acquisition will continue to be apparent for years to come.

Compliance with regulatory issues form an important component. Ensure you have changed your various elections or notifications as to the group that you are operating for tax purposes. This cannot be retrospectively changed, so it is crucial you get it right – or risk penalties from the tax office. Does the new business structure you have inherited match your future plans? If not, you need to think about what transactions are necessary and the timing of these.

Additionally, your structural and financing profile may not be able to meld easily to the profile you have acquired. Examine exactly what is the most effective structure on an ongoing basis – and make moves to implement it. Remedial action – what did you identify during the due diligence process as demanding attention?

A new acquisition typically involves a significant change in the current financing arrangements. Take a look at the financing strategy that is appropriate to fund the acquisition and refinance existing arrangements. The additional value you can drive may go some way to recouping the acquisition costs.

Steps to protect and enhance value

CFOs can use the following steps to protect and enhance the value available to shareholders in M&A transactions. The steps have been put together from the perspective of targets.

Targets should have an action plan to protect against potential unwelcome takeover offers. Independent valuations need to be kept up-to-date. In a recent deal PricewaterhouseCoopers participated in, significant revisions of the initial offer were required to put the deal on appropriate terms. Without any early involvement it is difficult to negotiate this extra value. Targets need to recognize that their ongoing trading price reflects certain discounts such as liquidity, size, and even conglomerate discounts. The offer must be assessed for reasonableness in light of those facts. Also an awareness of the likely takeover premiums, particularly those relevant to the industry, is necessary.

The shareholding structure needs to be evaluated as well. Having cornerstone shareholders who understand the true value of the business can protect targets from unwelcome and low value offers. Even in a formal takeover situation, the introduction of competitive tension can drive premiums upward. Studies show the introduction of competitive tension into auction-like situations can significantly increase premiums available to disposing shareholders.

There are a number of guidelines that help an acquirer arrive at a bid price. A careful consideration of the changing M&A market trends, historical trading and pricing multiples, industry rules of thumb, and competing third-party bidders are among the factors that can shape a buyer's pricing decisions. Motivations and objectives of both buyers and sellers vary from case to case and also affect pricing.

Intelligent assessment of the full range of these forces enables a buyer to price a deal effectively. Good acquisitions can enhance shareholder value by expanding geographical coverage, broadening distribution networks, advancing technological skills, and creating operating efficiencies. Bad ones can destroy the value of healthy companies. Companies today are making acquisitions that enhance their key market positions and are undergoing divestitures that extract non-core businesses.[67]

Diversification, by definition, implies a broadening of operations and scope. But unlike the diversification of the 1960s, which was financially driven, the M&A activity of the 1980s and 1990s have been market-driven. Statistics compiled from the Mergers and Acquisitions Data Base indicated that the average premium paid, above market value, for acquiring publicly held companies during the late 1970s and 1980s ranged from a high of 70 percent in 1979 to a low of about 40 percent in 1987. The 1990s premiums have averaged in the 35–50 percent range. This would imply that strategic valuations have been significantly higher than traditional financial analysis would suggest.[68]

A buyer cannot begin to identify synergies between combining organizations until it can compare their per unit costs and revenues by business line or activity. A fair assessment of relative performance requires understanding the key drivers of cost and their differences. However, a synergy estimate used in pricing an acquisition is merely that, an estimate; it is the realisation of the estimate that translates into value for an acquirer.

A synergy estimate used in pricing an acquisition is merely that, an estimate.

On a purely pragmatic basis, the premiums paid for publicly owned corporations are influenced by many strategic and qualitative factors other than purely financial ones. M&A is a vehicle for competitive positioning and operational efficiency when it is driven as part of an overall strategic game plan and is grounded on a thorough understanding of the economic value and risks of acquisition candidates and alternative growth options.

CASE STUDY 3.7 IBM[69]

In 2002, IBM completed 12 acquisitions at an aggregate cost of $3,958m. The largest acquisition was PricewaterhouseCoopers Consulting (PwCC). On October 1, 2002, the company purchased PricewaterhouseCoopers' (PwC) global business consulting and technology services unit, PwCC, for $3,474m. The acquisition of PwCC provides IBM with new expertise in business strategy, industry-based consulting, process integration and application management. The purchase price above includes an estimated amount of net tangible assets to be transferred of approximately $422m. The recorded amount of net tangible assets transferred to IBM from PwC on October 1, 2002, was approximately $454m higher than the estimate. IBM paid $2,852m of the purchase price in cash, $294m primarily in the form of restricted shares of IBM common stock and $328m in notes convertible into restricted shares of IBM common stock.

In connection with the acquisition, IBM incurred approximately $196m of pre-tax, one-time compensation costs for certain PwCC partners and employees. This amount relates to restricted stock awards and the compensation element of the convertible notes issued as part of the purchase consideration and was recorded in the fourth quarter of 2002. The portion of this amount recorded as part of sales, general and administrative expenses (SG&A) in the Consolidated Statement of Earnings as compensation expense for the convertible notes equals the difference between the fair value and the face value of the notes.

As a result of its acquisition of PwCC, IBM recorded a liability of approximately $601m in the fourth quarter of 2002 to rebalance its workforce and to vacate excess leased space. All employees affected by this action were notified as of December 31, 2002. The portion of the liability relating to IBM people and space was approximately $318m, and substantially all was recorded as part of SG&A in the Consolidated Statement of Earnings. The portion of the liability relating to acquired PwCC workforce and leased space was approximately $283m and was included as part of the liabilities assumed for purchase accounting.

	Amortisation years	PWC	Other
Current assets		1,197	264
Fixed non-current assets		199	102
Intangible assets			
Goodwill		2,461	364
Completed technology	3		66
Strategic alliances	5	103	
Non-contractual customer relationships	4 to 7	131	
Customer contracts and backlog	3 to 5	82	6
Other intangible assets	3 to 5	95	10
Total assets acquired		4,268	812
Current liabilities		560	208
Non-current liabilities		234	124
Total liabilities assumed		794	332
Net assets acquired		3,474	480
In-process research development			4
Total purchase price		**3,474**	**484**

FIGURE 3.18 ■ IBM's Acquisition of PricewaterhouseCoopers and other assets ($ million)

CASE STUDY `3.8` Exxon-Mobil[70]

On November 30, 1999, a wholly-owned subsidiary of Exxon Corporation merged with Mobil Corporation so that Mobil became a wholly-owned subsidiary of Exxon. At the same time, Exxon changed its name to Exxon Mobil Corporation.

As a condition of the approval of the merger, the US Federal Trade Commission and the European Commission required that certain property — primarily downstream, pipeline and natural gas distribution assets — be divested.

The carrying value of these assets was approximately $3bn and before-tax proceeds were approximately $5 bn. Net after-tax gains of $40m and $1,730m were reported in 2001 and 2000, respectively, as extraordinary items consistent with pooling of interests accounting requirements. The divested properties historically earned approximately $200m per year. The merger was accounted for as a pooling of interests.

In association with the merger between Exxon and Mobil, $410m pre-tax ($275m after-tax), $748m pre-tax ($525m after-tax) and $1,406m pre-tax ($920m after-tax) of costs were recorded as merger-related expenses in 2002, 2001 and 2000, respectively.

Charges included separation expenses related to workforce reductions (approximately 8,200 employees at year-end 2002), plus implementation and merger closing costs. The separation reserve balance at year-end 2002 of approximately $101m is expected to be expended in 2003. Merger-related expenses for the period 1999 to 2002 cumulatively total approximately $3.2bn pre-tax.

Pre-tax operating synergies associated with the merger, including cost savings, efficiency gains, and revenue enhancements, have cumulatively reached over $7bn by 2002. Reflecting the completion of merger-related activities, merger expenses will not be reported in 2003.

CASE STUDY `3.9` GlaxoSmithKline[71]

The combination of Glaxo Wellcome plc and SmithKline Beecham plc was treated as a merger at December 27, 2000 under UK GAAP.

Under merger accounting, the shares issued by GlaxoSmithKline plc to acquire Glaxo Wellcome and SmithKline Beecham were accounted for at par and no share premium arose; the shares acquired by GlaxoSmithKline in Glaxo Wellcome and SmithKline Beecham were similarly accounted for at the nominal value of the shares issued.

In the consolidated financial statements of GlaxoSmithKline, the results and net assets of Glaxo Wellcome and SmithKline Beecham were combined, at their book amounts, subject to alignment adjustments.

▶

In view of the proximity of the merger date to the financial year end date, and the relative insignificance of any business activity between December 27, 2000 and December 31, 2000, the accounting date of the merger was for practical purposes taken as December 31, 2000. The whole of the profit for the financial year 2000 of each of Glaxo Wellcome plc and SmithKline Beecham plc was deemed to relate to the period prior to the merger date.

Merger items, restructuring costs and divested businesses, manufacturing and other restructuring costs were incurred by GlaxoSmithKline during 2002 and 2001 in implementation of previously announced plans for restructuring of manufacturing and other activities. These costs were also incurred by Glaxo Wellcome and SmithKlineBeecham in 2000.

Merger integration costs relate to the integration of Glaxo Wellcome and SmithKline Beecham into a unified GlaxoSmithKline business. These costs include consultancy fees in respect of integration planning, severance costs, asset write-offs, costs related to the early vesting or lapse of performance conditions on share options and share incentive awards and costs of the program to encourage staff to convert Glaxo Wellcome and SmithKline Beecham share options into GlaxoSmithKline share options.

Integration costs were incurred in 2002 and 2001 relating to the integration of the Block Drug businesses. These costs include professional fees, severance costs and asset write-offs. Product divestment income arising in 2002 related to the finalization of the disposals of Famvir, Kytril and other products required in 2000 in order to obtain regulatory approval for the merger.

Asset-liability management: optimizing the balance sheet

Corporate business management is, in a sense, management of assets and liabilities of many sorts. A part of corporate planning is to understand whether the financial obligations or liabilities are in sync with investments or assets.

If short-term debt is incurred to finance long-term fixed assets, then increasing short-term interest rates will put undue pressure on liquidity, and is undesirable. Similarly, if long-term debt obligations are used to finance short-term assets like inventory, the company may be spending too much on debt, given a positively sloped term structure of interest rates.

Depository financial institutions such as banks, must ensure that the effective maturity of the assets portfolio is the same as that of the liabilities, so that a duration imbalance does not occur. For example, if long-term fixed-rate loans are made with short-term variable rate deposits, an unexpected increase in interest rates reduces the bank's enterprise value, since the market value of its asset portfolio will experience larger capital losses than that of its liabilities. If duration imbalance were reduced, the losses would have been curtailed.

Following the maturity-matching principle, non-financial firms should finance the fixed assets with long-term debt that matures as the useful life of the assets expires, and finance the short-term working capital assets with short-term debt. Therefore, balance sheet assets and liabilities need to be matched by tenure. In other words, the weighted average duration of assets and liabilities should be comparable. Intangible assets should be financed with equity. This way, the company immunizes its asset-liability structure from adverse volatility in market variables. The firm's financial flexibility is enhanced, overall financing costs are minimized, and the firm's default risk is reduced.

Asset-liability management is important, especially in investment and portfolio management, and is particularly applicable for financial institutions and banks that need to match asset and liability durations. Leading pension plans, for example, employ asset and liability management systems for optimizing their strategic decisions.[72]

Balance sheet restructuring is thus an exercise in gaining closer duration alignment between the assets and liabilities of the firm. Since the assets and its characteristics are less amenable to change, typically it is the liabilities that are adjusted to match asset durations. Off-balance-sheet assets and contingent liabilities are often included in a thorough analysis of overall asset-liability mismatches.

When new operating assets which have appropriate tenures are added to the company's asset base by incurring debt, then the asset-liability matching minimizes funding and interest rate risks. Debt is often recalled by corporates in response to lower interest rates, while new equity issuances consider issuance costs and the need for permanent capital injection requirements to fund long-term operations.

Balance sheet restructuring should consider tax implications of both domestic and off-shore financing sources, as well as special purpose vehicles (SPEs) or what are now dubbed variable interest entities (VIEs).

CASE STUDY 3.10 Merrill Lynch

Merrill Lynch routinely issues debt in a variety of maturities and currencies to achieve low-cost financing and an appropriate liability maturity profile. The cost and availability of unsecured funding may also be impacted by general market conditions or by matters specific to the financial services industry or Merrill Lynch.

In 2002, corporate credit spreads widened considerably with the potential to significantly impact the cost and availability of funding for financial institutions, including Merrill Lynch. Throughout the year, Merrill Lynch adhered to its established liquidity practices and had sufficient financial flexibility to avoid significant changes in the cost and availability of funding.

Merrill Lynch uses derivative transactions to more closely match the duration of borrowings to the duration of the assets being funded to enable interest rate risk to be ▶

managed within limits set by the Corporate Risk Management Group. Interest rate swaps also serve to adjust Merrill Lynch's interest expense and effective borrowing rate principally to floating rate.

Merrill Lynch also enters into currency swaps to hedge non-local-currency denominated assets that are not financed through debt issuance in the same currency. Investments in subsidiaries in non-US dollar currencies are also hedged to a level that minimizes translation adjustments in the Cumulative Translation Account

NOTES

1   George, Abraham (1996).

2   Harris and Raviv (1991).

3   Pinegar and Wilbricht (1989).

4   Booth *et al.* (2001).

5   Hatfield *et al.* (1994).

6   Kalotay, A, Logue D E, and Hiller, H L (1990).

7   Prowse (1998).

8   Leland, Hayne (1994).

9   Smithson and Chew (1992).

10 Shape and Nguyen (1995).

11 Helfert (2003).

12 Ibid.

13 Henry, D (2003).

14 Scovanner, D (1997).

15 Damodaran, A (1999).

16 Palepu, K (1986), and Denis, D J *et al.* (1993).

17 Pinegar and Wilbricht (1989).

18 Kalotay *et al.* (1990).

19 Galitz, L (1994).

20 White (2003).

21 Bernard 2002

22 Beaver in Fabozzi (2002).

23 Nissim and Ziv (2001).

24 Ogden et al. (2003).

25 Ibid.

26 Talmor and Titman (1990).

27 Damodaran, A (1999).

28 Ibid.

29 Vermaelen (1981); Dann and DeAngelo (1983).

30 Edwards C. (2003).

31 J P Morgan (2003).

32 Buzzell R, Gale B, and Sultan S (1975).

33 McKinsey and Company. *Marketers' Metamorphosis*. Updated internal document.

34 Kohli and Sahay (2000).

35 Nagle and Holden (2002).

36 Dolan and Simon (1996).

37 Nagle and Holden (2002).

38 Ibid.

39 Greenwood (2000).

40 In terms of the econometric estimation techniques to be applied to derive the price elasticity coefficient, Generalized Method of Moments (GMM) is preferable to Ordinary Least Squares (OLS) since it is a more robust estimator for such analysis.

41 Simon, H (1992).

42 Nolan and Simon (1996).

43 Tellis (1992).

44 Lambin, J (1976).

45 Kiewell and Roegner (2002).

46 Karayan (2002).

47 Ibid.

48 Thortveit, E and Schaefer, U (2002).

49 PricewaterhouseCoopers (2002).

50 James and Woodall (1997).

51 PricewaterhouseCoopers (2003d).

52 IBM Annual Report (2002).

53 DaimlerChrysler Annual Report (2002).

54 Toyota Annual Report (2002).

55 Nestlé Annual Report (2002).

56 Procter & Gamble Annual Report (2003).

57 GlaxoSmithKline Annual Report (2002).

58 Tregorgis, L (1998) and Mun, J (1993).

59 *Harvard Business Review* (Sept–Oct, 1998).

60 Mun, J (2002).

61 Ibid.

62 Rock, M *et al.* (1994).

63 Osterland, A (2002).

64 Lorange, P, Kotlarchuk, E, and Singh, H (1994).

65 Case, R (1990).

66 Stewart, R (2001).

67 Rock, R H (1994).

68 Edwards, W J (1994).

69 IBM Annual Report (2002).

70 Exxon-Mobil Annual Report (2002).

71 GlaxoSmithKline Annual Report (2002).

72 Mulvey and Simsek (2002).

CHAPTER 4

Risk management

Introduction

"In these uncertain times, CEOs across the globe still see new opportunities and are confident of their companies' abilities to seize them. Many expect to meet or beat internal earnings projections. But they are also mindful of the many threats to growth within that environment and cautious when it comes to putting their firms at risk."

PricewaterhouseCoopers, 6th Annual Global CEO Survey

Traditionally, there have been two strands of corporate risk management: financial and insurance. These risks have been managed in different parts of the organization: insurance matters are dealt with by the insurance or risk manager, while the corporate treasurer or finance director has had responsibility for financial risk management.[1]

Over the years, applied risk management has evolved with the times, and become more sophisticated, more analytical, and more objective. In the 1970s, risk managers started to pay more attention to active risk control, and risk management started to become more proactive than in the past. On the financial side, they saw a need to hedge against increasing economic volatility in the shape of fluctuating currency and commodity values. New financial derivative markets were born, and the discipline of financial risk management took off in corporate treasury departments and banks around the world.

In the 1980s, enterprises became more sensitized to political and country risk. In the late 1980s and early 1990s, the impact of major fluctuations in the global financial markets led to establishment of market risk management functions in the larger financial institutions.

With the new millennium, risk management has risen up the corporate agenda and has become a priority for organizations in a wide range of sectors. Almost all of the leading global multinationals, including financial institutions and corporates, have placed the function of overseeing risk management policy at the board level.

Corporate risk management has managed to shrug off its main function as a cost-cutting exercise. Increasingly, boards are realizing that it has strategic importance. The fact that some sophisticated financial institutions and corporations have chief risk officers and risk management committees that report to the board directly and themselves sit on the board is testimony to this.

Business and risk have always been inseparable, if not synonymous. But given current geopolitical instability, gyrating stock markets and the fragility of most new business models, even the most tough-minded entrepreneurs are struggling to remain sanguine.

In today's rapidly changing business climate, there is a need for an integrated approach to enterprise-wide risk management for enhancing strategic advantage. Risk management has often been too defensive, focusing on hazard risk rather than the upside potential involved with prudential positive risk taking.

Is it really true, though, that the corporate environment is markedly more risky than in earlier times? Has the increased scale of risk not been matched by advances in our understanding of how to cope with it? How can companies implement risk management procedures without stifling innovation? What should boards do to show a lead?

The lens through which managers and directors of a company view its financial and business risks and organizationally manage those risks define the firm's risk culture. In conventional corporate risk cultures, risk management is perceived as a cost centre whose primary purpose is the reduction of financial risks that are seen to be undesirable.

Corporate governance, product management, customer management, and knowledge management processes interact with the internal risk management process of the firm. Therefore, sound internal risk management requires independence of risk management decisions from risk-taking activities, to preserve the integrity of the risk management process. In practice, how a non-financial corporation leverages its risk management process as a non-core activity differs significantly from how a financial intermediary views risk management as a core business activity.

Risk measurement involves the quantification of certain risk exposures for the purpose of comparison to company-defined risk tolerances. The risks to which a firm is subject can change because of change in the composition of a company's assets or liabilities, or as a result of external factors affecting the cash-flows. These external factors include interest rates, exchange rates, prices for inputs, or other economic variables. The risk management process of a firm will always be targeted at decision variables (e.g., hedge ratios) that affect at least one dimension of the firm's financial condition: value, cash-flows, or earnings.

The risk management process is a dynamic one. A properly functioning risk management process includes risk audit, exposure oversight, and fine tuning of the process itself. This includes external audits of risk management policies and procedures, and internal reviews of quantitative exposure measurement models.

In some cases, a company's optimal risk control response to a divergence between actual and desired risk exposures is to take no action at all, if the cost of closing the gap is larger than the gap. Consequently, a well-functioning risk management process does not always yield actions that change the risk profile of the company. A company can use trading, clearing, and insurance products to manage risk exposures optimally through time.

As the finance function shifts focus from control to decision support, blue-chip companies are looking beyond traditional financial methodologies. Increasingly, treasury risk management functions utilize techniques for evaluating risks within an integrated framework. A broader, more structured approach to managing business risk boosts financial performance through better policy and decision making.

The level of sophistication in establishing corporate risk management operations varies among organizations. At one end of the spectrum are companies that manage risk in a reactive mode. They only implement new control processes when an unmanaged risk becomes a problem or results in a crisis.

The next level is where organizations attempt to understand the full extent of the risks facing them. They evaluate financial and operational risks, and search for best-practices. More sophisticated organizations understand the relationship between risk and change, and align business objectives with processes that are better equipped to achieve those objectives.

The next level again involves incorporation of opportunities into risk evaluation. Organizations evaluate their most sensitive drivers of shareholder value, and undertake new strategies and tactics designed to fully exploit those drivers. When appropriate, they change their business objectives to take advantage of identified business opportunities. These companies approach strategic decisions using the latest techniques for maximizing shareholder value.

At the most advanced level are companies that have an enterprise-wide risk management perspective. They integrate risk management more fully with the goals of achieving superior and sustainable shareholder value. They shift the responsibility for managing risk away from controllers, internal auditors, and compliance officers to a broader set of business leaders.

Companies make use of comprehensive real-time technology tools to support and facilitate the risk management process. They have extensive communication and organization-wide training programs to help their employees improve their risk management skills.

The generation of shareholder value is the result of complex inter-relationships between growth, risk, and return. Taking and managing risk is at the heart of shareholder value creation. Where risk is identified, many organizations continue to rely on financially focused risk mitigation strategies such as foreign exchange and capital structure practices that optimize only the financial risk exposures.

The key objective is to integrate an enterprise-wide and dynamic concept of risk into the existing focus on growth and return. Overall, an improved awareness of the alignment of an organization's objectives and risk profile provides a foundation from which market opportunities can be identified and shareholder value enhanced.

An effective control environment provides the discipline and structure needed.

It is the role of the board and executive management to provide guidance on the risk appetite and tolerance that define the extent of risk taking that the organization finds acceptable. An effective control environment provides the discipline and structure needed for risk management to succeed.

Identifying and estimating risk exposure

Business risks come in many forms. Some of these exposures are identifiable and amenable to approximate quantitative estimation, such as treasury risks, currency risks, interest rate risks or cash-flow risks. These are the "hard" risks.

However, other risks are primarily qualitative in nature, called "soft" risks. These soft risk classes include human resources, political risks, and some categories of strategic and operational risks. The process of developing a comprehensive enterprise-wide risk number is thus difficult to aggregate.

A systematic analysis of the major markets associated with each product line sets the stage for revenue risk factor identification. On the cost side, economic risk factors commonly addressed include the risks of changes in costs and prices, and financial risks associated with changes in interest and foreign exchange rates. For the global CFO, this aspect of risk has grown dramatically in complexity, because these factors can vary in their level and volatility by country and region.

An additional cost risk is that of excessive or inflexible production capacity due to high operating leverage. Economic down-turns leading to lower product demand causes idle capacity and lower margins. This affects earnings and cash-flows directly as it hurts revenue generation.

Traditionally, the measure used to estimate risk to a firm has been variance or volatility of cash-flows. However, this measure is uninformative about the source(s) of risk to the firm's cash-flows. Value at risk (VAR), cash-flow at risk (CFAR), or earnings at risk (EAR) are more informative and meaningful measures of risk to a firm's investments, cash-flows, and earnings respectively.

CFOs of non-financial corporations should provide CFAR and EAR measures along with other key business performance indicators.[2] DuPont uses earnings at risk (EAR) as its risk exposure metric.

A growing multiplicity of business risks have pushed multinationals to find more comprehensive approaches to estimating and managing business risks. But what exactly is business risk? Risk is a matter of perspective. Finance and operational managers, institutional and speculative investors, all see risks slightly differently. According to one report by the Economist Intelligence Unit, "business risk arises as much from the likelihood that something good *won't* happen as it does from the threat that something bad will happen."[3]

Corporate financial risk identification and exposure management is a critical corporate finance function. Risk identification is the process by which a company recognizes and, in some cases, detects the different financial risks to which it is exposed through the normal course of operating its business. Almost by definition, the risks that are most insidious for a company are those risks to which it is exposed that have not been identified.[4]

Risks can be left unidentified for reasons ranging from poor internal financial controls that allow the unnoticed booking of risky financial transactions, on or off balance sheet, to insufficient oversight of fundamental exposures. The process by which a company reviews, analyses, and discusses its risk profile is an indispensable means by which risks can be identified, and hence, managed.

In practice, financial losses can occur due to inadequate risk management. Had Barings properly identified the huge long position on Japanese equities accumulated in Singapore by a rogue trader Nick Leeson, the firm might not have gone bust. Had Procter & Gamble identified the massive interest rate risk affecting its treasury through a naked swap contract, the company might have avoided several hundred million dollars in losses.[5]

The risk groups

To plot particular risks, experts at PricewaterhouseCoopers divide the population of risks the company is exposed to into five main groups:[6]

■ strategic risks

■ financial risks

■ operational risks

■ commercial risks

■ technical risks.

Strategic risks include risks of plans failing, poor corporate strategies, weak marketing strategies, poor acquisition strategies, changes in consumer behaviour, adverse political or regulatory change. This group also includes adverse changes in government policies, such as taxation or foreign investment incentives, and a broad range of economic, financial, investment, and social policies that could affect the financial returns of the firm.

Financial risks include risks of financial controls failing, treasury risks, lack of counter-party or credit assessment, sophisticated financial fraud, and the effect of changes in macroeconomic factors.

Operational risks include risks of human error or omission, design mistakes, unsafe behaviour, employee practices risks, and sabotage.

Commercial risks include risks of business interruption, loss of a key executive, supplier failure, and lack of legal compliance.

Technical risks include risks of physical assets failing or being damaged, equipment breakdown, infrastructure failure, fire, explosion, pollution, or adverse *force majeure* events.

These risk groups are not mutually exclusive. For example, human factors – prime drivers of operational risks – are significant in many strategic and financial risks. Also, companies carry their histories with them: a business may have accumulated liabilities or assets, bad or good practices, weak or strong relationships, on-or off-balance sheet risk exposures. It is a perennial point of frustration for corporate risk managers that not all of these risks are amenable to accurate quantification. However, various analytical techniques are utilized to quantify as much of these risks as possible. In a dynamically linked world, past risks affect current exposure, and risks of all types affect strategic direction and, ultimately, the company's ability to generate shareholder value in future.

In terms of risk identification and measurement, it is important to understand that risk is a concept, not a particular statistical construct. Volatility of earnings can be estimated with standard deviations of returns, which is a traditional measure of risk.

Since there are many variables other than earnings that need to be managed, a multiple variable analog of the standard deviation point estimate is a risk correlation matrix. But it is of limited use as a measure of risk exposure for practical corporate financial management, since it is a statistical estimator of volatility, not an intuitive indicator of business risk levels.

The VAR measure

Because of these limitations of traditional risk measures, value at risk (VAR) has become a popular risk exposure identifier. The VAR measures the maximum level of loss that can occur in a given time period in currency terms, with a 95 percent confidence level, as a result of changes in the risk variables.[7]

VAR = (Initial investment) (Standard deviation) (Confidence level)

The VAR measure is useful because it is intuitively understandable. If the VAR of a certain set of risks is too high, hedging instruments can be used to bring it down to acceptable levels by reducing the standard deviation measure. Businesses operate to take risks and make profits. They take risks because they have expertise in their core business, and are comparatively advantaged in the market to undertake those risks. There is nothing wrong with taking desirable risks, as long as undesirable ones are prudently avoided. But we cannot distinguish desirable from undesirable risks unless a careful analysis is performed on the major risk exposures, and a comprehensive enterprise risk profile created.

Many financial and non-financial corporations have incurred significant losses by imprudently managing this process. Examples include the infamous collapse of Barings Bank Plc., and the derivative losses at Procter & Gamble. Business and financial risks come in many forms. There are some risks that the firm can avoid by hedging activities. All categories of financial risks are in this category.

Risk Budgeting

The revolution in risk management reflects the recognition that risk should be measured at the highest level, that is, firm-wide. The ability to measure total risk has led to a top-down allocation of risk, called *risk budgeting*.[8]

If the acceptable aggregate risk exposure for a company is $100 million during a quarter, as measured by VAR or CFAR, it can be allocated to different operating divisions or product lines. For a financial institution, total acceptable risk exposure can be allocated to different asset classes within the portfolio. This risk budgeting approach is spreading rapidly to the management of pension plans. Such an approach has all the benefits of VAR. It provides a consistent measure of risk across all sub-portfolios. It forces managers and investors to confront squarely the amount of risk they are willing to assume. It gives them tools to monitor their risk in real time. In order to hedge a budgeted level of risk exposure, the optimal hedge ratio is derived. The number of futures or options contracts required to hedge or counteract the exposure in the underlying instrument (for example, shares, commodities etc) is called the *hedge ratio*. The optimal hedge ratio will minimize the risk of the position.

Operational risks that cannot be affected

Most operational risks are also managed by firms. However, there are some risks that the firm cannot affect. These are systematic risks that result in changes in the value of assets, driven by risk factors that affect all bundles of cash-flows, such as changes in aggregate consumption growth, or economic downturn resulting in a fall in demand.

Other operational risks include problems in raw material supplies, internal labor disputes resulting in production stoppage, competitor pricing action adversely affecting demand, *force majeure* events, and a number of other environmental factors, all of which can neither be identified nor measured perfectly. For management of these issues, top management expertise and business judgment is relied upon, as they cannot be resolved with quantitative financial models alone.

Financial risks are more amenable to quantitative analysis, pro-active exposure identification, and management. For example, historical-cost-based balance sheet figures allow estimation of the risk that a company will violate a loan covenant requiring maintenance of a minimum ratio of debt to net worth.

In contrast to business risks that the firm must bear in order to operate its primary business, financial risks are those that non-financial firms are not usually in the business of bearing. These risks can be quantified, and are easier to avoid. Interest rate risk and foreign currency risk are the main categories of financial risks. Changes in interest rates or exchange rates affect corporate value as they impact the financial statements. For example, increases in interest rates will increase interest expenses on floating rate debt. This risk can be hedged with an interest rate swap contract. Depreciation in the foreign currency income streams will reduce the value of reporting currency income as accounting translation adjustments are made. This adverse effect can be avoided by engaging in a forward contract to lock-in the current exchange rate.

Market risk arises in the event of a change in some market-determined asset price, reference rate such as LIBOR, or an index. Any market determined price rate, or index value that impacts the cash-flows of an exposure is a risk factor. Liquidity risk occurs in the event that cash inflows and current cash balances are insufficient to cover cash outflow requirements, often necessitating desperate measures to generate temporary cash inflows.

Most firms, both financial and non-financial, have liquidity plans in their corporate financial planning process, designed to manage funding risks. The well publicized bankruptcy of Drexel Burnham Lambert Group occurred due to failure in funding risk management, and has only increased corporations' attention to this risk.[9] Another risk category is credit risk – the risk of the actual or possible non-performance by a firm.

Identifying all material risk exposures

There are alternative means of hedging various forms of financial risks with structured financial products that are combinations of derivatives such as options, forwards etc. The first step however, is to identify all material risk exposures. In practice, interest rate and exchange risks are easily identified. Metrics used to measure these risks are usually sensitivities that measure the change in value of assets or income to changes in underlying rates.

To estimate the sensitivity of fixed-income debt valuation to changes to interest rate movements, *effective duration* measures the percentage change in the value of debt to a one percentage change in interest rates. This is essentially an elasticity measure and takes into consideration the impact of embedded options. However, it assumes parallel shifts of the yield curve, which may not be realistic in some circumstances.

Effective duration = %change in value of debt / %change in interest rates (small change)

The *effective convexity* measure refines the effective duration measure with an additional adjustment to take into consideration the impact of embedded options in the debt instruments.

Effective duration + Effective convexity = %change in value of debt with embedded options/ %change in interest rates (large change)

For exchange rate risks, the impact of rate appreciation or depreciation on financial statement recognition of income or liabilities in the parent's reporting currency can be approximated by attempting to forecast probable ranges of rate changes and the resulting flow-through impact on reporting currency financial results.

Having thus identified the risks and quantified probable loss through VAR or other metrics, the question becomes which risks the management will choose to hedge. Insurance has been used traditionally as a risk management instrument for undesirable risk exposures, but excessive risk aversion can be expensive for corporate profitability as well, because hedging risks costs money as the risks are simply being transferred to someone else.

Until recently, companies managed risks largely in terms of possible solutions. An insurable risk might be the insurance manager's responsibility. If a risk seemed to be a financial control matter, the treasurer might deal with it. Risks touching on consumer relations might be managed as part of sales and marketing. Today, functionally segregating risk seems dated. The CFOs and other senior executives of many multinationals are learning to take a more integrated view of business risks and business risk management.

A solid business risk management program lowers the company's exposure to the classes of risk it is not in the business to take, and reshapes exposure to those it is in the business to take. The investment community may favor a stock if it understands the rationale underlying the total risk management effort – believing the company more likely to manage its cost base and produce future cash-flows. And customers may prefer to do business with a company seen to be managing risks that affect the service they receive, whether corporate reputation, financial stability, supply line, quality, or other risks.

Risk management means dealing with uncertainty. Companies grow large, and prosper only by managing huge amounts of risk. Blue chips earn their strong ratings because they do manage big risks, successfully and economically. However, companies also need to identify latent business risks that are not obvious on the surface.

Companies also need to identify latent business risks.

Scale of materiality

It takes a keen awareness of what risks might arise, where, and crucially, how material they are to the business. In order to manage business risks based on their materiality, the CFO works with the board and senior operating managers to devise an overall risk management strategy and reporting structure. It is vital to look at risk holistically, not pockets of risk measured on different scales. Map the business impact of each potential risk against its likelihood to get a scale of materiality (see Figure 4.1)

At one end, *catastrophic* losses are any failure of business strategy that leaves the organization unable to achieve its objectives: a rare event among larger companies. More common *disabling* events severely hamper the company's strategy for a period of, say, a year. A series of disabling events can spell catastrophe: when share price drops progressively, the company becomes vulnerable to take over, withdrawal of credit facilities, of other constraints that, sooner or later, can cause its downfall.

Further along the materiality scale, *significant* losses should be disclosed, but these do not seriously impair returns to shareholders: for example, a foreign exchange currency translation loss, or an unanticipated increase in the price of raw materials. Least material are

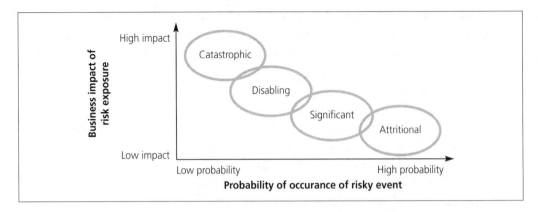

FIGURE 4.1 ■ Assessing the business materiality of different risk exposures

relatively frequent attritional losses, like small damage claims, workers' compensation and safety related losses. Though insignificant in themselves, these losses tend to be expense matters for the corporation as a whole.

Clearly, assessing the business impact of a risk involves more than simply estimating the immediate financial loss. Risks need to be viewed in terms of its short-, medium-, and long-term consequences, taking into account all factors and views of all stakeholders. For example, shareholders might be concerned about dividend flow, banks about leverage and equity value, and customers about management integrity and product quality.

A single, relatively minor human error or omission can develop into a multi-billion dollar event, putting an entire corporation's reputation at stake. Many well-publicised corporate losses demonstrate this. This ripple effect from one event to another illustrates the relationship between risks – reinforcing the case for an integrated approach.

Good judgment regarding risk exposures can only be made when good models are used to support identification and quantification of exposures. Equally, risk quantification models are only models, based on a range of assumptions. Management's experience must complement the technical exercise of quantifying risk. Quantitative and qualitative risks may have an equal business impact – the CFO needs to understand both.

It is relatively easy to produce quantified analyses of many business risks, such as those attached to volatility of foreign exchange, commodity, and interest rates.

Value at risk (VAR) – usually applied to financial and commodity management practices – is a statistical measure of the maximum expected loss under normal market conditions, over a defined period, within a defined level of probability. A direct measure of potential loss that extends across all types of financial instruments, it provides a common denominator for quantifying different risks.

VAR can be used to calculate risk-adjusted returns. For example, some organizations (especially in financial services) adjust financial returns for a particular product line or division by the VAR of the underlying cash-flows. This lets management weigh rewards against risks involved.

Cash flow at risk (CFAR)

VAR methodology can and should be applied to all enterprise cash-flows (cash-flow at risk, (CFAR)) subject to financial market risks – not just to financial instruments.

Many companies originally formulated foreign exchange hedging positions when their international business activity was relatively small and it was appropriate to view currency risk exclusively in terms of their home currency. But, too often, companies remain fixated on single currency risks without considering their global multi-currency exposures, increased revenues, and risk appetites.

Although it is necessary to analyse each type of exposure separately, you can gain competitive advantage by understanding how different risks inter-relate, and how they aggregate to define a company-wide risk profile, and how management's risk appetite changes as the business grows. Here CFAR is a big help.

As a component of risk management analysis, CFAR supports business strategy for non-financial corporations and promotes risk improvement initiatives. It assures managers that the actual value at risk is commensurate with what they expect to put at risk, and is in alignment with what shareholders and the board consider reasonable.

Research sponsored by Sedgwick Group shows that the impact of a major human factor loss can differ dramatically from one company to another.[10] A study of 15 major corporate incidents – including Pan Am's Lockerbie air crash, Union Carbide's Bhopal gas leak, and the explosion of Occidental's Piper Alpha North Sea oil platform – shows that, irrespective of industry type, companies fall into two distinct groups: recoverers and non-recoverers.

For *recoverers*, initial loss of shareholder value is recovered within two months of the incident. This can be attributed to market's confidence in management's ability to manage risks. In contrast, *non-recoverers* suffer an enduring drop in share prices. In most of these cases, the incident's potential adverse cash-flow impact is enormous.

Food for thought for CFOs. The stock market as well as creditors in the banking sector often form a collective opinion on management's ability to manage risks and steer the corporation from adverse consequences to its financial results. Since risk events can affect a company's solvency, investors' general view of management skill in handling risk seems to be crucial to share price performance. Through investor relations programs, the CFO must communicate evidence of management's capabilities and its risk management approach.

The stock market as well as creditors in the banking sector ... form a collective opinion on management's ability to manage risks.

Share value performance reflects investors' confidence in management's ability to generate future wealth. Risk contributes to share price volatility, so anything the company does to demonstrate competent risk management should improve its share price. Lower perceived risk means lower weighted average cost of capital (WACC), driving higher value. For the corporation's shareholders, risk is good – if managed and exploited for gain.

One technique CFOs use to monitor the returns of a particular product division is to examine the risk-adjusted return on capital. Any extraneous (as opposed to systematic) risks that the product division is taking can then be accounted for in the allocation of capital. For instance, the product division taking some relatively exotic risk, such as territorial or political exposure, must pay a premium: its return on capital is diminished compared to other divisions without that exposure.

Typically, different risks are shown to have different impacts on shareholders. Computing the effects of mitigating those risks lets you show the investment community the benefits of sound risk management. There is some evidence that by economically reducing its risk profile, the company bolsters certainty in future cash-flows at a moderate amount of additional cost, which should be reflected in determining shareholder value.

Off-balance-sheet (OBS) risks

Financial contracts are generally off-balance-sheet items, but each firm needs to understand the economic status and results of its hedging actions, and examine how these actions alter its competitive position.

Risks should be managed in the broader context of corporate strategy and corporate financial planning. Both on- and off-balance-sheet risks should be assessed. Off-balance-sheet (OBS) risks are not captured by the traditional accounting statements adequately, although US GAAP requires more disclosure on the impact of OBS transactions than accounting treatments in European or Asian countries.

Statement of Financial Accounting Standards (SFAS) 133, accounting for derivatives and similar instruments and hedging activities, now requires all derivatives to be recorded as either assets or liabilities at fair value. As the values change, the resulting gains or losses may be recognized immediately or deferred, depending on whether the derivative qualifies for classification as a hedge.[11]

Global financial markets have experienced a dramatic increase in volatility over the past two decades as a result of globalization and increased cross-border trade and financial flows. Given a firm's risk exposure, increased volatility of foreign exchange rates, interest rates, and commodity prices translates into increased volatility of firm value. Although risk management reduces volatility of enterprise value, there is wide variation in the use of risk management instruments across firms.

In general, it is neither necessary nor practical to attempt to quantify all OBS risks and liabilities, but the handful of primary ones should be identified and quantified. For example, any major contingent liability like a corporate guarantee on a subsidiary's debt obligations with a high likelihood of default by the subsidiary, should be included in the assessment of corporate risk profile.

Derivatives such as forwards, futures, options, and swaps are specialized OBS risk management tools that allow the firm to hedge many sources of market-wide financial risk.

In contrast, on-balance-sheet financial risk management tools include convertible bonds and hybrid debt issuances, while on-balance-sheet production risk management tools include loss prevention and control, joint ventures, technology choice, plant location, vertical integration etc. To analyse a firm's hedging incentives, it is important how both on- and off-balance sheet risk exposures are related to enterprise value.

OBS risks related to enterprise value

Different OBS risks are managed with different hedging instruments. Insurance policies are employed to hedge firm-specific risks like fires and lawsuits. Market-wide risks such as exposures to interest rates, foreign exchange rates, and commodity prices can be managed with the use of OBS derivatives instruments such as forwards, futures, swaps, and option contracts.

Buying a forward contract hedges the firm's exposure if its core business cash-flows are a negative function of the asset value. In contrast, writing a forward contract hedges the exposure if core business cash-flows are positively related to asset value. Buying a call plus writing a put on the same asset with the same exercise price and the same expiration date creates payoffs that are equivalent to those of buying a forward. This equivalence among puts, calls, and forwards is referred to as put-call parity.

Off-balance-sheet assets and liabilities, and the risks therefrom, have hitherto been largely hidden from the public eye in terms of formal disclosure. However, all that is changing. In the US, publicly listed companies are now required to disclose OBS assets, liabilities, and risks in their financial statements. This is also being adapted by the IAS, and likely to become mainstream worldwide. Companies will increasingly need greater understanding of their off-balance-sheet exposures.

During the last 25 years, off-balance-sheet financing has grown in popularity in US and Europe, taking such forms as securitizations, synthetic leases, and unconsolidated entities. However, new regulatory guidelines, as described above, require off-balance-sheet disclosure.

US SEC Adopts Rules on Disclosure of Off-Balance Sheet Arrangements and Aggregate Contractual Obligations (Jan, 2003):

■ The US SEC requires each annual and quarterly financial report required to be filed with the Commission, to disclose "all material off-balance sheet transactions, arrangements, obligations (including contingent obligations), and other relationships of the issuer with unconsolidated entities or other persons, that may have a material current or future effect on financial condition, changes in financial condition, results of operations, liquidity, capital expenditures, capital resources, or significant components of revenues or expenses."

The amendments approved by the Commission will require a registrant to provide an explanation of its off-balance sheet arrangements in a separately captioned subsection of the "Management's Discussion and Analysis" (MD&A) section in its disclosure documents. The amendments also will require registrants (other than small business issuers) to provide an overview of certain known contractual obligations in a tabular format.

The amendments will include a definition of "off-balance-sheet arrangements" that primarily targets the means through which companies typically structure off-balance-sheet transactions or otherwise incur risks of loss that are not fully transparent to investors. The definition of "off-balance-sheet arrangements" will employ concepts in accounting literature in order to define the categories of arrangements with precision. Generally, the definition will include the following categories of contractual arrangements:

- certain guarantee contracts
- retained or contingent interests in assets transferred to an unconsolidated entity
- derivative instruments that are classified as equity
- material variable interests in unconsolidated entities that conduct certain activities.

The amendments will require disclosure of off-balance-sheet arrangements that either have, or are reasonably likely to have, a current or future effect on the company's financial condition, changes in financial condition, revenues or expenses, results of operations, liquidity, capital expenditures or capital resources that is material to investors. That disclosure threshold is consistent with the existing disclosure threshold under which information that could have a material effect on financial condition, changes in financial condition or results of operations must be included in MD&A.

The amendments will require disclosure of the following specified information to the extent necessary to an understanding of off-balance-sheet arrangements and their material effects:

- The nature and business purpose of the registrant's off-balance-sheet arrangements
- The importance to the company for liquidity, capital resources, market risk or credit risk support or other benefits
- The financial impact and exposure to risk
- Known events, demands, commitments, trends or uncertainties that implicate the company's ability to benefit from its off-balance-sheet arrangements.

Consistent with the existing MD&A requirements, the amendments will contain a principles-based requirement that a company provide such other information that it believes is necessary for an understanding of its off-balance-sheet arrangements and their specified material effects.

In addition, the amendments will include a requirement for companies to disclose the amounts of payments due under specified contractual obligations, aggregated by category of contractual obligation, for specified time periods. The categories of contractual obligations to be included in the table are defined by reference to the applicable accounting literature.[12]

Disclosure in management's discussion and analysis about off-balance-sheet arrangements, contractual obligations and contingent liabilities and commitments

Agency: US Securities and Exchange Commission.

Summary: As directed by new Section 13(j) of the Securities Exchange Act of 1934, added by Section 401(a) of the Sarbanes-Oxley Act of 2002, we propose to require disclosure of off-balance sheet transactions, arrangements, obligations (including contingent obligations), and other relationships of an issuer with unconsolidated entities or other persons that have, or may have, a material effect on financial condition, changes in financial condition, revenues or expenses, results of operations, liquidity, capital expenditures or capital resources.

The new disclosure would be located in the "Management's Discussion and Analysis of Financial Condition and Results of Operations" ("MD&A") section in a company's disclosure documents. The proposals would require a registrant to provide, in a separately captioned subsection of MD&A, a comprehensive explanation of its off-balance sheet arrangements. The proposals also would require a company (other than small business issuers) to provide an overview of its aggregate contractual obligations and contingent liabilities and commitments.

Variable interest entities (VIEs)

The Financial Accounting Standards Board (FASB) in the US requires special purpose entities (SPE), now called variable interest entities (VIEs), to be consolidated onto the parent's balance sheets. VIE consolidation will also affect synthetic leases since the debt would now have to be recognized on the balance sheet.

Other OBS liabilities, such as loan guarantees are also mandated to be recognized as a liability for the fair market value of the obligation the company assumes. If commercial paper conduits (CPC) – the large multinational banks that aggregate and issue commercial paper – are required to consolidate VIEs, their capital and reserve requirements will increase accordingly.

While a healthy debt-to-equity ratio helps companies attract inexpensive sources of capital, OBS financing helps companies balance sheets look less levered than they really are, and diversifies funding sources.

Banks and credit agencies that penalize companies that are highly levered force them to use OBS financing. Specifically, a highly levered company may find lenders restricting capital, increasing interest rates, or adding conditions to the loan covenants. Credit rating agencies may down-grade their rating, and raising capital may become more difficult.

Securitization

Securitization is the packaging of debt backed by revenue streams into bonds. Companies that use asset securitizations, synthetic leases, or other common structured financing techniques often benefit from VIEs – the vehicles typically used to engineer the deals by taking the assets and debt off companies' balance sheets.

"The fundamental rationale for structured financing is the value it creates by unlocking otherwise inaccessible capital," argues Andrew Feldstein, head of structured financing at JP Morgan Chase.[13]

Structured finance allows companies to obtain more capital than they would get with straightforward equity or debt. It also allows companies to raise funds they might not otherwise have been able to raise, and that access to capital contributes to productivity, albeit at a higher risk.

Often, it is accounting, not economics, that drives common structured finance transactions such as synthetic leases, which reduce a company's cost of capital. In the US, since accounting treatment is different for book and tax purposes, synthetic leases increase net income and operating cash-flow because assets are depreciated for tax purposes, but not for accounting purposes. Although the asset remains off-balance-sheet, synthetic leases lower total cash-flow since the financing costs are usually higher.

Under US GAAP, the term of a synthetic lease can usually run no longer then seven years for the property to be excluded from the borrower's balance sheet. In theory, synthetic leases can be rolled over into new ones when the term is up. However, lenders may not be willing if they are worried about the company's ability to pay, since financing is extended against the company's corporate credit, instead of the underlying property.

Critics of synthetic leases point to its risks, which is using short-term financing to support what is normally a long-term asset. This mismatch between assets and liabilities can ultimately force a company to refinance at a much higher cost.

A recent study of securitization programs in the US and Europe by Standard and Poor's showed that all major banks, and many minor ones, conduct significant OBS securitizations through their own SPEs and CPCs. Conduit programs alone financed approximately $500bn in 2002 – none of which appeared on corporate or bank balance sheets. Not much appeared in the footnotes to financial statements either.[14]

However, securitization has evolved from a niche product used only by banks and project financiers into a flexible acquisition finance and balance sheet restructuring tool for non-financial corporations. It was first introduced in Europe in the mid-1980s when financial institutions began to issue bonds secured against mortgage payments and credit card receipts.

In the mid-1990s there were less than 50 asset-backed investors in Europe. Today there are well over 500, and interest is growing fast, particularly among European pension funds and insurance companies.[15]

The structure behind securitization transactions is often extremely complicated but the principle behind them is not. The company sets up a bankruptcy-remote special purpose vehicle (SPV) into which it transfers a pool of assets, for example credit card bills. The SPV issues bonds secured by these assets and then passes the proceeds back to the company via a loan.

All the revenue generated by the assets within the SPV is used to pay back the debt and cannot be used by the issuer. If the parent company goes bankrupt, the bondholders are allowed to control the insolvency proceedings through an administrative receiver so that any assets in the SPV go to them, not other creditors.

The global economic slowdown, and the resulting rise in corporate earning volatility, tends to increase demand for bonds that are stable and free from event-risk. Asset backed securities (ABS) meet the requirement. Whether ABSs are cheaper than other forms of debt depends largely on the structure and business of the company concerned.

For AAA-rated single business corporates, straight debt may be very attractively priced. However, for BBB-rated corporates – especially those able to split off the best bits of their business into a separate SPV – the cost savings can be significant, sometimes as much as 200 basis points. This is because the SPV will have a better credit rating than the parent.

The key advantage of securitization is not that it allows companies to raise debt at lower rates of interest, but that it enables them to raise much more of it.[16]

The key advantage of securitization is not that it allows companies to raise debt at lower rates of interest, but that it enables them to raise much more of it.

The longer maturity available on ABSs is another advantage. But there are a number of downsides to securitization. ABSs take a long time to arrange, require extensive road-showing by senior management, and securitization covenants can be extremely restricting. These covenants can include bans on acquisitions and divestitures, and limit capital investments or dividends. Therefore, in order to secure reasonably priced debt, companies have to cede a significant amount of operational control.

Issuing ABSs can also have a negative impact on a company's credit rating. If corporate cash-flows are pledged to pay back ABS debt, that leaves less cash sources to redeem other bonds. A non-investment grade company with a lower than BBB debt rating, or a non-rated company may, however, find ABS financing attractive.

In principle, any asset that produces revenues can be securitized. However, in practice, securitization only really works with assets producing extremely predictable cash-flows. Unfortunately, there are no fixed rules as to how volatile a revenue stream can be before it becomes too unpredictable to use for ABSs.[17]

Receivables such as invoices, rental, and ticket income, and long-term client contracts, are typical assets that back ABS issuances. Since these assets are not tangible physical assets, the receivables should be either due from a very large number of clients so that risk of non-payment is spread wide enough to avoid mass default, or from two or three large multi-national institutions or governments.

Just to give you a sense of size, the US securitization market had in excess of $6 trillion outstanding as of 2002.[18] In Asia, the ABS market is beginning to grow as well.

In the Asian market, for example, the Malaysian government has for many years been intent on upgrading the value added of manufacturing in the country. Hence the creation of *1st Silicon* by the state government of Sarawak. In year 2000, Nomura International provided a $250m seven-year asset backed bond issue, priced at 275 basis points over LIBOR, with a put and call option at the end of year five. Other senior debt ranks *pari passu* with the securitized bond issue. This was the first transaction in Asia to use the whole business securitization structure that has proven so effective in the UK and US in the last decade.[19]

A CFO survey of 180 senior financial executives on corporate financial reporting suggests that 42 percent of the companies in the survey used SPEs to keep debt off their balance sheets.[20]

CASE STUDY 4.1 Citigroup[21]

Citigroup and its subsidiaries are involved with several types of off-balance-sheet arrangements, including special purpose entities (SPEs), lines and letters of credit, and loan commitments. The principal uses of SPEs are to obtain sources of liquidity by securitizing certain of Citigroup's financial assets, to assist Citigroup's clients in securitizing their financial assets, and to create other investment products for Citigroup's clients.

SPEs may be organized as trusts, partnerships, or corporations. In a securitization, the company transferring assets to an SPE converts those assets into cash before they would have been realized in the normal course of business. The SPE obtains the cash needed to pay the transferor for the assets received by issuing securities to investors in the form of debt and equity instruments, certificates, commercial paper, and other notes of indebtedness.

Investors usually have recourse to the assets in the SPE and often benefit from other credit enhancements, such as a cash collateral account or over-collateralization in the form of excess assets in the SPE, or from a liquidity facility, such as a line of credit or asset purchase agreement.

Accordingly, the SPE can typically obtain a more favorable credit rating from rating agencies, such as Standard and Poor's and Moody's Investors Service, than the transferor could obtain for its own debt issuances, resulting in less expensive financing costs. The transferor can use the cash proceeds from the sale to extend credit to additional customers or for other business purposes.

The SPE may also enter into a derivative contract in order to convert the yield or currency of the underlying assets to match the needs of the SPE's investors or to limit or change the credit risk of the SPE. The company may be the counter-party to any such derivative. The securitization process enhances the liquidity of the financial markets, may spread credit risk among several market participants, and makes new funds available to extend credit to consumers and commercial entities.

Citigroup also acts as intermediary or agent for its corporate clients, assisting them in obtaining sources of liquidity by selling the clients' trade receivables or other financial assets to an SPE. Citigroup also securitizes clients' debt obligations in transactions involving SPEs that issue collateralized debt obligations.

In yet other arrangements, Citigroup packages and securitizes assets purchased in the financial markets in order to create new security offerings for institutional and private bank clients as well as retail customers. In connection with such arrangements, Citigroup may purchase, and temporarily hold assets designated for subsequent securitization.

Securitization is a process by which a legal entity issues certain securities to investors, which securities pay a return based on the principal and interest cash-flows from a pool of loans or other financial assets. Citigroup securitizes credit card receivables, mortgages, and other loans that it originated and/or purchased and certain other financial assets.

After securitization of credit card receivables, Citigroup continues to maintain account relationships with customers. Citigroup also assists its clients in securitizing the clients' financial assets. Citigroup may provide administrative, asset management, underwriting, liquidity facilities and/or other services to the resulting securitization entities, and may continue to service the financial assets sold to the securitization entity.

There are two key accounting determinations that must be made relating to securitizations. In the case where Citigroup originated or previously owned the financial assets transferred to the securitization entity, a decision must be made as to whether that transfer would be considered a sale under generally accepted accounting principles, resulting in the transferred assets being removed from the company's Consolidated Statement of Financial Position with a gain or loss recognized.

Alternatively, the transfer would be considered a financing, resulting in recognition of a liability in the company's Consolidated Statement of Financial Position. The second key determination to be made is whether the securitization entity should be considered a subsidiary of the company and be included in the company's Consolidated Financial Statements or whether the entity is sufficiently independent that it does not need to be consolidated.

If the securitization entity's activities are sufficiently restricted to meet certain accounting requirements to be considered a *qualifying special purpose entity (QSPE)*, the securitization entity is not consolidated by the seller of the transferred assets. Most of the company's securitization transactions meet the existing criteria for sale accounting and non-consolidation.

In January 2003, the Financial Accounting Standards Board (FASB) issued a new interpretation on consolidation accounting. The company participates in 4,249 securitization transactions, structured investment vehicles and other investment funds with its own and with clients' assets totalling $926.3bn at December 31, 2002.

CASE STUDY 4.2 IBM[22]

IBM periodically sells receivables through the securitization of loans, leases and trade receivables. The company retains servicing rights in the securitized receivables for which it receives a servicing fee. Any gain or loss incurred as a result of such sales is recognized in the period in which the sale occurs.

CASE STUDY 4.3 GE[23]

Off-balance-sheet arrangements are used in the ordinary course of business to achieve improved share owner returns. One of the most common forms of off-balance-sheet arrangements is asset securitization. The securitization transactions GE engages in are similar to those used by many financial institutions and are part of a $700bn annual market for asset-backed commercial paper.

GE uses sponsored and third-party entities to execute securitization transactions funded in the commercial paper and term markets. As part of this program, GE considers the relative risks and returns of each alternative and predominantly uses sponsored entities. These transactions could be readily executed through non-sponsored entities or term securitization at modest incremental cost.

Beyond improved returns, these securitization transactions serve as funding sources for a variety of diversified lending and securities transactions, transfer selected credit risk, and improve cash-flows while enhancing the ability to provide a full range of competitive products for GE's customers.

In a typical securitization transaction, GE sells high-quality financial assets to entities that have financed those purchases using low-cost, highly-rated commercial paper. The first step in the securitization process uses entities that meet the accounting criteria for qualifying special purpose entities (QSPE). Among other criteria, a QSPE's activities must be restricted to passive investment in financial assets and issuance of retained interests in those assets.

Under GAAP, consolidated in the sponsor's financial statements, they remain off-balance-sheet. GE sells selected financial assets to QSPEs. Examples include financing and credit card receivables and trade receivables. On the whole, the credit quality of such assets is equal to or higher than the credit quality of similar assets GE owns.

Qualifying special purpose entities raise cash by issuing retained interests – rights to cash-flows from the assets – to other SPEs GE sponsors that issue highly-rated commercial paper to third-party institutional investors. These SPEs use commercial paper proceeds to obtain retained interests in the financial assets of QSPEs, as well as financial assets originated by multiple third parties.

GE provides credit support for certain of these assets, as well as liquidity support for the commercial paper. In accordance with GE's contractual commitments to the qualifying entities, GE rigorously underwrites and services the associated assets, both those GE originates and those originated by other participants. All of the qualifying entities' assets serve as collateral for the commercial paper.

Support activities include credit reviews at acquisition and ongoing review, billing and collection activities— the same support activities that GECS employs for its own financing receivables. These entities are not consolidated in GE's reported financial statements. They are off-balance-sheet.

GE's sponsored SPEs are routinely evaluated by the major credit rating agencies, including monthly reviews of key performance indicators and annual reviews of asset quality. Commercial paper issued by these entities has always received the highest available ratings from the major credit rating agencies and at year-end 2002 was rated A–1+/P–1.

Assets held by SPEs include:

- receivables secured by equipment, commercial real estate and other assets;
- credit card receivables; and
- trade receivables.

In addition to being of high credit quality, these assets are diversified to avoid concentrations of risk. Examples of these assets include loans and leases on manufacturing and transportation equipment, loans on commercial property, commercial loans, and balances of high credit quality accounts from sales of a broad range of products and services to a diversified customer base.

Such assets totalled $42.2bn and $43.0bn at December 31, 2002 and 2001, respectively. Sales of securities assets to SPEs result in a gain or loss amounting to the net of sales proceeds, the carrying amount of net assets sold, the fair value of retained interests and servicing rights, and an allowance for losses.

Total securitization sales resulted in gains of $0.8bn and $1.3bn in 2002 and 2001, respectively, and are included in revenues net of any effects of replenishing securities credit card balances.

In addition to the securitization activities, Financial Guaranty Insurance Company (FGIC), an affiliate of GE that is a leader in the municipal bond insurance market, uses SPEs that offer municipalities guaranteed investment contracts with interests in high-quality, fixed maturity, investment-grade assets. FGIC actively manages these assets under strict investment criteria and GE Capital also provides certain performance guarantees. Total assets in sponsored FGIC entities amounted to $13.7bn and $13.4bn at December 31, 2002 and 2001, respectively.

GE provides financial support related to assets held by certain SPEs through liquidity agreements, credit support, performance guarantees and guarantee and reimbursement contracts. Net credit and liquidity support amounted to $27.2bn after consideration of participated liquidity and arrangements that defer liquidity draws beyond 2003, a reduction of $15.9bn from 2001. This amount includes credit support, in which GE provides recourse for a maximum of $16.9bn of credit losses in SPEs.

Potential credit losses are provided for in GE's financial statements. Based on management's best estimate of probable losses inherent in the portfolio, GE provided an allowance of $233m for recourse obligations at year end 2002.

Performance guarantees relate to letters of credit and liquidity support for guaranteed investment contracts and are subject to a maximum of $3.8bn at December 31, 2002. None of the GE sponsored SPEs is permitted to hold GE stock, and there are no commitments or guarantees that provide for the potential issuance of GE stock. These entities do not engage in speculative activities of any description, are not used to hedge GE's asset positions, and under GE integrity policies, no GE employee, officer or director is permitted to invest in any sponsored SPE.

Under FIN 46, Consolidation of Variable Interest Entities, new consolidation criteria will be applied to certain SPEs, which it defines as "Variable Interest Entities".

CASE STUDY 4.4 Ericsson[24]

Ericsson has a securitization program amounting to $250m with Eureka Securitization plc, under which Ericsson sells trade receivables in the US, UK, Dutch and German markets at an effective cost of one month LIBOR + 150 BP on a fully drawn basis. The program is settled on a weekly basis with new receivables sold to replace those collected during the week.

Eureka Securitization plc is externally managed and funded in the commercial paper market. As of December 31, 2002, the program was not utilized. The program is currently under review following the Moody's rating downgrade of Ericsson from Ba2 to B1 in February 2003.

Ericsson's long-term objective is to have a payment readiness of between 7 and 10 percent of net sales to adapt to changes in liquidity requirements. Payment readiness is an internal measure, defined as net liquidity plus long-term unused credit facilities (excluding undrawn committed facilities where Ericsson is not able to meet borrowing conditions) expressed as percentage of net sales. During periods of increased uncertainty, the payment readiness target may be significantly higher.

CASE STUDY 4.5 | Toyota[25]

Toyota's securitization program involves selling discrete pools of finance receivables or interests in lease receivables to wholly owned bankruptcy remote SPEs, which in turn sell the receivables to separate securitization trusts in exchange for the proceeds from securities issued by the trust.

The securities issued by the trust, usually notes or certificates of various maturities and interest rates, are secured by collections on the sold receivables. These securities, commonly referred to as asset-backed securities, are structured into senior and subordinated classes. Generally, the senior classes have priority over the subordinated classes in receiving collections from the sold receivables.

As of March 31, 2002, outstanding debt from asset-backed securitizations and notes payable related to securities finance receivables structured as collateralized borrowings totalled approximately ¥573.0bn and ¥138.1bn, respectively. On any payment date, the priority of payments made from available collections and amounts withdrawn from existing reserve funds or revolving liquidity notes, are as follows: servicing fee, note holder interest, allocation of principal, reserve fund account deposit, and excess amounts.

Therefore, the interests of note holders are subordinate to the servicer, but have priority over any deposits in a reserve fund, any draws against existing revolving liquidity notes, or any excess amounts. In addition, in most cases, note holders holding senior classes of notes are paid prior to any existing subordinate class (some transactions are structured so that the subordinate tranche is released pro rata with certain senior tranches).

Toyota may enter into swap agreements with the securitization trusts so that interest rate exposure remains with Toyota, and not the securitization trusts. This exposure may or may not be mitigated by other swap arrangements entered into by Toyota, and this is determined by Toyota's management.

The company's general exposure every month, is the notional balance of the security multiplied by the rate differential. However, in the case of a default by the securitization trust, the company's maximum exposure would be the interest due based on the outstanding notional value of underlying securities paid at the rate inherent in the swap agreement.

Toyota has continued to originate operating leases to finance new Toyota vehicles. These leasing activities are subject to residual value risk. Residual value risk arises when the lessee of a vehicle does not exercise the option to purchase the vehicle at the end of the lease.

The number of vehicles returned at the end of leases has grown in recent years. For example, fewer than 20 percent of vehicles leased by Toyota Motor Credit Corporation, Toyota's financing subsidiary located in the US, were returned at the end of the applicable lease period during fiscal 1996, compared to a return rate of approximately 50 percent during fiscal 2001 and 2002.

▶

To avoid a loss on a vehicle returned to Toyota at the end of the lease, Toyota must resell or re-lease the vehicle at or above the residual value of the vehicle. If Toyota is unable to realize the residual value for the vehicle, it will incur a loss at the end of the lease. This loss would offset any earnings on the lease. In recent years, the resale values of returned vehicles have been depressed, primarily because of an increased supply of used vehicles in the market that has depressed market prices.

In addition, sales incentives in the automotive industry, particularly in the US, increased substantially in fiscal 2002, adversely affecting resale values.

Financial risk management

Shareholder value is affected by financial market risk resulting from adverse changes in interest rates and exchange rates.

Equity markets reward those companies with predictable and steady growth in earnings and cash-flows over the longer term. When profitability is adversely affected by increased costs resulting from changes in currency, interest rates, or commodity prices, shareholders bear the brunt.

For example, the base currency value of capital invested by a multinational company is a function of prevailing exchange rates. Since foreign exchange is often the denominator of both revenues and costs in overseas business, exchange rate movements affect long-term corporate profitability. This is because exchange rate movements have a built-in structural impact on the consolidated earnings of the company.

When the financial policies of a company help operating units attain their business goals, the finance function contributes to shareholder value. When changes in currency rates and commodity prices force a company to lower their sales prices, for competitive reasons, the lower margin may have to be made up by financial hedging actions.

Both financial institutions and non-financial firms are subject to financial risks due to their exposure to interest rate and exchange rate movements. Shareholders face economic risk from these exposures. The corporate treasury management function identifies and deals with these risks and uncertainties in financial markets to protect the value of the firm. The board of directors often perform the policy making and oversight functions.

However, there is no uniform approach to financial risk management among companies today. Although we observe the current global best practices, the financial management objectives and the definitions of what is exposed to financial market risk vary from one organization to another. Consequently, what is hedged is subject to what is recognized as exposure.

The differences in what is recognized as exposure have a major impact on the overall hedging activity. Similarly, the time horizon for which exposures are recognized also varies among companies, with most emphasis placed on the current year's transactions.

As is all too common today, when management is under pressure to improve short-term profitability, even at the expense of paying far less attention to longer-term objectives, financial activities tend to be tactical in nature.

"There is very little incentive to implement longer-term strategic financial measures, and the main focus is to achieve the current year's budget goals. Senior management tends to no more than pay lip service to longer term hedging ideas that entail cash expenditures today."[26]

This management short-termism is compounded by restrictive accounting regulations that often preclude management from taking prudent longer-term hedging actions that could protect the economic viability of the firm.

International financial markets have undergone dramatic changes in the last decade, with information technology allowing the market to become globally integrated. Equity and debt financing now go well beyond domestic markets, tapping global capital markets that offer possibly cheaper source of funds.

Changes in exchange and interest rates exert considerable influence on the pricing, sourcing, manufacturing, and financing aspects of the business. As companies face unique risk exposures based on their industry dynamics, so do the financial markets fulfill the need of this diverse set of risk management needs by offering a wide array of hedging instruments such as forwards, futures, options, swaps, and a multitude of debt or hybrid securities. These financial instruments are available to qualified participants to limit financial price risks, reduce financing and hedging costs, and avail market opportunities.

With sound policies, management approaches, and controls, well-run companies are attempting to deal with different types of financial risks in an integrated fashion on a global level, thereby contributing to the shareholder value of their respective firms.[27]

Corporate treasury groups typically develop and implement sound hedging programs. Considerable importance is given to the management decision process in formulating hedging strategies to deal with a single exposure as well as a portfolio of exposures.

Measuring financial risks

Typically, these financial risks are measured using the duration-convexity approach or the value at risk approach. Critical components of risk measurement include:

■ mark-to-market valuation,

■ establishment of valuation reserves,

■ analysis of revenue to identify sources of risk,

■ measurement of exposure to changes in market prices of interest rates and exchange rates.

In general, the financial industry agrees more on how risk should be measured than how it should be controlled.[28]

For financial institutions, the Group of 30 recommendations relating to the measurement of financial risks suggests use of VAR methodology. It states:

"Market risk is best measured as 'value at risk' using probability analysis based upon a common confidence interval (e.g., two standard deviations) and time horizon (e.g., one day exposure). Components of market risk that should be considered across the term structure include: absolute price or rate change (delta); convexity (gamma); volatility (vega); time decay (theta); basis correlation; and discount rate (rho)."[29]

EXAMPLE

For example, consider a $500m position in a stock in which the amount that can be transacted in one day without adversely impacting prices is estimated to be $50m. So $500m/$50m = 10 days of price moves should be reserved against, which implies that on average there will be 10/2 = 5 days of price moves prior to sale. If the daily standard deviation of price moves is 1.5 percent, and if management decides on a reserve to a 95 percent confidence interval level, which is equivalent to 1.65 standard deviations of a normal distribution, then the reserve (VAR) level should be:

$$\$500m \times 1.65 \times 1.5\% \times \sqrt{10/2} = \$27.7m$$

Controlling financial risk

Once an adequate measurement of risk is available, the next logical question is how to control it. Two fundamental and complementary approaches are available. The first is for the board of directors or risk management committees to place detailed limits on the amount and type of risks that CFO and treasury team can take – limits on VAR, position size, vega, gamma, and so on.

The second is for board of directors or risk management committees to provide incentives to the CFO team to optimize the trade-off between return and risk. The latter approach, based on incentives, gives the CFO team members who are closer to the information required to make informed trade-off decisions, the flexibility to find combinations of risks that can maximize the return for a total risk level approved by senior management.

In order to assess the likelihood of extreme adverse market moves, the amount of value at risk is put under 'stress tests'. Stress testing involves using economic insight rather than strict reliance on statistics to generate scenarios against which to measure firm risk.

The advantage of using stress testing as a supplement to VAR is that it can pick up possible extreme events that can cause large losses to the firm's positions that may be missed by a purely statistical approach.

However, there is some scepticism regarding the use of VAR as an estimator for risk exposure and as a controlling mechanism, since market moves that cause losses of sufficient size to threaten a firm's stability are generally radical departures from recent historical experience. This still leaves the possibility of using stress testing or an extreme value version of VAR as a good controlling mechanism for those embarrassing losses that are based on large market moves.

When it comes to risk comparability, both VAR and stress tests offer advantages to more traditional metrics such as duration, since they allow meaningful comparison and aggregation between different businesses. As Thomas Wilson states in a recent article "traditional risk measures such as the value of a basis point or vega provide little guidance when trying to interpret the relative importance of each individual risk factor to the portfolio's bottom line or for aggregating the different risk categories to a business unit or institution level."[30]

The ability that VAR and stress tests can provide to aggregate risks correctly allows institutions to gain a deeper understanding of the relative importance of its different risk positions and to gauge better its aggregate risk exposure relative to its aggregate risk appetite.

VAR accomplishes these objectives by defining a common metric that can be applied universally across all risk positions or portfolios: the maximum possible loss within a known confidence interval over a given holding period.

Besides being able to be applied universally across all risk categories, including financial, market, operational, credit, and insurance risks, this metric is also expressed in units that are meaningful at all levels of management: dollars, or pounds, euros, or the relevant currency. It therefore serves as a relevant focal point for discussing risks at all levels within the institution, creating a risk dialogue and culture that is otherwise difficult to achieve given the otherwise technical nature of the issues.[31]

A supplement to the use of limits to control risk is the provision of an adequate capital cushion against potential losses due to financial risk exposure. This cushion is required for both earnings volatility and protection against large market moves. Earnings volatility measurement aligns well with VAR, while the impact of large market moves is a risk better measured by stress tests or the Delta-EVT method.

The influence of shareholders on boardrooms has grown substantially over the last two decades. Business performance is increasingly measured by reference to shareholder value. The rise in importance of financial performance benchmarks such as earnings per share growth or economic value added are indicative of this shift in emphasis.

Boards are more inclined to invest in projects where the return is greatest.

Boards are more inclined to invest in projects where the return is greatest. It is in this context that financial risk management makes significant contributions towards increasing the value of the business by minimizing earnings volatility.

Overall, financial risk management helps generate a business environment that is able to minimize both the likelihood and impact of risk occurrences that could decrease shareholder value. Managing for shareholder value is likely to change the orientation of financial risk management, since it becomes clear that not all exposures need to be minimized at all times, depending on the nature of the business, and any natural off-sets.

EXAMPLE

In this example, we calculate the value at risk (VAR) of the returns of a two-asset portfolio financial asset (see Figure 4.2).

	no.	Security A returns	Security B returns	Covariance (A, B)
Jan-02	1	8.00%	28.00%	−0.57%
Feb-02	2	9.00%	24.00%	−0.31%
Mar-02	3	10.00%	11.00%	0.01%
Apr-02	4	11.00%	11.00%	0.00%
May-02	5	12.00%	8.00%	−0.02%
Jun-02	6	13.00%	7.00%	−0.07%
Jul-02	7	14.00%	2.00%	−0.24%
Aug-02	8	15.00%	3.00%	−0.31%
Average return		11.50%	11,75%	
Standard deviation		2.45%	9.44%	
Correlation with A			−0.9269	
Total				−1.50%
Covariance				−0.21%
Correl coefficient				−0.9269
Portfolio weighting		0.5	0.5	
Portfolio variance				0.131%
Required VAR		95%		
Number of standard deviations		−1.6449		
Value at Risk (VAR)		−4.03%		
Diversified VAR (%)				3.613%
Portfolio Value				$5,000,000
Diversified VAR ($)				**$180,649**

Figure 4.2 ■ Value at risk (VAR)

CASE STUDY 4.6 | Citigroup[32]

At Citigroup, market risk is managed through corporate-wide standards and business policies and procedures. Market risks are measured in accordance with established standards to ensure consistency across businesses and the ability to aggregate like risks at the Citigroup or corporate level.

Each business is required to establish, and have approved by independent market risk management, a market risk limit framework, including risk measures, limits and controls, that clearly defines approved risk profiles and is within the parameters of Citigroup's overall risk appetite.

Citigroup's businesses, working in conjunction with independent Market Risk Management, must ensure that market risks are independently measured, monitored and reported to ensure transparency in risk-taking activities and integrity in risk reports. In all cases, the businesses are ultimately responsible for the market risks that they take and for remaining within their defined limits.

Citigroup's market risk encompasses liquidity risk and price risk, both of which arise in the normal course of business of a global financial intermediary. Liquidity risk is the risk that some entity, in some location and in some currency, may be unable to meet a financial commitment to a customer, creditor, or investor when due. Price risk is the risk to earnings that arises from changes in interest rates, foreign exchange rates, equity and commodity prices, and in their implied volatilities. Price risk arises in non-trading as well as trading portfolios.

CASE STUDY 4.7 | Siemens[33]

Prudent financial market risk management is a key priority for Siemens. Its international operations, financing activities and investments expose the company to financial market risks. Siemens defines "market risk" as the potential loss due to an adverse move in market rates. "Potential loss" for equity price risk is a decline in fair values due to an adverse move in market prices. For foreign exchange risk, a "potential loss" is defined as a decline in future cash-flows due to an adverse move in market rates. For interest rate risk, "potential loss" for fixed rate instruments is a decline in fair values, and, for variable rate instruments, a decline in future cash-flows.

Siemens' objective for managing financial risks is to capitalize on the opportunities available in the global markets for its products and services while proactively managing the associated financial market risks. Siemens Financial Services (SFS) uses credit default swaps to protect against credit risks stemming from its receivables purchase business.

Siemens' primary financial market risk exposures, after the application of its market risk management approach, are equity price risk from its investments in marketable securities and

▶

asset swaps; foreign exchange rate risk, particularly to the US dollar, the UK pound, and the Swiss franc; interest rate risk resulting from long-term fixed rate debt obligations denominated principally in the euro, and also long-term interest rate swaps based on three- to six-month euro LIBOR.

Siemens uses VAR to estimate foreign exchange market risk. The company has no material commodity price risk out of derivative instruments. SFS holds a minor foreign exchange trading portfolio which is subject to tight limits and which, as of September 30, 2002, had a VAR close to zero. Siemens also uses sensitivity analysis to measure financial market risk.

In the unlikely occurrence that all risk factors were to move simultaneously in an unfavorable direction, Siemens could potentially suffer a combined loss of €4,279m as of September 30, 2002 in comparison to a similarly calculated value of €4,462m as of September 30, 2001. Sensitivity analysis is a widely used risk measurement tool that allows management to make judgments regarding the risk positioning of the company as a whole. Sensitivity analyses approximate an answer to the question of how much could be lost if certain specified parameters were to be met under a specific set of assumptions.

The risk estimates calculated by Siemens assume a 20 percent decrease in the equity prices of all of investments in marketable securities and asset swaps; a simultaneous, parallel foreign exchange rates shift in which all currencies weaken against the euro by 10 percent; and a parallel shift of 100 basis points of the interest rate yield curves in all currencies.

Sensitivity analysis has known limitations. Siemens uses business experience, market information and additional analytics to manage risk exposure and mitigate the limitations of its sensitivity analysis. The limitations of sensitivity analyses including the risk-mitigating effects caused by correlation and diversification among different currencies, interest rate areas and equity prices, or among these different risk exposures are not taken into account. This leads to an overestimation of risk, since a simultaneous adverse shift in all currencies, yield curves and share prices is highly unlikely.

Unlike other more complex risk-modeling concepts, it applies only two shifts (up or down) in each risk category with the direction causing the adverse outcome chosen. While it is possible to apply more sophisticated risk measurement techniques, Siemens contends that sensitivity analysis gives its decision makers in its non-financial businesses a sufficient warning of potential losses that further detailed analyses using the specific facts of a given situation may be applied to determine if appropriate corrective actions are needed.

Sensitivity analyses offer a snap-shot of risk exposures at and between specific dates in time. However, there is continuous change in assets other than the trading portfolio. For example, positions are continually being opened and closed, assets and liabilities mature, or new interest rates take effect. Siemens accepts this limitation and whenever more current information is required, produces either updated sensitivity analyses or utilizes other management reporting options to understand in detail the effects of changing market conditions.

Siemens has investments in publicly traded companies, which are held for purposes other than trading. The company estimates that an adverse move in equity prices of 20 percent would reduce the value of these investments by 4129m.

Siemens' risk management approach is to pool and analyze interest rate and currency risk exposures of the business groups. Exceptions to this approach are made in the case of country-specific restrictions and similar considerations.

The pooled exposures are recorded on a real-time basis in a treasury management system maintained by the Treasury and Financing Services (TFS) division of SFS. This system allows the company to perform an ongoing mark-to-market valuation of interest rate and currency risks of all pooled transactions, as well as a measure of credit exposure to individual financial institutions.

Siemens' TFS acts as a platform, on an internal service basis, to provide a centralized link for all of the operating groups to the third-party financial institutions in its financial risk management activities. TFS enters into derivative financial instruments with third-party financial institutions to offset all pooled exposures using a value at risk (VAR) model. At TFS, functional and organizational separation of duties between transaction initiation, processing, risk controlling and accounting is in place.

Financial derivatives used by Siemens include forward exchange contracts, interest rate swaps, cross-currency swaps, forward contracts and options. Derivatives are used to manage the company's foreign currency and interest rate exposures, as well as less frequently for specific hedging strategies related to equity holdings. To a limited extent, interest rate swaps and asset swaps are used to transform liquidity invested on a short-term basis into the intended asset allocation.

Neither Siemens' operating groups nor its TFS are permitted to buy or sell exotic or illiquid instruments, or enter into such transactions. The company has a clearly defined approval process for new hedging products. Each new proposal to use a new hedging product must be prepared and reviewed by several departments prior to the initiation of its use. The implementation process includes these departments: Treasury and finance, back office, accounting and controlling, risk management, credit, tax, and legal.

Siemens' foreign currency transactions arise from its business groups as well as from investments and financing activities of Siemens as a whole. Foreign exchange risks are partly offset through the company's production facilities abroad, as well as through procurement and financing activities conducted in foreign currencies. Siemens defines foreign currency exposure as foreign currency denominated cash inflows and cash outflows from anticipated transactions for the next three months, firm commitments and balance sheet items.

The foreign currency exposure is determined from the point of view of the respective functional currencies of the Siemens' entity where the exposure exists. Siemens' group-wide guidelines require each entity to enter into foreign exchange contracts with TFS to cover at least 75 percent of its foreign currency exposure. The unhedged balances are reported to the ▶

corporate finance department, which monitors the overall net foreign exchange exposure of the company. In determining the company's foreign exchange sensitivity, Siemens aggregates the net foreign exchange risk exposure of the operations groups and TFS. Siemens calculates a parallel 10 percent alteration of foreign currencies and its impact on earnings.

To address the effects of foreign exchange translation risk in its risk management, the working assumption is that investments in Siemens' foreign-based operations are permanent and that reinvestment is continual. Whenever a divestment of a particular asset or entity is contemplated or made, Siemens incorporates the approximate value into its sensitivity analyses. Effects from currency fluctuations on the translation of net asset amounts into euros are reflected in the Siemens consolidated equity position.

Siemens' interest rate exposure results mainly from debt obligations and interest-bearing investments. The company measures interest rate risk using either a fair value sensitivity or a cash-flow sensitivity depending on whether the instrument has a fixed or variable interest rate. The company uses the fair value sensitivity calculation for fixed interest instruments to show the change in the fair value (defined as net present value) caused by a hypothetical 100-basis point shift in the yield curve.

The first step in this calculation is to use the yield curve to discount the gross cash-flows, meaning the net present value of future interest and principal payments of financial instruments with fixed interest rates. A second calculation discounts the gross cash-flows using a 100-basis point shift of the yield curve. In all cases, Siemens uses the generally accepted and published yield curves on the relevant balance sheet date. The cash-flow sensitivity shows the change in future cash-flows of financial instruments with a variable interest rate also assuming a 100-basis point shift of the yield curves.

The total fair value sensitivity as well as the total cash-flow sensitivity are generated by aggregating the sensitivities of the exposure denominated in various currencies. Siemens' fair value interest risk results primarily from its long-term fixed rate debt obligations. The company seeks to limit this risk through the use of derivative instruments which allow us to hedge fair value changes by swapping fixed rates of interest into variable rates of interest.

CASE STUDY 4.8 Hong Kong Shanghai Banking Corp. (HSBC)[34]

Market risk is the risk that foreign exchange rates, interest rates, or equity and commodity prices will move and result in profits or losses to HSBC. Market risk arises on financial instruments which are valued at current market prices (mark-to-market basis) and those valued at cost plus any accrued interest (accruals basis). Trading positions are valued on a mark-to-market basis.

In liquid portfolios, market values are determined by reference to independently sourced mid-market prices where it is reasonable to assume the positions could be sold at that price. In those instances where markets are less liquid and/or where positions have been held for extended periods, portfolios are valued by reference to bid or offer prices as appropriate. In relation to certain products, such as over-the-counter derivative instruments, there are no independent prices quoted in the markets.

In these circumstances market values are determined by reference to standard industry models, which typically utilize discounted cash-flow techniques to derive the market value. The models may be in-house developed or software vendor packages. In valuing transactions, prices may be amended in respect of those positions considered illiquid, having recognition of the size of the position vis-à-vis the normal market trading volume in that product.

The main valuation sources are securities prices, foreign exchange rates, and interest rate yield curves. In excess of 95 percent of HSBC's derivative transactions are in plain vanilla instruments, primarily comprising interest rate and foreign exchange contracts, where the mark-to-market values are readily determinable by reference to independent prices and valuation quotes.

In the limited number of circumstances where standard industry models are not available, and where there is no directly relevant market quotation, HSBC has developed its own proprietary models for the purposes of performing valuations. Such circumstances normally would be where HSBC has tailored a transaction to meet a specific customer need.

The models used are checked by the finance and operations departments and are subject to audit review on an ongoing basis to ensure that the model assumptions are, and remain, valid over the transaction life which is generally less than five years.

HSBC makes markets in exchange rate and interest rate instruments, as well as in debt, equities and other securities. Trading risks arise either from customer-related business or from position taking. HSBC manages market risk through risk limits approved by the Group Executive Committee. Traded Markets Development and Risk, an independent unit within the Corporate Investment Banking and Markets Operation, develops risk management policies and measurement techniques, and reviews limit utilization on a daily basis.

HSBC's risk limits are determined for each location and, within location, for each portfolio. Limits are set by product and risk type with market liquidity being a principal factor in determining the level of limits set. Only those offices with sufficient derivative product expertise and appropriate control systems are authorised to trade derivative products.

Limits are set using a combination of risk measurement techniques, including position limits, sensitivity limits, as well as VAR limits at a portfolio level. Similarly, options risks are controlled through full revaluation limits in conjunction with limits on the underlying variables that determine each option's value.

HSBC's VAR predominantly calculated on a variance/co-variance basis, uses historical movements in market rates and prices, a 99 percent confidence level, a ten-day holding

▶

period, takes account of correlations between different markets and rates within the same risk type, and is calculated daily.

The movement in market prices is calculated by reference to market data from the last two years. Aggregation of VAR from different risk types is based upon the assumption of independence between risk types. HSBC's VAR should be viewed in the context of the limitations of the methodology used.

The model assumes that changes in risk factors follow a normal distribution. This may not be the case in reality and may lead to an *underestimation* of the probability of extreme market movements. The model uses a ten-day holding period and assumes that all positions can be liquidated or hedged in ten days. This may not fully reflect the market risk arising from times of severe illiquidity, when a ten-day holding period may be insufficient to fully liquidate or hedge all positions.

The VAR model uses a 99 percent confidence level, and does not take account of any losses that might occur beyond this level of confidence. In addition, use of historical data as a proxy for estimating future events may not encompass all potential events, particularly those which are extreme in nature. The assumption of independence between risk types may not always hold and therefore results in VAR not fully capturing market risk where correlation between variables is exhibited.

VAR is calculated at the close of business, with intra-day exposures not being subject to intra-day VAR calculations on an HSBC basis; and VAR does not necessarily capture all of the higher order market risks and may underestimate real market risk exposure.

HSBC recognizes these limitations by augmenting the VAR limits with other position and sensitivity limit structures, as well as with *stress testing*, both on individual portfolios and on a consolidated basis. HSBC's stress testing regime provides senior management with an assessment of the impact of extreme events on the market risk exposures of HSBC.

CASE STUDY 4.9 | AT&T[35]

AT&T Corp. is exposed to market risk from changes in interest and foreign exchange rates, as well as changes in equity prices associated with previously affiliated companies. In addition, the company is exposed to market risk from fluctuations in the prices of securities, some of which AT&T monetized through the issuance of debt.

On a limited basis, AT&T uses certain derivative financial instruments, including interest rate swaps, options, forwards, equity hedges and other derivative contracts, to manage financial risk exposures. However, the company does not use financial instruments for trading or speculative purposes. All financial instruments are used in accordance with board-approved policies.

AT&T enters into foreign currency contracts to minimize its exposure to risk of adverse changes in currency exchange rates. AT&T is subject to foreign exchange risk on foreign-currency-denominated transactions, such as debt issued, recognized payables and receivables, and forecasted transactions. At December 31, 2002, AT&T's foreign currency market exposures were principally euros, Japanese yen, and Swiss francs.

The fair value of foreign exchange contracts is subject to the changes in foreign currency exchange rates. For the purpose of assessing specific risks, AT&T uses sensitivity analysis to determine the effects that market risk exposures may have on the fair value of its financial instruments and results of operations.

To perform the sensitivity analysis, AT&T assesses the risk of loss in fair values from the effect of a hypothetical 10 percent adverse change in the value of foreign currencies, assuming no change in interest rates.

The model to determine sensitivity assumes a parallel shift in all foreign currency exchange rates, although exchange rates rarely move in the same direction. Additionally, the amounts do not necessarily represent the actual changes in fair value AT&T would incur under normal market conditions, because all variables, other than the exchange rates, are held constant in the calculations.

AT&T uses interest rate swaps to manage the impact of interest rate changes on earnings and cash-flows. Sensitivity analysis is performed on the company's interest rate swaps to assess the risk of changes in fair value.

The model to determine sensitivity assumes a hypothetical 10 percent parallel shift in all interest rates. At December 31, 2002 and 2001, assuming a hypothetical 10 percent decrease in interest rates, the fair value of interest rate swaps would have decreased by $1m and $2m, respectively.

Typically, the decrease in fair value of underlying financial assets are largely offset by increases in the fair value of the underlying hedged debt. AT&T enters into combined interest rate foreign currency contracts to hedge its foreign-currency-denominated debt. Assuming a hypothetical 10 percent increase in interest rates, the fair value of the contracts would have decreased by $3m at December 31, 2002, and by a negligible amount at December 31, 2001.

The fair value of AT&T's fixed-rate long-term debt is sensitive to changes in interest rates. Interest rate changes would result in gains or losses in the market value of the debt due to differences between the market interest rates and rates at the inception of the obligation. Assuming a 10 percent downward shift in interest rates at December 31, 2002 and 2001, the fair value of AT&T's unhedged debt would have increased by $0.7bn and $1.0bn, respectively.

At December 31, 2002, AT&T had certain notes, with embedded derivatives, which were indexed to the market price of equity securities that AT&T owned. Changes in the market prices of these securities resulted in changes in the fair value of the derivatives. Assuming a hypothetical 10 percent increase in the market price of these equity securities, the fair value of the collars would have decreased by $46m and $112m at December 31, 2002 and 2001, ▶

respectively. Because these collars hedged the underlying equity securities monetized, the decrease in the fair value of the collars are largely offset by increases in the fair value of the underlying equity securities.

AT&T uses equity hedges to manage its exposure to changes in equity prices associated with various equity awards of previously affiliated companies. Assuming a hypothetical 10 percent decrease in equity prices of these companies, the fair value of the equity hedges (net liability) would have increased by $9m at December 31, 2002, and by a negligible amount at December 31, 2001. Because these contracts are entered into for hedging purposes, the increase in fair value would be largely offset by decreases in the underlying liabilities.

In order to determine the changes in fair value of AT&T's various financial instruments, including options, equity collars and other equity awards, AT&T uses certain financial modeling techniques, including Black-Scholes. The company applies rate sensitivity changes directly to its interest rate swap transactions and forward rate sensitivity to its foreign currency forward contracts.

CASE STUDY 4.10 General Electric (GE)[36]

GE uses derivative financial instruments to mitigate or eliminate certain financial and market risks, including those related to changes in interest rates and currency exchange rates. As a matter of policy, GE does not engage in derivatives trading, derivatives market-making or other speculative activities.

The US Securities and Exchange Commission requires that registrants provide information about potential effects of changes in interest and currency exchange rates.

GE uses sensitivity analysis or "shock tests," which model effects of interest rate and currency shifts on the reporting company. While the results of shock tests for changes in interest rates and currency exchange rates may have some limited use as benchmarks, they should not be viewed as forecasts.

One means of assessing exposure to interest rate changes is a duration-based analysis that measures the potential loss in net earnings resulting from a hypothetical increase in interest rates of 100 basis points across all maturities. This assumes a parallel shift in the yield curve. Under this model, with all else held constant, GE estimates that such an increase, including repricing in the securities portfolio, would reduce the 2003 net earnings of GE Commercial Services (GECS) based on year-end 2002 positions by approximately $184m; the pro-forma effect for GE was $61m.

GE's geographic distribution of operations is diverse. One means of assessing exposure to changes in currency exchange rates is to model effects on reported earnings using a sensitivity analysis. GE analyzes year-end consolidated currency exposures, including financial instruments designated and effective as hedges, to identify assets and liabilities denominated in other than their relevant functional currencies. Net unhedged exposures in each currency are then remeasured, generally assuming a 10 percent decrease (substantially greater decreases for hyperinflationary currencies) in currency exchange rates compared with the US dollar.

Changes in the currency translation adjustment reflect the effects of changes in currency exchange rates on GE's net investment in non-US subsidiaries that have functional currencies other than the US dollar. GE periodically invests available cash in GECS short-term borrowings. Such amounts are classified as cash equivalents in the GE Statement of Financial Position.

CASE STUDY 4.11 DaimlerChrysler[37]

The DaimlerChrysler Group is exposed to market risks from changes in foreign currency exchange rates and interest rates. To a minor degree the group is also exposed to changes in market prices of equity securities. These changes may adversely affect DaimlerChrysler's operating results and financial condition. The Group seeks to manage and control these risks primarily through its regular operating and financing activities, but, when it is appropriate, through the use of derivative financial instruments.

DaimlerChrysler evaluates these market risks by monitoring changes in key economic indicators and market information on an ongoing basis. In order to quantify the foreign exchange rate risk, interest rate risk and equity price risk of the group on a continuous basis, DaimlerChrysler's risk management control systems employ VAR analyses as recommended by the Bank for International Settlements.

The VAR calculations employed by DaimlerChrysler express potential losses in fair values and are based on the variance-covariance approach, assuming a 99 percent confidence level and a holding period of five days. Estimates of volatilities and correlations are primarily drawn from the RiskMetrics™ datasets and supplemented by additional exchange rate, interest rate, and equity price information.

DaimlerChrysler does not use financial instruments for speculative purposes. Following organizational standards in the international banking industry, DaimlerChrysler maintains risk management control systems independent of corporate treasury and with a separate reporting line.

The global nature of DaimlerChrysler's business activities results in cash receipts and payments denominated in various currencies. Cash inflows and outflows of the business segments are offset and netted if they are denominated in the same currency. Within the framework of central currency management, currency exposures are regularly assessed and hedged with suitable financial instruments according to exchange rate expectations, which are constantly reviewed.

▶

The net assets of the group, which are invested in subsidiaries and affiliated companies outside the euro zone, are generally not hedged against currency risks. However, in specific circumstances, DaimlerChrysler seeks to hedge the currency risk inherent in certain of its long-term investments.

DaimlerChrysler holds some equity securities as a part of its strategy to manage excess liquidity. The group hedges the risk inherent in these securities mainly through equity derivatives. According to international banking standards, DaimlerChrysler does not include investments in equity securities, which it classifies as long-term investments in the equity price risk assessment.

CASE STUDY 4.12 Toyota[38]

Toyota Corp. is sensitive to fluctuations in foreign currency exchange rates. In addition to the Japanese yen, Toyota is principally exposed to fluctuations in the value of the US dollar and the euro and, to a lesser extent, the British pound. Toyota's consolidated financial statements, which are presented in Japanese yen, are affected by foreign currency exchange fluctuations through both translation risk and transaction risk.

Changes in foreign currency exchange rates may positively or negatively affect Toyota's revenues, gross margins, operating costs and expenses, operating income, net income, and retained earnings.

Translation risk is the risk that Toyota's financial statements for a particular period or for a particular date will be affected by changes in the prevailing exchange rates of the currencies in those countries in which Toyota does business against the Japanese yen.

Even though the fluctuations of currencies against the Japanese yen can be substantial and, therefore, significantly impact comparisons with prior periods and among various geographic markets, the translation effect is a reporting consideration and does not reflect Toyota's underlying results of operations. Toyota does not hedge against translation risk.

Transaction risk is the risk that the currency structure of Toyota's costs and liabilities will deviate from the currency structure of sales proceeds and assets. Transaction risk relates primarily to sales proceeds from Toyota's non-domestic sales produced in Japan and, to a lesser extent, sales proceeds from Toyota's continental European sales produced in the UK.

Location of its production facilities in different parts of the world has significantly reduced Toyota's level of transaction risk. As part of its globalization strategy, Toyota has localized much of its production by constructing production facilities in the major markets in which it sells its vehicles. In 2001, Toyota produced 54 percent of its non-domestic sales outside Japan. In North America, 59 percent of vehicles sold in 2001 were produced locally. In Europe, 36 percent of vehicles sold in 2001 were produced locally.

Local operations permit Toyota to purchase many of the supplies and resources used in the production process in a manner that matches the currencies of local revenues with the currencies of local expenses. Toyota also enters into currency borrowings and other hedging instruments to address a portion of its transaction risk. This has reduced, but not eliminated, the effects of foreign currency exchange rate fluctuations, which in some years can be significant.

CASE STUDY 4.13 Intel[39]

Intel is exposed to financial market risks, including changes in currency exchange rates, interest rates and marketable equity security prices. To mitigate these risks, Intel utilizes derivative financial instruments, among other strategies. Other than warrants and other equity derivatives that Intel acquired for strategic purposes, the company does not use derivative financial instruments for speculative purposes.

Sensitivity analyses are performed on Intel's financial positions to determine potential impacts of adverse price movements in the financial markets. Intel generally hedges currency risks of non-US dollar-denominated investments in debt securities with offsetting currency borrowings, currency forward contracts, or currency interest rate swaps. Gains and losses on these non-US-currency investments would generally be offset by corresponding losses and gains on the related hedging instruments, resulting in negligible net exposure.

A substantial majority of Intel's revenue, expense and capital purchasing activities are transacted in US dollars. However, the company does enter into these transactions in other currencies, primarily the euro and certain other European and Asian currencies. To protect against reductions in value and the volatility of future cash-flows caused by changes in currency exchange rates, Intel has established transaction and balance sheet hedging programs.

Currency forward contracts and currency options are utilized in these hedging programs. Intel's hedging programs reduce, but do not entirely eliminate, the impact of currency exchange rate movements. Intel considers historical trends in currency exchange rates and determines reasonably possible adverse changes in exchange rates of 20 percent for the euro and certain other European, Asian and South American currencies and 10 percent for all other currencies that could be experienced in the near term.

Such adverse changes, after taking into account hedges and offsetting positions, would have resulted in an adverse impact on income before taxes of less than $10m as of the end of each of 2002 and 2001.

The primary objective of Intel's investments in debt securities is to preserve the principal while maximizing yields, without significantly increasing risk. To achieve this objective, the ▶

returns on a substantial majority of its marketable investments in long-term fixed rate debt securities are swapped to US dollar LIBOR-based returns.

Intel considered the historical volatility of the three-month LIBOR rate experienced in the past year and determined that it was reasonably possible that an adverse change of 80 basis points, approximately 57 percent of the rate at the end of 2002, could be experienced in the near term. A hypothetical 0.80 percent (80-basis-point) increase in interest rates, after taking into account hedges and offsetting positions, would have resulted in a less than $5m decrease in the fair value of Intel's investments in debt securities as of the end of 2002 and an approximate $10m decrease as of the end of 2001.

CASE STUDY 4.14 Nestlé[40]

Financial risk management is an integral part of the way the Nestlé Group is managed.[41] The board establishes the group's financial policies and the executive board establishes objectives in line with these policies.

An Asset and Liability Management Committee, under the supervision of the CFO, is then responsible for setting financial strategies, which are executed by the centre treasury and the affiliated companies.

Approved Treasury Management Guidelines define and classify Nestlé's risks as well as determine, by category of transaction, specific approval, limit and monitoring procedures. In the course of its business, the group is exposed to financial market risks, credit risk, settlement risk and liquidity risk.

Financial market risks are essentially caused by exposures to foreign currencies, interest rates and commodity prices. Foreign currency transaction risk arises because affiliated companies sometimes undertake transactions in foreign currencies such as the import of raw materials, the export of finished goods, and the related borrowings. Translation exposure arises from the consolidation of the Nestlé group accounts into Swiss francs.

Interest rate risk comprises the *interest price risk* that results from borrowing at fixed rates and the *interest cash-flow risk* that results from borrowing at variable rates. Nestlé's commodity price risk arises from transactions on the world commodity markets mainly for securing the supplies of green coffee and cocoa beans necessary for the manufacture of some of the group's products. These risks are mitigated by the use of derivative financial instruments.

Credit risk arises because a counterparty may fail to perform its obligations. The group is exposed to credit risks on financial instruments such as liquid assets, derivative assets, and its trade receivable portfolios. Credit risk is managed by investing liquid assets and acquiring derivatives with high credit quality financial institutions in accordance with the Nestlé group's Treasury Management Guidelines.

The Nestlé group is not exposed to concentrations of credit risk on its liquid assets as these are spread over several financial institutions. Trade receivables are subject to credit limits, control and approval procedures in all the affiliated companies. Due to its large geographic base and number of customers, the group is not exposed to material concentrations of credit risk on its trade receivables.

Nestlé's settlement risk results from the fact that the group may not receive financial instruments from its counterparties at the expected time. This risk is managed by monitoring counterparty activity and settlement limits, and managing presettlement counterparty exposures. Liquidity risk arises from the fact that a counterparty may not be able to unwind or offset a position because of inadequate market depth or disruption or refinancing problems. This risk is managed by limiting exposures in instruments that may be affected by liquidity problems and through actively matching the funding horizon of debt with incoming cash-flows.

As a result of its strong credit ratings, the Nestlé group does not expect any refinancing issues. The group has several benchmarks and approval requirements for borrowing and investing as well as for using derivatives. In general, affiliated companies may borrow in their respective local currencies up to six months forward while group management approval is required for longer terms and for any indebtedness in foreign currency as well as for interest and foreign exchange derivatives on such positions.

The affiliated companies may also hedge their foreign currency exposures up to six months forward but they must obtain approval of group management for longer maturities. The affiliated companies must repatriate all their excess liquidities to Nestlé group finance companies or require the approval of the group management for the rare cases where they may have a justification to invest them locally.

The Asset and Liability Management Committee reviews and decides the currency and interest rate framework of Nestlé's intragroup loans portfolio on a monthly basis. With regard to commodity price exposures, group management defines the hedging policy for affiliated companies. The policy is sufficiently flexible to allow management to rapidly adjust hedges following possible changes in raw material needs.

CASE STUDY 4.15 GlaxoSmithKline[42]

In GlaxoSmithKline, foreign currency transaction exposure arising on normal trade flows both in respect of external and intra-group trade is not hedged. GlaxoSmithKline's policy is to minimize the exposure of overseas operating subsidiaries to transaction risk by matching local currency income with local currency costs.

For this purpose, intra-group trading transactions are matched centrally and intra-group payment terms are managed to reduce risk. Exceptional foreign currency cash-flows are hedged selectively under the management of Corporate Treasury. A significant proportion of group borrowings, including the commercial paper program, is in US dollars, to benefit from the liquidity of US dollar denominated capital markets. Certain of these and other borrowings are swapped into other currencies as required for group purposes. The group seeks to denominate borrowings in the currencies of its principal overseas assets.

Borrowings denominated in, or swapped into, foreign currencies which match investments in overseas group assets are treated as a hedge against the relevant net assets. Based on the composition of net debt at December 31, 2002, a 10 percent appreciation in sterling against major currencies would result in a reduction in the group's net debt of approximately £145m. A 10 percent weakening in sterling against major currencies would result in an increase in the Group's net debt of approximately £177m.

GlaxoSmithKline's policy on interest rate risk management requires that the amount of net borrowings at fixed rates increases with the ratio of forecast net interest payable to trading profit. The group uses a limited number of interest rate swaps to redenominate external borrowings into the interest rate coupon required for group purposes. The duration of these swaps matches the duration of the principal instruments. All interest rate derivative instruments are accounted for as hedges of the relevant assets or liabilities.

The group manages centrally the short-term cash surpluses or borrowing requirements of subsidiary companies and uses forward contracts to hedge future repayments back into originating currency. Sensitivity analysis considers the sensitivity of the group's net debt to hypothetical changes in market rates and assumes that all other variables remain constant. Based on the composition of net debt at December 31, 2002 a one percentage point (100 basis points) increase or decrease in average interest rates would result in a negligible change in the group's annual interest expense.

Equity investments classified as current assets are available for sale and the group manages disposals to meet overall business requirements as they arise. The group regularly monitors the value of its equity investments and only enters into hedges selectively with the approval of the board.

The group continues to benefit from strong positive cash-flow. Group net debt would have decreased significantly in the year to December 31, 2002, except for the group's purchase of its own shares in the market of £2,220m. The financial assets and liabilities at

December 31, 2002 are representative of the treasury policies and strategies of GlaxoSmithKline, applied consistently during the year. There were no significant changes in such policies throughout the year.

In 2002 the employee share ownership trusts (ESOTs) did not make any market purchases of shares in GlaxoSmithKline plc (2001: £795m). The shares are held by the trusts to satisfy future exercises of options and awards under the group share option and award schemes. A proportion of the shares held by the trusts are in respect of options where the rules of the scheme require the company to satisfy exercises through market purchases rather than the issue of new shares.

The shares held by the trusts are matched to options granted and diminish the dilutive effect of new share issues on shareholders' capital and earnings. At the 2002 Annual General Meeting, shareholders renewed approval for GlaxoSmithKline to make market purchases of its own shares.

In September 2002, the £4bn share repurchase program announced in October 2001 was completed. On October 23, 2002, GlaxoSmithKline announced a further share repurchase program of £4bn. The exact amount and timing of future purchases will depend on market conditions and other factors. In 2002, GlaxoSmithKline purchased 155.7m shares for cancellation, at a total cost of £2,220m.

Operational risk management

Operational risk arises as a result of risks from business operations, as opposed to financing decisions. The aim of operational risk management is to help organizations identify and mitigate potentially adverse events ahead of time, thus achieving strategic goals.

Operational risks are unique to each business based on:

■ industry,

■ competitive structure,

■ customer demographics,

■ demand and supply conditions,

■ sensitivity to economic conditions,

■ product elasticities to various factors,

■ level of complexity in product development and delivery,

■ intangible issues such as intellectual rights, level of human capital intensity, etc.

Therefore, no one measure of operating risk can fit all enterprises. However, we can profile general elements of operational risk management that are applicable to most companies. These include risk identification, risk assessment, risk response, and risk finance (see Figure 4.3).

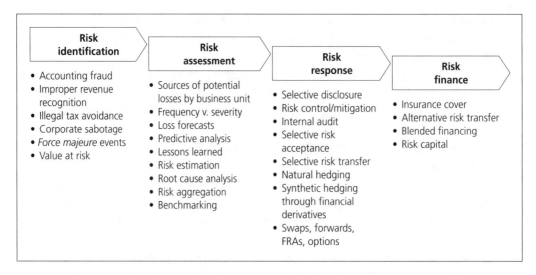

FIGURE 4.3 ■ Profiling elements of the risk management process

Many markets are inherently unpredictable. Changing patterns of supply and demand can leave companies with excess inventory, order backlog problems, or sudden rises in demand. As a result, the core operations need to be responsive to the needs of the marketplace. Managing capacity is at the heart of sound business management. Optimizing capacity utilization through careful operational management minimizes one aspect of operational risks naturally.

Operational risk management is a relatively new management discipline with the goal of enhancing management performance through the early identification and avoidance of business disruption. Its specific focus is on failure of people, processes, systems, or external events.[43]

In the 1980s and 1990s, much of the focus of corporate risk management revolved around designing and implementing control frameworks, managing insurance portfolios, and meeting corporate governance standards. But in the dawn of the twenty-first century, leading companies are rethinking the nature of risk, risk management, and operations management. There is a greater awareness of operational risks as managers walk the fine line between success and failure – the difference between making the numbers and falling short.

As the pace of change continues to accelerate, many organizations are now finding that they can no longer afford to take a solely defensive attitude to risk. While control frameworks are a necessary first step in managing risk, many organizations now need to manage risk for strategic advantage, to improve customer satisfaction and increase shareholder value.[44]

By its nature, operational risk management is the integration of risk management with core operations management. As well as offering a structure for designing and implementing controls that support business objectives, operational risk management can also help ensure that organizations deliver shareholder value. Risk management and corporate strategy are becoming more closely aligned than ever before.

Operational risk estimation and management has been a challenge for financial services firms as well as non-financial corporations due to methodological issues and infrequency of events that lead to large operational losses. However, operational losses have been occurring at respected firms in the US and Europe. Companies such as Barings, Prudential, Procter & Gamble, and Kidder Peabody have suffered notable financial losses due to operational risks, underscoring the danger of ignoring this area in the corporate financial planning process.

Reducing the risk of operational losses

The primary objective of risk mitigation is to reduce the risk of operational losses, thus supporting decision-making for strategic advantage for the company. Leading firms seek to turn their risk profiles into a competitive advantages, seeking to build shareholder value through more effective organizations. In this process, management of financial risks is necessary but not sufficient to secure the firm's financial performance from adverse results. Operational risks must be managed as well.

Operational risks must be managed as well.

In fact, there is now a growing recognition that a major source of earnings volatility is not due to financial risk. It is not due to the way a firm finances its business, but rather the way a firm operates its business, and is called operational risk.[45]

Operational risk estimation involves segregation of corporate risks into regular value-adding process events that usually carry high-frequency but low-impact risks, and irregular or unusual losses which are of the low-frequency high-impact type. These two separate categories of events can be separately modeled using the VAR framework and aggregated to represent total operational risk of the firm.

The operating loss distribution uses the continuous probability distributions and estimates the VAR from operational risk exposure using the delta-normal method. The excess loss distribution is derived using the VAR from discrete probability distributions by applying extreme value theory. A schematic diagram of the process is presented in Figure 4.4.

Operational risk has generally come to be understood to mean the risk of loss from inadequate or failed internal processes, people, and systems from external events. Strategies to improve earnings that do not address the related risk may not provide the expected increase in the value of the firm because actions to increase earnings may also lead to an increase in undesirable risk.

These often include elements that are within management control, but the pervasive nature and broad variety of operational risks faced by businesses is difficult to exactly quantify. This is a relatively new and difficult area of corporate risk management.

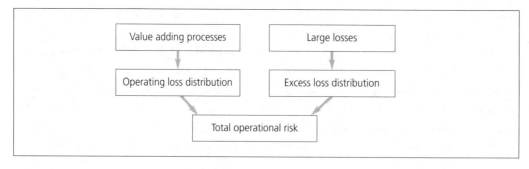

FIGURE 4.4 ■ Operational risk estimation

Operational losses are measured by the direct economic loss and indirect expense associated with business interruptions and legal risk. Some also include immeasurable exposures such as reputation risk.

EXAMPLE

Some notable examples of losses from operational risk include:[46]

- Bank of Credit and Commerce International (BCCI): $17bn loss in 1991 due to management fraud.
- Long Term Capital Management (LTCM): $4bn market loss in 1998 due to overexposure to leverage, sovereign, model, liquidity, and volatility risk.
- Texaco Inc.: $3bn loss in 1984 due to litigation risk.
- Sumitomo Corporation: $2.8bn loss in 1996 due to excessive trading of copper.
- Metallgesellschaft: $1.8bn loss in 1991–93 due to liquidation of oil supply contracts.

Other high-profile corporate losses due to inadequate operational risk management include:

- Drexel Burnham Lambert's $1.3bn loss during 1993–98.
- Barings' fatal loss of $1.0bn leading to its collapse in 1995.
- General Motors' $1.2bn loss in 1996.

The above examples demonstrate the importance of operational risk identification and management in corporations.

Other types of operational risk

Operational risk is also the risk that failures in computer systems, internal supervision and control, or *force majure* events will impose unexpected losses on a firm's financial or derivative positions.[47] Other operating risks may include excessive operating leverage and legal risks. For example operating leverage may be managed a by prudent mix of fixed versus variable costs. Legal risk is the risk that a firm will incur loss if a contract it thought was enforceable is actually not, or as a result of counter-party default.

Intellectual risk arises when personnel with specialized knowledge leave the firm, making it difficult for the firm to manage the assignments or projects. At the core of risks facing the business is the risk that the business will lose customers resulting in possible market share erosion. Customer losses can occur due to competitive conditions or market demand conditions.

Operational risk encompasses elements like pricing risk. Supply chain risks are adverse events that may occur at any point along a physical supply chain, or the chain that connects inputs to the firm's production process to its outputs. Outsourcing certain production functions may be necessary to optimize internal resources. Process inefficiencies often cause resource leakage and waste. Inability to identify the principle causes of operating weakness may be cited as an operational risk.

Similarly, inability to effectively execute the business plan increases financial risks of the business, while management's ability to target the right product and customer segments for maximum marginal revenue and profit growth lowers risks to the business plan.

Operational risks are also minimized when management monitors operational performance metrics unique to the business in real time, and takes corrective action promptly if misalignments are discovered compared to targets. For example, if inventories are trending up sharply, the production and raw material line-up must commensurately be lowered to avoid expensive stock build-up.

Operational risk management includes corporate governance, risk estimation, operational controls, process execution, and operational effectiveness. In this continuum, we need to develop and execute a disciplined approach that selectively retains some of the operational risks, while other risk elements are transferred through alternative risk transfer mechanisms such as insurance. Figure 4.5 is a schematic representation of this process.

If operations are not managed efficiently, this creates sub-optimality downstream. Total quality management (TQM) and just in time (JIT) manufacturing processes are operational models that help lower operational risks of mismanagement in process flow.

Operational risk has a unique set of data availability and characteristics, complex causation considerations, subjective control variables, and a different notion of portfolio and transaction views. The move toward enterprise-wide risk management emphasizes the fact that operational risks, unlike credit and market risks, touch or are touched by everyone in the organization. Operational risk management is beginning to pave the way for enhanced shareholder value with the use of best of breed practices.

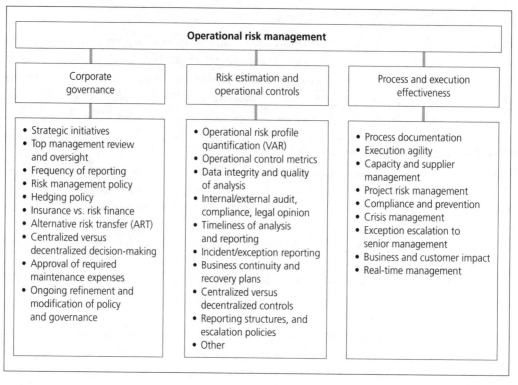

FIGURE 4.5 ■ Operational risk management

Key trends

According to empirical research conducted recently, the best firms are making heroic strides toward risk definition, data collection, aggregation, and first-level analysis. Key trends, particularly for financial firms, include:[48]

■ Enterprise-wide risk management and operational risk recognition are on the rise.

■ Early consensus is beginning to emerge on the definition of operational risk.

■ Companies and risk managers have recognized the value of operational risk data and are creating internal risk loss event database systems.

■ External commercially available databases have become available.

■ Corporations have begun to set up internal accounting codes to trace losses resulting from operational risk.

■ Firms have begun to track risk issues on both corporate and business line levels.

■ Organizations use external risk data (commercial vendors) to supplement their internal risk loss data for statistical analysis in support of experimental risk capital calculations.

■ Regulators are beginning to impose industry standards and guidelines for handling operational risk, data, and capital for financial institutions.

■ Risk mitigation is being enhanced through the interpretation of operational risk data.

■ Incentives are being developed for operational risk management through performance measures such as risk capital attribution and links to incentive compensation.

■ Insurance risk managers recognize that they need operational risk data for effective evaluation of insurance and risk finance hedge structures.

■ New risk information measures and technology applications have begun to emerge for improved operational risk management decision making.

■ Firms are recognizing the upside value in proactively managing operational risk.

Line management should have responsibility for strategy and day-to-day management of operational risk, both anticipated and unanticipated. In contrast, corporate management is usually in the best position to capture an enterprise-wide perspective of the firm's risk profile, including the larger scale impact of operational inter-dependency and concentration risks, and capitalize on economies of scale in hedging the risk.

There is no "one size fits all" solution, however, for mitigating and managing a corporation's operational risk exposure. This is due to the varied nature of businesses representing manufacturing, agriculture, financial, and other service sectors that cover the entire range of low to high technology applications in their operational processes.

Different organizations face different risks including the degree of geographic dispersion, operational complexity, process effectiveness, control structures, level of competitive threats etc. That caveat notwithstanding, what is clear at the boardroom level is that strong risk management is an essential part of good corporate governance, and something that helps to protect shareholder value. There is also a growing recognition of the need to ensure that an effective framework of management controls and supervision is in place.

The aim of operational risk management is to ensure that the varied exposures to operational risk faced by an organization are identified and addressed in the most efficient way possible. The achievement of this goal is dependent on management taking positive action to consider what steps should be taken to optimize an organization's exposure to operational risk so that shareholder value gains can be maximized.

While risk management at an operational level often focuses on the smooth and efficient running of an organization, attention is not always paid to management of operational risk within the context of an enterprise-wide view of risk. Operational risk is too often framed at an operational level within organizations. As a result, it remains apart from strategic considerations.

Attention is not always paid to management of operational risk within the context of an enterprise-wide view of risk.

In today's world, organizations need to focus on an approach to risk management that is aligned with forward-looking growth strategies for achieving competitive advantage. This approach should go hand in hand with maintaining operational resilience – the ability to handle operational stress. Overall, organizations that achieve greater stability in operations have a better foundation to compete more competently in the market, and provide high service levels to their customers.[49]

The consequences of not managing operational risk properly go beyond financial losses. Failure at the level of operational continuity can lead to a loss of reputation among the public at large and the shareholders, in turn affecting the brand. In the event of a problem, organizations may find it very difficult to recover damage to market share or brand value, or regain competitive advantage after an unexpected shock.

Drivers of change

As we move into the twenty-first century, the rate of change is becoming one of the most important issues facing management. According to Chris Frost and others of PricewaterhouseCoopers, some of the drivers of change that have increased exposure to operational risk for organizations across most industries around the world include:

- globalization,
- growth of e-business,
- competition,
- increased regulation,
- increased awareness of uninsurable risks,
- increased level of litigation,
- greater focus on corporate accountability,
- managing public expectations.

The constantly changing nature of today's global economy is not well suited to the cautious, risk-averse entrepreneur. The need for flexibility and the ability to embrace continuous change has introduced a whole new set of challenges for executives around the world as they come under increasing competitive pressure in the global marketplace. These challenges have reshaped the way in which risk is perceived.

Research has shown that many of the organizations that are successful in the constantly changing business environment place a premium on innovation, risk-taking, and entrepreneurship, and strive to develop a "break-through" culture – a culture where ongoing experimentation thrives.

The benefits of prudential risk-taking are clear. Progress – economic or otherwise – implies risk-taking of some kind, to mark a break from convention and change for the better. Not only are there tangible rewards at the end of the process that may come from experimentation and the creation of new products, organizations also benefit from the confidence and experience acquired in the process.

As organizations continue to need to take risks, top management and boards should try to avoid stifling this need by being over-defensive. One very important cost of a risk management approach that focuses on risk elimination when it is not appropriate to do so, is a negative impact on initiative, innovation, and entrepreneurship.

Excessive emphasis on avoiding failure can ultimately lead to failure, because survival of most businesses is dependent on management taking risks in pursuit of opportunities. Risk taking is integral in the process of creating shareholder value.[50]

The main reason for implementing operational risk management should not be to merely defend an organization against hazard risks. Defensive strategies alone – for example, headcount reduction on cost-cutting-exercises – cannot lead to the generation of substantial competitive advantage. Dynamic boards of companies everywhere are revising their values at a strategic level in order to achieve sustainable competitive advantage.

According to PricewaterhouseCoopers,[51] at present, risk management practices at many of the world's largest organizations still tend to be based around a narrow definition of risk, namely, the downside aspects of risk. In recent years, executives in a wide range of diverse sectors including oil, biotechnology, mutual funds, consumer products, and banking have launched major initiatives to improve their approach to the management of risk. These initiatives focus on actively managing risks that must be taken in the pursuit of opportunity and ultimately, profit.

This contrasts with the more traditional notion of risk management which involves protecting the organization from losses through control procedures and hedging techniques.

Different perspectives

From management's perspective, each business risk issue can be viewed from three different perspectives:[52]

■ *Risk as opportunity:* the risk and return trade-off is apparent. Risk as opportunity reflects the outlook of senior management and strategists. Managing risk as an opportunity is an offensive function which necessitates actions taken by management to achieve positive gains. Opportunities can be identified by examining the risks faced by the firm.

■ *Risk as uncertainty:* determine how to be proactive in preventing uncertain future events from having a negative impact. It is the governing perception among the senior CFO team members and line management responsible for sales and operations. Monthly or quarterly targets may not be achieved due to uncertain external or internal events.

■ *Risk as hazard:* associated with compliance and prevention functions such as internal audit, financial controllers, insurance, and security. There needs to be contingency plans in place in the event of adverse events occurring.

Managing the upside risk, in some ways, can be seen as an "offensive" strategy, demanding management decisions designed to exploit opportunities and achieve positive gains. On the other hand, managing the downside risks is often a "defensive" response and covers the prevention or mitigation of hazards arising from failures, incidents, and actions of employees and others that can generate loss.

In some industries, risk taking is prevalent and encouraged, as there is a greater focus on opportunity risks. In many cases, there are formal risk management procedures in place. The extremely dynamic nature of some vertical industries such as entertainment and telecommunications creates great uncertainty and performance pressure. To be successful demands quick action and substantial commitment of resources. Executives now realize that some of the biggest risks they face relate to lost opportunities caused by failure to act quickly and decisively enough.

Formal risk management techniques are harder to develop in other industries. For example, some investment projects with substantial uncertainty of payoffs require the application of real options techniques to assess viability (see Chapter 3 for more on real options).

Whilst senior executives have a natural inclination to be positive-minded about future opportunities, corporate boards and executive committees have a responsibility to ensure that all risk across the continuum is managed prudently. This can only occur if risk is understood, estimated, and reported across the business risk continuum.

Risk is inherent in every business. Although the nature and extent may differ, risk is as applicable to a small retailer as it is to a multinational conglomerate. An organization takes risks in order to pursue opportunities to earn returns for its owners. Striking a balance between risk taking and return is key to maximizing shareholder wealth.

Corporate risk management includes multiple dimensions, as shown in Figure 4.6.

As noted above, many organizations have suffered crises in recent years. However, some of them had highly regarded internal audit, compliance, and legal functions, as well as complex array of control processes. But these control-focused frameworks do not capture the complexity of risk taking and risk management.

In particular, control functions that tend to rely heavily on the use of detailed checklists to determine whether appropriate controls are in place struggle to handle the impact of change, and tend to employ a bottoms-up approach, thus missing the "big-picture" from an enterprise-wide perspective.

Senior management is typically not engaged in the process. And checklist-based approaches are often too static – constantly waiting for the next version to be updated following changes to company policy, law, or control models.

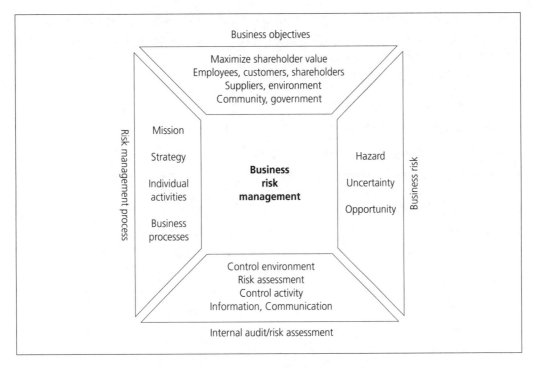

FIGURE 4.6 ■ The multiple dimensions of corporate risk management

The new desire among senior managers to view risk from a holistic, or enterprise-wide perspective is a trend that has developed in the last few years. However, risk integration does not just happen of its own accord. It is invariably the result of deliberate management strategy and execution. Business risk management can be characterized as a form of risk management that realigns the relationship between risk, growth, and return to an organization's advantage.

Risk integration does not just happen of its own accord.

It is important to be pragmatic about the reality of executive business decisions: not all decisions will be correct. Some decisions will, in retrospect, prove to have been wrong. The objective is to minimize the impact of those value-destroying events.

Taking into account areas of uncertainty, a key objective is to ensure that organizations achieve greater consistency in their financial performance. The main goal is not to eliminate risk, therefore, but rather to be proactive in the assessment and management of risk for strategic advantage.

Over the last two decades, organizations in most sectors have found it necessary to embrace a program of almost constant change, encompassing downsizing, business process reengineering, new quality management, mergers and acquisitions activity, outsourcing, and so on. Experience has shown that an organization's exposure to operational risk increases as the rate of change increases. The rate of change itself can alter the risk profile of an organization.

Some of the drivers of change have been:

- introduction of new technology,
- new distribution and delivery channels,
- increasing use of inexperienced temporary staff,
- increasing transaction volumes.

Drivers of shareholder value are:

- sales growth,
- operating profit margin,
- cash tax rate,
- working capital,
- fixed assets,
- cost of capital,
- growth duration period.

Organizations are increasingly dependent on their operational processes being available 24 hours a day, 7 days a week. Even a brief, unplanned outage of a local area network (LAN), for example, can lead to process breakdowns affecting an organization's ability to take customer orders, dispatch goods, or complete credit checks.

One of the goals of operational risk management, therefore, is to ensure greater business continuity. By allowing organizations to keep a stricter rein on their operations and maintain continuity – operational resilience – significant competitive advantages may be gained. Operational resilience is defined as the ability of a business process to adjust or recover quickly from adverse events.

A firm is made up of business units that are comprised of value-adding processes. The business model for operational risk measurement framework uses the value-adding processes of the business unit as the unit of analysis for measuring operational risk. For each value-adding process, an earnings figure is available. But operational risk measurement deals with risk factors that result in losses for the value-adding process, and measures the variability of earnings due to these losses.

Delta – EVT

The measurement methodology of the operational risk framework provides a way of calculating the measures of risk for the factors defined through the business unit analysis. The operational risk measurement methodology is called Delta-EVT™.[53]

Delta-EVT involves the use of two familiar analytical techniques:

■ the delta method and extreme value theory (EVT)

■ the calculation of a threshold.

The process involves estimation of probable losses from known and assignable events using the delta method, and estimation of losses from unassignable random and unlikely events using EVT. Since the assignable losses are generally high frequency events, delta models are able to do a good job of estimation.

In Delta-EVT, EVT is used to deal with the tails of the loss distribution, and to set the minimum loss threshold that defines a minimum large loss. EVT includes a parametric model that, given a series of large losses, can be used to predict the occurrence of losses that have not yet happened.

Low-frequency, high-impact losses are usually unassignable because they are due to rare events or control breakdowns that occur infrequently and seldom repeat.

A large loss due to a particular non-standard risk factor may occur once in several years, and a business unit that had not experienced such a large loss would have no way of measuring the risk. The EVT measurement model is used to address this problem.

Steps for implementing the Delta-EVT method are as follows:[54]

■ Establish the business model with value-adding processes and activities, and any available historical large losses.

■ Determine the risk factors for the major activities in the value-adding processes and their relation to earnings (earnings function).

■ Estimate operational losses using uncertainty of the risk factors propagated to the earnings at risk (EAR), using the delta method.

■ Set the threshold for operating losses from the processes using the risk factor uncertainties and operating losses from the delta method, and filter the large losses using the threshold.

■ Create a set of excess losses greater than the threshold using plausible scenarios based on actual historical losses, external events, and near misses, and model them using EVT.

The delta method can be used to generate the volatility for daily or monthly profit and losses due to operational risk. Using a 99 percent confidence level, three standard deviations would yield a VAR for this operational risk. This is the maximum daily or monthly loss

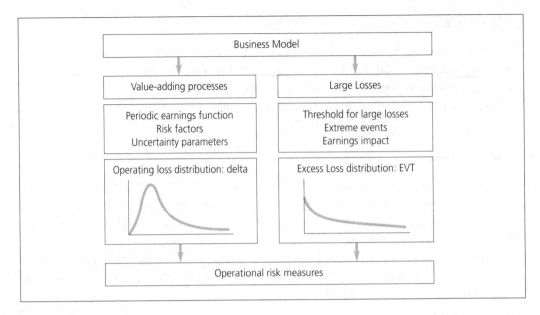

FIGURE 4.7 ■ Operational risk

(P&L impact) due to operational risk. It can be extended to an annual figure by using the 'square root of time' rule.

$$\text{VAR}_{\text{annual}} = \text{VAR}_{\text{monthly}} \sqrt{12}$$

The delta method is based on classic error propagation and can be used to measure the risk in operations due to errors and omissions. The EVT methodology is a multi-period extreme loss model that uses the generalized pareto distribution (GPD) as one of the extreme value distributions to fit losses.

The measures from Delta-EVT are loss measures from the two loss-generating sources – value adding processes and rare events, and includes the following:

■ Excess value at risk (EVAR)

Different from market VAR, operational VAR is based on discrete stochastic processes rather than continuous ones. Operational VAR is generated through the aggregation of two processes: the severity and frequency of operational losses.[55]

> *Operational VAR is based on discrete stochastic processes rather than continuous ones.*

The principle of sub-additivity can be applied to operational risk aggregation. This ensures that the sum of two or more risks should be less than or equal to risks individually. Therefore, the simple sum of individual risk exposures will represent a conservative measure of risk aggregation as it would over-estimate overall risks.

Earnings at Risk (EAR) can be substituted for VAR for corporates that have non-liquid asset portfolios. Probably the most popular approach in performance measurement is the one developed by Bankers Trust (now Deutsche Bank) in the 1980s. It is known as risk adjusted return on capital (RAROC).

RAROC = Risk adjusted return/capital

An alternative measure is the risk adjusted return on risk adjusted capital (RARORAC):

RARORAC = Risk adjusted return/Risk adjusted capital
        = (Net income – Expected losses)/VAR

RARORAC simply adjusts earnings taking into consideration the expected losses, and divides by the risk capital represented by the VAR figure.

An important concept within risk adjusted performance measurement (RAPM) is the marginal RAPM:

Marginal RAPM = change in profit/change in VAR

CASE STUDY 4.16 HSBC[56]

The Hong Kong Shanghai Banking Corporation (HSBC) follows a systematic set of policies regarding operational risk management. Credit risk is the risk that a customer or counterparty will be unable or unwilling to meet a commitment that it has entered into with HSBC. It arises principally from lending, trade finance, treasury, and leasing activities. HSBC has dedicated standards, policies, and procedures to control and monitor all such risks.

HSBC's Group Credit and Risk Management Committee is mandated to provide a high-level centralized management of credit risk for HSBC on a global basis.

Group Credit and Risk is headed by a group general manager who reports to the group chief executive, and its responsibilities include the following.

Formulation of high level credit policies: These are embodied in HSBC standards with which all HSBC subsidiaries are required to comply in formulating their own more detailed credit policies and procedures, which are written in each HSBC subsidiary's dedicated credit policy manuals. The credit policies and procedures are monitored by Group Credit and Risk.

Establishment and maintenance of HSBC's large credit exposure policy: This sets controls at the HSBC level on exposures to customers and customer groups and on other risk concentrations. HSBC's policy, which is designed to be more conservative than the internationally accepted regulatory standards, is required to be adopted by all the banking subsidiaries within HSBC.

Issue of lending guidelines: which provide HSBC subsidiaries with clear guidance on HSBC's attitude towards and appetite for lending to, amongst others, different market sectors, industries, and products. Each HSBC subsidiary and major business unit is required to ▶

produce its own lending guidelines which conform with HSBC guidelines and which are regularly updated and provided to all credit and marketing executives.

An independent review and objective assessment of risk: Group Credit and Risk undertakes an independent assessment of all commercial non-bank credit facilities over designated limits originated by all HSBC's subsidiaries, prior to the facilities being offered to the customer. The business may not proceed without the concurrence of Group Credit and Risk. Similarly, renewals and reviews of commercial non-bank facilities over designated levels are subject to review by and concurrence of Group Credit and Risk.

Control of exposures to banks and financial institutions: HSBC's credit and settlement risk limits to counterparties in the financial and government sectors are approved centrally, to optimize the use of credit availability and to avoid excessive risk concentration. A dedicated unit within Group Credit and Risk controls and manages these exposures on a global basis using centralized systems and automated processes. Full authority is devolved to this unit by the respective HSBC subsidiaries.

Control of cross-border exposures: Control of country and cross-border risk is also managed by a dedicated unit within HSBC Group Credit and Risk using centralized systems, through the imposition of country limits with sub-limits by maturity and type of business. Country limits are determined by taking into account economic and political factors, together with local business knowledge. Transactions with countries deemed to be higher risk are considered on a case-by-case basis.

Control of exposure to certain industries: Group Credit and Risk controls HSBC's exposure to the shipping and aviation industries, and closely monitors exposures to other industries or products such as telecoms and commercial real estate. Controls, such as restrictions on new business or the capping of exposure within HSBC subsidiaries, are introduced where necessary.

Maintenance of HSBC's universal facility grading process: HSBC's grading structure contains seven grades, the first three of which are applied to differing levels of satisfactory risk. Of the four unsatisfactory grades, grades 6 and 7 are non-performing loans. In the case of banks, the grading structure involves nine tiers, five of which cover satisfactory risk. It is the responsibility of the final approving executive to approve the facility grade. Facility grades are subject to frequent review, and amendments, where necessary, are required to be undertaken promptly.

Review of efficiency and effectiveness of subsidiaries' credit approval processes: Regular reports are provided to Group Credit and Risk on the credit quality of the local portfolios and corrective action is taken where necessary. Reporting is also to senior executives on aspects of the HSBC loan portfolio. Reports are produced for senior management, including the Group Executive Committee, Group Audit Committee and the board, covering:

- risk concentrations and exposures to industry sectors,
- large customer group exposures,
- emerging market debt and provisioning,
- large non-performing accounts and provisions,

- specific segments of the portfolio: commercial real estate, telecoms, aviation, shipping, credit cards, as well as ad hoc reviews as necessary,
- country limits and cross-border exposures,
- management and direction of credit-related systems initiatives.

HSBC has a centralized database of large corporate, sovereign, and bank facilities and is currently rolling out a new standard corporate credit application system.

Provision of advice and guidance to HSBC's subsidiaries: In order to promote best practice throughout HSBC, advice is given and procedures approved where necessary on numerous credit-related issues such as:

- regulatory issues,
- environmental policy,
- credit scoring,
- new products,
- training courses,
- credit-related reporting.

In each of HSBC's subsidiaries, local management is responsible for the quality of its credit portfolio. Each major subsidiary has an appointed chief credit officer, who reports to the local CEO, with a functional reporting line to the group general manager, Group Credit and Risk. Each subsidiary has established a credit process involving credit policies, procedures, and lending guidelines conforming with HSBC requirements, and credit approval authorities delegated from the board of directors of HSBC Holdings to the local CEO.

The objective is to build and maintain risk assets of high quality where risk and return are commensurate. Each subsidiary is responsible for the assets in its portfolio, including any subject to central control by Group Credit and Risk, and for managing its own risk concentrations on a market sector, geographical and product basis. Each HSBC subsidiary has systems in place to control and monitor its exposures at the customer and counterparty level.

Special attention is paid to the management of problem loans. Where deemed appropriate, specialist units are established by HSBC subsidiaries to provide intensive management and control in order to maximize recoveries of doubtful debts. Regular audits of subsidiaries' credit processes are undertaken by HSBC's Internal Audit function. Such audits include consideration of the completeness and adequacy of credit manuals and lending guidelines, together with an in-depth analysis of a representative sample of accounts in the portfolio to assess the quality of the loan book and other exposures.

Individual accounts are reviewed to ensure that the facility grade is appropriate, that credit procedures have been properly followed, and that where an account is non-performing, provisions raised are adequate. Internal Audit will discuss any facility grading it considers should be revised at the end of the audit and its subsequent recommendations for revised grades must then be assigned to the facility.

CASE STUDY 4.17 Citigroup[57]

Similar to HSBC, Citigroup has instituted a thorough and systematic risk management structure. At Citigroup, operational risk is defined as the risk of loss resulting from inadequate or failed internal processes, people, or systems, or from external events. It includes reputation and franchise risks associated with business practices or market conduct that the Company may undertake with respect to activities as principal, as well as agent, or through a special purpose vehicle.

The management of operational risk is not new. Businesses have typically managed operational risk as part of their standard business practices. However, management of operational risk has begun to evolve into a distinct discipline with its own risk management structure, tools, and processes, much like credit and market risk.

In February 2002, the Citigroup Operational Risk Policy was issued, codifying the core governing principles for operational risk management and providing the framework to identify, control, monitor, measure, and report operational risks in a consistent manner across the company.

The core operational risk principles, which apply without exception to all of Citigroup's businesses, are:

- senior business managers are accountable for managing operational risk;
- Citigroup has a system of checks and balances in place for operational risk management including an independent operational risk oversight function, reporting to the Citigroup chief risk officer, and an independent audit and risk review function;
- each major Citigroup business segment must have approved business specific policies and procedures for managing operational risk including risk identification, mitigation, monitoring, measurement, and reporting, as well as processes for ensuring compliance with corporate policies and applicable laws and regulations.

The operational risk policy and its requirements facilitate the aggregation of operational risks across products and businesses and promote effective communication of those risks to management, including the Citigroup Risk Management Committee, and Citigroup's board of directors. It also facilitates Citigroup's response to the requirements of emerging regulatory guidance on operational risk.

Credit risk is the potential for financial loss resulting from the failure of a borrower or counter-party to honor its financial or contractual obligation. Credit risk arises in many of the company's business activities including lending activities, sales and trading activities, derivatives activities, and securities transactions settlement activities, and when the company acts as an intermediary on behalf of its clients and other third parties.

The credit risk management process at Citigroup relies on corporate-wide standards to ensure consistency and integrity, with business-specific policies and practices to ensure applicability and ownership. For corporate clients and investment banking activities across the organization, the credit process is grounded in a series of fundamental policies, including:

- ultimate business accountability for managing credit risks;
- joint business and independent risk management responsibility for establishing limits and risk management practices;
- single centre of control for each credit relationship that coordinates credit activities with that client, directly approves or consents to all extensions of credit to that client, reviews aggregate exposures, and ensures compliance with exposure limits;
- portfolio limits, including obligor limits by risk rating and by maturity, to ensure diversification and maintain risk/capital alignment;
- a minimum of two authorized credit-officer signature requirements on extensions of credit – one from a sponsoring credit officer in the business and one from a credit officer in independent credit risk management;
- uniform risk measurement standards, including risk ratings, which must be assigned to every obligor and facility in accordance with Citigroup standards;
- consistent standards for credit origination, measurement, and documentation, as well as problem recognition, classification, and remedial action.

These policies apply universally across corporate clients and investment banking activities. Businesses that require tailored credit processes, due to unique or unusual risk characteristics in their activities, may only do so under a credit program that has been approved by independent credit risk management. In all cases, the above policies must be adhered to, or specific exceptions must be granted by, independent credit risk management.

The current credit exposure arising from derivatives and foreign exchange contracts is represented by the current mark-to-market (i.e. the current cost of replacing all contracts), and is reported as a component of Trading Account Assets. At year-end 2002, Citigroup's current credit exposure arising from derivative and foreign exchange contracts was $37.5bn, after taking into consideration the benefit of legally enforceable master netting agreements, as well as cash collateral posted under legally enforceable margin agreements.

Additionally, for purposes of managing credit exposure on derivative and foreign exchange contracts, particularly when looking at exposure to a single counter-party, Citigroup measures and monitors credit exposure taking into account the current mark-to-market value of each contract plus a prudent estimate of its potential change in value over its life.

This measurement of the potential future exposure for each credit facility is based on a stressed simulation of market rates and generally takes into account legally enforceable risk-mitigating agreements for each obligor such as netting and margining.

Citigroup's credit exposure on derivatives and foreign exchange contracts, including both the mark-to-market and the potential future exposure, is primarily to professional counter-parties in the financial sector, with 74 percent arising from transactions with banks, investment banks, governments and central banks, and other financial institutions. Approximately 90 percent of the exposure is investment grade.

As part of its overall risk management activities, Citigroup makes use of credit derivatives and other risk mitigants to hedge portions of the credit risk in its portfolio, in addition to outright asset sales. The effect of these transactions is to transfer credit risk to creditworthy, independent third parties.

CASE STUDY 4.18 Ericsson[58]

Ericsson evaluates risk exposure on a geographic segment level. Regarding outstanding exposure by region, of its total outstanding customer finance credit exposure as of December 31, 2002, 52 percent related to Latin America (Mexico and Brazil represent 20 percent respectively of the total global exposure), 25 percent to Western Europe, 13 percent to Central and Eastern Europe/Middle East/Africa, 7 percent to Asia/Pacific, and 3 percent to North America.

Ericsson has a significant presence in emerging markets. Customers in these markets frequently request financial support from the company as a result of unavailability of financing from local financial markets or cross-border financing sources. Banks are generally reluctant to bear the risk that political events could prevent customers in these markets from fulfillling their payment obligations.

These political risks are partially mitigated by obtaining risk coverage for Ericsson's financing arrangements from various export credit agencies, regional development banks and institutions such as the World Bank Group, including the Multilateral Investment Guarantee Agency (MIGA) and the International Finance Corporation (IFC).

Financial instruments carry an element of risk in that counterparties may be unable to fulfill their obligations. Ericsson Treasury Services mitigates these risks by investing excess liquidity primarily in government bonds and treasury bills, commercial papers, and corporate bonds, with short-term ratings of at least A-2/P-2 and long-term ratings of at least A. No credit losses were incurred during 2002.

CASE STUDY 4.19 Merrill Lynch[59]

Growth, consistent returns and capital are jeopardized if risk is not controlled. Merrill Lynch's market, credit, and operating risk management framework seeks to reduce volatility in its operating performance and lower its cost of equity by managing risks both within and across businesses.

Merrill Lynch limits its risk profile by diversifying risk and revenue sources, growing fee-based and recurring revenues, and minimising the break-even point by carefully managing fixed costs. Other risk management objectives include focussing its trading activities on client-driven business, limiting proprietary risk-taking, and closely monitoring its long-term exposure to illiquid assets.

Merrill Lynch continuously looks for opportunities to strengthen its worldwide market and credit risk controls, with particular attention to avoiding undue concentrations. At all levels of the organization, Merrill Lynch recognizes that sound corporate governance and oversight policies are critical to effectively managing risk and protecting the interests of shareholders.

CASE STUDY 4.20 DaimlerChrysler[60]

DaimlerChrysler holds a variety of interest rate sensitive assets and liabilities to manage its liquidity and cash needs of the day-to-day operations. A substantial volume of interest rate sensitive assets and liabilities is related to the leasing and sales financing business operated by DaimlerChrysler Services. The leasing and sales financing business enters into transactions with customers which primarily result in fixed-rate receivables. DaimlerChrysler's general policy is to match funding in terms of maturities and interest rates.

However, for a limited portion of the receivables portfolio, the funding does not match in terms of maturities and interest rates. As a result, DaimlerChrysler is exposed to risks due to changes in interest rates.

DaimlerChrysler coordinates operational funding activities of the industrial business and financial services at the group level. It uses interest rate derivative instruments, such as interest rate swaps, forward rate agreements, swaptions, caps and floors, to achieve the desired interest rate maturities and asset/liability structures. Value-at-risk (VAR) figures are calculated for Daimler-Chrysler's 2002 and 2001 portfolio of interest rate sensitive financial instruments.

The company computes the average exposure based on an end-of-quarter basis. In 2002, the average and period-end VAR of Daimler-Chrysler's portfolio of interest rate sensitive financial instruments decreased, primarily due to less volatile interest rates and a reduced mismatch in terms of interest rate maturities between both, the receivables from the Group's leasing and sales financing business and the respective funding of that business.

CASE STUDY 4.21 Toyota[61]

Toyota's sales financing and finance lease receivables consist of retail instalment sales contracts secured by passenger cars and commercial vehicles. Collectability risks include consumer and dealer insolvencies and insufficient collateral values (less costs to sell) to realize the full carrying values of these receivables. As a matter of policy, Toyota maintains an allowance for doubtful accounts and credit losses representing Toyota's management's estimate of the amount of asset impairment in the portfolios of finance, trade, and other receivables.

Toyota determines the allowance for doubtful accounts and credit losses based on a systematic, ongoing review and evaluation of operational risk performed as part of the credit-risk evaluation process, historical loss experience, the size and composition of the portfolios, current economic events and conditions, the estimated fair value and adequacy of collateral, and other pertinent factors.

This evaluation is inherently judgmental and requires material estimates, including the amounts and timing of future cash-flows expected to be received, which may be susceptible to significant change. Although management considers the allowance for doubtful accounts and credit losses to be adequate based on information available, additional provisions may be necessary due to:

- changes in management estimates and assumptions about asset impairment;
- information that indicates changes in the expected future cash-flows; or
- changes in economic and other events and conditions.

A prolonged economic downturn in North America and Western Europe could increase the likelihood of credit losses exceeding original estimates. To the extent that sales incentives remain an integral part of sales promotion with the effect of reducing new vehicle prices, resale prices of used vehicles and, correspondingly, the collateral value of Toyota's sales, financing and finance lease receivables could experience downward pressure. If these factors require a significant increase in Toyota's allowance for doubtful accounts and credit losses, it could negatively affect future operating results of the financial services operations.

CASE STUDY 4.22 Intel[62]

Financial instruments that potentially subject Intel to concentrations of credit risk consist principally of investments in debt securities, derivative financial instruments and trade receivables.

In order to minimize risks, Intel generally places its investments with high-credit-quality counter-parties and, by policy, limits the amount of credit exposure to any one counter-party based on Intel's analysis of that counter-party's relative credit standing.

Intel's investments in debt securities with original maturities of greater than six months consist primarily of A and A2 or better-rated financial instruments and counter-parties. Investments with original maturities of up to six months consist primarily of A1 and P1 or better-rated financial instruments and counter-parties. Government regulations imposed on investment alternatives of Intel's non-US subsidiaries, or the absence of A and A2 rated counter-parties in certain countries, result in some minor exceptions.

Credit-rating criteria for derivative instruments are similar to those for investments. The amounts subject to credit risk related to derivative instruments are generally limited to the amounts, if any, by which a counter-party's obligations exceed the obligations of Intel with that counter-party. At December 28, 2002, Intel's debt investments were placed with approximately 200 different counter-parties. Intel's practice is to obtain and secure available collateral from counter-parties against obligations, including securities lending transactions, whenever Intel deems it appropriate.

A majority of Intel's trade receivables are derived from sales to original equipment manufacturers of computer systems, cellular handsets and handheld computing devices, telecommunications and networking communications equipment, and peripherals. The company's three largest customers accounted for approximately 38 percent of net revenue for 2002, an increase from 35 percent for 2001.

CASE STUDY 4.23 Royal Dutch-Shell[63]

Shell Group's operating companies insure against most major property and liability risks with the Group's captive insurance companies. These companies reinsure part of their major catastrophe risks with a variety of international insurers. The effect of these arrangements is that uninsured losses for any one incident are unlikely to exceed $400m.

Enterprise-wide risk management (EWRM)

The most basic requirement of strategic risk management is a clear policy on the firm's approach to risk: senior management must take a view of the sort of risks they want the firm to manage, and those it will transfer to other parties.

To some extent, the answer will depend on the firm's line of business, and the management would normally want the firm to bear those risks unique to its own particular business. The answer will also depend on the size of the firm's exposures to different risks, and on its capability to handle them.[64]

Enterprise-wide risk management covers the factors shown in Figure 4.8.

Uncertainty abounds in today's economy. Every organization is, to some extent, in the business of risk management. As a business continually changes, so do the risks. Stakeholders increasingly want companies to identify and manage their business risks, so that they can achieve the business goals with high certainty.

The term "risk" includes any event or action that will adversely affect an organization's ability to achieve its business objectives and execute its strategies successfully. Risk management is a strategic tool that can increase profitability and smooth earnings volatility.[65] Senior management must manage the ever-changing risks if they are to create, protect, and enhance shareholder value.

If the firm fails to manage its risks well, its staff will start looking for jobs elsewhere, its suppliers will avoid longer-term commitments, and its customers will look for alternative sources of supply, all of which are obviously detrimental to the firm. The firm therefore needs a good risk management policy and process to protect its core business.[66]

In January 2000, the Financial Executives Institute in the UK released the results of a survey on audit committee effectiveness. Respondents, who were primarily CFOs and

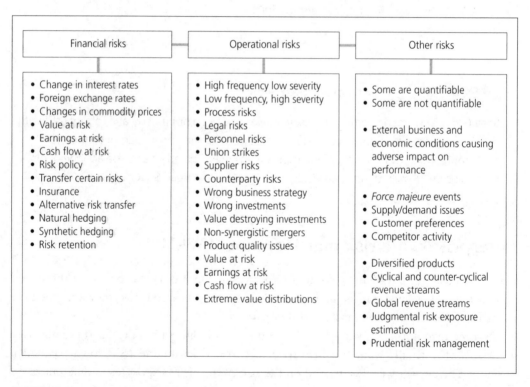

FIGURE 4.8 ■ Enterprise-wide risk management

controllers, ranked "key areas of business and financial risk" as the most important for audit committee oversight.[67]

With the speed of change increasing for all companies in the new economy, senior management must deal with a myriad of complex risks that have substantial consequences for their organizations. These forces include:

- technology and the internet,
- increased worldwide competition,
- freer global trade and investment,
- financial derivative instruments,
- industry deregulation,
- organizational restructuring,
- higher customer expectations,
- shorter business cycles, and
- mergers and acquisitions.

Collectively, these forces are stimulating considerable change and creating an increasingly risky and turbulent business environment. As the internet and e-commerce come of age, companies are rethinking their business models, core strategies, and target customer bases. E-commerce provides businesses with new opportunities as well as more uncertainty and risks.

Historically, risk management in even the most successful companies has tended to be in "silos" – insurance risk, technology risk, financial risk, operational risk, environmental risk – all managed independently in separate compartments. Traditionally, most organizations have viewed risk management as a specialized and isolated activity. Coordination of risk management has usually been nonexistent, and the identification of new risks have been sluggish.[68] A new model, enterprise-wide risk management (EWRM), manages risks in an integrated and coordinated manner for the entire organization.

In the new risk management paradigm, risk management is not fragmented, it is integrated and coordinated across the organization. Risk management is a continuous process, rather than an ad hoc activity according to perceived need. Finally, risk management is more broadly focused on all business risks, rather than narrowly focused only on insurable risks and financial risks.

EWRM takes a structured and disciplined approach that aligns strategy, processes, people, technology, and knowledge, with the purpose of evaluating and managing the uncertainties that could either negatively or positively influence achievement of the organization's objectives. In addition, the Big Five accounting firms have produced documents expounding the value of EWRM.

EWRM takes a structured and disciplined approach.

EWRM defined

EWRM strives to consolidate, integrate, and optimize the corporate risk exposures and their management. Some leading practitioners define EWRM as:

> "… a structured and disciplined approach that aligns strategy, processes, people, technology, and knowledge with the purpose of evaluating and managing the uncertainties the enterprise faces as it creates value…. It is a truly holistic, integrated, forward-looking and process oriented approach managing all key business risks and opportunities – not just financial ones – with the intent of maximizing shareholder value for the enterprise as a whole".[69]

EWRM consolidates the risk management process organizationally. Independent risk management in the form of EWRM plays the role of analyzing aggregate information of institutional risk exposures and policing compliance of actual exposures with predetermined tolerance limits. Leading banks with both lending and derivative portfolios, for example, have independent credit risk management functions so that loans and derivatives transactions with the same counterparty are considered together when the bank's risk exposure to that counterparty is assessed.

For firms that are relatively inactive in derivatives activity, or hold derivatives only to directly offset the exposures of balance sheet liabilities or assets, the treasury can take responsibility for risk management as the independent corporate fiduciary. Pro-active participation of the legal department in the risk management process is important for contractual enforcement and administration of policy compliance.

Risk management and corporate finance are inextricably related, with corporate finance being the backbone of the strategy of risk management. Indeed, the first principles of corporate finance – the Modigliani-Miller (MM) capital structure irrelevance propositions – tell us that value-maximizing firms should not spend money to manage their risks, under certain restrictive assumptions of market efficiency.[70] Unfortunately the MM propositions are only of theoretical interest. In practice, risk management really does help companies protect shareholder value. An important part of building strategic capability is having the right enterprise technology in the risk management process.

In practice, the financial, business, and operating risks are correlated, and not mutually exclusive domains. Corporate risks are best managed if the complete risk profile can be viewed holistically.

This can be likened to the optimal portfolio selection process for equity investments, where stocks are not selected based on individual returns in isolation, but as part of their contribution to the overall portfolio returns and risks. Similarly, corporate risks ought to be looked upon as an overall portfolio of risk exposures forming the integrated enterprise risk profile. The correlations between different risks are such that it is inappropriate to simply add the risk exposures across the different risk categories. For example, VAR levels cannot be summed for different risk variables to derive total risk estimates, as that would, in most cases, over-estimate the overall risk exposures.

The need and desirability of an integrated corporate or enterprise risk management apparatus has been acknowledged for some time now by academics, practitioners, and leading companies such as Chase Manhattan Corp., DuPont, Microsoft Corp., United Grain Growers Ltd., and Unocal Corp. These companies have implemented comprehensive EWRM systems.[71]

Integrated risk management requires quantification of risk exposure and probable financial loss across the different risk classes on a common basis. In other words, if quantification of exchange rate risk of loss is denominated in a currency metric such as VAR, other risks such as interest rate risk should be quantified in the same currency metric, so that overall risk exposure can be assessed on a consistent basis.

While the old paradigm was a silo approach to risk management – with each risk considered in isolation – the new EWRM approach is holistic, integrating the various risks across the organization and designing risk response strategies. Leading companies that are using EWRM such as Chase, Microsoft, Unocal, and DuPont were surveyed by the Financial Executives' Institute (FEI). The results showed that each company believed it was creating, protecting, and enhancing value by managing enterprise-wide risks.

Value can be created, protected, and enhanced by knowing risks, knowing how those risks relate to each other and whether offsets occur, and knowing the risk tolerance level of the company and its stakeholders. Value can also be created, protected, and enhanced by knowing the effect risks have on both financial position and earnings, knowing the probabilities of achieving an earnings goal, and knowing the likelihood and significance level of each risk.

In addition, knowing whether inconsistencies exist across the company in risk management, and knowing whether resources are being efficiently allocated, add value in strategic financial planning and operational execution. Because of the wide variations between companies in terms of operations, culture, risk tolerance, and other unique factors, a cookbook recipe for implementing EWRM is not feasible. It has to be tailored to each business based on its unique characteristics.

To manage effectively in today's business environment, companies should make a formal dedicated effort to identify all their significant risks. Microsoft, for example uses scenario analysis to identify its material business risks. Its Risk Management Group identifies various risk scenarios, initiates the thinking about those scenarios, and emphasizes face-to-face time with individual business units.

This approach allows the Risk Management Group to be aware of "perhaps 90 percent of the risks facing Microsoft" according to Microsoft's treasurer. At Chase, managers at various levels complete self-assessment scorecards to identify their unit's risks. Unocal requires annual risk assessments in each business unit, identifies the areas of greatest risk, and devises steps to manage those risks. Identification of the major risks, ranking them by importance in terms of financial impact along with their chance of occurrence produces the risk map.[72]

In practice, focussing on the low-frequency, high-severity risks is an effective risk management strategy. Microsoft and United Grain Growers (UGG) acknowledge that some risks are just not measurable, due to data availability issues.

VAR and stress testing

The most developed areas for risk measurement are in financial risks, and the most common approaches for measuring and assessing financial risk are VAR and stress testing. VAR was originally developed for use in financial institutions to enable them to assess their capital at risk in different financial market transactions and their risk adjusted rates of return.

The intuitive appeal of this technique is that it is understandable, from a business point of view, since it presents a currency figure to identify risk levels, and therefore is now finding much wider application.

VAR is a currency measure of potential loss from adverse market moves in an everyday market environment. Stress testing examines the worst case scenario. Microsoft, Chase, and DuPont use VAR to assess corporate risks in an EWRM framework. DuPont relies on its risk philosophy to drive risk awareness. A component of this philosophy is the link between risk management and corporate strategy: "The company is expected to manage risks at levels that are consistent with business strategy and not engage in activities that are inconsistent with the corporate financial risk management policy".[73]

As the company's risk exposure is quantified and aggregated in the EWRM process, its risk profile or risk map generates absolute aggregate levels of potential financial loss with their probabilities of occurrence. Transaction-intensive financial firms can rely on a risk concept like VAR to derive intuitively plausible risk exposure measures. However, many non-financial firms find it intractable to reliably aggregate exposures. In practice, it becomes more difficult then, to manage natural business risk exposures using EWRM.

The essence of EWRM is the management of overall institutional risk across all risk categories and business units.[74] Operationalizing an EWRM system for the enterprise requires collaboration among business units, standardization of procedures, and setting up new systems to facilitate both centralized control and centralized risk management. Setting up EWRM systems can therefore involve major upheaval and considerable expense. Nonetheless, firms that have established them are reaping significant benefits.

The degree to which a firm is subject to interest rate risk depends crucially on the capital structure of the firm – the amount of debt the firm issues, and the maturities of those instruments. Determining optimal risk tolerance levels is difficult, and often requires specialized subjective judgment. Analytical techniques help and guide that process. Because risk management is an ongoing process, the risks to which a firm is subject and stakeholders' tolerance for those risks will evolve over time.

The dynamic nature of corporate risk management thus supports the corporate business process over time by anticipating possible adverse impacts and taking appropriate action to avoid them. Most businesses are, in practice, selective risk managers.

Popular measures

In terms of ex post performance measurement, the levels of return or earnings alone do not address the means by which those returns were attained. In the performance assessment process, it is important to identify how much risk was taken to attain those returns. The concept of risk adjusted returns has thus been used as a classical method to evaluate performance. Popular measures to assess risk adjusted returns include return-to-risk ratio, Sharpe ratio, Sortino ratio, and risk adjusted return on capital (RAROC).

The *return-to-risk* ratio uses a statistical measure of risk. It is the ratio of average historical returns to the standard deviation of returns. Here, the return measure could be corporate net income, EBIT, or operating income:

Return-to-risk ratio = Average historical return/Standard deviation of returns

The *Sharpe Ratio* is quite similar to the return-to-risk ratio, and reveals corporate excess returns per unit of risk:

Sharpe ratio = [Average historical return – Average risk-free rate]/ Standard deviation
of returns

The *Sortino ratio* is essentially the same as the Sharpe ratio, but with one important difference – total risk is defined as downside risk only, not overall volatility. It therefore uses downside semi-standard deviation in the denominator:

Sortino ratio = Average excess return/Risk of downside

Where:

Average excess return = Average historical return – Average risk-free rate
Downside risks = Downside semi-standard deviation of returns

The *risk adjusted return on capital (RAROC)* uses the VAR concept to derive a measure of risk exposure called capital at risk (CAR). Its risk adjusted return measure is:

RAROC = Actual net income/Actual capital at risk

We can relate the RAROC measure to economic profit or EVA:

EVA = (RAROC – Cost of capital) × (Total capital)

Where, the cost of capital is the weighted average cost of capital of the company.

Insurance and alternative risk transfer (ART) products are important strategic and tactical risk management tools. Unlike derivatives, insurance is useful primarily for situations in which a firm is concerned about a possible future deviation of actual risks from tolerance levels. In fact, insurance solutions are rapidly evolving toward full integration with derivatives and securitization control solutions.[75]

Selective risk management is a commonly observed feature in well-capitalized firms whose primary business pertains in some way to financial intermediation or risk bearing. For example, one problem with traditional insurance has been disputes over the nature of the insurable interest. A firm seeking unconditional coverage of a potential adverse event can seek a guarantee rather than a traditional insurance policy. In a guarantee, the policy of the insurer is to pay first and ask questions later.

In a guarantee, the policy of the insurer is to pay first and ask questions later.

ART has improved the ability of firms to obtain total risk control solutions from insurance companies. ART refers to any of three recent innovations in insurance markets:

- the development of integrated total risk solutions

- the provision of liquidity and 'finite-risk' facilities, and

- the evolution of alternative sources of financing insurance risk.

Because risks are correlated, "blended layering" allows firms to identify an insurer that will write a "basket policy" covering some blended layer of loss across multiple risk categories.

An EWRM system includes a centralized data warehouse in which to store all position, credit, and transaction data. In addition, analytics are required to process the data into meaningful exposure estimates at the aggregate company level. It is practically very difficult to avoid adding risks together unless we have an integrated approach that takes risk correlations into account.

VAR is most suited to financial institutions that have large portfolios of traded financial instruments that are traded on fairly liquid markets and market to market, so their positions and different exposures are straightforward to value and their profits and losses easy to ascertain.

In contrast, non-financial corporations can also use VAR as a risk estimation methodology even though most corporates have substantial asset holdings that are not traded in organized markets, and therefore cannot be valued by marking to market. By using Monte Carlo simulation as an estimation methodology, VAR risk exposure levels can be identified for corporates.

Cash flow at risk (CFAR)

According to some leading academics and practitioners, a VAR system could be used by non-financial corporates to manage their fixed-income positions, FX positions, derivative positions, credit risks, and liquidity or cash-flow risks.[76] The last is called cash-flow at risk (CFAR). CFAR is the lowest likely cash-flow over a specified period at a chosen confidence level.

Since we are thinking in terms of operating cash-flows, we can also think of CFAR in terms of the risks of missing targets in our business plans.[77] A CFAR system consists of a method of simulating cash-flows based on certain assumptions about underlying risk factors and the sensitivities of cash-flows to those risk factors. A CFAR system can be applied to the firm as a whole and take account of correlations among individual cash-flows.[78] As more multinationals adopt EWRM policies for operating companies to follow, they learn that they must spend more time managing a dynamic business risk profile.

The Basel II Capital Accord

Financial institutions, particularly depository financial institutions, are subject to much more stringent regulatory guidelines compared to non-financial corporates. In the four years since it was introduced by the Basel Committee for Banking Supervision, the Basel II Capital Accord has evolved as a complex set of recommendations for Banks in Europe, the Americas, Asia, and around the globe.

According to a report by KPMG International, the Basel II Accord will likely create a variety of regulatory compliance for banks, resulting in implications for operational risk management.[79] Key areas to be affected are:

■ Banks will be asked to implement an enterprise-wide risk management framework that ties regulatory capital to economic capital.[80]

■ Non-banks outside the scope of Basel II will not face its compliance challenges.

■ Global banks could experience extended trends toward securitization as financial institutions adapt to Basel II requirements.

Jörg Hashagen, head of KPMG's Basel Initiative, expects the complexity of the new Basel II Accord, as well as its interdependencies with International Financial Reporting Standards (IFRS), to make its implementation rather involved.

> "For a bank, a project will be driven by the structure of its business, beginning with its strategy and encompassing its risk management and capital calculation methods, business processes, data requirements, and IT systems. With a structured and disciplined approach, banks can begin to achieve the Basel Committee's intended benefits of enhanced risk management and lower capital requirements. Such changes, in turn, could influence banks' strategies, customer relations, and, over time, their business models."[81]

As the Basel II (2003) Capital Accord is a refinement from the Basel I (1998), the Basel Committee on Banking Supervision moves closer to its goal of aligning banking risks and their management with capital requirements. By redefining how banks worldwide calculate regulatory capital and report compliance to regulators and the public, Basel II is intended to improve safety and soundness in the financial system by placing increased emphasis on banks' own internal control and risk management processes and models, minimum capital requirements (Pillar I), supervisory review (Pillar II) process, and market discipline (Pillar III).

Basel II's three pillars are defined below.[82]

Pillar I sets out minimum regulatory capital requirements – the amount of capital banks must hold against risks at 8 percent of capital-to-risk-weighted-assets. The formula is presented in Figure 4.9.[83]

Pillar II defines the process for supervisory review of an institution's risk management framework and, ultimately, its capital adequacy. It sets out specific oversight responsibilities for the board and senior management, thus reinforcing principles of internal control and other corporate governance practices established by regulatory bodies in various countries worldwide.

Pillar III aims to bolster market discipline through enhanced disclosure by banks. It "sets out disclosure requirements and recommendations in several areas, including the way a bank calculates capital adequacy and its risk assessment methods." Enhanced comparability and transparency are the intended results.

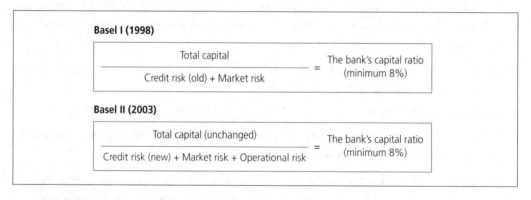

FIGURE 4.9 ■ Calculation of minimum capital requirements

CASE STUDY 4.24 DuPont[84]

DuPont believes that financial risk management must be integrated, and that risk management must be integrated into the business strategies and operations. Although not all risks can be fully integrated enterprise-wide, DuPont realizes that the process of examining risks is portable. Its experience with quantitative measures for financial risk, such as VAR, led it to examine property and casualty insurable risks with a process, examine those risks collectively, and attempt to apply more quantitative analysis to those risks.[85]

DuPont has a corporate policy of retaining significant risks in areas where it has a competitive advantage, for example, managing property and casualty risks. It self insures itself from these risks. DuPont focuses on low-frequency, high-severity risks because those are the ones with the potential to have significant financial impact, while the company manages the high-frequency, low-severity risks quite well.

DuPont did a best practices study and found that while a number of companies were making progress in managing risks, no company felt it had completely achieved the goal.[86]

DuPont uses Measurisk.com, an application service provider for risk exposure analysis, for its risk estimation. In addition to complying with SFAS 133, DuPont is able to calculate and report fair values for derivative instruments and hedged exposures, measure hedge effectiveness, and develop scenarios to view alternative hedging programs.

Risk management is a strategic tool that can increase profitability and smooth earnings volatility, claims vice president and treasurer of DuPont, Susan Stalnecker. The company believes that financial risk management must be integrated into the business strategies and operations.

DuPont conducted a global best practices study and found that while a number of companies were making progress in managing risks, no company felt it had completely achieved that goal. Since VAR is more suitable for financial institutions that have liquid trading portfolios, earnings at risk (EAR) was felt to be more suitable for non-financial corporations that have mostly non-trading illiquid asset portfolios.[87]

DuPont now has EAR estimation capabilities using world-class methods, data, and models. It works with Measurisk.com which provides analytical support. EAR calculates the maximum potential earnings loss, within a certain confidence interval, caused by adverse movements of market factors. EAR allows DuPont to quantify the exposures it faces from risks such as changes in interest rates, currency, or commodity prices. This quantification assesses the effect of these exposures on DuPont's earnings and cash-flow.

SFAS 133 – the US derivatives and hedging reporting accounting standards – will actually help DuPont in several ways. In addition to complying with the new SFAS, DuPont will be able to calculate and report fair values (as required by SFAS) for derivative instruments and hedged exposures, measure hedge effectiveness, and develop scenarios to view alternative hedging programs.

DuPont can quantify EAR for any quarter just from market movements. A benefit of using EAR is better integration or aggregation of risks. DuPont did not want risk to be managed only at a business unit level, because on an enterprize-wide level, the company can have natural offsets. Viewing risks on an enterprize-wide basis using a common metric (EAR) allows DuPont's managers to see offsetting risks, and prevents over- or under-hedging any single position.

Risk exposures are converted into earnings per share at risk. This view allows DuPont's top management to see how each risk element is likely to affect the EPS next quarter of next year. It also demonstrates the effect of any hedging on earnings per share expectations.

Underlying exposure (US$)	Gross EPS at risk (EAR)	Hedged	Net EPS at risk (EAR)
Interest rates	0.03	0.00	0.03
Commodity prices	0.17	0.07	0.10
Currency rates	0.14	0.14	0.00
Net revenue	0.16	0.00	0.16
Total	**0.50**	**0.21**	**0.29**

Figure 4.10 ▥ DuPont's enterprise-wide risk exposure and management

Note that in Figure 4.10 the total risk exposure is US$0.50 per share without any risk mitigation. Management can relate this information to its own risk appetite to determine if this level of EAR per share is acceptable. If management chooses to hedge $0.21 per share, then the remaining exposure is $0.29 per share. The impact can be seen for each risk type. Using this approach, DuPont can manage EAR to a specified level.

A similar approach can be applied to determine the probability that actual earnings will equal expectations. Assume DuPont expected $670m in earnings, but management wanted to know how financial risk would affect that amount. EAR reveals that DuPont is 95 percent confident that earnings will be at least $545m. The difference is due to EAR. Clearly, CFOs, risk management committees and boards can use this information to determine how much risk they are willing to bear.

Monte Carlo simulation of historical earnings can estimate the probability that earnings will fall below the expected $670m. DuPont estimated that all enterprize-wide risks create a 30 percent probability that earnings will fall below the expected level of $640m. This type of information can be invaluable in determining how to manage the enterprize-wide risk profile. It also helps optimize the proportion of risk exposures to be managed proactively via controls or retroactively via hedging instruments, financing and other techniques.

Even for EAR estimation, stress testing is necessary because some statistical techniques are not relevant when considering low frequency, high impact events.

CASE STUDY 4.25 Citigroup[88]

The Citigroup Risk Management framework recognizes the wide range and diversity of global business activities by balancing strong corporate oversight with defined independent risk management functions at the business level. The risk management framework is grounded on the seven principles shown in Figure 4.11, which apply universally across all businesses and all risk types:

The Citigroup chief risk officer, with the assistance of risk management functions at the Citigroup-level, is responsible for:

■ establishing standards for the measurement, approval, reporting and limiting of risk;
■ appointing independent risk managers at the business-level;
■ approving business-level risk management policies;
■ approving business risk-taking authority through the allocation of limits and capital, and
■ reviewing, on an ongoing basis, major risk exposures and concentrations across the organization.

Risks are regularly reviewed with the independent business-level risk managers, the Citigroup Risk Management Committee, and, as appropriate, with the Citigroup board of directors.

The independent risk managers at the business-level are responsible for establishing and implementing risk management policies and practices within their business, while ensuring

Risk management principle	How it is done
1 Integration of business and risk management	Risk management is integrated within the business plan and strategy
2 Risk ownership	All risks and resulting returns are owned and managed by an accountable business unit
3 Independent oversight	Risk limits are approved by both business management and independent risk management groups
4 Policies	All risk management policies are clearly and formally documented
5 Risk identification and measurement	All risks are measured using defined methodologies, including stress testing
6 Limits and metrics	All risks are managed within a limit framework
7 Risk reporting	All risks are comprehensively across the organization

FIGURE 4.11 ■ Seven principles of Citigroup's risk management framework

consistency with Citigroup standards. The business risk managers have dual accountability—to the Citigroup Chief Risk Officer and to the head of their business unit.

The Citigroup Risk Management Committee is chaired by the Citigroup chief risk officer, and its members include senior business and risk managers across the organization. Its objectives include the review of the major risk exposures of Citigroup, particularly those that cut across business lines; the review of current and emerging risk issues; and the ongoing review of the risk management infrastructure, including policies, people and systems. The scope of risks covered includes, but is not limited to:

■ *corporate credit risks* including obligor exposures vis-à-vis limits, risk ratings, industry concentrations, and country cross-border risks;

■ consumer credit risk including product concentrations, regional concentrations, and trends in portfolio performance;

■ counterparty pre-settlement risk in trading activities including distribution and underwriting risks.

Price risks include earnings or the economic impact of changes in the level and volatilities of interest rates, foreign exchange rates and commodity, debt and equity prices on trading portfolios and on investment portfolios. *Liquidity risk* includes funding concentrations and diversification strategy

Risks resulting from the underwriting sale and reinsurance of life insurance policies are also important. Other risks include legal and litigation risks, technology risks, operational risks, and franchise risks. Additional risk exposures may include specific matters identified and reviewed in the audit and risk review process.

At Citigroup, price risk in non-trading portfolios is measured predominantly through EAR and factor sensitivity techniques. These measurement techniques are supplemented with additional tools, including stress testing and cost-to-close analysis.

Business units manage the potential earnings effect of interest rate movements by managing the asset and liability mix, either directly or through the use of derivative financial products. These include interest rate swaps and other derivative instruments that are designated and effective as hedges. The utilization of derivatives is managed in response to changing market conditions as well as to changes in the characteristics and mix of the related assets and liabilities.

EAR is the primary method for measuring price risk in Citigroup's non-trading portfolios (excluding the insurance companies). EAR measures the pre-tax earnings impact of a specified upward and downward instantaneous parallel shift in the yield curve for the appropriate currency assuming a static portfolio.

Citigroup generally measures this impact over a one-year and five-year time horizon under business-as-usual conditions. The EAR is calculated separately for each currency and reflects the repricing gaps in the position as well as option positions, both explicit and embedded. US dollar exposures in the non-trading portfolios are calculated by multiplying the gap between interest sensitive items, including assets, liabilities, derivatives and off-balance-sheet instruments, by 100 basis points.

Non-US dollar exposures are calculated utilizing the statistical equivalent of a 100 basis point change in interest rates and assuming no correlation between exposures in different currencies. Citigroup's primary non-trading price risk exposure is to movements in the US dollar and Mexican peso interest rates.

Citigroup also has EAR in various other currencies; however, there are no significant risk concentrations in any other individual non-US dollar currency. Citigroup estimates the impact to it's pre-tax earnings from a 100 basis point increase or decrease in the US dollar yield curve. As of December 31, 2002, for example, the company estimates that the potential impact on pre-tax earnings over the next 12 months is a decrease of $822m from an interest rate increase and an increase of $969m from an interest rate decrease.

The potential impact on pre-tax earnings for periods beyond the first 12 months is an increase of $460m from an increase in interest rates and a decrease of $380m from an interest rate decrease. The change in EAR from the prior year primarily reflects the change in the asset/liability mix to reflect Citigroup's view of interest rates.

CASE STUDY 4.26 Siemens[89]

Siemens' approach to managing financial market risk is part of its overall enterprise-wide risk management system and begins with its managing board, which has oversight over all of the company's operations. The company CFO sits on this board and has specific responsibility for the financial market risk management organization.

The managing board retains ultimate accountability but for practical business purposes delegates responsibilities to central functions and to the business groups. Specialist departments (at the corporate level and within the operations groups) support the business groups and have responsibility for risk policy setting, risk oversight and developing tools and standards for risk management.

Day-to-day risk management activities are generally conducted at the operational level within the business groups in accordance with policies and procedures established by the specialist departments. Internal Audit regularly reviews the adequacy and efficiency of Siemens' risk management and control systems. The company recognizes that its local managers often have access to timelier business and capital markets intelligence relevant to their respective regional marketplaces. This understanding permits them to identify and rapidly act on opportunities in the local markets for its goods and services as well as in local markets for sources and uses of funds.

▶

Siemens therefore entrusts the management of its various business groups with a certain degree of decision-making flexibility, within clearly defined limits, regarding interest rate and foreign exchange risk positions. For example, each business group has in place carefully structured foreign exchange risk origination and hedging guidelines that conform to a model policy developed by the corporate finance department. These policies apply equally to all of its business groups including both operations groups and Siemens Financial Services. The actions of the business groups are regularly audited to ensure compliance with the risk management policies and other standard business controls.

CASE STUDY 4.27 Merrill Lynch[90]

Risk-taking is an integral part of Merrill Lynch's core business activities. In the course of conducting its business operations, Merrill Lynch is exposed to a variety of risks including market, credit, liquidity, operational, and other risks that are material and require comprehensive controls and ongoing management.

The responsibility and accountability for these risks remain primarily with the businesses. The Corporate Risk Management (CRM) group, along with other control units, works to ensure that these risks are properly identified, monitored, and managed throughout Merrill Lynch. To accomplish this, CRM has established a risk management process, which includes:

- a formal risk governance organization that defines the oversight process and its components;
- a regular review of the entire risk management process by the Audit Committee of the board of directors;
- clearly defined risk management policies and procedures supported by a rigorous analytical framework;
- communication and coordination between the business, executive, and risk functions while maintaining strict segregation of responsibilities, controls, and oversight; and
- clearly articulated risk tolerance levels as defined by a group composed of executive management which are regularly reviewed to ensure that Merrill Lynch's risk taking is consistent with its business strategy, capital structure, and current and anticipated market conditions.

The risk management process, combined with CRM's personnel and analytic infrastructure, work to ensure that Merrill Lynch's risk tolerance is well-defined and understood by the firm's businesses as well as by its executive management. Other groups, including Corporate Audit, Finance, Legal and Treasury, work with CRM to establish and maintain this overall risk management control process. While no risk management system can ever be absolutely complete, the goal of CRM is to make certain that risk-related losses occur within acceptable, predefined levels.

Merrill Lynch's risk governance structure is comprised of the Audit Committee, the Management Group, the Risk Oversight Committee (ROC), the business units, CRM, and various corporate governance committees.

The Audit Committee is comprised entirely of external directors and has authorized the ROC to establish Merrill Lynch's risk management policies. The Management Group establishes risk tolerance levels for the firm and authorizes material changes in Merrill Lynch's risk profile. This group also ensures that the risks assumed by Merrill Lynch are managed within these tolerance levels and verifies that Merrill Lynch has implemented appropriate policies for the effective management of risks. The Management Group must approve all substantive changes to risk policies, including those proposed by the ROC. The Management Group pays particular attention to risk concentrations and liquidity concerns.

The ROC, comprised of senior business and control managers, and currently chaired by the Chief Financial Officer, oversees Merrill Lynch's risks and ensures that the business units create and implement processes to identify, measure, and monitor their risks. The ROC also assists the Management Group in determining risk tolerance levels for the firm's business units and monitors the activities of Merrill Lynch's corporate governance committees, reporting significant issues and transactions to the Management Group and the Audit Committee. Various other governance committees exist to create policy, review activity, and ensure that new and existing business initiatives remain within established risk tolerance levels.

Corporate Risk Management (CRM) is an independent control function responsible for Merrill Lynch's market and credit risk management processes both within and across the firm's business units. The co-heads of CRM report directly to the CFO who chairs the ROC and is a member of the Management Group. Market risk is defined to be the potential change in value of financial instruments caused by fluctuations in interest rates, exchange rates, equity and commodity prices, credit spreads, and/or other risks.

Credit risks are defined to be the potential for loss that can occur as a result of impairment in the creditworthiness of an issuer or counterparty, or a default by an issuer or counterparty on its contractual obligations. CRM also provides Merrill Lynch with an overview of its risk for various aggregate portfolios and develops and maintains the analytics, systems, and policies to conduct all risk management functions.

CRM's chief monitoring and risk measurement tool is Merrill Lynch's Risk Framework. The Risk Framework defines and communicates Merrill Lynch's risk tolerance and establishes aggregate and broad risk limits for the firm. Market risk limits are intended to constrain exposure to specific asset classes, market risk factors, and VAR.

Credit risk limits are intended to constrain the magnitude and tenor of exposure to individual counterparties and issuers, types of counterparties and issuers, countries, and types of financing collateral. Risk framework exceptions and violations are reported and investigated at pre-defined and appropriate levels of management.

CASE STUDY 4.28 Microsoft[91]

Microsoft is exposed to foreign currency, interest rate, and equity price risks. A portion of these risks is hedged, but fluctuations could impact Microsoft's results of operations and financial position. Microsoft hedges the exposure of accounts receivable and a portion of anticipated revenue to foreign currency fluctuations, primarily with option contracts.

The company monitors its foreign currency exposures daily to maximize the overall effectiveness of its foreign currency hedge positions. Principal currencies hedged include the euro, Japanese yen, British pound, and Canadian dollar. Fixed income securities are subject to interest rate risk. The portfolio is diversified and consists primarily of investment grade securities to minimize credit risk.

Microsoft routinely uses options to hedge its exposure to interest rate risk in the event of a catastrophic increase in interest rates. Many securities held in the Company's equity and other investments portfolio are subject to price risk. Microsoft uses options to hedge its price risk on certain highly volatile equity securities.

Microsoft uses a VAR model to estimate and quantify its market risks. The VAR model is not intended to represent actual losses in fair value, but is used as a risk estimation and management tool. The model used for currencies and equities is geometric Brownian motion, which allow incorporation of optionality of these exposures. For interest rates, the mean reverting geometric Brownian motion is used to reflect the principle that fixed-income securities prices over time revert to maturity value.

VAR is calculated by, first, simulating 10,000 market price paths over 20 days for equities, interest rates, and foreign exchange rates, taking into account historical correlations among the different rates and prices. Each resulting unique set of equities prices, interest rates, and foreign exchange rates is applied to substantially all individual holdings to reprice each holding. The 250th worst performance (out of 10,000) represents the VAR over 20 days at the 97.5th percentile. Several risk factors are not captured in the model, including liquidity risk, operational risk, credit risk, and legal risk.

A substantial amount of Microsoft's equity portfolio is held for strategic purposes. The company attempts to hedge the value of these securities through the use of derivative contracts such as collars.

The company has incurred substantial impairment charges related to certain of these securities in fiscal 2002 and fiscal 2001. Such impairment charges have been incurred primarily for strategic equity holdings that the company has not been able to hedge.

The VAR amounts are used as a risk management tool and reflect an estimate of potential reductions in fair value of the company's portfolio. Losses in fair value over a 20-day holding period can exceed the reported VAR by significant amounts and can also accumulate over a longer time horizon than the 20-day holding period used in the VAR analysis.

The VAR numbers are shown separately for interest rate, currency, and equity risks. These VAR numbers include the underlying portfolio positions and related hedges. Historical data is used to estimate VAR. Given reliance on historical data, VAR is most effective in estimating risk exposures in markets in which there are no fundamental changes or shifts in market conditions.

An inherent limitation in VAR is that the distribution of past changes in market risk factors may not produce accurate predictions of future market risk.

Figure 4.12 sets forth the VAR calculations for substantially all of Microsoft's positions.

The total VAR for the combined risk categories is $908m at June 30, 2002 and $759m at June 30, 2001. The total VAR is 34 percent less at June 30, 2002 and 19 percent less at June 30, 2001 than the sum of the separate risk categories for each of those years in Figure 4.12, due to the diversification benefit of the combination of risks. The reasons for the change in risk in portfolios include:

■ larger investment portfolio size,
■ higher foreign exchange exposure due to stronger non-US currencies, and
■ asset allocation shifts.

| US$ millions | As of June 30, | | Year ended June 30, 2002 | | |
Risk categories	2001	2002	Average	High	Low
Interest rates	$363	$472	$435	$535	$333
Currency rates	58	310	162	310	58
Equity prices	520	602	584	757	488

Figure 4.12 ■ VAR calculations – Microsoft

CASE STUDY 4.29 Ericsson[92]

Ericsson's enterprise-wide risk management is governed by a policy approved by its board of directors. The Finance Committee of the board is responsible for the continuous monitoring of its financial exposures and for approving certain matters regarding investments, loans, guarantees, and customer financing commitments.

Internally, the Corporate Treasury and Corporate Customer Finance functions manage financial risks and the group's financial assets and liabilities, and issue policies governing consolidated companies. The Corporate Treasury function's principal role is to ensure that the group has sufficient financing in place through loans and committed credit arrangements, to actively manage the group's liquidity as well as financial assets and liabilities, and to manage and control financial exposures in a manner consistent with underlying business risks and financial policies.

Ericsson Treasury Services has established treasury centres in Stockholm, Dublin, Singapore and Dallas, for cash management and handling of hedging activities. The major part of the risks assumed by Ericsson Treasury Services are hedged in the financial markets, but it may also take positions in the financial markets within the framework of the policy established by the board of directors.

The risk mandate, SEK200m, is based on a five percent change in exchange rates against the total foreign exchange position and a one percentage point change in interest rate. As of December 31, 2002, the market risk amounted to SEK116m. This is also complemented by a VAR calculation given a confidence level of 99 percent and a one-day horizon.

Ericsson's Corporate Customer Finance function's main objective is to find suitable third-party financing solutions for its customers and to minimize recourse to Ericsson. The Corporate Customer Financing function operates in all market areas to support the business in the early stages of negotiations. To the extent customer loans are not immediately provided by banks, the consolidated subsidiary Ericsson Credit AB manages the bulk of Ericsson's own outstanding vendor credits. The exposure from outstanding vendor loans and credit commitments are monitored centrally by the Corporate Customer Finance function.

CASE STUDY 4.30 DaimlerChrysler[93]

DaimlerChrysler has an enterprise-wide risk management (EWRM) system. It is an integrated risk management system which produces an enterprize-wide risk exposure status report called risk report, detailing a real-time corporate risk exposure profile, adequately detailed at the different risk classes.

Within the framework of their global activities and as a result of the increasingly intense competition in all markets, the business units of the DaimlerChrysler Group are exposed to a great number of risks, which are inextricably linked with corporate business.

Effective management and control instruments, combined within a uniform risk management system which is continuously improved, are deployed for the early detection, evaluation and management of risks. The risk management system is an integral part of the overall planning, control and reporting process in all relevant legal units and central functions. It is aimed at the systematic detection, assessment, controlling, and documentation of risks. Taking defined risk categories into account, risks are identified by management of the business units and segments, and the key associated companies, and assessed with respect to the likelihood of occurrence and the possible extent of damage.

The communication and reporting of relevant risks is controlled by value limits set by management. Within the framework of risk management, measures are developed and initiated as required to avoid, reduce and prevent risks. The key risks are monitored in the framework of risk monitoring. The aim of the group's risk management system is to enable corporate management to identify key risks at an early stage and initiate counter measures.

Compliance with uniform group guidelines, as defined in a risk management manual applicable for the entire group, is checked by the internal audit department. In addition, external auditors test the early risk detection system integrated into the risk management system for its fundamental suitability for early detection of developments that could jeopardise the continued existence of the company.

To manage and control the group as a whole and its business units, DaimlerChrysler employs modular and closely integrated management tools. The implemented control system with its performance standards promotes cross-divisional transparency and comparability as well as capital market-oriented investment control within the DaimlerChrysler Group.

CASE STUDY 4.31 HSBC[94]

All of HSBC's activities involve analysis, evaluation, and management of some degree of risk or combination of risks. The most important types of risk are credit risk (which includes cross-border risk), liquidity risk, market risk, and operational risk. Market risk includes foreign exchange, interest rate, and equity price risks.

HSBC's risk management policy is designed to identify and analyze credit risk, liquidity and market risk, operational risk and other risks, to set appropriate risk limits, and to monitor these risks and limits continually by means of reliable and up-to-date administrative and information systems.

HSBC continually modifies and enhances its risk management policies and systems to reflect changes in markets and products. Training, individual responsibility and accountability, and a disciplined cautious and conventional culture of control lie at the heart of HSBC's management of risk.

The Group Executive Committee, comprising executive directors and group general managers appointed by the board of directors, formulates risk management policy, monitors risk, and regularly reviews the effectiveness of HSBC's risk management policies.

CASE STUDY 4.32 Procter & Gamble[95]

As a multinational company with diverse product offerings, Procter & Gamble is exposed to market risks, such as changes in interest rates, currency exchange rates, and commodity pricing.

To manage the volatility related to these exposures, Procter & Gamble evaluates exposures on a consolidated basis to take advantage of logical exposure netting. For the remaining exposures, the company enters into various derivative transactions in accordance with Procter & Gamble's policies in areas such as counterparty exposure and hedging practices.

Derivative transactions are accounted for under SFAS 133, Accounting for Derivative Instruments and Hedging Activities, as amended and interpreted. Procter & Gamble does not hold or issue derivative financial instruments for speculative trading purposes.

At inception, Procter & Gamble formally designates and documents the financial instrument as a hedge of a specific underlying exposure. The company formally assesses, both at inception and at least quarterly on an ongoing basis, whether the financial instruments used in hedging transactions are effective at offsetting changes in either the fair value or cash-flows of the related underlying exposure. Fluctuations in the derivative value generally are offset by changes in the fair value or cash-flows of the exposures being hedged. This offset is driven by the high degree of effectiveness between the exposure being hedged and the hedging instrument. Any ineffective portion of an instrument's change in fair value is immediately recognized in earnings.

Procter & Gamble has established strict counterparty credit guidelines and normally enters into transactions with investment grade financial institutions. Counterparty exposures are monitored daily and downgrades in credit rating are reviewed on a timely basis. Credit risk arising from the inability of a counterparty to meet the terms of the company's financial instrument contracts generally is limited to the amounts, if any, by which the counterparty's obligations exceed the obligations of the company. The company does not expect to incur material credit losses on its risk management or other financial instruments.

Procter & Gamble's policy is to manage interest cost using a mix of fixed-rate and variable-rate debt. To manage this risk in a cost-efficient manner, the company enters into interest rate swaps in which it agrees to exchange, at specified intervals, the difference between fixed and variable interest amounts calculated by reference to an agreed upon notional principal amount.

Interest rate swaps that meet specific conditions under SFAS 133 are accounted for as fair value hedges. Accordingly, the changes in the fair value of these agreements are immediately recorded in earnings. The mark-to-market values of both the fair value hedging instruments and the underlying debt obligations are recorded as equal and offsetting gains and losses in the interest expense component of the income statement. The fair value of the company's interest rate swap agreements was $322 at June 30, 2003 and $231 at June 30, 2002. All existing fair value hedges are 100 percent effective. As a result, there is no impact to earnings due to hedge ineffectiveness.

Procter & Gamble manufactures and sells its products in a number of countries throughout the world and, as a result, is exposed to movements in foreign currency exchange rates. The purpose of the company's foreign currency hedging program is to reduce the risk caused by short-term changes in exchange rates. Procter & Gamble primarily utilizes forward exchange contracts and purchased options with maturities of less than 18 months and currency swaps with maturities up to five years. These instruments are intended to offset the effect of exchange rate fluctuations on forecasted sales, inventory purchases, intercompany royalties and intercompany loans denominated in foreign currencies. The company also utilizes the same instruments for purposes that do not meet the requirements for hedge accounting treatment. In these cases, the change in value of the instruments offsets the foreign currency impact of intercompany financing transactions, income from international operations and other balance sheet revaluations.

Procter & Gamble hedges its net investment position in major currencies and generates foreign currency interest payments that offset other transactional exposures in these currencies. To accomplish this, the company borrows directly in foreign currency and designates a portion of foreign currency debt as a hedge of net investments in foreign subsidiaries. In addition, certain foreign currency swaps are designated as hedges of the company's related foreign net investments.

EAR and CFAR estimation

Cash-flow at risk (CFAR) is the general term used to describe models which quantify the underlying risks of an enterprise, and express these risks as a maximum loss of an objective measure at a given probability. The objective measure is generally some common, intuitive measure, such as cash-flow, EBIT, earnings per share, or net equity. The model output is the probability density function for EBIT, from which maximum losses at various probabilities can be observed.

Although calculation methodologies are not uniform, there are standard practices that are widely observed. EAR and CFAR are talked about a lot, but are not widely implemented. There is little uniformity in implementation because the underlying models are necessarily company and balance sheet specific. The cash-flows and balance sheet of an airline, for example, will have little in common with those of a construction company or bank.

EAR and CFAR are talked about a lot, but are not widely implemented.

EAR calculates the maximum potential earnings loss, with a certain probability, caused by the adverse movements of market factors. A comprehensive EAR estimation would individually value each derivative position and aggregate the risk exposures by adjusting for risk correlations. Market factors that can cause earnings volatility are interest rates, exchange rates, commodity prices, etc. This quantification assesses the effect of these exposures on earnings or cash-flows from operations.

DuPont quantifies EAR in any given quarter just from market movements. To do so, it looks at all cash-flows within an identifiable market risk factor and aggregates exposures to validate any natural offsets. Then simulations are run integrating market factors, volatilities, and correlations, to see how they could potentially impact earnings. Risk exposure optimization is achieved when the EAR is at a level which the management team is comfortable with.

Since we do not have publicly available information that is detailed enough about a company's derivative positions, we define EAR in a more simplistic way. We define EAR as the threshold earnings level which would be exceeded per period with a 95 percent probability. Alternatively, earnings would be less than this amount per period with a 5 percent probability. The earnings shortfall therefore is the difference between the targeted earnings per period and the EAR, with a 5 percent probability.

EXAMPLE

In the this example we collect the previous 36 months of earnings data for XYZ Corp. and use *Palisades'* BestFit analytical software to determine the appropriate probability distribution for the earnings data.

The data is presented in Figure 4.13.

XYZ Corp.

Month	Normalized Earnings ($M)	Month	Normalized Earnings ($M)
Jan-01	25	Jul-02	48
Feb-01	30	Aug-02	51
Mar-01	43	Sep-02	33
Apr-01	44	Oct-02	10
May-01	48	Nov-02	−5
Jun-01	38	Dec-02	−10
Jul-01	32	Jan-03	0
Aug-01	45	Feb-03	20
Sep-01	36	Mar-03	40
Oct-01	47	Apr-03	29
Nov-01	44	May-03	66
Dec-01	50	Jun-03	33
Jan-02	52	Jul-03	8
Feb-02	53	Aug-03	33
Mar-02	50	Sep-03	26
Apr-02	47	Oct-03	21
May-02	46	Nov-03	14
Jun-02	46	Dec-03	46

XYZ Corp.: Data analysis for EAR

	Fit	Input
Function	33.191	N/A
Shift	N/A	N/A
min	−15.860	N/A
m.likely	47.000	N/A
max	68.433	N/A
Minimum	−15.860	−10.000
Maximum	68.433	66.000
Mean	33.191	34.417
Mode	47.000	33.000 [est]
Median	35.612	39.000
Std. Deviation	17.886	17.685
Variance	319.894	304.076
Skewness	−0.417	−0.866
Kurtosis	2.400	3.132

FIGURE 4.13 ■ Determining the appropriate probability distribution

XYZ Corp.'s monthly earnings for the previous three years follow a triangular distribution, as shown in Figure 4.14.

The left tail of the distribution gives us the 5 percent probability area for EAR calculations, which shows a 5 percent probability that earnings will fall below $0.42m per quarter.

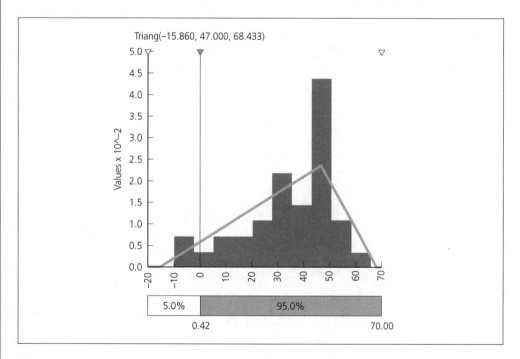

FIGURE 4.14 ■ Triangular distribution

EXAMPLE

In this example, we calculate the EAR for DaimlerChrysler Corp. The earnings data for 18 quarters are presented in Figure 4.15.

DaimlerChrysler Corp.

Quarter	Normalized Earnings (EUR Billion)
2Q03	€ 0.109
1Q03	€ 0.588
4Q02	€ 0.327
3Q02	€ 0.780
2Q02	€ 1.108
1Q02	€ 2.503
4Q01	−€ 0.039
3Q01	€ 1.103
2Q01	€ 0.731
1Q01	−€ 2.357
4Q00	−€ 0.299
3Q00	€ 0.327
2Q00	€ 1.748
1Q00	€ 1.705
4Q99	€ 1.615
3Q99	€ 1.511
2Q99	€ 1.474
1Q99	€ 1.626

FIGURE 4.15 ▪

Based on the Chi-squared, the Kolmogorov-Smirnov, and the Anderson-Darling tests, the logistic distribution was the best fit to the normalized earnings data as shown in Figure 4.16.

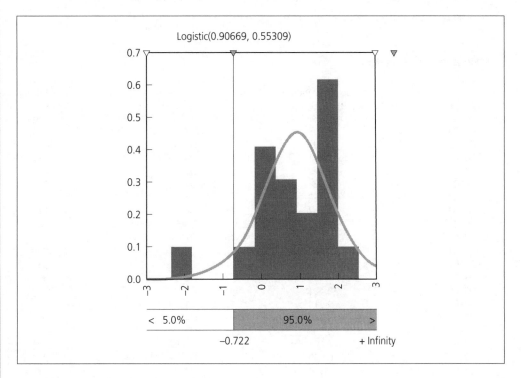

FIGURE 4.16 ■ Logistic distribution as best fit

The quarterly EAR for DaimlerChrysler is €722m, since there is a 5 percent probability that earnings will fall below €722m.

EXAMPLE

In this example, we calculate the EAR for Microsoft Corporation using 60 quarters of annualized trailing 12-month normalized earnings data (see Figure 4.17).

Microsoft Corp. ($ million)

Quarter	Trailing 12-month normalized earnings	Quarter	Trailing 12-month normalized earnings
Q4–03	9,993	Q2–96	1,838
Q3–03	9,597	Q1–96	1,636
Q2–03	9,541	Q4–95	1,453
Q1–03	9,272	Q3–95	1,447
Q4–02	7,829	Q2–95	1,307
Q3–02	6,369	Q1–95	1,223
Q2–02	6,082	Q4–94	1,146
Q1–02	6,423	Q3–94	1,049
Q4–01	7,345	Q2–94	1,036
Q3–01	9,689	Q1–94	983
Q2–01	9,624	Q4–93	953
Q1–01	9,436	Q3–93	898
Q4–00	9,421	Q2–93	834
Q3–00	9,214	Q1–93	773
Q2–00	8,746	Q4–92	708
Q1–00	8,293	Q3–92	637
Q4–99	7,785	Q2–92	582
Q3–99	6,940	Q1–92	520
Q2–99	6,360	Q4–91	463
Q1–99	5,510	Q3–91	404
Q4–98	4,490	Q2–91	355
Q3–98	4,190	Q1–91	316
Q2–98	3,895	Q4–90	279
Q1–98	3,503	Q3–90	245
Q4–97	3,454	Q2–90	211
Q3–97	2,956	Q1–90	184
Q2–97	2,476	Q4–89	171
Q1–97	2,310	Q3–89	155
Q4–96	2,195	Q2–89	152
Q3–96	2,004	Q1–89	140

FIGURE 4.17 ▪

Based on chi-squared distribution fitting criterion, the inverse Gaussian distribution has the best fit and shows a 5 percent probability that Microsoft's normalized annual earnings will fall below $200m (see Figure 4.18).

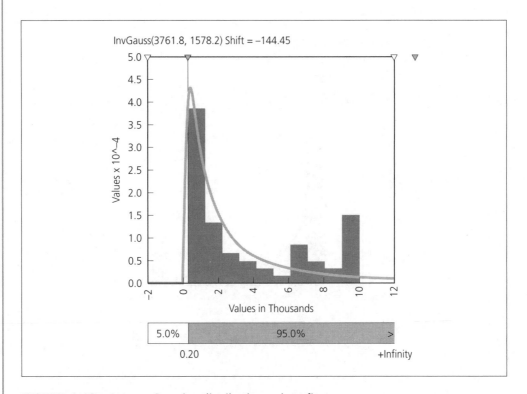

FIGURE 4.18 ■ Inverse Gaussian distribution as best fit

However, for the Microsoft normalized earnings data, based on the Anderson-Darling distribution fitting criterion, the log-normal distribution has the best fit and shows an EAR of $210m per annum, with a 5 percent probability (see Figure 4.19).

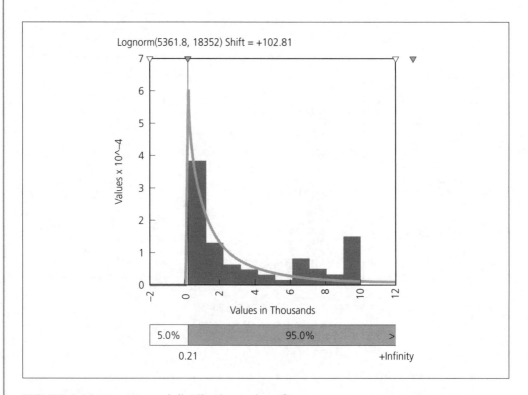

FIGURE 4.19 ■ Log-normal distribution as best fit

Based on the Kolmogorov-Smirnov distribution fitting criterion, we find that the Beta-general distribution has the best fit with a $150m EAR per annum for Microsoft, at a 5 percent probability (see Figure 4.20).

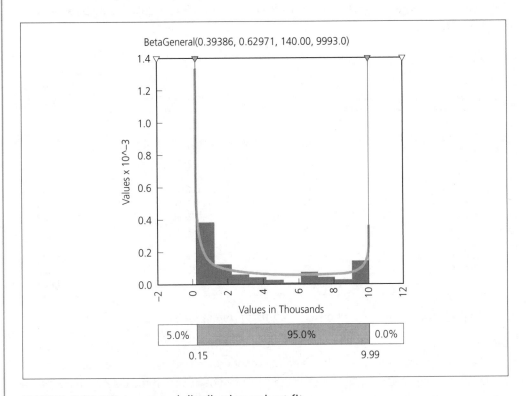

FIGURE 4.20 ■ Beta-general distribution as best fit

We therefore conclude that there is a 5 percent probability that Microsoft's earnings will fall below $150 to $210 m per quarter. The Earnings at Risk per quarter of the earnings shortfall will be the difference between the projected earnings and the actual earnings.

EXAMPLE	

In this example, we estimate the (CFAR of Royal Dutch/Shell Group of companies. The company's reported quarterly cash-flow from operations for 26 quarters are presented in Figure 4.21.

Royal Dutch/Shell Corp. ($m)

Quarter	Cash flow from operations	Quarter	Cash flow from operations
Q2–03	5,425	Q1–00	3,859
Q1–03	6,688	Q4–99	4,579
Q4–02	4,398	Q3–99	2,430
Q3–02	5,604	Q2–99	2,164
Q2–02	3,152	Q1–99	1,886
Q1–02	3,211	Q4–98	5,693
Q4–01	4,171	Q3–98	2,896
Q3–01	3.534	Q2–98	2,824
Q2–01	4,539	Q1–98	3,316
Q1–01	4,689	Q4–97	2,930
Q4–00	6,184	Q3–97	6,171
Q3–00	4,097	Q2–97	3,546
Q2–00	4,219	Q1–97	4,083

FIGURE 4.21 ■ Reported quarterly cash flow from operations

Since the cash-flow from operations data are not normalized, and include one-time non-recurring items, the volatility is higher than it would have been if the data were normalized.

According to the chi-squared distribution fitting criterion, the extreme value distribution is the best fit and presents a 5 percent probability that cash-flow from operations will be less than $2.27bn per quarter. If the projected cash-flow from operations is $5.50bn, then the CFAR is approximately $3.23bn with a 5 percent probability level (see Figure 4.22).

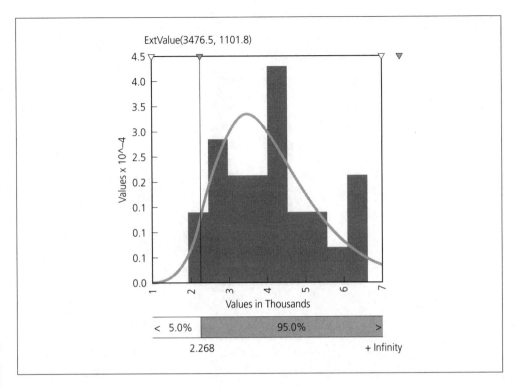

FIGURE 4.22 ■ Extreme value distribution as best fit

According to both the Anderson-Darling and the Kolmogorov-Smirnov distribution fitting criteria, the Weibull distribution is the best fit and presents a 5 percent probability that cash-flow from operations will be less than $2.24bn (see Figure 4.23).

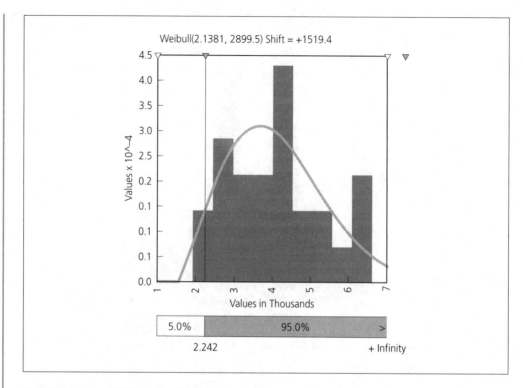

FIGURE 4.23 ■ Weibull distribution a best fit

Risk hedging strategies

Financial contracts are intended to hedge the financial market risk exposures of the business from potential negative impact on cash-flow, earnings, and equity prices.

Derivatives are powerful instruments at the CFO's disposal that allow the restructuring of the corporate risk profile in an efficient manner. They allow companies to transfer unwanted risks optimally to those parties that are willing to take them on. Hedging techniques basically allow a company to take offsetting positions to an existing exposure, so that the uncertainty of adverse payoffs can be minimized.[96]

Dealing in derivative financial instruments is a significant part of capital market activity globally. Derivatives allow companies and investors to transfer and acquire risks synthetically; they also enable banks and other financial institutions to manage the risks incurred in their normal operations, such as balance sheet lending.

Financial derivatives have revolutionized global capital markets. The emergence of substantial markets in forwards/futures, options, swaps, and other derivative financial instruments (DFIs) have altered the conduct of financial management and investment activities substantially. The significant economic benefits of DFIs are that they:[97]

■ permit the unbundling of, and trading in, risk attributes;

■ have the ability to hedge price risks, and synthesize investments with greater efficiency and lower costs;

■ increase the liquidity of and encourage trading in financial assets.

The current size of the global derivatives markets is very large, and the markets continue to grow strongly. Current trends include the development of products to unbundle new types of risk such as credit and insurance to facilitate trading and hedging in these assets.

DFIs are generally utilized for a number of purposes:

■ hedging,

■ synthetic asset exposure,

■ speculation,

■ arbitrage.

Hedging entails the use of derivatives to transfer the risk of the underlying asset to eliminate the exposure to price movements.

Synthetic asset exposure entails the use of derivatives to acquire exposure to the price fluctuation in the underlying asset without the necessity of investing in the underlying asset itself.

Speculation involves using derivatives to acquire exposure to price fluctuations. Derivative contracts are not inherently speculative, but are capable of being used to take positions in anticipation of price changes.

Arbitrage involves using derivatives to exploit price discrepancies between the asset or cash markets. The objective is to lock in profits on a risk-free basis.

In practice, both hedging and synthetic asset exposure applications constitute the major use of DFIs.

All financial contracts have potential cash-flow impacts. However, depending on their accounting treatment, the book impact is deferred, amortized, or accounted for at a future date in the income statement or the balance sheet equity. Regardless of the accounting treatment, the net economic exposure is the same, except for differences caused by the timing of the tax impact.

Financial instruments, such as forward and option contracts on currencies, can effectively alter the currency risk associated with the underlying asset, liability, or planned future transaction. Similarly, interest rate swaps, caps, and forward rate agreements (FRAs) can alter the risk between fixed- and floating-rate transactions.

Other instruments, such as cross-currency interest rate swaps, impact both currency and interest rate risks. Depending on the accounting treatment of these financial contracts, they may be measured through a mark-to-market process and reflected in the income statement.

These derivatives are being utilized to tailor existing financial exposures so that they have more desirable properties and payoff structures. Changing relationships between corporates and providers of financial derivatives are driving the biggest changes in the way derivative products are packaged.

Investors pointing accusing fingers are just about the last thing any corporate needs right now. So when Warren Buffett, whose rare pronouncements can have a profound effect on the investment community, warns against the use of derivatives there is bound to be an unwelcome impact for those corporate treasurers willing to embrace them.[98]

Growing fears over risk have led many corporates to take a conservative stance toward hedging. Most leading corporations actually have a corporate policy of not trading financial derivatives for speculative purposes, and prohibit their treasuries to operate as a profit centre.

Add to this the burden of accounting for derivatives under FAS 133 and IAS 39, that have basically made the use of derivatives a more involved accounting disclosure exercise, and you have corporates unwilling to use financial derivatives. While some highly sophisticated corporates have made extensive use of these instruments – Siemens is one example – a recent survey by *Corporate Finance Magazine* found the use of credit derivatives was nowhere near as extensive as some bankers supposed.

The use of credit derivatives was nowhere near as extensive as some bankers supposed.

Siemens hedges its trade exposure with derivatives. Innovation has been taken to mean devising new products. But in the current climate, it has come to mean something else entirely. In derivatives, as in so many other areas where banks provide services to corporates, the emphasis has shifted away from product. So the innovations coming from the provider side are not in the form of new types of product, but in a new way of approaching the corporates' requirements.

Antonio Polverino, managing director and head of corporate derivative marketing at JP Morgan, explains that CFOs, finance directors and treasurers in large corporations now have an enormous workload, since they are involved in a very wide range of markets and products. "It therefore makes little sense for a bank to provide coverage through different salespeople for FX, interest rates, and credit derivatives," he says. "A holistic, client-centered model, coupled with a strong product platform and a constant dialog, is essential in order to help corporations best address their risk management needs."[99]

For hedging risks, stock incentive-related structured products have been used by many corporates. Monetization, which is a synthetic alternative to a sale, is also used frequently. Balance sheet asset-liability matching and M&A derivative transactions are other areas where structured products are used. Many of the structured products usually originate from a tax or accounting perspective.

Credit Default Swaps

Credit Default Swaps (CDSs) have emerged as one of the primary building blocks of the bond and loan sectors, serving as a vital tool for banks and investors to manage credit risk or accept exposure to lucrative opportunities. CDSs are popular with bankers because they can lower their exposure to a specific client without the client knowing that the loan has been sold on. CDSs are also a kind of insurance agreement that permits banks and investors to shield themselves against default risk. Banks are usually the primary purchasers of cover, while insurers have been the leading vendors. As the market has grown, however, CDSs have become tradable securities. In theory, there is no limit to the number of CDSs that can be composed on a specific risk, so the CDS market is frequently more liquid than that of the underlying securities. The worth of outstanding credit derivatives, mostly CDSs, has increased significantly in recent years, according to a report by the International Swaps and Derivatives Association (ISDA).[100]

Corporate treasurers and CFOs are taking an increasingly sophisticated approach to balance sheet optimization. As corporate sophistication increases, and corporates are more open to innovation, financial institutions put in more measures to work towards meeting their needs. Banks internally become more sophisticated to meet a more specialized and sophisticated set of demands. The increased sophistication right now comes from the ability to tailor any product to meet specific needs in terms of specific tax, accounting treatments, and so on.

The IAS 39 standard

IAS 39, the international accounting standard for derivatives reporting, will have a significant impact on hedging policies, as well as improving internal controls and the quality of external information. The standard is likely to lead to increased centralization of risk management processes. This is the potential upside for the corporate treasury – moves to comply with the new rules will also mean an added emphasis on best practice in treasury.

EXAMPLE

Since its highs in 2002, the US dollar has depreciated significantly against the euro until mid-2003. European companies with investments in the US have seen the euro equivalent of their investments fall significantly as a result of the depreciation in the US dollar. While this fall does not directly affect net profit or loss under most local European GAAPs, it will deplete the equity of the consolidated group, which can lead to breaches of funding covenants and loss of value. Many CFOs and treasurers are thus revisiting the idea of hedging their investments and earnings in foreign subsidiaries.

While hedging the net investment in a foreign subsidiary is economically appealing, the accounting requirements introduced by IAS 39, which all listed EU corporates will be required to adopt by 2005, introduce new considerations for corporates.

Under IAS 39, all derivative instruments must be carried at fair value in the balance sheet and changes in fair value are reflected in the income statement unless the derivative instrument qualifies for hedge accounting. Changes in the value of net investments due to movements in foreign exchange rates are reflected directly in the balance sheet equity. Therefore, a hedging strategy that does not qualify for hedge accounting, will result in a mismatch between the income statement and balance sheet impact. Thus, many European corporates will be interested in qualifying for hedge accounting under IAS 39 in order to minimize any profit and loss volatility resulting from their hedging strategy.

Under IAS 39, the earnings of a foreign subsidiary are not a hedgeable item. Thus, a corporate cannot enter into a derivative strategy and designate the earnings of a foreign subsidiary as the hedged item.

Traditionally, companies have used combinations of different strategies to hedge their investment in foreign subsidiaries. For example, the parent company issues debt denominated in the subsidiary's local currency in order to hedge its net investment. This strategy eliminates foreign currency risk by creating a short liability position in the subsidiary's local currency to offset the long position in the net investment.

Forward contracts are often used to hedge foreign currency risk. For example, a German corporate enters into a euro-yen, six-month forward contract to buy yen at a currently agreed forward exchange rate, thus locking in the rate against any adverse fluctuation.

Under IAS 39, the fair value of the forward contract is recognized on the balance sheet. At initiation, this is likely to be zero. At each balance sheet date, the value of the forward is adjusted to fair value or marked to market. Generally, there are no upfront cash-flows to enter a forward contract.

Currency and interest rate swaps are strategies that reduce foreign currency or interest rate risk and can provide the desired stability in cash-flows against adverse price risk. Swaptions provide additional flexibility but for an upfront cost for the optionality.

Risk management as integral to the business

The link between risk management and shareholder value argues strongly for the CFO taking responsibility for developing an integrated approach. The objective of managing business risk is to maximize shareholder value. So, risk management, an integral part of the business, should not be isolated from business management.

View the world from a risk perspective, but do not put all your effort into minimizing risk. For shareholders, risk is good – if commensurate with an adequate level of return. The CFO must embed corporate risk management within the financial planning process in achieving corporate goals and reducing volatility of outcomes.[101]

The best CFOs view risk as a business asset to be managed and exploited for gain – turning conventional wisdom on its head. Eliminating risk is not only expensive, it simultaneously eliminates the opportunity for profit.

Risk exposures can be viewed as an asset or as a liability (see Figure 4.24). A corporation's risk appetite or level of risk aversion is driven by its corporate culture. The board and senior management often set the tone and direction as to how much risk is acceptable.

CFO 2000 research highlights risk management as an important issue for CFOs. In certain areas, including financial control and environmental risks, most survey respondents said their companies aim to minimize risks. Innovative business strategies and hedging techniques are utilized to manage exposures optimally. But in overall business and financial risk management, 20 percent of CFOs say that their companies accept an above average degree of risk – nearly matching the 27 percent whose companies accept below average risk. The toughest question comes when determining the company's risk appetite in specific terms that guide subsequent events.[102]

Many companies lack clear policies for hedging business risks. CFOs need to propose and get agreement from the board in terms of defining the company's risk appetite in each treasury activity. Often boards are risk averse and recommend a low risk exposure policy with very low probability of catastrophic losses.

For example, the stop loss limit for foreign exchange transaction exposure may be set at 2.5 percent of forecast group profit: approved investments may include forwards, futures, options, and spot foreign exchange contracts and currency options, or currency swaps and swaptions. Appropriate parameters can thus be set for hedging foreign currency flows on a committed basis.

However, implementing risk policy – and adhering to limits imposed by agreed risk appetite – is easier said than done. In practice, companies decide management's risk appetite in different ways, but the process involves balancing various factors. As custodians

Risk as an asset	Risk as a liability
We must manage risks to:	*We must manage risks to:*
seize opportunities	reduce possibility of loss
maximize value	protect value
attract investors	reassure investors
beat competition	avoid falling behind
push to the limits	stay in control
proactively anticipate risk events	react quickly to risk events

FIGURE 4.24 ■ Looking at business risks from both sides

of shareholders' funds, the CFOs and other managers perform broad due diligence, ensuring that adequate capital is allocated to the core business – the primary risk area – that is, risks the company is in the business to take.

In addition, it is important to understand that greater risks bring greater nominal returns – in the ultimate test of risk management, taking a risk should bring future cash-flows that exceed the company's cost of capital by a particular benchmark or hurdle rate. This rate may be the company's overall marginal weighted average cost of capital or the project's specific risk adjusted cost of capital.

Finally, the most economic way to manage each risk must be considered. For example, the treasury may choose to deal with foreign currency exposure without using hedging instruments, having weighed the associated administrative and other costs against potential rewards.

The financial services industry shows how positive risk management can create and protect shareholder value. Billions of dollars turn over every day in the foreign exchange market, but less than 5 percent relate to corporations trading goods and services between countries.[103]

All other transactions originate from financial institutions and are traded amongst themselves in anticipation of arbitrage profits: they turn foreign exchange hedging instruments into an asset for gain. For every bank that errs by failing to manage the volatility of these instruments, many more are making substantial, sustained gains for shareholders. However, managing business risk to produce a return for everyone's benefit takes the discipline of an integrated approach.

Risk classes

Risk classes may be grouped in various ways, but in general fall under treasury, human resources (HR), sales and marketing, health, safety, and environment, production and operations, legal, and business strategy and planning (see Figure 4.25).

Disciplined risk taking

Leading companies intermittently review their risk management philosophies – in particular – the risk-taking stance. Capital that is employed in the business must be consistent with balance sheet strength, operating position, and investors' expectations. Disciplined risk taking involves bringing together perspectives and knowledge of risk in a range of risk-classes. Who has a broad perspective on this diverse set of business risk classes across the whole corporation?

Business risk management combines a little science with a great deal of subjective judgment.

In the area of risk management, CFOs fulfil responsibilities for tax and treasury, for corporate insurance, and for capital investment decisions. So, they are exposed to techniques for quantifying risks and modeling the effects of risk management actions. Business risk management combines a little science with a great deal of subjective judgment.

Risk classes	Specific risk exposures
Treasury	Liquidity Foreign exchange Interest rate Credit
HR	Succession planning Training and development Hiring and firing Employment practices liability
Sales and marketing	Revenue growth Brand Customer satisfaction
Health, safety and environment	Working conditions Plant safety Environmental protection
Production and operations	Tangible and intangible processes Day-to-day business continuity
Legal	Contracts Compliance Legal liability issues
Business strategy and planning	Strategic risks Investments and divestments

FIGURE 4.25 ■ Classification business risks

Formal quantitative techniques are becoming established, as we have covered in this chapter. But this new discipline remains complex. No single approach suits every company. A corporate risk management process may be viewed in four inter-linked phases. It is designed to reinforce the fact that risk management is not only about analytical models and risk management techniques like hedging and insurance, but should fit with corporate strategy and help boost shareholder value.

The corporate risk management cycle includes strategy, analysis, implementation, and monitoring (see Figure 4.26).

The risk management cycle is not static, but evolves over time as the business' tactical conditions change constantly. Dynamic risk management works real-time, ensuring that the company's exposures to possible adverse conditions are managed ahead of time. In such a changing environment, risk analysis, improvement and monitoring, linked to review of risk strategy, is a real-time effort, not a conventional annual or quarterly event.

(See Chapter 6 for more on real-time performance management.)

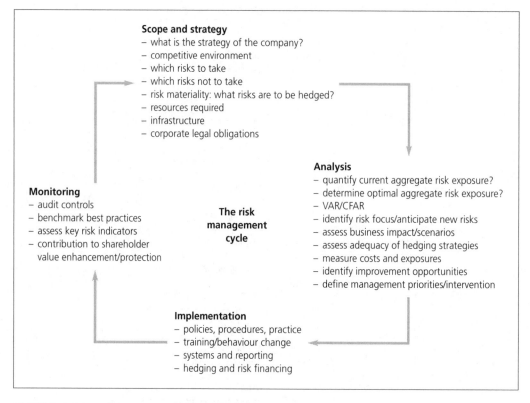

Scope and strategy
– what is the strategy of the company?
– competitive environment
– which risks to take
– which risks not to take
– risk materiality: what risks are to be hedged?
– resources required
– infrastructure
– corporate legal obligations

Monitoring
– audit controls
– benchmark best practices
– assess key risk indicators
– contribution to shareholder
  value enhancement/protection

The risk management cycle

Analysis
– quantify current aggregate risk exposure?
– determine optimal aggregate risk exposure?
– VAR/CFAR
– identify risk focus/anticipate new risks
– assess business impact/scenarios
– assess adequacy of hedging strategies
– measure costs and exposures
– identify improvement opportunities
– define management priorities/intervention

Implementation
– policies, procedures, practice
– training/behaviour change
– systems and reporting
– hedging and risk financing

FIGURE 4.26 ■ The corporate risk management cycle

Traditional risk management approaches do not address the need to manage risk in a forward-looking and proactive way across the organization. Internal audit, for example, traditionally focuses on financial risk rather than general business and operational factors. It is often viewed negatively, and perceived to have a policing role.

Adoption of risk management frameworks from a strategic standpoint can enhance a company's external image. Publicizing the high standards of risk management that are used within the organization can confer competitive advantages in the capital market.

Three main options

In support of protecting shareholder value, alternative risk management mechanisms are often applied by companies. Organizations have three main options when choosing an insurance strategy:

■ risk retention,

■ risk transfer,

■ risk financing.

Risk retention can either mean proactive management of risk through loss control, or establishing an internal provision for loss, or both.

Risk transfer involves shifting the risk burden to a third party. Insurance is the most popular form of risk transfer involving the outsourcing of the funding of a loss. The insured pays a risk premium in exchange for shedding the risk to the insurer.

Risk financing can involve a mixture of risk retention and risk transfer. It involves a repayment obligation. For example, reinsurance for low-frequency, high-severity risks such as natural disasters involves a retention risk on the initial loss layers, and a transfer of risk on the higher layers.

Risk financing can take many forms, and products can usually be tailored to a company's specific needs.[104]

▪ *Contingent capital* is an agreement between a company and an investor (typically an insurance company) that, when a certain trigger event occurs, the company gains the right to raise capital from the investor. The money must be paid back, typically with interest. Unlike a line of credit with a bank, the form of the financing is usually flexible – it can be structured as subordinated debt, senior debt, of preferred equity.

▪ *Catastrophe (CAT) bonds* involves cash-flows that are linked to the occurrence of a natural disaster. These securities pay a higher yield than conventional bonds – in exchange, investors risk losing interest, principal, or both if a catastrophe occurs.

▪ *Finite risk* is a reinsurance product that focuses on specific, hard-to-insure risks. Contracts are often multi-year, and include an upper limit. Finite risk deals are often motivated by the desire for favorable tax or accounting treatment.

Figure 4.27 shows a generic model of risk hedging and is a useful way to begin to think about partitioning risk exposures for risk retention or risk transfer decisions.

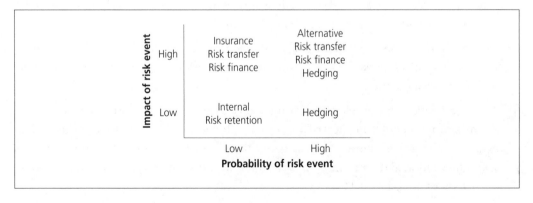

FIGURE 4.27 ▪ Risk hedging strategy matrix

The first and most basic decision facing an organization is whether to hedge or not. Often the board of directors or the risk management committee will develop carefully thought-out policies and guidelines on this. Clearly, some risks are outside the control of management but have an important ongoing impact on business operations. Hedging these risks, therefore, is central in responsible risk management in general.

The next stage involves making a distinction between low-severity, high-frequency risks versus high-severity low-frequency risk events. Organizations with high turnovers seek to retain high-frequency, low-severity risk exposures that pose a regular but low level of financial loss to the organization.

It could be argued that these are the business risks the organization is in the business of bearing because of its specialist knowledge, capacity, assets, and competence. Most organizations can quantify the probable magnitude of this loss and have in place methods to proactively manage down the risk and the loss.

In fact, according to research by PricewaterhouseCoopers, as organizations have become more proactive in managing risk, they have decided to retain more risk rather than transfer risk to third parties, traditionally large insurers.[105]

Insurance as a risk hedging strategy

This research also suggests that, as multinationals have developed in size and have increasing resources at their disposal, they have realized that 'self-insurance' – the setting up of an internal fund or provision, for loss can be a far more efficient way of financing risk. By self-insuring, some organizations have reported savings of millions of dollars in insurance premiums.

There are at least three deficiencies with using insurance as a risk hedging strategy:[106]

■ Insurance has come to be associated with irresponsible behaviour. In the past, buying insurance was often an excuse for not managing risk proactively, since all of it was transferred to a third party, and risk was effectively eliminated by paying large premiums. Today, however, such an approach is clearly becoming untenable.

■ Insurance is not necessarily the best financial instrument to maximize shareholder value, since the derivatives market offers many customizable risk-management instruments that can offer more attractive options.

■ Many organizations now seek cover for intangible assets such as brand protection, reputation, and intellectual property. Traditionally, however, the insurance industry has focused on hazards or perils. Many organizations have become disillusioned with the lack of innovation and customization within the insurance markets, and have turned to alternative risk transfer (ART) solutions.

Insurance, then, is often viewed as too defensive for today's economic climate of harsh competition, and increasing pressure on management to deliver performance improvement and shareholder value.

A new trend in the area of risk financing is the integrated approach to both finance and insurance risks. Traditionally, organizations have tended to approach risk from a separate, departmental perspective. The risk manager has tended to buy insurance, while the treasurer has traditionally hedged financial variables that may have an impact on the organization, such as interest rate volatility and currency rate volatility. However, managers now have a better awareness of how risks in their 'risk portfolio' impact one another. This integrated approach is becoming increasingly important as organizations want to show their shareholders they are managing risks in a consistent fashion.

New innovative risk financing techniques can immediately increase shareholder value. An example is financing environmental remediation costs. Many firms across sectors are affected by environmental liabilities. Some innovative products cap these costs and, in the process, remove uncertainty for shareholders by eliminating the need to hold an on-balance-sheet loss provision.

Innovative reinsurance service providers are now turning their attention to financing operational risks for banks, following the rise in interest in operational risk management. This is a challenging area. Banks are in the business of voluntarily taking on financial risks and retaining them. In this context, transferring risk runs counter to their core business and objectives. However, banks are now exploring alternative risk transfer (ART) strategies, in conjunction with the reinsurance market.[107]

A wide range of innovative 'alternative' products are being utilized by organizations to selectively hedge and finance different risk exposures. The main ones include:

- multi-year, multi-line insurance,
- finite risk programs,
- derivatives.

Multi-year, multi-line insurance products integrate different insurance risks, such as property and liability, into a single program. The result is a greater partnership approach between the insurer and the insured. Organizations that agree to assume or retain more risk often find that they can get the interest of the insurance market in risks that are not conventionally insurable. *Finite risk programs* involve a financing deal between the insurer and the insured, thus avoiding the win–lose proposition of conventional 'risk transfer' arrangements. For instance, a fund set aside for losses is invested, with both parties enjoying the investment gains if no claim is made.

> *Finite risk programs involve a financing deal between the insurer and the insured.*

A variety of *derivatives* are now available which give organizations more choice in the hedging decision process. A benefit of this approach is the flexibility of options arrangements where a very large notional amount can be hedged at a cost which is an insignificant fraction of the amount of the notional.

Recent research suggests that cost-conscious companies are increasingly relying on natural hedges to manage exposure to currency risks. They are forsaking derivatives for natural hedges – matching revenues and costs for the same currency or offsetting losses in one currency with gains in another.[108]

Since most multinationals have centralized their treasury operations, at least on a regional basis, risk managers can now better understand how transactions in one currency offset those in another. They can erect natural hedges with access to data from inter-company and third party transactions within the various countries in which the multinational operates.

The second reason is that the cost of derivatives can be prohibitive. Hedging everything can lead to costs greater than those of unhedged exposures. Therefore it is necessary to be selective in hedging with derivatives.

Companies can and do use hedges to reduce transaction exposure – the impact of currency fluctuations on cash-flows. Natural hedges are less effective, however, at reducing translation risk – the impact of variations in exchange rates on a multinational's reported earnings and shareholders' equity.

According to surveys conducted by the Association of Finance Professionals (AFP), the use of financial instruments to hedge risk has declined since FAS 133 took affect in June 2000. Much of the decline reflects the sharp fall in interest rates since then, since most financial hedges are intended to offset the risk of rising interest rates. Some of the decline in use of currency derivatives are a result of the advent of the euro, which has supplanted currencies in many European countries. But evidence points to the increasing use of centralized treasury operations, which enable companies to take greater advantage of natural hedges.[109]

Recent research on US-based corporations, conducted by CFO Research Services suggests that interest in alternative risk financing is rising. The main drivers are the increasing cost and declining availability of insurance, and the accompanying rise in self insurance. Many companies are having difficulty obtaining sufficient insurance coverage.

"Of course, alternative risk financing may not be the right choice in every instance. Some may find that simple self-insurance is cheaper or more attractive given the regulatory environment in their industry. But for others, these products will provide a helpful tool for managing cash-flow, mitigating risks, and saving money. As a greater number of companies develop innovative ways of using risk financing, alternative risk financing may become a more prominent feature of the risk management landscape, and not merely a temporary alternative to costly insurance."[110]

┌─ **CASE STUDY 4.33** Gillette[111]

Gillette, which has approximately 60 percent of its sales coming from outside the US, uses its in-house bank in Zurich to centralize and net transaction risk. The residual net transaction exposure is hedged primarily through forward contracts.

As for translation risk, Gillette no longer makes much use of derivatives for managing this risk as far as earnings are concerned. Gillette's basic policy on that is to use more of the natural types of hedging. Those hedges mainly involve pricing and sourcing policies.

Expense and earnings volatility are Gillette's prime considerations here. The challenge of hedging translation risk to earnings with financial derivatives is compounded by the fact that the US dollar tends to move in broad cycles against other major currencies like the euro, yen, sterling pound, etc. If one consistently hedges revenues and expenses in a major currency with forwards, one could incur several years of losses on those forwards under these circumstances.

Neither treasury centralization nor natural hedges, however, can insulate corporate balance sheets from currency exposure. Gillette does use currency forward contracts and debt instruments to hedge against the translation risk posed by assets primarily in countries where interest rates are lower than the US.

Gillette benefits from that exposure because the company benefits from lower interest costs and exchange on the hedge offsets the net investment in the country. But for countries where rates are higher than the US, that formula does not work and losses may arise from currency exposure.

┌─ **CASE STUDY 4.34** Toyota[112]

Toyota uses derivatives in the normal course of business to manage its exposure to foreign currency exchange rates and interest rates. The accounting is complex and continues to evolve. In addition, there are the significant judgments and estimates involved in estimating fair value in the absence of quoted market values. These estimates are based upon valuation methodologies deemed appropriate in the circumstances, but the use of different assumptions may have a material effect on the estimated fair value amounts.

Toyota's accounting policy is to record a write-down of such investments to realizable value when a decline in fair value below carrying value is other than temporary. In determining if a decline in value is other than temporary, Toyota considers the length of time and the extent to which the fair value has been less than the carrying value, the financial condition and prospects of the company, and Toyota's ability and intent to retain its investment in the company for a period of time sufficient to allow for any anticipated recovery in market value.

▶

Toyota is exposed to market risk from changes in foreign currency exchange rates, interest rates and certain commodity and equity security prices. In order to manage the risk arising from changes in foreign currency exchange rates and interest rates, Toyota enters into a variety of derivative financial instruments.

Toyota monitors and manages these financial exposures as an integral part of its overall risk management program, which recognizes the unpredictability of financial markets and seeks to reduce the potentially adverse effect on Toyota's operating results. The financial instruments included in the market risk analysis consist of all of Toyota's cash and cash equivalents, marketable securities, finance receivables, securities investments, long-term and short-term debt, and all derivative financial instruments.

Toyota's portfolio of derivative financial instruments consists of foreign exchange forward contracts, foreign currency options, interest rate swaps, interest rate currency swap agreements and interest rate options. Anticipated transactions denominated in foreign currencies that are covered by Toyota's derivative hedging are not included in the market risk analysis. Although operating leases are not required to be included, Toyota includes these instruments in determining interest rate risk.

Toyota has foreign currency exposures related to buying, selling and financing in currencies other than the local currencies in which it operates. Toyota is exposed to foreign currency risk related to future earnings or assets and liabilities that are exposed due to operating cash-flows and various financial instruments that are denominated in foreign currencies. Toyota's most significant foreign currency exposures relate to the US and Western European countries.

Toyota uses a VAR analysis to evaluate its exposure to changes in foreign currency exchange rates. The VAR of the combined foreign exchange position represents a potential loss in pre-tax earnings that are estimated to be ¥25.2bn as of March 31, 2001 and ¥24.0bn as of March 31, 2002.

Based on Toyota's overall currency exposure (including derivative positions), the risk during the year ended March 31, 2002 to pre-tax cash-flow from currency movements was on average ¥25.0bn, with a high of ¥26.7bn and a low of ¥22.9bn.

The VAR was estimated by using a variance/covariance model and assumed a 95 percent confidence level on the realization date and a ten-day holding period. Toyota changed the model used for calculation of VAR from the "variance/covariance" method to the "Monte Carlo simulation" method because Toyota introduced a new system it considers more effective for risk management purposes.

Toyota is subject to market risk from exposure to changes in interest rates based on its financing, investing, and cash management activities. Toyota enters into various financial instrument transactions to maintain the desired level of exposure to the risk of interest rate fluctuations and to minimize interest expense. Certain exchange traded future and option contracts, interest rate caps and floors, along with various investments, have been entered into to reduce the interest rate risk related to these activities.

The potential decrease in fair value resulting from a hypothetical 100 basis point upward shift in interest rates would be approximately ¥38.3bn as of March 31, 2001 and ¥28.3bn as of March 31, 2002.

There are certain shortcomings inherent to the sensitivity analyses Toyota treasury performs. The model assumes interest rate changes are instantaneous parallel shifts in the yield curve. However, in reality, changes are rarely instantaneous. Although certain assets and liabilities may have similar maturities or periods to repricing, they may not react correspondingly to changes in market interest rates. Also, the interest rates on certain types of assets and liabilities may fluctuate with changes in market interest rates, while interest rates on other types of assets may lag behind changes in market rates.

Finance receivables are less susceptible to prepayments when interest rates change and, as a result, Toyota's model does not address prepayment risk for automotive related finance receivables. However, in the event of a change in interest rates, actual loan prepayments may deviate significantly from assumptions used in Toyota's financial model.

Commodity price risk is the possibility of higher or lower costs due to changes in the prices of commodities, such as nonferrous (e.g. aluminium), precious metals (e.g. palladium, platinum and rhodium) and ferrous alloys (e.g. steel), which Toyota uses in the production of motor vehicles. Toyota does not use derivative instruments to hedge the price risk associated with the purchase of those commodities and controls its commodity price risk by holding minimum stock levels.

Toyota holds investments in various available-for-sale securities which are subject to price risk. The fair value of available-for-sale securities was approximately ¥718.6bn as of March 31, 2001 and the fair value of available-for-sale equity securities was approximately ¥564.4bn as of March 31, 2002. The potential change in the fair value of these investments, assuming a 10 percent change in prices, would be approximately ¥71.9bn as of March 31, 2001 and ¥56.4bn as of March 31, 2002.

CASE STUDY 4.35 Nestlé[113]

Derivative financial instruments are mainly used to manage Nestlé's operational exposures to foreign exchange, interest rate and commodity price risks. Some derivatives are also acquired with the aim of generating short-term profit.

All derivative financial instruments are carried at fair value, being the market value for listed instruments or valuation based on mathematical models, such as option pricing models and discounted cash-flow calculations for unlisted instruments. These models take into consideration assumptions based on market data.

▶

The instruments consist mainly of currency forwards and options, commodity futures and options, interest forwards, options and swaps, as well as interest rate and currency swaps. Hedge accounting is applied to derivative financial instruments that are effective in offsetting the changes in fair value or in cash-flows of the hedged items. The effectiveness of such hedges is verified at regular intervals and at least on a quarterly basis.

Fair value hedges are derivative financial instruments that hedge the currency risk and/or the interest price risk. The changes in fair value of fair value hedges are recognized in the income statement. The hedged item also is stated at fair value in respect of the risk being hedged, with any gain or loss being recognized in the income statement.

Cash-flow hedges are derivative financial instruments that hedge the currency risks of anticipated future export sales, cash-flow risks of anticipated future purchases of industrial equipment, the currency and/or commodity risk of future purchases of raw materials as well as the cash-flow risk from changes in interest rates. The effective part of the changes in fair value of cash-flow hedges are recognized in equity, while any ineffective part is recognized immediately in the income statement. When the hedged item results in an asset or in a liability, the gains and losses previously recognized in equity are included in the measurement cost of the asset or of the liability.

As a result of the short business cycle of the Nestlé Group, the majority of the transactions outstanding at the balance sheet date are expected to occur in the next period. Otherwise the gains and losses previously recognized in equity are removed from equity and recognized in the income statement at the same time as the hedged transaction.

Hedges of the net investment in a foreign entity are currency derivative financial instruments that hedge the translation exposure on the net investment in affiliated companies. The changes in fair value of such derivatives are recognized in equity until the net investment is sold or otherwise disposed of.

Trading derivatives comprise two categories.

■ The first one includes derivatives that are acquired in connection with the risk management policies of the Group but for which hedge accounting is not applied because they are either not designated or not effective as hedging instruments. For example hedge accounting is not applied to foreign exchange derivatives that manage the currency exposure of some recognized financial assets or liabilities.
■ The second category relates to derivatives that are acquired with the aim of achieving benchmark objectives of trading portfolios.

IBM[114]

IBM operates in approximately 35 functional currencies and is a significant lender and borrower in the global markets. In the normal course of business, the company is exposed to the impact of interest rate changes and foreign currency fluctuations, and to a lesser extent equity price changes. The company limits these risks by following established risk management policies and procedures including the use of derivatives and, where cost-effective, financing with debt in the currencies in which assets are denominated. For interest rate exposures, derivatives are used to align rate movements between the interest rates associated with the company's lease and other financial assets and the interest rates associated with its financing debt. Derivatives are also used to manage the related cost of debt. For foreign currency exposures, derivatives are used to limit the effects of foreign exchange rate fluctuations on financial results.

IBM does not use derivatives for trading or speculative purposes, nor is it a party to leveraged derivatives. Further, the company has a policy of only entering into contracts with carefully selected major financial institutions based upon their credit ratings and other factors, and maintains strict dollar and term limits that correspond to the institution's credit rating. When viewed in conjunction with the underlying and offsetting exposure that the derivatives are designed to hedge, the company has not sustained a material loss from these instruments.

In its hedging programs, the company employs the use of forward contracts, futures contracts, interest rate and currency swaps, options, caps, and floors, or a combination thereof depending upon the underlying exposure.

IBM issues debt on the global capital markets, principally to fund its financing lease and loan portfolio. Access to cost-effective financing can result in interest rate and/or currency mismatches with the underlying assets.

To manage these mismatches and to reduce overall interest cost, IBM primarily uses interest-rate and currency instruments, principally swaps, to convert specific fixed-rate debt issuances into variable-rate debt (i.e. fair value hedges) and to convert specific variable-rate debt and anticipated commercial paper issuances to fixed rate ones (i.e. cash-flow hedges).

The resulting cost of funds is lower than that which would have been available if debt with matching characteristics was issued directly. The weighted-average remaining maturity of all swaps in the debt risk management program is approximately four years.

A significant portion of IBM's foreign currency denominated debt portfolio is designated as a hedge of net investment to reduce the volatility in stockholders' equity caused by changes in foreign currency exchange rates in the functional currency of major foreign subsidiaries with respect to the US dollar. The company also uses currency swaps and foreign exchange forward contracts for this risk management purpose.

▶

IBM's operations generate significant non-functional currency, third-party vendor payments, and intercompany payments for royalties, and goods and services among the company's non-US subsidiaries and with the parent company. In anticipation of these foreign currency cash-flows and in view of the volatility of the currency markets, IBM selectively employs foreign exchange forward and option contracts to manage its currency risk. At December 31, 2002, the maximum remaining maturity of these derivative instruments was less than 18 months, commensurate with the underlying hedged anticipated cash-flows.

IBM uses its Global Treasury Centers to manage the cash of its subsidiaries. These centers principally use currency swaps to convert cash-flows in a cost-effective manner. In addition, the company uses foreign exchange forward contracts to hedge, on a net basis, the foreign currency exposure of a portion of the company's non-functional currency assets and liabilities.

The terms of these forward and swap contracts are generally less than one year. The changes in fair value from these contracts and from the underlying hedged exposures are generally offsetting and are recorded in Other (income) and expense in the Consolidated Statement of Earnings.

IBM is exposed to certain equity price changes related to certain obligations to employees. These equity exposures are primarily related to market value movements in certain broad equity market indices and in the company's own stock. Changes in the overall value of this employee compensation obligation are recorded in the sales, general and administrative (SG&A) expense in the Consolidated Statement of Earnings.

Although not designated as accounting hedges, IBM utilizes equity derivatives, including equity swaps and futures to economically hedge the equity exposures relating to this employee compensation obligation. To match the exposures relating to this employee compensation obligation, these derivatives are linked to the total return of certain broad equity market indices and/or the total return of the company's common stock. These derivatives are recorded at fair value with gains or losses also reported in the SG&A expense in the Consolidated Statement of Earnings.

IBM holds warrants in connection with certain investments that, although not designated as hedging instruments, are deemed derivatives since they contain net share settlement clauses. During the year, the company recorded the change in the fair value of these warrants in net income.

Ericsson[115]

Ericsson uses different financial instruments to hedge group financial exposures arising from business operations, group funding and asset-liability management. The company defines the financial instruments as either primary or derivative.

Primary instruments are mainly loans, investments and foreign exchange spot transactions. As a complement to the primary instruments, Ericsson uses derivative instruments to reduce its financial exposures. Derivatives used are mainly currency swaps, interest rate futures, and interest rate swaps. The use of other types of derivatives is limited.

Except for the SEK200m risk mandate given to Ericsson Treasury Services, all risk associated with Ericsson's use of financial instruments corresponds to actual and forecasted currency and interest rate commitments.

Ericsson classifies financial risks as either market risk, credit risk, country risk or funding and liquidity risk. Market risk is divided into three categories:

■ foreign exchange risk,
■ interest rate risk,
■ risk related to Ericsson's share price.

Ericsson is domiciled in Sweden, reports in SEK, and currently conducts business in more than 140 countries. It has significant revenues, costs, assets, and debt in currencies other than SEK, which result in substantial foreign exchange exposures. Fluctuations in exchange rates between SEK and foreign currencies affect its earnings. It is Ericsson's policy to reduce this effect to the extent possible through a variety of hedging activities.

Foreign exchange risks are classified as economic exposure, transaction exposure, or translation exposure. Ericsson is dependent on the development of exchange rates in SEK and on economic conditions in Sweden. As of December 31, 2002, approximately 47 percent of all employees were located in Sweden, while Sweden accounted for only 6 percent of total sales in 2002.

Ericsson's exports from Sweden are normally invoiced in foreign currencies. With this substantial SEK-denominated cost base, a gradually stronger SEK exchange rate during 2002 had a negative impact on the company, compared to Ericsson's competitors with costs denominated in euros or US dollars.

Both committed and forecasted transaction exposures are hedged to safeguard business margins and to reduce volatility in earnings. Due to the stronger SEK, the effects of hedging during 2002 increased earnings by approximately SEK2bn, calculated by comparing the average hedged rates on the hedge contract portfolio as of January 1, 2002, with average spot rates during 2002.

As of December 31, 2002, anticipated net transaction exposures were hedged for the next 9–12 months, giving Ericsson time to react to fluctuations in foreign exchange rates by ▶

changing prices or renegotiating contracts with customers and vendors. Unrealized currency forwards carried a positive market value of approximately SEK3bn at year-end, 2002.

Hedging activities are centralized to Ericsson Treasury Services as much as possible. The local companies enter into currency forward agreements with Ericsson Treasury Services, which in turn reverses these transactions in the financial markets. In general, internal sales from Sweden to subsidiaries operating outside Sweden are made in the same currency as the local company use when selling to the external customer, in order to minimize the exposure in the non-Swedish companies.

Ericsson has many subsidiaries operating outside Sweden. The value of such foreign investments is exposed to exchange rate fluctuations, which affects the Consolidated Balance Sheet and Income Statement when translated to SEK. Translation exposure in foreign subsidiaries is hedged according to the following policy established by Ericsson's board of directors:

> "Monetary net income in subsidiaries is translated using the temporal method (translation effects in investments affecting the income statement) and is hedged to 100 percent.

> Equity in subsidiaries is translated using the current method (translation effects are reported directly in stockholders' equity in the balance sheet) and is hedged up to 20 percent in selected companies."

The translation differences reported in equity during 2002 were –SEK4.9bn, mainly due to a stronger SEK.

Ericsson is exposed to interest rate risks through market value fluctuations of certain balance sheet items and through changes in interest expenses and revenues. Interest rate risks are managed centrally by Ericsson Treasury Services. The net debt position was –SEK5.6bn at the end of 2002. In managing Ericsson's interest rate exposure, the company uses derivative instruments, such as forward rate agreements, interest rate swaps and futures.

Ericsson aims to avoid risk in the form of a mismatch between fixed and floating interest-bearing balance sheet items. To achieve this, having large gross interest revenues and costs, Ericsson strives to a position where all interest rates are floating.

CASE STUDY 4.38 RoyalDutch/Shell[116]

US accounting standard, FAS 133, as amended, which requires all derivative financial instruments, with certain exceptions, to be recorded in the Statement of Assets and Liabilities (as assets or liabilities in respect of risk management activities) at their fair value, has been adopted by Shell from the beginning of 2001. Adoption of the standard did not have a significant effect on the group's Financial Statements and the transition adjustment as at January 1, 2001 was negligible.

Shell Group companies use derivatives in the management of interest rate risk, foreign currency risk and commodity price risk. The carrying amount of all derivatives, other than those meeting the normal purchases and sales exception, is measured using market prices.

Those derivatives qualifying and designated as hedges are either:

- a "fair value" hedge: a hedge of the fair value of a recognized asset or liability or of an unrecognized firm commitment;
- a "cash-flow" hedge: a hedge of the variability of cash-flows to be received or paid related to a recognized asset or liability or a forecasted transaction; or
- a "foreign currency" hedge: a hedge of the foreign currency exposure of a recognized asset or liability or of an unrecognized firm commitment (fair value hedge) or of the variability of foreign currency cash-flows associated with a forecasted transaction, a recognized asset or liability, or an unrecognized firm commitment (cash-flow hedge).

The effective portion of a change in the carrying amount of a cash-flow hedge is recorded in other comprehensive income, until income reflects the variability of underlying cash-flows; any ineffective portions are taken to income.

A change in the carrying amount of a fair value hedge is taken to income, together with the consequential adjustments to the carrying amount of the hedged item. A change in the carrying amount of a foreign currency hedge is recorded on the basis of whether the hedge is a fair value hedge or a cash-flow hedge. A change in the carrying amount of other derivatives is taken to income.

Shell Group companies formally document all relationships between hedging instruments and hedged items, as well as risk management objectives and strategies for undertaking various hedge transactions. The effectiveness of a hedge is also continually assessed. When effectiveness ceases, hedge accounting is discontinued.

CASE STUDY 4.39 GlaxoSmithKline[117]

GlaxoSmithKline's contingent liabilities, comprising guarantees, discounted bills and other items arising in the normal course of business, amounted to £138m at December 31, 2002, and £90m at year-end 2001.

The GlaxoSmithKline Group has entered into forward foreign exchange contracts in order to swap liquid assets and borrowings into the currencies required for group purposes.

At December 31, 2002, the GlaxoSmithKline Group had outstanding contracts to sell or purchase foreign currency having a total notional principal amount of £1,937m (2001: £7,312m). The majority of contracts are for periods of 12 months or less.

At the end of the year the GlaxoSmithKline Group had a number of currency swaps in place in respect of medium-term debt instruments. Borrowings denominated in, or swapped into, foreign currencies which match investments in overseas GlaxoSmithKline Group assets are treated as a hedge against the relevant net assets and exchange gains or losses are recorded in reserves.

To manage the fixed/floating interest rate profile of debt, the GlaxoSmithKline Group had several interest rate swaps outstanding with commercial banks at December 31, 2002.

The GlaxoSmithKline Group does not believe it is exposed to major concentrations of credit risk. The group is exposed to credit-related losses in the event of non-performance by counterparties to financial instruments, but does not expect any counterparties to fail to meet their obligations.

The GlaxoSmithKline Group applies board-approved limits to the amount of credit exposure to any one counterparty and employs strict minimum credit worthiness criteria as to the choice of counterparty.

Statement of Financial Accounting Standard No. 133, "Accounting for Derivative Instruments and Hedging Activities" (SFAS 133) as amended by SFAS 137 and SFAS 138 and as interpreted by the Derivatives Implementation Group, was adopted by the GlaxoSmithKline Group with effect from January 1, 2001.

SFAS 133 establishes accounting and reporting standards for derivative instruments, including certain derivative instruments embedded in other contracts and for hedging activities. Under UK GAAP, some derivative instruments used for hedging are not recognized on the balance sheet and the matching principle is used to match the gain or loss under these hedging contracts to the foreign currency transaction or profits to which they relate.

SFAS 133 requires that an entity recognize all derivatives as either assets or liabilities in the consolidated balance sheet and measure those instruments at fair value. Changes in fair value over the period are recorded in current earnings unless hedge accounting is obtained. The GlaxoSmithKline Group does not designate any of its derivatives as qualifying hedge instruments under SFAS 133. SFAS 133 prescribes requirements for designation and documentation of hedging relationships and ongoing assessments of effectiveness in order to qualify for hedge accounting.

The GlaxoSmithKline Group also evaluates contracts for 'embedded' derivatives, and considers whether any embedded derivatives have to be bifurcated, or separated, from the host contracts in accordance with SFAS 133 requirements. If embedded derivatives exist and are not clearly and closely related to the host contract, they are accounted for separately from the host contract as derivatives.

Gains and losses related to the fair value adjustments of all derivative instruments are classified in the consolidated statement of income and cash-flows in accordance with the nature of the derivative.

The fair value of derivative instruments is sensitive to movements in the underlying market rates and variables. The GlaxoSmithKline Group monitors the fair value of derivative instruments on a periodic basis. Derivatives including interest rate swaps and cross currency swaps are valued using standard valuation models, counterparty valuations, or third party valuations. Standard valuation models used by the group consider relevant discount rates, the market yield curve on the valuation date, forward currency exchange rates and counterparty risk. All significant rates and variables are obtained from market sources.

All valuations are based on the remaining term to maturity of the instrument. Foreign exchange contracts are valued using forward rates observed from quoted prices in the relevant markets when possible. The group assumes parties to long-term contracts are economically viable but reserves the right to exercise early termination rights if economically beneficial when such rights exist in the contract.

CASE STUDY 4.40 Exxon-Mobil[118]

Exxon-Mobil's size, geographic diversity and the complementary nature of the upstream, downstream and chemicals businesses mitigate its risk from changes in interest rates, currency rates, and commodity prices. The company relies on these operating attributes and strengths to reduce enterprise-wide risk. As a result, the company makes limited use of derivatives to offset exposures arising from existing transactions.

Exxon-Mobil does not trade in derivatives nor does it use derivatives with leverage features. The company maintains a system of controls that includes a policy covering the authorization, reporting, and monitoring of derivative activity. The company's derivative activities pose no material credit or market risks to ExxonMobil's operations, financial condition, or liquidity. Interest rate, foreign exchange rate, and commodity price exposures arising from derivative contracts undertaken in accordance with the company's policies have not been significant.

▶

The fair value of derivatives outstanding and recorded on the balance sheet was a net receivable of $20m before-tax and a net payable of $50m before-tax at year-end 2002 and 2001, respectively. This is the amount that Exxon-Mobil would have received or paid to third parties if these derivatives had been settled. These derivative fair values were substantially offset by the fair values of the underlying exposures being hedged. The company recognized a before-tax loss of $35m and a before-tax gain of $23m related to derivative activity during 2002 and 2001, respectively.

The losses/gains included the offsetting amounts from the changes in fair value of the items being hedged by the derivatives. The fair value of derivatives outstanding at year-end 2002 and losses recognized during the year are immaterial in relation to the corporation's year-end cash balance of $7.2bn, total assets of $152.6bn, or net income for the year of $11.5bn.

ExxonMobil is exposed to changes in interest rates, primarily as a result of its short-term debt and long-term debt-carrying floating interest rates. The company makes limited use of interest rate swap agreements to adjust the ratio of fixed and floating rates in the debt portfolio. The impact of a 100 basis point change in interest rates affecting the corporation's debt would not be material to earnings, cash-flow, or fair value.

ExxonMobil conducts business in many foreign currencies and is subject to foreign currency exchange rate risk on cash-flows related to sales, expenses, financing, and investment transactions. The impacts of fluctuations in foreign currency exchange rates on ExxonMobil's geographically diverse operations are varied and often offsetting in amount. The corporation makes limited use of currency exchange contracts to reduce the risk of adverse foreign currency movements related to certain foreign currency debt obligations. Exposure from market rate fluctuations related to these contracts is not material.

ExxonMobil makes limited use of commodity forwards, swaps and futures contracts of short duration to mitigate the risk of unfavorable price movements on certain crude, natural gas and petroleum product purchases and sales. Commodity price exposure related to these contracts is not material.

ExxonMobil makes limited use of derivatives. Derivative instruments are not held for trading purposes nor do they have leverage features. When the company does enter into derivative transactions, it is to offset exposures associated with interest rates, foreign currency exchange rates and hydrocarbon prices.

The gains and losses resulting from the changes in fair value of these instruments are recorded in income, except when the instruments are designated as hedging the currency exposure of net investments in foreign subsidiaries, in which case they are recorded in the cumulative foreign exchange translation account, as part of shareholders' equity.

The gains and losses on derivative instruments that are designated as fair value hedges (i.e. those hedging the exposure to changes in the fair value of an asset or a liability, or the changes in the fair value of a firm commitment), are offset by the gains and losses from the changes in fair value of the hedged items, which are also recognized in the Income Statement.

Most of these designated hedges are entered into at the same time that the hedged items are transacted. They are fully effective and, in combination with the offsetting hedged items, they result in no net impact on income. In some situations, the corporation has chosen not to designate certain immaterial derivatives used for hedging economic exposure as hedges for accounting purposes due to the excessive administrative effort that would be required to account for these items as hedging transactions. These derivatives are recorded on the balance sheet at fair value and the gains and losses arising from changes in fair value are recognized in income. All derivatives activity is immaterial.

The method of translating the foreign currency financial statements of the corporation's international subsidiaries into US dollars is prescribed by GAAP. Under these principles, it is necessary to select the functional currency of these subsidiaries. The functional currency is the currency of the primary economic environment in which the subsidiary operates. Management selects the functional currency after evaluating this economic environment. Downstream and chemicals operations normally use the local currency, except in highly inflationary countries, primarily Latin America, as well as in Singapore, which uses the US dollar, because it predominantly sells into the US dollar export market.

Upstream operations also use the local currency as the functional currency, except where crude and natural gas production is predominantly sold in the export market in US dollars. These operations, which use the US dollar as their functional currency, are in Malaysia, Indonesia, Angola, Nigeria, Equatorial Guinea, and the Middle East countries.

CASE STUDY 4.41 Procter& Gamble[119]

Procter & Gamble is exposed to market risks, such as changes in interest rates, currency exchange rates and commodity prices. Derivative positions are monitored using techniques including market valuation, sensitivity analysis and VAR modeling.

The tests for interest rate and currency rate exposures are based on a Monte Carlo simulation VAR model using a one-year horizon and a 95 percent confidence level. The model incorporates the impact of correlation and diversification from holding multiple currency and interest rate instruments, and assumes that financial returns are normally distributed. Estimates of volatility and correlations of market factors are drawn from the *RiskMetrics*™ dataset as of June 30, 2003. In cases where data is unavailable in *RiskMetrics*, a reasonable proxy is included.

▶

Interest rate swaps are used to hedge underlying debt obligations. Certain currency interest rate swaps are designated as hedges of the company's foreign net investments.

Based on the Procter & Gamble's overall interest rate exposure as of and during the year ended June 30, 2003, including derivative and other instruments sensitive to interest rates, the company does not believe a near-term change in interest rates, at a 95 percent confidence level based on historical interest rate movements, would materially affect the company's financial statements.

Procter & Gamble's corporate policy prescribes the range of allowable hedging activity. The company primarily uses forward exchange contracts and purchased options with maturities of less than 18 months. In addition, the company enters into certain currency swaps with maturities of up to five years to hedge inter-company financing transactions. Procter & Gamble also uses purchased currency options with maturities of generally less than 18 months and forward exchange contracts to hedge against the effect of exchange rate fluctuations on inter-company royalties and to offset a portion of the effect of exchange rate fluctuations on income from international operations.

Based on the Procter & Gamble's overall currency rate exposure as of and during the year ended June 30, 2003, including derivative and other instruments sensitive to currency movements, the company does not believe a near-term change in currency rates, at a 95 percent confidence level based on historical currency rate movements, would materially affect the company's financial statements. Raw materials used by Procter & Gamble are subject to price volatility caused by weather, supply conditions, political and economic variables, and other unpredictable factors. The company uses futures, options and swap contracts to manage the volatility related to the above exposures. Commodity hedging activity is not considered material to the company's financial statements.

NOTES

1   Frost *et al.* (2001).

2   Asaf (1997).

3   EIU (1995).

4   Culp, C (2001).

5   Culp, C *et al.* (1998).

6   PriceWaterhouseCoopers (1997).

7   Jorion, P (1997).

8   Jorion (2003)

9   Culp, C (2000).

10   Knight and Pretty (1996).

11   Fridson and Alvarez (2002).

12   US Securities and Exchange Commission documents (2003).

13   Reason, T (2002).

14   Fink, R (2002).

15   Olivier, C (2001).

16   Ibid.

17   Ibid.

18   Final, C (2002).

19   Johnson, M (2001).

20   Fink, R (2002).

21   Citigroup Annual Report (2002).

22   IBM Annual Report (2002).

23   General Electric Annual Report (2002).

24   Ericsson Annual Report (2002).

25   Toyota Annual Report (2002).

26   George, Abraham (1996).

27   George, Abraham (1996).

28   Allen, S (2003).

29   Group of 30 (1993). The G-30 is a private non-profit organization which studies international eco-
      nomic and financial issues, and is headed by 30 senior representatives of the international
      business, regulatory, and academic communities.

30   Wilson, T (1998).

31   Ibid.

32   Citigroup Annual Report (2002).

33   Siemens Annual Report (2002).

34   HSBC Annual Report (2002).

35   AT&T Annual Report (2002).

36   General Electric Annual Report (2002).

37   DaimlerChrysler Annual Report (2002).

38   Toyota Annual Report (2002).

39   Intel Annual Report (2002).

40   Nestlé Annual Report (2002).

41   Nestlé's consolidated accounts comply with International Financial Reporting Standards (IFRS)
      issued by the International Accounting Standards Board (IASB) and with the Standing
      Interpretations issued by the International Financial Reporting Interpretations Committee
      (IFRIC) of the IASB. The accounts are prepared on an accrual basis and under the historical cost
      convention, except derivative financial instruments, investments held for trading, available-for-
      sale investments and recognized assets and liabilities subject to fair value hedges that are stated
      at their fair value.

42   GlaxoSmithKline Annual Report (2002).

43 Hoffman D (2002).

44 Frost *et al*. (2001).

45 King, J L (2001).

46 Hoffman D (2002).

47 Culp C (1999).

48 Hoffman, D (2002).

49 Frost, C *et al*. (2001).

50 Asaf and Bertoneche (1997).

51 Frost, *et al*. (2001).

52 Ibid.

53 King, J L (2001).

54 Ibid.

55 Cruz, M G (2002).

56 HSBC Annual Report (2002).

57 Citigroup Annual Report (2002).

58 Ericsson Annual Report (2002).

59 Merrill Lynch Annual Report (2002).

60 DaimlerChrysler Annual Report (2002).

61 Toyota Annual Report (2002).

62 Intel Annual Report (2002).

63 RoyalDutch/Shell Annual Report (2002).

64 Dowd (1998).

65 Stalnecker, S chapter 4 in Barton (2002).

66 Campbell and Kracaw (1993).

67 Barton *et al*. (2002).

68 Ibid.

69 DeLoach (2000).

70 Culp, C (2001).

71 Barton (2001).

72 Barton (2002).

73 Ibid.

74 Paul-Choudhury (1996) and Williams (1996).

75 Culp, C (2001).

76 Dowd, K (1998).

77 Linsmeier and Pearson (1996).

78 Dowd, K (1998).

79 KPMG (2003).

80 "Economic Capital" is the capital banks set aside as a buffer against potential losses inherent in a particular business activity – making a loan, for example, or underwriting a currency.

81 KPMG (2003).

82 Ibid.

83 Bank for International Settlements (BIS) (2003).

84 DuPont Annual Report (2002).

85 Barton *et al*. (2003).

86 Ibid.

87 Ibid.

88 Citigroup Annual Report (2002).

89 Siemens Annual Report (2002).

90 Merrill Lynch Annual Report (2002).

91 Microsoft Annual Report (2002).

92 Ericsson Annual Report (2002).

93 DaimlerChrysler Annual Report (2002).

94 HSBC Annual Report (2002).

95 Procter & Gamble Annual Report (2003).

96 Asaf S (1997).

97 PricewaterhouseCoopers (2003b).

98 Foote (2003).

99 *Corporate Finance Magazine*, (2002) June.

100 Batchelor (2004)

101 Asaf and Bertoneche (1998).

102 CFO 2000 research.

103 CFO (1997).

104 CFO Research Services (2003).

105 Frost, *et al*. (2001).

106 Ibid.

107 Culp (1999) and Frost (2001).

108 Fink, R (2003).

109 Ibid.

110 CFO Research Services (2003).

111 *Corporate Finance Magazine* (2002 June).

112 Toyota Annual Report (2002).

113 Nestlé Annual Report (2002).

114 IBM Annual Report (2002).

115 Ericsson Annual Report (2002).

116 Royal-Dutch/Shell Annual Report (2002).

117 GlaxoSmithKline Annual Report (2002).

118 Exxon-Mobil Annual Report (2002).

119 Procter & Gamble Annual Report (2003).

CHAPTER 5

Financial reporting, planning, and control

Introduction

Financial reporting has much to do with ethics and public trust, because even the most strict accounting regulations are not foolproof, leaving corporate management with many techniques to fine tune the numbers. Best-in-class global multinationals realize that transparency and accountability are the cornerstones of building integrity. Corporations have an obligation to provide shareholders and stakeholders with the information they need to properly evaluate the company and its performance.

Many of the companies reviewed in this book have internal and external auditors reporting directly to the board of directors, and have instituted a culture of accountability and integrity in everything they do. As accounting practices gain visibility, the role of the finance function will gain further importance. Shareholders want their companies to deliver real performance, not illusory performance that comes from manipulating the numbers.

Corporate financial reporting has come under increasing scrutiny in recent years, as many high-profile firms such as WorldCom, Enron, and Anderson committed fraudulent accounting reporting and financial management practices. In response, accounting standards are being made more stringent in the US, Europe, and other countries. Best practices in financial reporting follows not only ethical accounting practices, but leans toward the conservative presentation of financial results.

We have seen that companies that follow best practices in financial reporting recognize the limitations of accrual-based accounting measures like net income and earnings per share (EPS). Many of these companies complement GAAP accounting results with economic value added (EVA) measures, and financial measures with non-financial metrics.

Best practice companies also measure risk exposure with advanced methodologies like value at risk (VAR) and earnings at risk (EAR), and report off-balance-sheet financing techniques clearly, so that investors and financiers can understand the actual overall financial health and strength of the business.

Best-in-class companies are adopting real-time financial performance reporting. These advanced systems can report the status of global treasury operations and risk exposure levels at the touch of a button. They can pinpoint financial and non-financial metrics within a balanced scorecard framework, allowing management to pinpoint issues through exception reporting capabilities.

Real-time financial reporting also supports financial control in real-time. Best-in-class finance departments perform rolling forecasts, and view the entire organization minute-by-minute. Adoption of these advanced financial management techniques are a *sine qua non* for companies that aspire to emulate the best in the business. When presenting management's expectations of the future of the company, the long-term financial plan summarizes these expectations and their impact on the bottom line. However, prophesizing is risky business. Therefore, we see carefully crafted "safe-harbor" statements like the following example, adapted from Exxon-Mobil's 2002 annual report:

EXAMPLE

Forward-looking statements: ExxonMobil[1]

Statements in this discussion regarding expectations, plans and future events or conditions are forward-looking statements. Actual future results, including production growth; financing sources; the resolution of contingencies; the effect of changes in prices; interest rates and other market conditions; and environmental and capital expenditures could differ materially depending on a number of factors, such as the outcome of commercial negotiations; changes in the supply of and demand for crude oil, natural gas, and petroleum and petrochemical products; and other factors discussed above and under the caption "Factors Affecting Future Results" in Item 1 of ExxonMobil's 2002 Form 10-K.

Financial reporting: GAAP convergence

The future of corporate reporting is all about transparency – the clear, complete, relevant information about corporate performance that investors and other stakeholders are demanding. Are you ready to meet the demand?

Key questions for CFOs include the following:

- Can management articulate the company's complete value proposition – how it creates and manages value?

- Do analysts and investors understand the company's value proposition?

- How does the company's corporate reporting compare to that of its competitors?

- What measures does management have to gauge performance against the company's value proposition?

- Does management have adequate systems in place to capture the performance data it needs?

- Is management using its performance data to manage against the company's most important value drivers?

- What must management do to develop a corporate reporting strategy that embraces the principles of transparency?

Companies are under pressure to create and preserve value for their shareholders. How that value is measured and communicated – the essence of corporate reporting – is changing. For global multinationals, the task of understanding financial accounting practices in different countries will become easier, soon.

Recent research by the big six accounting firms shows that an overwhelming majority of countries – over 90 percent of a total of 59 countries surveyed – intend to converge with *International Financial Reporting Standards (IFRS)*. The findings, taken from GAAP Convergence 2002, found that this convergence will initially apply to listed companies only, to be followed by privately held firms.[2]

Corporate sustainability the latest buzz-word in corporate governance.

Corporate performance reporting is increasingly coming under scrutiny. Corporate sustainability – the latest buzz-word in corporate governance – is being defined as managing for the long-term vitality of the business, and is receiving a high level of attention from executives in North America and Europe. A recent survey of 103 European- and 150 US-based CFOs found that:[3]

- European multinationals place more focus on the economic, social, and environmental impact of their products and services than US firms.

- US multinationals place more emphasis on long-term profitability, management oversight, and compensation than their European counterparts.

PricewaterhouseCoopers has developed a framework for understanding how companies create and define value today, a new approach to performance measurement and corporate reporting called *ValueReporting*™.

The historical cost accounting framework fails to provide all the information the markets need to properly assess value. Corporate executives believe their shares are undervalued. Investors want more information to make decisions about the companies they invest in.

Analysts often find themselves caught between the interests of investors and the interests of their corporate clients. Without a broader perspective, the markets end up translating current earnings into stock prices, leading to volatility and rewarding short-term financial results rather than long-term value creation.

Beyond financial reporting

ValueReporting challenges companies to disclose information on the performance measures that they themselves use to manage their businesses—to adopt a philosophy of greater transparency. It provides a framework for companies to evaluate and communicate the financial *and* non-financial industry drivers of value to the markets.

ValueReporting addresses the gap between the current financial reporting model and the market's demand for more information. It calls for greater disclosure about market dynamics, corporate strategy, and intangible, non-financial drivers of stakeholder value such as customer satisfaction, market share, and employee retention.

The potential benefits of providing such information include enhanced credibility, longer-term investment interest, improved access to capital and higher share prices. Without such a qualitative perspective, investors are left to "guess" at the key drivers responsible for a company's current market valuation and expected future potential.

By going beyond the elements of traditional financial statements, such a framework provides greater room for management to analyse and directly address the broader concerns of investors. Its use helps deliver a deeper sense of the health of the company through metrics, industry information, strategy, and likely outcomes, assisting investors in understanding the rationale behind management decisions.

Business and financial planning

Almost every company has a five-year business plan which is typically broken out into quarterly or monthly versions. This is required by banks and creditors for credit rating, loan covenants, and other long-term capital financing. However, with business conditions changing fast, there is a high degree of uncertainty the further forward you go. CFOs agree on one thing: once you get beyond two years, it is so fuzzy that the numbers are rarely ever right.

There is no doubt that there is a connection between quality of management and ability to forecast, says John Daniels, vice president of commercial banking at Bank of America.[4]

For companies that can develop superior forecasts, the process of business planning is very useful to force management to see a longer-term view of the business, and as a process that the enterprise uses to operationalize high-level strategy. It pushes the finance function to deliver strategic decision support, and thus helps make dynamically optimal resource allocation decisions so that the best growth opportunities get priority.

> "Comprehensive business modeling represents the missing link to effective business execution"[5]

However, forecasting the business environment two to five years hence, and developing the underlying assumptions and drivers for the corporate long-term business plan is risky business, because of the uncertainty inherent in the economic, financial, and political environments. Although we try to be as objective as possible, our own views of the future often influence our judgments about the outcomes.

> "No one knows what the future holds, and those who claim to know, at least beyond quite a short perspective, are charlatans. For not only are we all curious about the future, but we also carry an implicit set of expectations about it in our heads. We are all prisoners of some idea of the future that is inherent in our view of the present."[6]

Clearly, a great deal of circumspection is needed in developing a pragmatic long-term business plan. Business modeling represents how a business works and functions, created in such a way that it can productively be used as a means to simulate the company's current and future financial condition.

The ability of executives, planners, managers, and analysts to model and test operational and financial planning assumptions for their business is fundamental to good decision making. And while strategy deployment and performance measurement are facilitated in a balanced scorecard, a comprehensive business model is required to show managers how to realize their strategic objectives and improve corporate performance.

The strategic business plan integrates, among others, marketing, pricing, tax planning, and capital investment planning into the financial planning process. As a result, the plan not only establishes a basis for operational budgets and internal resource allocations, but concurrently creates the analytical framework for shareholder value maximising financial and operating decisions.

A strategic business and financial plan is based on a detailed analysis of the competitive environment. The plan also delineates clearly the corporation's business in an analytical framework for potential acquisition and divestiture decision making.

Industry demand, market share, product mix, selling prices, cost of goods, operating and capital expenses, and financial resource requirements are quantified. Working capital needs, stockholder dividends, financial obligations, and debt repayment needs are based on financial projections that are developed according to management's strategic plans for the company.

This framework provides a solid foundation for analyzing the corporation's internal operations at both the business unit and consolidated levels, and concurrently permits the company to evaluate the impact on shareholder value of alternative strategic moves.

In practice, revenue and profitability objectives are set quarterly and annually for up to five years as standard practice. In order to manage the business, every corporation has a business planning process, but the nature of corporate business planning has changed dramatically over the last couple of decades.

What was essentially an annual accounting and budgeting exercise in financial and operational target setting and management, has now become the quintessential decision-support function that synthesizes strategy, operations, and financial management to create superior long-term shareholder value.

Ideally, even before a new corporate strategy is deployed throughout an organization, the strategy is validated against an existing business model. Actions defined by the strategy are mapped into the business model, and resource requirements are determined and measured against existing capacities.

If the existing operations and financial capacity cannot support the strategic objectives, either the strategy must be adjusted or the operations must be improved or expanded to accommodate these objectives. Business plans are optimized by looking at various scenarios and choosing the one that best fits the mandate.

Once the strategic plan and the operational business model are synchronised, an organization can move forward with a fully articulated strategy coupled with an operational plan to achieve the strategy. However, without tying strategy with operations, a balanced scorecard cannot be an effective tool.

A comprehensive business modeling solution combines the operational and financial information of an enterprise. It is capable of modeling activities, pricing, resources, outputs of goods or services, costs, resource capacities, revenue and profitability, asset and liability, leverage, cash flow, capital investments and returns, and other key metrics.

Without tying strategy with operations, a balanced scorecard cannot be an effective tool.

In addition, for companies focused on shareholder value, it is vital that the business model solution can calculate the cost of capital, the effects of tax planning, and economic profit (economic value added – EVA) of the business unit.

The complete business modeling solution

A complete business modeling solution supports many performance management initiatives including:

■ strategic decision analysis and support,

■ operational planning and resource capacity management,

■ customer and product profitability,

- impact of alternative pricing strategies,

- EVA analysis,

- activity-based costing and target costing,

- activity-based management,

- budgeting and planning,

- rolling forecasts,

- optimization capabilities for key decision variables,

- risk exposure estimation,

- operational results tracking,

- key value drivers.

Until recently, business modeling solutions primarily used profitability as the key measurement criterion for decision making and improvement initiatives. The balance sheet was not brought into the equation, and business models were not designed to consider EVA.

However, as powerful as the EVA concept is, superior performance is achieved not only by bold strategic initiatives, but also by the thousands of decisions that create shareholder value at all levels of the organization every year. This war of inches must be fought not only by the top executives, but by all employees.

The conglomerates of the 1980s have deleveraged and divested themselves of grand ideas of the proverbial diversified company, as the synergies that were expected from mergers did not come to fruition because their business plans were flawed. Fortune 500 companies are now focusing ever more on their core businesses.

Most businesses, even those that are not multinationals, do operate internationally as a result of raw materials procurement needs or customer base dispersion. This results in more complex global planning requirements. The interplay between business strategy and financial strategy needs to reflect the reality of the requirements of business operations.

Mature companies, for example, face financial dynamics that deliver healthy cash flows from operations and are therefore able to pay dividends to shareholders, while additional financing requirements are fulfilled by debt issuance or bank financing.

Some companies reduce the costs of capital by off-balance-sheet transactions such as securitizing receivables or adding sweeteners like warrants or options to incremental equity or debt issuances. However, venture capital or growth firms cannot afford to churn out high levels of cash due to capital spending requirements that result in profitable operations but very meagre cash positions.

Poor working capital management can result in a high-growth and profitable enterprise to become cash strapped. Business plans therefore need to balance the objectives of high revenue and earnings growth on the one hand and sustainable growth on the other.

Superior business planning not only develops and utilizes an effective set of value-based financial and operational performance metrics against which to control variances from the plan, it uses careful judgment as to the appropriate benchmarks against which to compare results. EVA and cash flow return on investment (CFROI) are metrics that have gained pre-eminence in the last ten or so years as ones that cannot be easily manipulated by accounting conventions, and revenue and expense recognition tricks.

Competitive analysis is an adjunct that puts the numbers in perspective for benchmarking purposes. Optimal tax planning and treasury management functions support optimization of the cash flow retention and return maximization. Positive net present value generating zero-based capital budgeting policies are in order in most cases of investment decision making. Business planning, in the end, is all about results, primarily financial but also concerning customer and employee satisfaction.

Results based leadership has been a basic management guide in the 1990s. Business plans must be realistic but not complacent, challenging but achievable. Competitive activity, changes in economic conditions, and operational efficiency assumptions form part of the upside and downside views that would be generated from the base case assumptions.

Simulation analysis is conducted by leading corporations, where alternative courses of action and their probable impact on long-term profitability and cash positions can be generated real-time. However, financial control is an important element of successful business plan execution. In order to create the right checks and balances, companies should undergo periodic audits by external auditors that report directly to the board of directors.

However, no amount of planning can replace the practical do-ability part of the equation. Execution is the critical success factor. The Japanese excelled at manufacturing excellence because the *keiretsus* (enterprise groups) had business plans that were realistic, although inter-locked by financial strangleholds on each other. The people who will execute the plan must believe in the plan, and their goals and visions must be aligned with those of the corporation.

The value each person adds to the company must be clear and rewards commensurately dispensed. Only through integrated strategic, operational, and financial planning can corporations attain perfection in operational execution and financial results. This perfection is achieved when business plans are developed and executed so that the shareholders and employees are financially rewarded, and customers satisfied beyond their expectations.

The CEO is responsible to the board of directors for the strategic plans of the company. Therefore, the CEO is the chief long-range planner, with support from the senior management team.

In general, it is desirable that the business planning group be multi-disciplinary, including marketing, product development, strategy, finance, human resources, sales, operations, and research. Flexibility and creativity are necessary for development of dynamic business plans.

Selecting the proper planning horizon

You may be asking, just how far ahead should a company plan? Since the business environment has become more dynamic and volatile, some experts suggest that the planning horizon ought to be shorter than the usual five-year period. There may be some merit to that argument, but, it still does not answer the question.

Each business has characteristics that can be identified in determining the time period of planning. Obviously, companies plan ahead only so far as is useful. Surveys on this subject indicate that among companies that do long-range business and financial planning, the most common planning period is five years, although the trend is toward a greater distance into the future[7] It is also common practice to break-out the five-year plan into quarterly and monthly periods.

Some of the factors that serve as a guide in selecting the proper planning horizon are:

- lead time for product development,

- life span of product or service,

- market development time,

- development time for raw materials and components,

- time required for construction of physical infrastructure,

- payout period for capital investments.

Many companies find it practical to update the strategic plan on an annual basis. In effect, one year is dropped and a new year is added. Each year, as new perceptions of the business or new opportunities or threats emerge, the new factors are studied and incorporated into the planning process and resultant plan.

Financial planning optimizes the financial and operational performance of the firm. The financial plan provides guidance in regard to the cash flow, liquidity, leverage, and risk-exposure profile of the firm. It thus helps management to see the areas of performance gap, and potential financial consequences of decisions taken or about to be taken, and allows management to make optimal business decisions in alignment with the financial capabilities of the firm.

Financial plans assist in planning for growth, including the required funds for capital expenditure, operating expenditure, and working capital. It indicates in advance of needs, the extent and duration of funds required from outside sources and thus permit the securing of more advantageous loans. The extent and duration of funding availability is then matched to investment needs.

For example, cash budgets point out peaks or seasonal fluctuations in business activity that make larger investments in inventories and receivables necessary. It indicates the time and extent of funds needed to meet maturing obligations, tax payments, and dividend or interest payments. But financial planning is increasingly being computerised, and integrated into the enterprise-wide planning framework.

Best-in-class enterprise-wide planning and budgeting solutions provide capabilities for collaborative revenue forecasting, dynamic expenses steering, visibility to financial commitments, and synchronization of operating activities and decisions with the financial outlook. For example, financial planning estimates funding requirements of the business, the timing and amounts of capital expenditures on projects, and the earnings they will produce, forecasts the future profitability of the enterprise, highlights the financial and operational risks, assesses financial capacity to enter into purchase transactions of assets or businesses, maximizes the profitability of operations through focusing resources on high-margin segments or products, decides how the firm will finance Capex, debt payments, dividends, stock repurchases, and on the whole, manages disciplined growth over time.

Finanical planning balances the amount and timing of future cash outflows against net cash inflows from operations and external sources such as proceeds from debt or equity issues. The external funding requirement is the plug that balances the need for funds with the source of funds. Thus, a firm's leverage may vary over time depending on its funding requirements.

Financial planning is not only about asset and liability optimization, but also determines what levers to optimally pull and when, so that the year-end financial objectives are met. There is a revenue side, a cost side, and a cash flow side to the equation. The annual budget, for example, is a key driver to ensure that costs are in line with business plan targets. Financial planning also includes an element of control, since a plan that is not properly implemented and monitored will not allow management to attain financial targets. This is because management will not know how far actual results differ from the target.

In view of the ongoing need to replace and add to productive capacity, over a full operating cycle, the capital expenditures reported in a company's statement of cash flows are ordinarily at least as great as the depreciation charges shown on its income statement. On depreciation, which is an accrual rather than a cash expense, accounting standards leave companies considerable discretion regarding the depreciable lives they assign to their property, plant, and equipment. Sale and leaseback accounting is commonly used for individual assets.

Adding working capital to cash flow analysis frequently reveals problems that may not be apparent from observing the trend of earnings before interest, taxes, depreciation and amortization (EBITDA) or net income plus depreciation. Aside from seasonal variations, the amount of working capital needed to run a business represents a fairly constant percentage of a company's sales.

A rise in working capital requirements reduces operating cash flow, even though EBITDA may rise steadily. A surge in accounts receivable, would similarly reduce operating cash flow. Management can prop up sales by liberalizing credit terms to the company's existing customers. If the company does not finance increases in receivables and inventories resulting from sales growth by extending its payables or drawing down cash, it must do so by adding to its borrowing.

In practice, just as cost containment is important to meeting earnings guidance, so is earnings management. Most companies use some form of earnings smoothing policy so that their earnings and dividends are not excessively volatile.

These smoothing techniques include favorable treatment of various accounting revenue and expense recognition items, depreciation treatment, off-balance-sheet financing or asset-liability recognition, book value versus current value adjustments of various assets, tax planning, creation of reserves, etc.

Financial planning processes develop and leverage enterprise technology to create meaningful business intelligence around actual business performance and future forecasts of the financial impact of alternative capital investments that are made in alignment with business strategy.

Often, non-traditional solutions are required to manage different business risks. Innovative approaches require that companies commit themselves to bearing risks that their customers, employees, or counterparties seek to shed. Management requires a means of structuring, valuing, and mitigating those risks as part of the financial planning process, thus creating a competitive edge.

EXAMPLE

Peter Tufano of Harvard Business School has demonstrated several examples where leading global companies have solved non-traditional business problems through innovative financial planning and financial engineering.[8] In Tufano's study, Rhone-Poulenc, the leading French life sciences and chemical company guaranteed a minimum return to its employees on stock options to engender confidence in its under-valued stock.

Consider the case of Cemex, the largest cement producer in Americas and the second largest industrial company in Mexico. In 1992, when Cemex announced its strategic acquisition of two Spanish cement manufacturers, its stock fell dramatically in response. The market under-valuation was both extreme and crippling. In order to communicate confidence to the investors, Cemex sold investors put options on its stock allowing them to sell their stock back at any time over the next year for a fixed price.

In effect, Cemex committed to buy back its shares, guaranteeing a minimum price to any investor who bought the put. In order to hedge the risk of a plummeting stock price, Cemex's financial advisors, J P Morgan, issued and backed Equity Buyback Obligation Rights (EBORs).

The array of plans and budgets

Corporate financial plans are stated in terms of financial statements. Because virtually every corporate action has financial implications, a vital part of any financial plan is determining whether the plan is attainable given market constraints in demand or supply, pricing leverage, and the company's limited resources. Companies typically prepare a wide array of plans and budgets.

Pro forma financial statements – described in more detail in the next example in this chapter – are the most widely used vehicles for financial forecasting. A pro forma statement is simply a prediction of what the company's financial statements will look like at the end of the forecast period, given a certain number of assumptions regarding the future. The pro forma format displays the information in a logical, internally consistent manner.

A major use of pro forma statements is to determine the company's future need for financing. Another use is to determine forecasted cash flows so that a company valuation can be made. Determination of the affordability for dividend payout is another use of pro forma statements.

Most corporate five-year or three-year financial plans are made on a monthly or quarterly basis to take business seasonality into consideration. The monthly or quarterly figures are then aggregated into annual figures. Forecasts of key variables over the projection period are often driven by the revenue forecast in the income statement. The rationale for this percent-of-sales approach is a tendency for all variable costs and most current assets and current liabilities to vary in close proportion to changes in revenue or sales. For other variables that are not positively correlated with sales, some independent forecasts of such variables are required.

As we demonstrate in the next example, the first step in a percent-of-sales forecast is to examine the historical data to determine which variables have consistently varied as a near-constant proportion to revenues in the past. This enables the forecaster to decide which items can safely be forecasted as a percent of sales, and which ones need to be independently forecasted.

Forecasting sales itself is one of the most important elements in the pro forma financial planning process. Usually a "base case" or most-probable scenario for sales is made by the internal sales operations team, where macro-economic environment, competitive dynamics, and product demand trends are taken into consideration.

Usually, an "up-side case" and a "down-side" case are developed.

Once the "base-case" pro forma statements are completed, sensitivity analysis is conducted to ascertain the impact of changes in key assumptions on earnings, cash flows, or financing needs. Usually, an "up-side case" and a "down-side" case are developed that represent an optimistic and a pessimistic management view.

Sensitivity analysis

Sensitivity analysis encourages management by exception: it enables managers to determine which forward-looking assumptions most strongly affect the forecast, and which are secondary. Sensitivity analysis has its uses, but it is important to realize that forecasts seldom err on one assumption at a time. That is, whatever events throw one assumption in a financial forecast off the mark will be likely to affect other assumptions as well.

Leading companies go a step further, by applying scenario and simulation analysis to pro forma financial statements. Instead of manipulating one assumption at a time, scenario analysis broadens the perspective to look at how simultaneous changes in a number of assumptions might affect the results in response to a particular economic event. This allows management to achieve a deeper understanding of dynamic effects on the corporation's financial results resulting from multiple unexpected scenarios.

This sort of scenario analysis allows management to conduct "stress-testing" of the financial impact from adverse changes in the business environment. Management can thus see the expected changes in the financial health of the business, resulting from pursuit of the business strategy. The last step in the analysis is to generate a separate forecast for each scenario. The result is a limited number of detailed financial projections describing the range of contingencies the business faces.

Often, management must conform to the financial realities, and amend its original business strategies due to the fact that it may not be financially feasible to pursue them. The company may not be able to afford it. This is where operating plans and financial plans merge – or often collide – to create a coherent strategy that is internally consistent, sustainable, and achievable.

Simulation analysis allows management to answer questions like: "What is probability that the company will achieve its 'base-case' or 'up-side case' pro forma financial projections?" As we will see in the next example, Monte Carlo and Latin hypercube simulation techniques allow us to answer these questions relatively easily.

EXAMPLE

Let's look at a fairly high-level view of the five-year business and financial plan for XYZ corporation. The financial statements are presented in Figure 5.1.

XYZ Corp. ($ Million)	Actual	Forecast				
Income Statement	**2003**	**2004**	**2005**	**2006**	**2007**	**2008**
Net revenue	1,000	1,060	1,124	1,191	1,262	1,338
- Cost of goods sold	410	435	461	488	518	549
= Gross profit	590	625	663	703	745	790
- Sales, general, and admin	120	127	135	143	151	161
= EBITDA	470	498	528	560	593	629
- Depreciation and amort.	90	104	120	138	158	180
= EBIT	380	394	408	422	436	449
- Interest expense	12	24	33	52	89	162
+Interest Income	-	48	86	179	356	710
= Income before Taxes	368	418	462	548	702	997
- Taxes	129	146	162	192	246	349
= Net Income	239	271	300	356	456	648
Beg. Retained earnings	100	315	560	830	1,151	1,561
Dividends	24	27	30	36	46	65
Ending retained earnings	315	560	830	1,151	1,561	2,144
Balance Sheet	**2003**	**2004**	**2005**	**2006**	**2007**	**2008**
Cash and cash equivalents	-	529	955	1,983	3,951	7,887
Current assets	150	159	169	179	189	201
Property, plant, and equip.	900	1,040	1,198	1,376	1,577	1,802
Accumulated depreciation	300	404	524	661	819	999
Net fixed assets	600	636	674	715	757	803
Total assets	750	1,324	1,798	2,877	4,898	8,890
Current liabilities	70	74	79	83	88	94
Debt	180	371	503	805	1,371	2,489
Stock	400	563	656	1,158	2,287	4,746
Retained earnings	100	315	560	830	1,151	1,561
Equity	500	879	1,216	1,988	3,438	6,307
Total Liabilities and equity	750	1,324	1,798	2,877	4,898	8,890

XYZ Corp. ($ Million)	Actual	Forecast				
Free Cash Flow	**2003**	**2004**	**2005**	**2006**	**2007**	**2008**
Net Income	239	271	300	356	456	648
+ Interest expense	12	24	33	52	89	162
+ Income taxes	129	146	162	192	246	349
- Interest income	0	48	86	179	356	710
= EBIT	380	394	408	422	436	449
- Cash taxes	133	138	143	148	152	157
= NOPAT	247	256	265	274	283	292
+Depreciation and amort.	90	104	120	138	158	180
= Gross cash flow	337	360	385	412	441	472
- Increase in net working capital		5	5	5	6	6
- Capex		140	158	178	201	226
= Free cash flow		215	222	229	235	240

FIGURE 5.1 ■ Financial statements

The company currently has a 24 percent debt-to-assets ratio, and plans to increase its leverage to 28 percent. This assumption is built into the five-year pro forma business plan (see Figure 5.2).

XYZ Corp. ($ Million)	Actual	Forecast					
Valuation	**2003**	**2004**	**2005**	**2006**	**2007**	**2008**
Return on equity	47.9%	30.9%	24.7%	17.9%	13.3%	10.3%
Retention rate	90.0%	90.0%	90.0%	90.0%	90.0%	90.0%
Sustainable growth rate	43.1%	27.8%	22.2%	16.1%	11.9%	9.2%
Debt Ratio	24.00%	28%	28%	28%	28%	28%
Cost of Debt	6.5%					
Cost of Equity	12.4%					
WACC	10.11%					
Corporate Value	$ 3,383					

FIGURE 5.2 ■ Five-year pro forma business plan

Assumptions for the five-year business plan are shown in Figure 5.3.

XYZ Corp. ($ Million)			
Assumptions	**2003**		**2003**
Net revenue growth	6%	Current liabilities	70
Current year sales	$1,000	Equity	400
Interest rate on debt	7%	Beg retained earnings	100
Dividend payout ratio	10%	Current assets	150
Tax rate	35%	Property, plant, and equip.	900
Cost of goods sold / net revenue	41%	Accumulated depreciation	300
SG&A / net revenue	12%		
Depreciation rate	10%		
Liquid asset interest rate	9%	Sustainable growth rate	4%
Current assets / net revenue	15%	Target Debt to asset ratio	28%
Current liabilities / net revenue	7%		
Net fixed assets / net revenue	60%		
PP&E / net revenue	90%		

FIGURE 5.3 ■ Assumptions

Based on the pro forma business plan, discounted free cash flow valuation shows a total firm valuation of $3,383m.

Although this example is at an aggregate level, actual business plans of mid-to-large size companies are much more detailed and includes hundreds of line items.

Segments of the long-range financial plan includes the following:

■ trend of revenues and profits,

■ capital investments,

■ cash flows and financing requirements,

■ key financial ratios,

■ risk analysis,

■ breakdown by business unit, product-line, geography,

■ financial position.

The long-range financial plan includes a listing of capital investments (Capex and Opex) required to attain the revenue and profit objectives. The investment amount should include working capital requirements (cash invested in receivables and inventory, less the amount of accounts payable).

There is a growing trend in industry toward eliminating working capital by shrinking inventories and receivables.[9] If the company plans to pursue such a strategy, that goal should be built into the business plan, since it will have a significant impact on capital requirements.

The long-range plan includes cash requirements for each year of the plan. This is one of the most crucial parts of the long-range plan, for management must know about the risks of future indebtedness as well as the need to issue stocks or bonds. It presents overall statistics that indicate changes in the company's valuation based on free cash flow projections, changes that may break loan covenants, and changes that may increase the company's risk profile.

Business planning includes an analysis of likely competitive response, capital cost overruns, sales fluctuations, raw materials scarcity, technological change, and deterioration of margins as risk elements. Competing products may cause deterioration of margins due to pricing pressure.

The financial statements from the business plan are often used by banks, creditors, credit-rating agencies, or potential merger partners, to determine financial position and prospects. At a more tactical level, the annual budgeting process interlocks subsidiary plans to form the corporate level budget. Business budgeting finds the most efficient course through which efforts of the business may be directed to achieve annual corporate revenue-expense objectives. Management is guided by the budget during the course of the year to remain on the charted course as nearly as possible. However, conditions change rapidly in business; the actions of customers and competitors cannot be entirely controled. Therefore, the beginning-of-the-year business plan and budget may require revisiting, as appropriate.

At the highest level, the annual budget is the method by which the company implements its long-range plan. The goals set forth in the long-range plan are used as the basis for the annual budget, given funding limitations. In the budgeting process, revenues, costs, levels of operation, facilities, financial resources, and personnel are all considered and interrelated.

Components of the budget

The budget contains the following subsidiary budgets:

- sales budget,

- production budget,

- purchase budget,

- labor budget,

- manufacturing expense budget,

- inventory budget,

- selling, general, and administrative budget,

- research and development budget,

- capital and operating expense budget,

- cost of goods sold budget,

- cash budget.

These subsidiary budgets roll up to a set of planned financial statements. The annual planning cycle integrates these division-level plans and forms the total company picture.

The consolidated plan is thus the summation of the division-level plans, and is evaluated at the corporate level. Some reiteration is typically necessary to arrive as an acceptable plan. Discussions are held with the functional supervisors or department heads to clarify any seemingly out-of-line condition. Upon approval by top management, the plan is presented to the board of directors for approval. When the overall plan is considered satisfactory at top management and board of directors levels, the respective divisions are notified of the approved plan.

Once the budget is approved, the business enters a new phase.

Once the budget is approved, the business enters a new phase. The budget must be attained, so the budget becomes a control tool against which to measure actual performance. Variances in each month or quarter are analysed, and corrective actions taken whenever necessary. Real-time business planning systems allow management to get information about these variances in a more timely fashion, and allows course-corrections more effectively.

Dynamic financial models capture the characteristics of the business, and allow companies to determine business strategies appropriate to their risk tolerance. Traditional business representations project expected outcomes. Dynamic financial models add to this by modeling:

■ variability,

■ interaction of risks,

■ relationships between products and services,

■ the effect of risk control mechanisms (pricing, insurance and dividend policy).

Companies use dynamic financial models to capture the characteristics of their business and to manage strategic, operational, and financial risks. Projected key performance indicators (KPIs) are continually monitored to ensure that both the probable outcome and the likely variability match the overall risk tolerance of the organization.

Making optimal financial decisions

In this section, we briefly review some of the financial modeling techniques and analytics that have been successfully applied by leading companies to make optimal financial decisions. A financial model is essentially a set of inter-related variables that have complex interconnections.[10]

In practice, the balance sheet, income statement, and cash flow statement are connected in one large integrated financial model of the corporation's assets, liabilities, revenues, expenses, cash inflows, and cash outflows. These financial models, however, are usually deterministic, that is, they do not have stochastic or simulation capabilities.

Various assumptions are used to forecast this integrated model into future periods on a pro forma basis. Most companies use a financial system for planning and analysis. *Hyperion*, *White Plains*, *SAP*, and *PeopleSoft* are examples of such systems that manage the accounting-based financial data. However, these financial systems usually do not allow sophisticated optimization analysis, but rather are large databases for general ledger transaction data input and organized data output based on accounting conventions.

Optimization is a powerful analytical tool because it allows management to see what are the most desirable levels of various variables within management's control that maximize shareholder value. Linear and non-linear programing can be used to maximize the choice variable, subject to selected constraints. But these models assume continuous functions, are deterministic, and static. To be useful in realistic management decision making, the modeling technique of choice is multi-period stochastic programing with discontinuous functions.

This allows the modeling of "if-then-else" type logical decision functions in the financial planning model. For example, cost of debt is not a monotonically increasing function of leverage, but a step-function of leverage levels and credit ratings.

In addition, pro forma financial models require forecasts of various uncertain variables, and the accuracy of these forecasts are greatly improved if appropriate probability distributions are assigned to each financial variable based on historical actual volatilities. Stochastic elements are thus an essential improvement in the financial modeling process.

Forecasting techniques

In practice, sophisticated econometric forecasting techniques, such as Generalized Autoregressive Conditional Heteroskedasticity (GARCH), Box Jenkins Autoregressive Fractionally Integrated Moving Average Models (ARFIMA) or Hodrick-Prescott (HP) filters, are useless in corporate pro forma financial statement forecasting because, to be useful, they require a minimum of 200 time series data points to be effectively applied. These econometric forecasting techniques, however, have found some use in financial market price series forecasting. Dynamic programing, stochastic dynamic programing, chaos theory, and neural networks are all useless for corporate applied financial planning for the same reason.

Pro forma corporate financial statement forecasts are therefore made mostly by crude methods such as percent of sales method where key variables such as accounts receivable, inventories, accounts payable, fixed assets, etc. are related to sales forecasts by some formula. Top-line revenue forecasts are made very realistically with a bottom-up method with operational inputs on potential sales growth. They are also made top-down, with economic and industry revenue growth projections along with market share assumptions. Once these forecasts are approved by the company management, the financial planning model, with literally hundreds of accounting variables and inter-connections, churns out likely financial position statements.

Although business conditions can change rapidly, many surprises that affect organizational performance can be predicted using available data and technologies. By predicting future performance from plans based on the current and perceived business environment, contingencies can be drawn up in advance and applied as appropriate. The ability to recognize and exploit changing business conditions is the driving force behind *rolling forecasts* – which also deliver the benefit of reducing or eliminating the annual budgeting process.

According to Hackett Best Practices research, however, only 23 percent of organizations make use of this proven best practice. When forecasting, many organizations focus solely on financial results, such as revenue and cost measures. As with planning, effective forecasting requires modifying and developing plans to achieve strategic goals.[11]

These strategic goals may in turn need to be revised as planning assumptions change. Realistic business plans indicate funding requirements, cash flow projections, corporate valuation, financial leverage, profitability, liquidity, and operational metrics.

The state-of-the-art financial modeling technique applied at this point is simulation. Simulations basically run the financial model literally thousands of times based on the likely volatilities in selected financial variables, and present a view of a distribution of probable earnings for the next few reporting periods. It can answer questions like: given the corporate financial model and its assumptions, what is the probability that our earnings next quarter will meet expectations?

Monte Carlo and Latin hypercube techniques are most often applied for financial plan simulations, although the latter is preferable in terms of robust sample distributions. There are many commercially available software packages such as *Crystal Ball* and *Palisades' Risk Optimizer* that perform financial planning model simulations.

The next step after simulations is to have the model answer questions about key financial policy areas. The model can provide the optimal levels of leverage that minimize the overall cost of capital, or the optimal short-term and long-term debt mix within the debt structure itself. Financial planning models incorporate a limited number of financial variables and exclude most off-balance-sheet considerations.

The optimal answers can be useful as guidelines to optimality, which has then to be further tweaked in light of other qualitative constraints. But that has much to do with refinements under management judgment.

The point here is that optimization analytics can be useful to provide baseline guidance on optimality. There are many commercial software packages, such as Crystal Ball's OptQuest, Palisade Software's Risk Optimizer, GAMS, Excel solver, etc., that can handle many of these optimization problems.

Treasury management

The environment within which corporates must conduct their day-to-day business is continually changing. In order to stay competitive and deliver the required value to shareholders, CFOs must assess the impact of these change factors across the organization's entire value chain.

Examples of some of the key change factors or drivers impacting all industry sectors are:

■ globalization of markets,

■ new regulatory requirements (e.g. FAS 133, IAS 39),

■ new avenues to market (i.e. e-business),

■ consolidation across and within industry sectors,

■ mergers, acquisitions and divestments/spin-offs,

■ increased emphasis on shareholder value,

■ continued push into emerging markets,

■ competitive pressure to reduce non-core units,

■ outsourcing non-core functions.

These external drivers have both a direct and indirect impact on Treasury. As other areas of the organization, particularly the business units and other head office functions, react to these external change drivers, the projects that they initiate will often impact other process areas creating internal change drivers.

The challenge for the treasurer is to assess the impact on the existing financial risks generated by the business and the treasury framework used to manage them. In addition, advances in banking products/services and treasury systems constantly alter what is recognized as best practice or leading edge in terms of treasury practice standards.

All of the above places an expectation on the treasurer to reassess how effective the existing treasury processes and activities are in meeting the changing requirements of the business and its stakeholders. Many of the world's leading corporations have designed and implemented a new dynamic risk management framework to meet the existing and future requirements of the business. The integrated treasury function is shown in Figure 5.4.

Best practices and standards in treasury management can vary significantly from one corporation to another just as size, geographical spread, industry sector and management's risk appetites vary. However, according to PricewaterhouseCoopers, there are some common fundamental objectives in terms of treasury processes and practices that all corporates should be seeking to achieve:[12]

- centralization of their transaction execution activities around structures;

- the introduction of truly regional service capability and cash management structures;

- development of e-capabilities and functionality of package treasury management systems to achieve significant enhancement in efficiency through the automation and integration of processes;

- Utilization of tools like a balance scorecard to monitor and measure treasury's contribution to the organization's shareholder value enhancement objectives/targets.

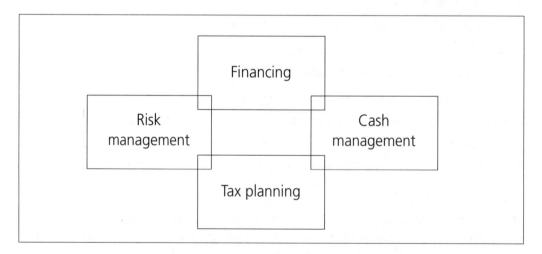

FIGURE 5.4 ■ The integrated treasury function

The move by corporations to centralize their transaction execution activities around structures like shared service centres and integrate the focus of the head office function, tax, treasury, financial and legal, while still attempting to provide the necessary decision support to the business has created an interesting dynamic for treasurers. The challenge for the treasurer is to find a balance between cost effectiveness and value added support to the business.

The introduction of truly regional service capability and cash management structures by a number of the leading banks means that many corporations are still over-banked and destroying value through high bank charges and inefficient cash management practices.

The advances in sophistication in recent years, including the development of e-capabilities and functionality of package treasury management systems, have been significant. Such systems are key enablers to achieving significant enhancement in efficiency through the automation and integration of processes. Enterprise-wide systems vendors have introduced treasury system functionality.

Enterprise-wide systems vendors have introduced treasury system functionality.

Many corporations are beginning to utilize tools like a balance scorecard to monitor and measure treasury's contribution to the organization's shareholder value enhancement objectives/targets. A balanced set of key performance indicators (KPIs) provides financial and non-financial benchmarks for treasury.

According to PricewaterhouseCoopers, companies planning to improve treasury efficiencies should:

■ review and reconfirm the treasury requirements for the business, leading to a high-level design of an organization (i.e. policies, processes, reporting), systems and banking solution to meet those requirements;

■ confirm existing risk profile of business and treasury practices;

■ understand internal and external change drivers;

■ develop alternative models taking account of the good practice standards applied by the world's leading corporate treasury finance operations, focusing on aspects of policy, organization, reporting, process, technology and banking solutions;

■ evaluate models based on criteria set by the user (i.e. control, cost/benefits, etc.);

■ develop high-level design from preferred model;

■ expand the high-level design into a detailed solutions definition, which will form the basis of the implementation plan. (This involves performing a gap analysis of the high-level design against the current state to develop a detailed specification and change plan for the treasury operations.)

▶

■ undertake the work necessary to set up the new organization, reporting, processes, systems and banking arrangements. In this phase, work closely with the system and banking vendors and apply best practice project and change management standards to ensure an efficient migration to the new structure. This includes the use of project plans, status reports and the development and delivery of communication and training plans to ensure that new processes are understood, accepted, and acted upon at all levels.

Improving treasury operations

Improving treasury operations entails a thorough assessment of the current state of treasury operations, capabilities, and level of efficiency. The desired goal or end state may be to move to a real-time globally-integrated treasury platform. This would require modifications in the organization's structure, processes, banking structures, and other issues. Once the objectives are set, an integrated migration plan is necessary.

With regard to treasury activities, both an external macroeconomic and an internal microeconomic perspective are warranted. The macroeconomic allocation is focussed on funds available from the general economy at any time. Of course, funds can be sourced from abroad as well, but in that case, foreign currency and interest rate exposures and their associated hedging plans need to be considered.

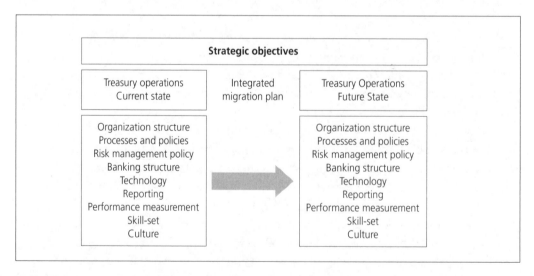

FIGURE 5.5 ■ Improving treasury management

Once available funds are defined, the internal microeconomic allocation process of where to commit the funds within the organization becomes the focus. Like control activities, treasury activities cut across all functions of the organization, as they impact financing and investing activities of the company. Therefore, measuring treasury performance is vital – how else can you know whether the risk management approach is adding value?

An international study of corporate treasury control and performance standards conducted by PricewaterhouseCoopers illustrates that treasury risk management approaches vary widely: 66 percent of respondents actively manage underlying business risks, 28 percent take a fully hedged approach, and 1 percent take on risk unrelated to any underlying business exposure. Across all companies and territories, a major focus is on using derivative products to manage core treasury risks. But only 40 percent of corporations apply formal control parameters, such as limit controls, to these activities.[13]

The new treasury management model is dynamic. "Break out of the treasury silo, mix things up with line managers and be ready to shift financing strategies on a dime."[14] These are some of the prescriptions for success in treasury today, provided by a group of CFOs interviewed by *Treasury and Risk Management* magazine back in 2001. The survey included CFOs from a range of industries and regions, whose companies are in distinctly varying states of financial health.

CFOs say that their growing responsibilities for corporate performance beyond the financial realm put a greater burden on their treasurers to keep the cash flowing and the financing flexible on a day-to-day basis.

The Operating Cycle & Cash Flow Timeline

The operating cycle consists of the day-to-day activities pertaining to the acquisition of materials and/or resources, their transformation into saleable goods, their marketing, and the ensuing collection of revenues.

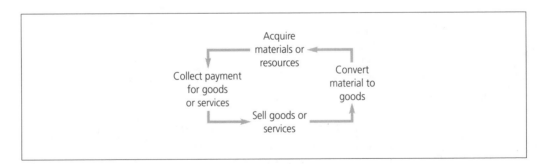

FIGURE 5.6 ■ The Operating Cycle

Float refers to the total time interval from the time resources are purchased at the beginning of a company's operating cycle until the time payment is received for goods and services at the end of a company's operating cycle. These include:

- invoicing float,
- collection float,
- payment float,
- disbursement float.

A company typically benfits from shortening all types of float associated with cash inflows, and lengthening all types of float associated with cash outflows. *Cash Conversion Efficiency* measures the efficiency with which a company converts sales into cash.

Cash Conversion Efficiency = cash flow from operations / sales

The *Cash conversion cycle* measures liquidity from another perspective. It calculates the time required for a company to convert cash outflows necessary to produce goods into cash inflows through collection of accounts receivable.

More demands on treasurers

In a tight budgetary environment, treasurers typically review all vendor contracts and purchasing operations, and try to squeeze profits out of joint ventures to keep expenses associated with closing unprofitable plants within budget. CFOs demand continuously creative financing structures from their treasurers, of course.

In a dynamic business environment, corporates should not build static financing and capital structure models that may have worked historically but may not be optimal going

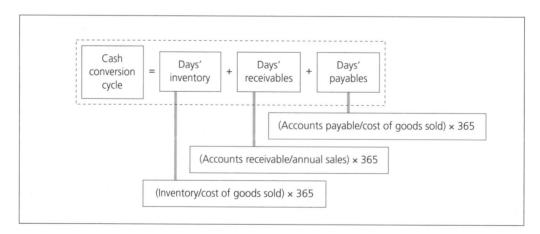

FIGURE 5.7 ■ Cash conversion cycle

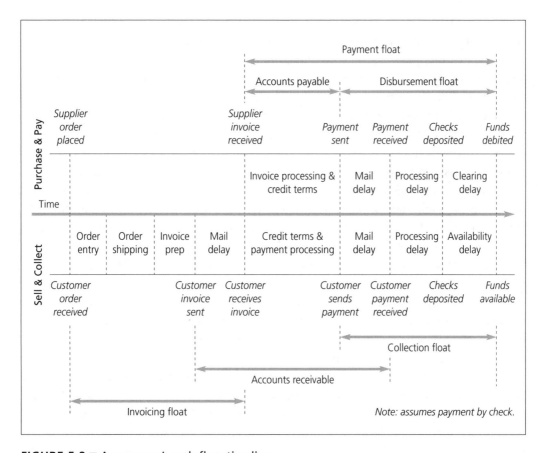

FIGURE 5.8 ■ A company's cash flow timeline

forward. Optimal financing structures need to be rebalanced and reoptimized as external financial conditions and internal funding requirements change. Corporate treasurers provide additional flexibility to financial decision making by arranging on- or off-balance-sheet risk management structures, and being vigilant about anything that could change the risk profile of the business.

There is little to be gained for a corporation that seems to do something clever in the treasury area only to end up having to write off a derivative instrument or record a loss associated with a foreign exchange hedging transaction. It is a difficult mandate, especially since business is more complex because of the speed at which companies have to react to change.

Sell-side analysts want information about how the business is running and the financials. Even as they stretch their treasurers to the limit, CFOs are quick to point out that treasury's primary responsibility is to ensure that cash flows are adequate for business operations at all times. This includes seasonality in demand and supply, as well as special business need for liquidity that might occur. Treasurers need to make sure their companies have liquidity where they need it and do so in the most cost-effective manner, but treasurers also need to be prudent risk takers.

Often, treasurers are so protective of the downside that they do not advocate the upside. Treasurers should suggest profitable hedging opportunities when "natural accounting hedges" are in place. Typically, cash balances and foreign currency exposures are dynamic throughout a given month, but treasurers must have enough confidence in their forecasting methodologies to take advantage of slight movements in currencies before actual inter-company settlement of overseas transactions. Tax issues form an integral component for treasury activities. In a sense, the treasurer is also the tax planner. We discuss optimal tax planning in Chapter 3.

Leading treasury management practices include financial risk management. The treasurer requires an analytical and an intuitive feel for risk correlations and their cash flow and earnings impact. Many operational risks are managed by line managers, but the treasurer integrates and manages those risks in the aggregate, so that selective risk management may be undertaken. Risk mapping or risk profiling aids these companies in devising appropriate capital structures.

The treasurer provides thought leadership on the capital structure, helping to determine the weighted average cost of capital and the cost of the different pieces of capital. The capital structure analytic is not new, but integrating that and the risk mapping with the capital structure thought process is certainly new.[15]

Collaboration between the treasury department and the operational units will only become more important in the future, promoting prudent balance sheet thinking. Treasury management is very much about performing a balancing act – that of efficient cash management, which requires application of analytical and strategic thinking to structure solutions that minimize adverse risks. Executing this according to board approved corporate guidelines requires financial discipline.

The importance of the treasurer's role goes beyond number crunching for day-to-day cash needs. Like CFOs, treasurers nowadays are increasingly aware of the implications of their work in creating shareholder value and maintaining good corporate governance.

Many companies in the Asia-Pacific region were humbled since the 1997 financial crisis. One of the root causes of their troubles was poor financial risk management, either seeking

EXAMPLE

ABB, the Swedish-Swiss power and industrial equipment giant carries out its Asian-Pacific treasury operations out of Singapore. The ABB Treasury Centre ensures that cash-short subsidiaries are internally funded from the surplus of subsidiaries elsewhere in the region. It also checks the foreign exchange commitments of its Asian units, working with them to hedge their risk with forward and options contracts.[16]

short-term funding for long-term projects or over-exposure to foreign exchange, or both. And then there is Enron's disastrous off-balance-sheet transactions. Best-in-class treasury management practices, as reviewed in this chapter, provide guidance.

New technology

New technologies have played a significant role in improving treasury management. Today, backed by fast-evolving technology, a treasurer has the ability to know more, do more, and decide more independently. Through enterprise resource planning (ERP) systems, information about a company's operations, supply chain and accounting are easily accessible.

As treasury software vendors compete amongst themselves in both price and quality, automated cash management processes are getting commoditized. ERP modules that power shared service centres are pervasive and getting cheaper. Oracle, for example, recently cut the price of its business management software by 75 percent due to fierce competition. Corporates that prefer to transfer specialized functions outside, rather than running their own shared services, outsource the process to banks, and even accounting firms.

Managing liquidity is getting easier. Treasurers of multinational or large local corporations can now perform in-country sweeping and arrange local currency pooling in many countries. They can also do cross-border, even cross-regional, US-dollar pooling around the clock.

Banks enable automatic investing of balances in overnight investment instruments, or they can actively manage short-term excess funds in investment-grade US commercial paper. Foreign exchange transactions may be done over the internet with the promise of straight-through processing (STP). Treasury integrators even automatically input hedging information into FAS 133-compliant general ledgers.

Emerging treasury and risk management technologies allow more efficient fund management operations, so that enterprise-wide risks can be managed efficiently, and in real time.

Active tax planning, as an integral part of the corporate treasurer's overall risk management function, is crucial in order to realize opportunities for tax savings. If left as an afterthought, tax has the potential to significantly erode the commercial benefits achieved on a pre-tax basis.

For example, subsidiaries fall into either of two legal structures governing US multinationals: check-the-box (CTB) and controlled foreign corporation (CFC). The two categories make a distinction whether a US multinational is a partnership or a corporation, and each has its own tax treatment. Lending between CFC and CTB entities is not tax efficient.

Subsidiaries fall into either of two legal structures governing US multinationals.

In a CFC, any cash that moves away, or that is construed as an active investment into another entity, will be viewed as a deemed dividend back to the parent. If it is deemed dividend, there are complex calculations to see what its tax implications are, but the simple conse-quence is, about 34 percent of the amount will be exposed. That amount practically negates whatever cost benefits a pooling structure offers. CTB seems to have a better way to move funds across regions, and even from the regions to the US. Lending from CFC to CFC, or CTB to CTB is not much of an issue. But in each instance, a tax analysis needs to be per-formed to see if it makes sense to do so.

The vigilance of treasurers is growing. The drive for efficiency through treasury hardware and software upgrades has been a notable trend in treasury management in the last few years. There has been an ongoing focus among companies on investing significantly in terms of IT infrastructure, enterprise resource planning systems, and using their rich func-tionality to optimize relationships with clients and customers. Not surprisingly, multinational corporations are the heaviest spenders in IT systems.

Liquidity management in a developing market context – focus on China[17]

No treasurer can afford to underestimate the importance of liquidity management, but when it comes to developing markets many find the unfamiliar rules and regulations challenging. Of all the developing markets, the People's Republic of China (China) best illustrates the dilemma for corporate treasurers. The same techniques for liquidity management as used in North America or Europe cannot be applied wholesale to China.

There are issues with definitions and demarcation zones. The practice of web-based liquidity management is giving way to the concept of working capital management. Many companies now recognize that how fast and efficiently receivables are collected is an integral part of working capital management, not just a processing factory which requires excellent operational support.

Unfortunately, for many companies operating in China, the historic restrictions on access to this market have led to a very fragmented corporate structure. Typically, major foreign operators in this market may have many subsidiaries, some wholly owned, some joint ventures with a variety of local partners. The activities of these subsidiaries vary, some being production centers and others operating as sales/marketing or retail distribution outlets.

Chinese regulations for the time being continue to distinguish between different types of operation (a subsidiary's scope of business will be tightly defined by its Chinese business license) and therefore this means companies are unable to create a true holding company structure where finances for a group of companies can be efficiently centralized and managed as is common practice in developed markets, although it is now possible to centralize some activities such as human resource management and sales activities.

On a day-to-day cash management level, each subsidiary will probably have its own board of directors and separate banking relationships. This can make monitoring of cash balances difficult as well as making it very hard to consolidate liquidity. Whereas in deregulated markets, cash rich operations could (via the intermediary of a bank account and pooling or cash concentration structures) be used to fund cash hungry parts of the business, these approaches are hard to achieve effectively in China. This is because:

■ There is no financial holding company structure available.
■ Transfers of funds between subsidiaries are subject to restrictions.
■ Inter-company loans from the parent are subject to withholding tax. Exacerbating the issue is China's heavily regulated interest rate environment in which margins or charges paid by the banks are centrally determined by the People's Bank of China (the Central Bank) which means there are unusually wide spreads between deposit and lending rates in this market. The consequences of over-funding an initially cash hungry start-up with capital injections are therefore punitive.
■ Exchange controls on the capital account and the requirement that capital must have been injected in accordance with the approved business plan before a dividend can be paid, together with minimum capitalization rules, mean that thin capitalization is not an option either.

For many major multinationals, the only long-term solution is to embark on a corporate restructuring resulting ultimately in a divisional structure. This can involve buying out partners in joint ventures so it can be a time-consuming and lengthy exercise with inherent tax complications if cross-provincial mergers are involved.

Direct inter-company lending between subsidiaries is, in general, not allowed in China. However, a relatively recent change in regulations has come to the rescue of customers with multiple legal entities and operations. Entrusted loans allow related parties to lend to and borrow from each other via a third party. The mechanism is simple and is initiated by an entity with surplus cash placing a deposit with a bank for on-lending to a designated company. There is a prescribed rate referenced to the Central Bank's lending rate. The intermediary is allowed to charge a set fee (a specified range) for the administration of the service, but all the credit risk is effectively taken by the lending entity.

In China, these restrictions and reporting requirements also apply to inter-company flows and one of the consequences is that it is very hard for companies to meet objectives in terms of implementing global netting. Nonetheless, with careful planning and the use of electronic settlement and balance monitoring systems, much can be done to improve the regularity and monitoring of cross-border cash flows.

Every market has its own idiosyncrasies and most cash management services have ways to manage the idiosyncrasies and inefficiencies. *Lockbox*, one of the most prevalent receivables management tools in the world was born out of the inefficiencies of the US postal system. Developing markets normally impose a higher cost of capital or borrowing and therefore efficient cash management is a necessity in these markets.

Technology is radically changing the way treasury processes are managed and efficient application of new technology is all-important for the cost-conscious corporate. Concepts such as centralisation and outsourcing are transforming the industry. Corporate treasury's role has never been more important. The *Corporate Finance Magazine* presented inaugural Awards for Excellence in Corporate Treasury.[18] The companies featured in the awards were as follows:[19]

Category	Best-in-class treasuries
STP and technology integration	Daimler Chrysler
	ACE
	Cisco Systems
Treasury strategy	British Petroleum (BP)
	Harley-Davidson
	Hutchison-Whampoa
Working capital management	Agilent
	Dell
	BASF
Foreign exchange	Shell
	General Electric (GE)
Operational efficiency	Hewlett-Packard (HP)
	The McGraw-Hill Cos.
	Cargolux
Outsourcing	Coca-Cola

Rapid advances in the technology available to treasurers has led to rapid change in the way treasury is run. Putting new technology to work frequently involves upheaval and restructuring, but keeping up with the pace of technological change is vital.

Straight through processing (STP) – some examples

For those treasuries that can quickly adopt – and adapt to – new technology there is a clear advantage. Processes become simpler, time is saved and costs reduced. Their investment in new technology is seen to save money. Implementing straight through processing has been a long-term treasury goal.

To achieve straight through processing (STP) the Daimler Chrysler group has implemented standardized treasury processes and controls worldwide, along with a uniform treasury system. STP of settlement instructions takes place via an interface between the treasury system and the bank's e-banking platform. The company has also put in place state-of-the-art security controls: deal initiation, confirmation and settlement are strictly segregated.

ACE Europe, part of the Bermuda-based insurer ACE Group has a universal payments system. Developed in-house, this system provides a consistent and borderless payment mechanism across the various business units. It allows staff in 16 countries, and from disciplines as disparate as claims, accounts receivable, and purchase ledger to access similar payment screens. The in-built system security and front-end bank code validation allows the staff involved to concentrate on their core competencies without needing to be payment experts. ACE achieves its high rate of STP through the combination of its universal payment system, its central pool of banking expertise, and by having single file access to 14 automated clearing-houses in Europe.

BP's treasury strategy is to leverage the scale of the company to add value through running highly efficient global cash management processes and accessing the financial markets directly through its own professional dealing capability. BP's treasury acts as the BP Group's internal bank. On a daily basis, the treasury manages global pooling of the cash and foreign exchange positions of the BP business world wide operations.

BP's foreign exchange and cash and debt balances are then net centrally and the residual positions are passed on to BP's dealing room to trade out directly into the financial markets. The dealing operations trade on their own account as well as to meet BP's requirements, ensuring the best pricing from other market counterparties. To achieve flexibility, and to provide both business and tax efficiency, the company actually runs two interconnected in-house banks, one in the UK and one in the US, as well as a highly rationalized cash concentration structure using key partnership banks.

Harley Davidson's treasury management is highly thought of for its awareness of new trends and willingness to adapt to new technologies. Hutchison-Whampoa's strength is in cash management portfolio. Cisco Systems has been successful in applying technology to streamline and automate its processes.

Created in 1999 after being spun-off from Hewlett-Packard, California-based Agilent develops and manufactures high-tech equipment. Doing business in 110 countries, it generates annual revenue of $6bn. To make itself independent within the time frame laid out for the spin-off, Agilent needed to deal with the wide range of systems and processes it had inherited from its parent.

So Agilent replicated what was in place at HP, with standardization and automation left until a later date. In Europe, this left the company with accounts payable centralized and payments outsourced, but with processes such as accounts receivable and payroll left with local

Agilent invested in a single ERP platform company-wide.

banks. Even at just one bank per country that made 15 banks across Europe. The result was very high finance-costs-to-revenues ratio. So Agilent decided simplification, standardization and automation were necessary and invested in a single ERP platform company-wide.

Agilent's treasury master accounts are automatically zero-balanced each day to a London-domiciled euro or dollar concentration account. So the treasury manages a single concentrated position and invests surplus balances. Automating the daily zero balancing has also cut the amount of transaction-processing work in the treasury.

Best-known in the finance world for the success of its direct-to-customer business model, Dell has also established a strong reputation in treasury circles. Dell has taken a progressive approach to treasury technology. Several years ago the company implemented an impressive treasury intranet, and in doing so provided a model that has since been followed by a number of others. For Dell's treasury, this pioneering intranet means more effective global communication and information integration.

In order to optimize its working capital processes, BASF group has put in place an umbrella facility credit arrangement. All excess cash is placed in short-term loan deposits, with minimal cash held in the current account. Mid-to long-term funding is managed through inter-company loans and banking credits are all kept under 365 days. Shell's treasury centre has state-of-the-art foreign exchange operations. General Electric's treasury runs class-leading foreign exchange operations.

Hewlett Packard's treasury team are continually striving to drive higher levels of automation in their daily processes. For example, the recent automation of the interface with the inter-company netting application. Forthcoming developments include the development of an interface between the company's ERP system and its treasury management system, in order to take short-term cash-flow forecast information directly into the daily cash position worksheets.

A recent benchmarking study using data from the Hackett Group shows that the typical treasury function has 6.3 full-time equivalent headcount per billion dollars of revenue whereas HP's treasury function has just 1.2 which is deemed to be 'world-class.'

McGraw-Hill uses the internet to provide balance and transaction information, and shared service centres for its back-office processing.

Cargolux carries out efficient management of receivables – and hence optimization of working capital – through the early adoption of e-billing. The company has a US dollar sweep system which has enhanced liquidity management. The group is now focussing on developing a more automated medium- and long-term cash forecast tool. The ultimate objective is to update the cash forecast and net currency exposures from each rolling forward business plan. It will also further roll-out and implement e-billing and e-payables systems to improve transparency and input timeliness of data in its treasury systems.

Coca-Cola's treasury group demands strict adherence to its treasury procedures manual in order to comply with the group's audit requirement. Other disciplines in place ensure the outsource provider has access to sufficient resources in terms of core skills and that the group optimizes its purchasing power. The treasury group is also expected to be at the forefront of treasury technology, but any implementation of platform upgrades must be achieved via carefully coordinated work plans. Having chosen agency treasury services as its outsourcing option, Coca-Cola treasury keeps hold of key strategic decisions but is able to focus on re-engineering treasury throughout the group.

Some authors have listed best practices in cash management as follows:[20]

■ area-concentration banking,

■ consolidate bank accounts,

■ controlled disbursements,

■ electronic funds transfer,

■ lockbox collections,

■ on-line access to bank account information,

■ positive pay system,

■ proliferate petty-cash boxes,

■ utilize an investment policy,

■ zero-balance accounts.

In treasury management, the authors list the following best practices:[21]

■ access bank account information in the internet;

■ automate employee retirement plan enrolment;

■ avoid delays in check posting;

■ centralize foreign exchange management;

■ consolidate insurance policies;

■ grant employees immediate retirement plan eligibility;

■ install a treasury workstation;

■ negotiate faster deposited check availability;

■ optimize cash management decisions through the internet;

■ use internet-based cash flow analysis software;

■ use internet-based options pricing services;

■ use internet-based risk measurement services;

■ use internet-based technical analyzis services;

■ use internet-based treasury management services;

■ use web broadcasting for public reporting.

Outsourcing selected treasury operations is a strategic option that more companies are considering. There are issues of control and accountability, and the important determination of what functions are core *vis-à-vis* those that are non-core.

Latest research suggests that:[22]

■ Treasury outsourcing means outsourcing operational treasury and cash management activities, not policy or strategy.

■ Corporate treasuries outsource in order to do more with less, access a core skill set, and focus on adding value.

■ There are three types of treasury outsourcing: treasury system outsourcing, corporate treasury outsourcing, and agency treasury.

■ Changes in corporate governance will drive corporates to reengineer their treasury processes and lead to an improved quality of documented treasury procedures.

■ A tight procedures manual, spelling out who is responsible for what, is crucial for successful outsourcing projects.

Treasury functions that are operational can be put into a set of guidelines, whether it be front, middle, or back-office. Banks provide treasury outsourcing services, and do so profitably.

Companies need efficient treasuries, and to have treasuries as integrated as possible, as highly-automated as possible, and as integrated with other products and transaction services as possible. While some corporates may not have in-house excellence in certain process-oriented aspects of treasury operations, banks provide this integration and automation.

If corporate activities reach a certain level of complexity, it might make sense to outsource, but as long as treasury operations are internally efficient compared to industry standards, treasury outsourcing may not add value, since a small staff and a highly automated process may suffice.

However, treasury outsourcing can be less expensive than keeping the function in-house with comparable levels of quality and efficiency. Automated treasury platforms are expensive. Medium-sized companies can access the type of technology which allows STP without actually buying the entire platform.

Treasury functions range from raising funds on capital markets to the fringes of the payables and receivables ledger. Unloading non-value-adding processes allows treasury staff to manage the balance sheet properly and implement new initiatives.

Managing the banking relationship

Treasury management is also about managing the banking relationships, especially since the costs of banking services appear to be getting less friendly. The 2002–03 edition of the Blue Book of Bank Prices shows the significant increases in prices of banking services in 2003.[23] Some companies that traditionally paid for services by leaving balances on deposit have been shocked to discover that money is now being debited from their accounts to pay bank fees.[24]

Banks have been creative in introducing new fees. Along with other interest rates, the earnings credit rate (ECR) – the value banks assign to balances – has fallen so low that it no longer covers the cost of bank services for most accounts. With the ECR hovering between 1 and 2 percent, banks are covering their rising expenses by charging customers.

In response, many companies are following a popular strategy: instead of letting each business unit buy services from local banks at local prices, these corporates organize a central treasury and buy services at much lower bulk rates. However, by leaving larger balances in the demand deposit accounts, a growing number of sophisticated treasuries are using formulas that factor in both the ECR and the cost of moving money into and out of investments. These organizations optimize treasury cash management by leaving balances in accounts when it is more rewarding to do so. Web-based cash management service and online cash management practices allow companies to economize on costs.

The importance of the treasurer's role goes beyond number crunching for day-to-day cash needs. Like CFOs, treasurers nowadays are increasingly aware of the implications of their work in creating shareholder value and maintaining good corporate governance.

Multinational corporations are pushing their banks and subsidiaries to support a consolidated, centralized global treasury operation in which cash belongs to the parent corporation and a small specialized treasury staff can see and control every balance. Increasing numbers of multinationals are opting for on-screen, real-time data availability, fewer banks, and concentrated funds.

According to latest studies, the wave of treasury consolidation is being driven by four pressures:[25]

■ corporate need for tight liquidity management;

■ corporate need for quicker handling of transaction, resulting in the requirements for automation and STP;

■ lower banking fees resulting from global consolidation of treasury operations;

■ Ability to reduce internal staff costs by automating standard processes

CASE STUDY 5.1 Cola-Cola[26]

Coca-Cola HBC outsourced its treasury process work prior to the company's relocation from London to Athens in April 2002. Coca-Cola HBC outsourced everything that was process-driven including back-office settlement, currency buying and selling, and commercial paper issuance. The more structural work such as bond issuance as well as certain derivative transactions remain in-house, but basically everything that flows on from that is outsourced.

Coca-Cola HBC outsourced non-value-added process-related treasury work in order to do more with less staff, accessing a concentration of a core skill set, and allowing treasury to focus on adding value.

CASE STUDY 5.2 HSBC[27]

Liquidity relates to the ability of a company to meet its obligations as they fall due. Management of liquidity in HSBC is carried out at local level in individual companies instead of on a consolidated basis because the range of currencies, markets, and time zones across which HSBC operates means that resources may not readily be transferred across HSBC to meet liquidity needs.

HSBC requires operating entities to maintain a strong liquidity position and to manage the liquidity structure of their assets, liabilities, and commitments so that cash flows are appropriately balanced and all funding obligations are met when due. It is the responsibility of local management to ensure compliance with local regulatory and Group Executive Committee requirements.

HSBC's liquidity is managed on a daily basis by local treasury functions, with the larger regional treasury sites providing support to smaller entities where required. Compliance with liquidity requirements is monitored by local Asset and Liability Policy Committees which report to Group Head Office on a regular basis.

This process includes:

- projecting cash flows by major currency and a consideration of the level of liquid assets in relation thereto;
- maintenance of strong balance sheet liquidity ratios;
- monitoring of depositor concentration both in terms of the overall funding mix and to avoid undue reliance on large individual depositors;
- maintenance of liquidity contingency plans.

These plans include the identification of early indicators of liquidity problems and actions which are to be taken to improve the liquidity position at this stage, together with the actions which the entity can take to maintain liquidity in a crisis situation while minimizing the long-term impact on its business.

Current accounts and savings deposits payable on demand or at short notice form a significant part of HSBC's overall funding. HSBC places considerable importance on the stability of these deposits, which is achieved through HSBC's diverse geographical retail banking activities and by maintaining depositor confidence in HSBC's capital strength.

Professional markets are accessed for the purposes of providing additional funding, maintaining a presence in local money markets and optimizing asset and liability maturities.

CASE STUDY 5.3 Citigroup[28]

Citigroup's primary source of incremental capital resources is its net earnings. Other sources include proceeds from the issuance of trust preferred securities, senior debt, subordinated debt, and commercial paper. Citigroup can also generate funds by securitizing various financial assets including credit card receivables and other receivables generally secured by collateral such as single-family residences and automobiles.

Citigroup uses these capital resources to pay dividends to its stockholders, to repurchase its shares in the market pursuant to board-of-director approved plans, to support organic growth, to make acquisitions, and to service its debt obligations.

Management of liquidity at Citigroup is the responsibility of the corporate treasurer. A uniform *liquidity risk management policy* exists for Citigroup and its major operating subsidiaries. Under this policy, there is a single set of standards for the measurement of liquidity risk in order to ensure consistency across businesses, stability in methodologies, and transparency of risk.

Management of liquidity at each operating subsidiary and/or country is performed on a daily basis and is monitored by corporate treasury.

A primary tenet of Citigroup's liquidity management is strong decentralized liquidity management at each of its principal operating subsidiaries and in each of its countries, combined with an active corporate oversight function.

Along with the role of the corporate treasurer, the Global Asset and Liability Committee (Global ALCO) undertakes this oversight responsibility. The Global ALCO functions as an oversight forum for Citigroup's CFO, chief risk officer, corporate treasurer, independent senior treasury risk officer, and the senior corporate and business treasurers and risk managers.

One objective of the Global ALCO is to monitor and review the overall liquidity and balance sheet position of Citigroup and its principal subsidiaries and to address corporate-

▶

wide policies and make recommendations back to senior management and the business units. Similarly, ALCOs are also established for each country and/or major line of business.

Each major operating subsidiary and/or country must prepare an annual funding and liquidity plan for review by the corporate treasurer and approval by the independent senior treasury risk officer. The funding and liquidity plan includes analysis of the balance sheet as well as the economic and business conditions impacting the liquidity of the major operating subsidiary and/or country. As part of the funding and liquidity plan, liquidity limits, liquidity ratios, market triggers, and assumptions for periodic stress tests are established and approved.

Liquidity limits establish boundaries for potential market access in business-as-usual conditions and are monitored against the liquidity position on a daily basis. These limits are established based on the size of the balance sheet, depth of the market, experience level of local management, the stability of the liabilities, and liquidity of the assets. Finally, the limits are subject to the evaluation of the entities' stress test results. Generally, limits are established such that in stress scenarios, entities need to be self-funded or net providers of liquidity.

A series of standard corporate-wide liquidity ratios have been established to monitor the structural elements of Citigroup's liquidity. For bank entities, these include measures of liquid assets against liquidity gaps, core deposits to loans, long-term assets to long-term liabilities, and deposits to loans. In addition, several measures exist to review potential concentrations of funding by individual name, product, industry, or geography.

For the parent company, insurance entities and the broker-dealer, there are ratios established for liquid assets against short-term obligations. Triggers to elicit management discussion have been established against these ratios. In addition, each individual major operating subsidiary or country establishes targets against these ratios and may monitor other ratios as approved in its funding and liquidity plan.

Market triggers are internal or external market or economic factors that may imply a change to market liquidity or Citigroup's access to the markets. Citigroup market triggers are monitored by the corporate treasurer and the independent senior treasury risk officer, and are discussed with the Global ALCO.

Appropriate market triggers are also established and monitored for each major operating subsidiary and/or country as part of the funding and liquidity plans. Local triggers are reviewed with the local country or business ALCO and independent risk management.

Periodic liquidity stress testing is performed for each major operating subsidiary and/or country. The scenarios include assumptions about significant changes in key funding sources, credit ratings, contingent uses of funding, and political and economic conditions in certain countries. The results of stress tests of individual countries and operating subsidiaries are reviewed to ensure that each individual major operating subsidiary or country is self-funded or a net provider of liquidity.

In addition, a *contingency funding plan* is prepared on a periodic basis for Citigroup. The plan includes detailed policies, procedures, roles and responsibilities, and the results of corporate stress tests. The product of these stress tests is a menu of alternatives that can be utilized by the corporate treasurer in a liquidity event.

Citigroup's funding sources are well-diversified across funding types and geography, a benefit of the strength of the global franchise. Funding for the parent and its major operating subsidiaries includes a large geographically diverse retail and corporate deposit base, a significant portion of which is expected to be long-term and stable and is considered core. Other sources of funding include collateralized borrowings, securitizations (primarily credit card and mortgages), long-term debt, and purchased/wholesale funds.

CASE STUDY 5.4 | GE[29]

The major debt-rating agencies evaluate the financial condition of GE and of GE Capital Corporation (GE Capital), the major public borrowing entity of GECS, differently because of their distinct business characteristics. Factors that are important to the ratings of both include the following:

■ cash generating ability – including cash generated from operating activities;
■ earnings quality – including revenue growth and the breadth and diversity of sources of income;
■ leverage ratios – such as debt to total capital and interest coverage;
■ asset utilization – including return on assets and asset turnover ratios.

Considering those factors, those major rating agencies continue to give the highest ratings to debt of both GE and GE Capital (long-term credit rating AAA/Aaa; short-term credit rating A-1+/P-1).

One of GE's strategic objectives is to maintain these ratings on debt issued by GE and GE Capital. GE's Triple-A rating lowers its cost of borrowings and facilitates access to a variety of lenders. GE manages its businesses in a manner consistent with maintaining these Triple-A ratings.

To support the GE Capital rating, at the end of 2002, GE was contractually committed to maintain the ratios of earnings to fixed charges at GE Capital at a specified level. To build equity, the GECS board of directors intends to reduce GECS dividend payments to GE to 10 percent of operating earnings.

Global commercial paper markets are a primary source of liquidity for GE and financial services. GE Capital is the most widely-held name in those markets and is the principal issuer of financial services debt. Financial services debt composition as of December 31, 2002 were: senior notes 52 percent, commercial paper 31 percent, and Other (principally current portion of long-term debt), 17 percent.

▶

During 2002, GE Capital issued approximately $88bn of long-term debt in US and international markets. These funds were used primarily to reduce the amount of commercial paper outstanding by $33bn and to fund acquisitions and new asset growth. GE targets a ratio for commercial paper of 25 percent to 35 percent of outstanding debt based on the anticipated composition of its assets.

GE Capital anticipates issuing approximately $60bn of long-term debt using both US and international markets during 2003. The proceeds from such issuances will be used to fund maturing long-term debt, additional acquisitions, and asset growth. The ultimate amount of debt issuances depend on the growth in assets, acquisition activity, availability of markets, and movements in interest rates.

GE's alternative sources of liquidity are sufficient to permit an orderly transition from commercial paper in the unlikely event of impaired access to those markets.

Funding sources on which GE could rely would depend on the nature of such a hypothetical event, but include $54bn of contractually committed lending agreements with highly-rated global banks and investment banks, an increase of $21bn since December 31, 2001, as well as other sources of liquidity, including medium- and long-term funding, monetization, asset securitization, cash receipts from lending and leasing activities, short-term secured funding on global assets, and potential asset sales.

CASE STUDY 5.5 | Merrill Lynch[30]

Merrill Lynch manages funding globally to assure liquidity at all times, across market cycles and through periods of financial stress. Merrill Lynch's primary liquidity objective is to ensure that all unsecured debt obligations maturing within one year can be repaid without issuing new unsecured debt or requiring liquidation of business assets. In order to accomplish this objective, Merrill Lynch has established a set of liquidity practices which are outlined below.

Merrill Lynch regularly reviews its mix of assets, liabilities and commitments to ensure the maintenance of adequate long-term capital, which includes portions of deposits, the non-current portion of long-term debt, and equity capital. The following items are generally financed with long-term capital:

- the portion of trading and other current assets that cannot be self-funded in the secured financing market, considering stressed market conditions;
- long-term, less liquid assets, such as goodwill, fixed assets and loans;
- regulatory capital requirements;
- collateral on derivative contracts that may be required in the event of changes in ratings or movements in underlying commodity prices;
- portions of commitments to extend credit based on the probability of draw-down.

In assessing the appropriate tenor of its financing liabilities, Merrill Lynch seeks to ensure sufficient matching of its assets based on factors such as holding period, contractual maturity, and regulatory restrictions, and limit the amount of liabilities maturing in any particular period.

Merrill Lynch also considers circumstances that might cause contingent funding obligations, including early repayment of debt. The company's vast majority of indebtedness is considered senior debt as defined under various indentures. Included in its debt obligations are structured notes issued by Merrill Lynch with returns linked to other debt or equity securities, indices, or currencies. Merrill Lynch could be required to immediately settle a structured note obligation for cash or other securities under some circumstances. Merrill Lynch typically hedges these notes with positions in the underlying instrument.

Merrill Lynch seeks to ensure availability of sufficient alternative funding sources to enable the repayment of all unsecured debt obligations maturing within one year without issuing new unsecured debt or requiring liquidation of business assets. The main alternative funding sources to unsecured borrowings are repurchase agreements, securities loaned, and other secured borrowings, which require pledging unencumbered securities held for trading or investment purposes.

Merrill Lynch also maintains a separate liquidity portfolio of US Government and agency obligations and asset-backed securities of high-credit quality that is funded with debt with an average maturity greater than one year. These assets may be sold or pledged to provide immediate liquidity to the firm to repay maturing debt obligations. In addition to this portfolio, the firm monitors the extent to which other unencumbered assets are available as a source of funds during a liquidity event.

Merrill Lynch also maintains a committed, multi-currency, unsecured bank credit facility. The facility totalled $3.5bn at December 27, 2002 and $5.0bn at December 28, 2001. Merrill Lynch elected to reduce the amount of its credit facility in 2002 and offset this reduction by an increase in the liquidity portfolio of unencumbered securities. Merrill Lynch's credit facility contains covenants, including a minimum net worth requirement, with which Merrill Lynch has maintained compliance at all times. The credit facility does not, however, require Merrill Lynch to maintain specified credit ratings.

Merrill Lynch is the primary issuer of all unsecured, non-deposit financing instruments that are used primarily to fund assets in subsidiaries, some of which are regulated. The benefits of this strategy are enhanced control, reduced financing costs, wider name recognition by creditors, and greater flexibility to meet variable funding requirements of subsidiaries. Where regulations, time zone differences, or other business considerations make this impractical, some subsidiaries enter into their own financing arrangements.

Merrill Lynch recognizes that regulatory restrictions may limit the free flow of funds from subsidiaries, where assets are held, to Merrill Lynch and also between subsidiaries. For

▶

example, a portion of deposits held by Merrill Lynch bank subsidiaries fund securities that can be sold or pledged to provide immediate liquidity for the banks. However, there are regulatory restrictions on the use of this liquidity for non-bank affiliates of Merrill Lynch. Merrill Lynch takes these and other restrictions into consideration when evaluating the liquidity of individual legal entities and Merrill Lynch.

Merrill Lynch strives to continually expand and globally diversify its funding programs, markets, and investor and creditor base to minimize reliance on any one investor base or region. Merrill Lynch diversifies its borrowings by maintaining various limits, including a limit on the amount of commercial paper held by a single investor. Merrill Lynch benefits by distributing a significant portion of its debt issuances through its own sales force to a large, diversified global client base. Merrill Lynch also makes markets by buying and selling its debt instruments.

In order to ensure that both daily and strategic funding activities are appropriate and subject to senior management review and control, Merrill Lynch reviews its liquidity management in Asset/Liability Committee meetings with senior treasury management and presents a financing plan to the Finance Committee of the Board of Directors. Merrill Lynch also closely manages the growth and composition of its assets and sets limits on the availability of unsecured funding at any time. Merrill Lynch finally maintains a contingency funding plan that outlines actions that would be taken in the event of a funding disruption.

CASE STUDY 5.6 | Ericsson[31]

Ericsson maintains sufficient liquidity through cash management, investments in highly liquid fixed income securities, and by having sufficient committed and uncommitted credit lines in place for potential funding needs.

Ericsson defines liquidity as cash and short-term investments up to 12 months. Under US GAAP, liquidity is defined as cash and short-term investments up to three months.

During 2002, liquidity decreased by SEK2.7bn to SEK66.2bn and net liquidity, after deduction of short-term, interest-bearing financial liabilities, increased by SEK9.5bn to SEK52.7bn, mainly due to the SEK29bn of net proceeds from the rights issue in September.

Ericsson finances its operations externally principally by borrowing directly in the Swedish and international bank and debt capital markets.

CASE STUDY 5.7 | ABB[32]

The ABB Group Treasury Services offers in-house banking services to ABB companies in 12 countries in the region. Being an in-house bank means all ABB units need only to contact the ABB Treasury Centre for foreign exchange and money-market transactions. ABB uses an electronic trading platform at the treasury intranet page of the ABB website. The intranet integrates financial- and treasury-related information and serves as an automated trading and reporting platform. The intranet application gives ABB management a comprehensive, real-time view of its foreign exchange risk exposures. This is especially helpful for ABB, since its financial risk exposures are not so much due to internal or commercial cash flow volatility, as to adverse foreign exchange fluctuations.

ABB keeps a low FX risk tolerance. All its business units are required to hedge every committed cash flow, and they come to treasury for mandatory trading. Forward contracts normally have a tenure of three to six months. In turn, the treasury centre conducts active risk management with banks, either for its own trading gains or hedging.

Covering FX exposures gives a company greater comfort to manage excess liquidity. Many leading treasuries have cash concentration arrangements. Active use of loans and deposits for inter-company funding is also a common practice. This means taking deposits from subsidiaries in surplus, and uses them to offer loans to subsidiaries in deficit. For example, if a Canadian unit is long on cash, it will place deposits with the treasury headquarters, which the company will use to finance Australia, Japan, or any other country that is short. As in arranging foreign exchange transactions, the subsidiaries and the treasury centre can efficiently use the intranet for loans and deposits.

Regional pooling is often an efficient way to aggregate funding in each region. This helps promote regional equilibrium in cash management, while the headquarters can dive in to support any imbalances, as needed. However, there are some difficulties in regional pooling arrangements. Cross-border pooling is often highly regulated, especially in developing or emerging market currencies that do not enjoy capital market convertibility.

Often, returns from investment options for the amount concentrated in a regional account will not be much different from yields available through domestic instruments. It is difficult for the treasury to offer a better rate on a cross-border structure, because local markets often quote quite attractive rates.

CASE STUDY 5.8 Nokia[33]

Nokia's treasury department is responsible for risk, cash and liquidity management and funding for Nokia's operations, and does not trade for profit for its treasury services. But its role in preserving and creating shareholder value is clearly stated in the group's annual report. The treasury function supports this aim by minimizing the adverse effects caused by fluctuations in the financial market on the profitability of the underlying businesses, and thus on the financial performance of Nokia.

Nokia enforces a monthly reporting cycle that collects foreign exchange exposure data from the affected companies. Nokia has a treasury policy according to which its sales companies are invoiced in their local currency, which concentrates the foreign exchange risk to factories and distribution centres. This way, the risk is not spread out across the region. The reporting cycle projects FX exposures for up to 12 months. The net position is then hedged in financial markets through forward and options contracts, rarely exceeding one year.

Nokia uses the VAR methodology to assess the foreign exchange risk. Nokia uses a risk management module called *Q-Risk*, provided by SunGard, a vendor of treasury integration systems. Nokia hedges almost all of its currency exposures. In addition to VAR, the company implements stress-testing as well, and remains prepared for major discontinuities in terms of market price risk.

After Nokia's global ERP implementation, subsidiaries all over the world post invoices on Nokia's SAP system. *BankLink* then extracts the invoice data from SAP, generates the appropriate payments and remittance advices, and executes them on behalf of group companies globally. Cost efficiency is achieved through netting internal payments, or payments between Nokia subsidiaries. Netting refers to lumping remittances, which reduces transaction fees.

CASE STUDY 5.9 Marks & Spencer[34]

Marks and Spencer's board approves treasury policies and senior management directly controls day-to-day operations. The board delegates certain responsibility to the Treasury Committee, comprising two members of the board, one non-executive director and the director of corporate finance. The Treasury Committee is empowered to take decisions, as necessary, within that delegated authority.

Marks and Spencer's financial instruments, other than derivatives, comprise borrowings, cash and liquid resources, and various items, such as trade debtors and trade creditors, that arise directly from its operations. The main purpose of these financial instruments is to raise finance for the group's operations.

Marks and Spencer's treasury also enters into derivatives transactions, principally interest rate and currency swaps and forward currency contracts. The purpose of such transactions is to manage the interest rate and currency risks arising from the Group's operations and financing. It has been, and remains, the Marks & Spencer's policy that no trading in financial instruments shall be undertaken.

The main financial risks faced by the group relate to interest rates, foreign exchange rates, liquidity, counter-party and the financial risks associated with the financial services operation. The policies and strategies for managing these risks are summarized as follows.

Interest rate risk in respect of debt on the retail balance sheet is reviewed on a regular basis. At the balance sheet date interest obligations in respect of the property securitization and the Eurobond issued in sterling were at fixed rates. The current group policy for debt raised to finance the operation of financial services is to maintain the majority of this portion of debt as floating rate and this is achieved with the help of interest rate swaps.

Marks and Spencer's currency exposure arising from exports from the UK to overseas subsidiaries is managed by using forward currency contracts to hedge between 80 percent and 100 percent of sales for periods averaging ten to 15 months forward. Imports are primarily contracted in sterling and only economic exposures arise. The group is increasing the proportion of imports contracted in local currencies and a policy is in place for the hedging of these exposures, principally using forward currency contracts.

Marks and Spencer does not use derivatives to hedge balance sheet and profit and loss account translation exposures. Where appropriate, borrowings are arranged in local currencies to provide a natural hedge against overseas assets.

The objective is to ensure a mix of funding methods offering flexibility and cost effectiveness to match the needs of the group. Operating subsidiaries are financed by a combination of retained profits, bank borrowings, commercial paper and medium-term notes and securities loan notes. Commercial paper issuance is backed by committed bank facilities totalling £385.0m.

The objective is to reduce the risk of loss arising from default by counter-parties. The risk is managed by using a number of banks and allocating each a credit limit according to credit rating criteria. These limits are reviewed regularly by senior management. Dealing mandates and derivative agreements are agreed with the banks prior to deals being arranged.

Interest rate exposures for financial services are managed, as far as practical, by matching the periods of borrowings and their interest basis with that of the customer debt. Interest rate swaps are used to convert fixed income from personal loan customers to short-term variable income to match short-term variable rate borrowings.

CASE STUDY `5.10` Toyota[35]

Historically, Toyota has funded its capital expenditures and research and development activities primarily through cash generated by operations. Toyota expects to fund its capital expenditures and research and development activities in fiscal 2003 primarily through cash and cash equivalents on hand, operating cash flow, and issuance of debt instrument.

Toyota funds its financing programs for customers and dealers, including leasing programs, from both operating cash flow and through borrowings by its finance subsidiaries. Toyota seeks to expand its ability to raise funds locally in markets throughout the world by expanding its network of finance subsidiaries.

CASE STUDY `5.11` Shell[36]

Shell Group companies, in the normal course of their business, use financial instruments of various kinds for the purposes of managing exposure to currency, commodity price, and interest rate movements. The group has Treasury Guidelines applicable to all group companies and each group company is required to adopt a treasury policy consistent with these guidelines.

These policies cover:

- financing structure,
- foreign exchange and interest rate risk management,
- insurance,
- counterparty risk management and derivative instruments,
- treasury control framework.

Wherever possible, treasury operations are operated through specialist Shell Group regional organizations without removing from each group company the responsibility to formulate and implement appropriate treasury policies.

Each Shell Group company measures its foreign currency exposures against the underlying currency of its business (its "functional currency"), reports foreign exchange gains and losses against its functional currency, and has hedging and treasury policies in place which are designed to minimize foreign exchange exposure so defined. The functional currency for most upstream companies, and for other companies with significant international business, is the US dollar, but other companies normally have their local currency as their functional currency.

The financing of most Shell Operating Companies is structured on a floating-rate basis and, except in special cases, further interest rate risk management is discouraged. Apart from forward foreign exchange contracts to meet known commitments, the use of derivative financial instruments by most Shell Group companies is not permitted by their treasury policy.

Some Shell Group companies operate as traders in crude oil, natural gas, oil products and other energy-related products, using commodity swaps, options and futures as a means of managing price and timing risks arising from this trading. In effecting these transactions, the companies concerned operate within procedures and policies designed to ensure that risks, including those relating to the default of counter-parties, are minimized.

Other than in exceptional cases, Shell's use of derivative instruments is generally confined to specialist oil and gas trading and central treasury organizations which have appropriate skills, experience, supervision and control and reporting systems.

CASE STUDY 5.12 Nestlé[37]

Nestlé is currently in the process of centralizing its treasury operations worldwide. With a core business of food and beverages, Nestlé had a local organizational approach for production and sales. However, in recent years, external legal, regulatory and technological changes have encouraged the sharing of certain functions among several operational units.

Internally Nestlé is under-going a business process reengineering program known as GLOBE (Global Business Excellence). The GLOBE program seeks to improve the performance and operational efficiency of the group's business worldwide.

Nestlé is concentrating its treasury functions in five regional platforms worldwide: Europe (seven countries); the Middle East (Dubai); US and Canada (Glendale); Latin America (Panama); and South Asia (Manila). Nestlé has decided to rationalize its banking relationships and choose one bank per country for its cash management needs.

Many multinational corporates would like to appoint a so-called 'universal bank' which would be able to manage global treasury operations, for example, means of payment, cash pools, etc., in every country. However, the reality is that such a universal bank for cash management does not exist, especially for companies like Nestlé with sales and cash collection requirements in almost every country in the world.

CASE STUDY 5.13 Cisco[38]

In 2002, Cisco Systems completed globalization of its treasury operations by bringing in Asia-Pacific and Latin America. The company now has just one primary bank per region: Morgan for Asia-Pacific, Citibank for Latin America, SEB for Scandinavia, and Citi and Bank of America for the US, the Middle East, and the rest of Europe. This consolidation is saving Cisco more than $5m annually across all regions through better liquidity management, a reduction in idle balances, increased repatriation of funds, and improved spread on foreign exchange transactions.

To tighten liquidity management, Cisco uses just-in-time funding for operating disbursements wherever possible. The company also cut its banking fees by consolidating activity with regional banks. In Asia-Pacific, Cisco now outsources all foreign exchange activity to one bank, getting preset and externally auditable rates and attractive pre-negotiated spreads.

In addition, fund concentration has brought automation. Cisco has seen a quantum shift from manual transaction processing to value-added activities. Although Cisco's suite of web-based tools, which it built in-house in lieu of implementing a treasury workstation, still does not provide visibility of all bank balances in one place, the company is actively working to achieve.

CASE STUDY 5.14 DuPont[39]

The DuPont Co. has reduced its number of treasury centres from six to two – Wilmington and Singapore. The company has also consolidated its back office processing in a single location: Asturias, Spain. The company uses a single global treasury system – Sungard's *Quantum*. Every authorized employee sees the same information real-time, and the information is updated continually as different regions operate in different time zones.

DuPont's cash management, hedging, and financing were separate activities. Surplus Asian cash was always invested in Asia. Now DuPont invests globally; if a US dollar invested in Asia earns less than it would earn in London, DuPont transfers the funds to the UK. The company uses global information to improve investment returns.

CASE STUDY 5.15 GlaxoSmithKline[40]

GlaxoSmithKline plc is a UK based business, reporting in sterling and paying dividends out of sterling profits. The role of Corporate Treasury in GlaxoSmithKline is to manage and monitor the group's external and internal funding requirements and financial risks in support of group corporate objectives.

Treasury activities are governed by policies and procedures approved by the board and monitored by a Treasury Management Group. GlaxoSmithKline maintains treasury control systems and procedures to monitor foreign exchange, interest rate, liquidity, credit, and other financial risks.

GlaxoSmithKline operates globally, primarily through subsidiary companies established in the markets in which the group trades. Due to the nature of the group's business, with patent protection on many of the products in the group's portfolio, the group's products compete largely on product efficacy rather than on price. Selling margins are sufficient to cover normal operating costs and the group's operating subsidiaries are substantially cash generative. Operating cash flow is used to fund investment in the research and development of new products as well as routine outflows of capital expenditure, tax, dividends, and repayment of maturing debt. The group will, from time to time, have additional demands for finance, such as for share purchases and acquisitions.

GlaxoSmithKline operates at low levels of net debt. In addition to the strong positive cash flow from normal trading activities, additional liquidity is readily available via its commercial paper program. Current back-up facilities, including committed lines of credit, support issuance under the $10bn commercial paper program of up to $4bn. The group also has an uncommitted euro medium-term note program of £5bn, of which £1,807m was in issue at December 31, 2002, and plans to establish a similar uncommitted borrowing program in the US during 2003.

The objective of treasury activity is to manage the post-tax net cost/income of financial operations to the benefit of group earnings. Corporate Treasury does not operate as a profit centre. GlaxoSmithKline uses a variety of financial instruments, including derivatives, to finance its operations and to manage market risks from those operations. Financial instruments comprise cash and liquid resources, borrowings, and spot foreign exchange contracts.

A number of derivative financial instruments are used to manage the market risks from treasury operations. Derivative instruments, principally comprising forward foreign currency contracts, interest rate and currency swaps, are used to swap borrowings and liquid assets into the currencies required for group purposes and to manage exposure to funding risks from changes in foreign exchange rates and interest rates.

▶

GlaxoSmithKline balances the use of borrowings and liquid assets having regard to:

■ the cash flow from operating activities and the currencies in which it is earned;
■ the tax cost of intra-group distributions;
■ the currencies in which business assets are denominated; and
■ the post-tax cost of borrowings compared to the post-tax return on liquid assets.

Liquid assets surplus to the immediate operating requirements of group companies are invested and managed centrally by Corporate Treasury. Requirements of group companies for operating finance are met whenever possible from central resources. External borrowings, mainly managed centrally by Corporate Treasury, comprise a portfolio of long and medium-term instruments and short-term finance.

GlaxoSmithKline does not hold or issue derivative financial instruments for trading purposes and the group's Treasury policies specifically prohibit such activity. All transactions in financial instruments are undertaken to manage the risks arising from underlying business activities, not for speculation.

The GlaxoSmithKline Group invests centrally managed liquid assets primarily in government bonds and short-term corporate debt instruments with a minimum short-term credit rating of A-1/P-1 from Standard and Poor's and Moody's Investors' Services respectively.

The group manages its net borrowing requirement through a portfolio of long and medium-term borrowings, including bonds, together with short-term finance under the US dollar commercial paper program. In 2002, a £500m, 4.875 percent coupon bond and two US dollar denominated, floating rate bonds totalling $495m were issued under the European Medium Term Note Program. The group also raised $500m floating rate debt through a private financing arrangement.

The group's medium-term borrowings mature at dates between 2004 and 2008, the private financing matures in 2032, and the long-dated sterling bond matures in 2033. The private financing may be redeemed by GlaxoSmithKline at any time and, in particular, in the event of any accelerating event that would increase the cost of funding for the group.

The group also has outstanding $500m of Flexible Auction Market Preferred Stock (Flex AMPS) and $400m of Auction Rate Preference Stock (ARPS), originally issued in 1996. $250m of the Flex AMPS may be redeemed by GlaxoSmithKline at any time after July 2003. The remainder of the Flex AMPS and the ARPS may be redeemed by GlaxoSmithKline at any time.

GlaxoSmithKline's long-term debt rating is AA from Standard and Poor's and Aa2 from Moody's Investors' Services. The agencies' short-term rating for paper issued under the group's commercial paper program is A-1+ and P-1 respectively.

Hewlett-Packard[41]

HP has centralized its global treasury operations. Before this centralization, 90 percent of treasury staff were spending their time on processing and data gathering, and just 10 percent on value-added services. HP centralized its treasury operations by pulling staff into three shared service centres – California, London, and Singapore – which allowed the company to hone specialized skills, maintain adequate back-up, and segregate duties.

HP's global treasury activity now flows into and out of a single software system from Wall Street Systems. Balances in every HP account in the world can be seen through one EDI interface, provided by JP Morgan Chase. Consolidation has brought a high degree of automation, thereby increasing the efficiency of treasury operations.

HP's treasury finances subsidiaries around the globe from a single legal entity which serves as an in-house bank. The treasury system automatically credits or charges interest to subsidiaries based on balances invested or borrowed.

HP's operating subsidiaries maintain accounts with one primary banking partner in each country. All of a subsidiary's accounts are either zero-balanced or notionally pooled daily into a special treasury account at that bank.

HP's treasury software automatically triggers a payment instruction when the target balance for one of these pools is breached – either it funds the local treasury account or sweeps excess cash into the in-house bank. In contrast to many companies that attempt to minimize the number of bank accounts, HP actually added new accounts as it created new treasury accounts.

Some benchmarks measure efficiency by the number of account used – the less the better. However, the account structure reflects the legal structure of the company, therefore the segregation of transactions into different accounts can be more efficient and lead to better controls. As long as there are automated processes behind the daily reconciliation and movement of funds, it does not necessarily lead to higher costs.

For HP, treasury consolidation reduced banking fees. Global visibility allows the company to see what it is charged all over the globe, and indicates in which regions or countries the company should negotiate lower banking fees. The most significant benefit was better management of working capital. The company has saved interest expense and achieved gains in interest income through the consolidation of funds at the in-house bank.

Financial control and audit

From a CFO perspective, a company's control environment is the corporate atmosphere in which the accounting and other controls exist, and in which the financial statements are prepared. It reflects management's commitment to an effective system of internal control.

There are seven basic elements that are necessary to meet the broad objectives of good internal accounting control – objectives that include safeguarding the assets against loss arising from intentional or unintentional errors, and producing reliable financial records for internal use and for external reporting purposes.[42]

1   Competent and trustworthy personnel with clearly defined lines of authority and responsibility.
2   Adequate separation of duties:
    ■ Separation of operating responsibility from financial record-keeping;
    ■ separation of custody of the assets;
    ■ separation of the authorization of transactions from the custody of any related assets;
    ■ separation of duties within the accounting function.
3   Proper procedures for authorization of transactions.
4   Adequate records and documents.
5   Proper physical control over both assets and records.
6   Proper procedures for adequate record keeping.
7   A staff that can provide independent verifications.

Good control systems usually incorporate multiple channels of assessment to ensure information accuracy and objectivity. For example, a CFO can usually corroborate earnings estimates during an accounting period by monitoring cash flow trends. Close interaction with functional and divisional managers is an absolute necessity in validating the organization's control systems and in allocating financial resources.

Effective control mechanisms are based on the science of real-time financial and operational reporting, ethical reporting, and in the art of good people skills. This art helps the CFO understand the true funding needs of divisional chief executives in the context of the entire organization.

Internal audit is a key part of prudent business management and planning. The financial planning process breaks down if there is questionable data integrity in the financial system. Having a real-time financial system in place that leverages data into meaningful and timely information helps in identifying unfavorable revenue or expense trends before they get too much out-of-line. This process, in itself, helps control and discipline the financial management process. It is also prudent to have external audits performed on both accounting and business process integrity, as it supports management thinking from an objective and unbiased external perspective.

Business planning and control are important factors for goal or target setting for corporate-wide or divisional cost-reduction initiatives. The audit committee of the board of directors serves as an additional line of defence in the struggle for candid financial reporting. In reality, rather than laying down the accounting law (or GAAP), the auditors typically wind up negotiating with management to arrive at a point where they can convince themselves that the bare minimum requirements of good practice have been satisfied. Ultimately, the responsibility for the existence of proper controls rests with the board of directors, the senior operational and financial management, the internal auditor, and the independent auditor.

In reviewing internal controls, the greatest amount of time is usually spent in analyzing and evaluating the very detailed controls that exist. A tension exists between the benefits of robust and effective controls on the one hand, and process efficiencies from quick decision making on the other. The latter often requires "streamlining" of controls, and is somewhat at odds with the control mentality. The ability to strike the optimal balance between these competing objectives is a hallmark of successful corporations around the world.

Given the responsibilities of the board of directors and top management, the ultimate purpose of control systems is to aid in meeting the business goals and objectives. Hence, control systems should include all levels of planning and related control. These levels can, in general, be included in three broad classes:

1 *Strategic* – board of directors and top management who plan and control:

  ▦ organizational structure

  ▦ corporate goals and objectives

  ▦ long-range business planning

  ▦ marketing policy

  ▦ management policy

  ▦ financial policy.

2 *Tactical* – board of directors and senior management who plan and control:

  ▦ annual profit plans

  ▦ executive-personnel policies

  ▦ capital expenditure

  ▦ annual research and development plans.

3 *Operational* – where planning and control involves:

  ▦ credit approval practices

  ▦ treatment of uncollectible accounts

  ▦ Purchasing procedure

  ▦ Billing procedure

  ▦ Salary and wage authorization

  ▦ Pension plan management.

CASE STUDY 5.17 Citigroup[43]

Citigroup's CEO and CFO evaluate the effectiveness of the company's disclosure controls and procedures.

Based on such evaluation, the CEO and CFO determine whether the company's disclosure controls and procedures are effective in alerting them on a timely basis to material information relating to the company (including its consolidated subsidiaries) required to be included in the company's reports filed or submitted under the Exchange Act.

CASE STUDY 5.18 Marks & Spencer[44]

Marks & Spencer's board has overall responsibility for the group's approach to assessing risk and systems of internal control, and for monitoring their effectiveness in providing shareholders with a return that is consistent with a responsible assessment and mitigation of risks.

This includes reviewing financial, operational, and compliance controls, and risk management procedures. The role of executive management is to implement the board's policies on risk and control, and present assurance on compliance with these policies. Further independent assurance is presented by an internal audit function, which operates across the group, and the external auditors. All employees are accountable for operating within these policies.

Because of the limitations that are inherent in any system of internal control, this system is designed to manage, rather than eliminate, the risk of failure to achieve corporate objectives. Accordingly, it can only provide reasonable but not absolute assurance against material misstatement or loss.

The board has established an ongoing process for identifying, evaluating and managing the significant risks faced by the group. As an integral part of planning and review, management from each business area and major project identify their risks, the probability of those risks occurring, the impact if they do occur, and the actions being taken to manage those risks to the desired level. This information is communicated upwards on a filter basis, culminating in a comparison with the executive directors' assessment of the group's risks and discussion by the board of the group risk profile.

Whilst the board maintains full control and direction over appropriate strategic, financial, organizational and compliance issues, it has delegated to executive management the implementation of the systems of internal control within an established framework. The board has put in place an organizational structure with formally defined lines of responsibility and delegation of authority. There are also established procedures for planning, capital expenditure, information and reporting systems, and for monitoring the group's businesses and their performance. These include:

- communication of the group's strategy, objectives and targets;
- appointment of employees of the necessary calibre to fulfill their allotted responsibilities;
- review by operating divisions of their annual and three-year operating and capital plans with the relevant executive directors prior to submission to the board for approval. This includes the identification and assessment of risks;
- regular consideration by the board of year-end forecasts;
- monthly comparison of operating divisions' actual financial performance with budget;
- clearly defined capital investment control guidelines;
- operating policies and procedures;
- reporting of accounting and legal developments to the board;
- review of treasury policies by the Treasury Committee with changes approved by the board;
- review of social, environmental and ethical matters by the Corporate Social Responsibility Committee.

On behalf of the board, the Audit Committee examines the effectiveness of the group's:

- assessment of risk by reviewing evidence of risk assessment activity and a report from internal audit on the risk assessment process;
- systems of internal control primarily through agreeing the scope of the internal audit program and reviewing its findings, reviews of the annual and interim financial statements and a review of the nature and scope of the external audit.

Any significant findings or identified risks are closely examined so that appropriate action can be taken. The work of the internal audit department is focussed on areas of priority as identified by risk analysis and in accordance with an annual audit plan approved each year by the Audit Committee and by the board. The board receives a full report from the chief internal auditor each year on the department's work and findings and regular interim updates on specific issues.

The external auditors are engaged to express an opinion on the financial statements. They review and test the systems of internal financial control and the data contained in the financial statements to the extent necessary to express their audit opinion. They discuss with management the reporting of operational results and the financial condition of the group and present their findings to the Audit Committee.

CASE STUDY 5.19 Royal-Dutch/Shell[45]

Shell Group's approach to internal control is based on the underlying principle of line management's accountability for risk and control management. The group's risk and internal control policy explicitly states that the group has a risk-based approach to internal control and that management in the group is responsible for implementing, operating and monitoring the system of internal control, which is designed to provide reasonable but not absolute assurance of achieving business objectives.

Established review and reporting processes bring risk management into greater focus and enable the Conference (meetings between the members of the Supervisory Board and the Board of Management of Royal Dutch and the Directors of Shell Transport) regularly to review the overall effectiveness of the system of internal control and to perform a full annual review of the system's effectiveness.

At Shell Group level and within each business, risk profiles which highlight the perceived impact and likelihood of significant risks are reviewed each quarter by the Committee of Managing Directors and by the Conference. Each risk profile is supported by a summary of key controls and monitoring mechanisms. A risk-based approach to internal control continues to be embedded within the businesses.

In addition, non-Shell operated ventures and affiliates are encouraged to adopt processes consistent with the group's approach. The group's approach to internal control also includes a number of general and specific risk management processes and policies. Within the essential framework provided by the Statement of General Business Principles, the group's primary control mechanisms are self-appraisal processes in combination with strict accountability for results.

These mechanisms are underpinned by controls including group policies, standards and guidance material that relate to particular types of risk, structured investment decision processes, timely and effective reporting systems, and performance appraisal. Examples of specific risk management processes include the Group Issue Identification and Management System, by which reputation risks are identified and monitored.

A common Health, Safety and Environment (HSE) Policy has been adopted by Shell companies. All companies have HSE management systems in place and for major installations the environmental component of such systems has been certified to international standards. The Shell Group Financial Control Handbook establishes standards applicable across the group on the application of internal financial controls.

A procedure for reporting business control incidents enables management and the Group Audit Committee to monitor incidents arising as a result of control breakdowns and to ensure appropriate follow-up actions have been taken. Lessons learned are captured and shared as a means of improving the group's overall control framework. A formalized self-appraisal and assurance process has been in place for many years at Shell. The process was reviewed and updated in 2002.

Each year the management of every business unit provides assurance as to the adequacy of financial controls and reporting, treasury management, risk management, HSE management and the Statement of General Business Principles, as well as other important topics.

Any business integrity concerns or instances of bribery or illegal payments are to be reported. The results of this process and any qualifications made are reviewed by the Group Audit Committee and support representations made to the external auditors.

In addition, internal audit plays a critical role in the objective assessment of business processes and the provision of assurance. Audits and reviews of group operations are carried out by Shell Group Internal Audit to provide the Group Audit Committee with independent assessments regarding the effectiveness of risk and control management.

CASE STUDY 5.20 Exxon-Mobil[46]

Exxon-Mobil's management is responsible for establishing and maintaining adequate internal controls and procedures for the preparation of financial reports. Accordingly, comprehensive procedures and practices are in place. These procedures and practices are designed to:

- provide reasonable assurance that the corporation's transactions are properly authorized;
- the corporation's assets are safeguarded against unauthorized or improper use; and
- the corporation's transactions are properly recorded and reported to permit the preparation of financial statements in conformity with US GAAP.

Internal controls and procedures for financial reporting are regularly reviewed by management and by the ExxonMobil internal audit function and findings are shared with the Board Audit Committee.

In addition, PricewaterhouseCoopers, the company's independent accountant, who reports to the Board Audit Committee, considers and selectively tests internal controls in planning and performing their audits. Management's review of the design and operation of these controls and procedures in 2002, including review as of year-end, did not identify any significant deficiencies or material weaknesses, including any deficiencies which could adversely affect the corporation's ability to record, process, summarize, and report financial data.

Optimize amid changing operating conditions

Businesses operate in a continuously changing operating environment. As new opportunities spring up and are capitalized upon by industry leaders, so do unforeseen risks that can adversely impact the business. Not all of these external or internal variables can be forecasted adequately, but some of these potential changes can be anticipated in the business strategy and financial planning process.

"Continuous change" is the operating term here. Amid incessant changes taking place in the economic, competitive, and market environments, no business can optimize its financial and operating management with a static strategy, business plan, or operational plan. Changing operating conditions are effectively incorporated into the business planning process in two ways.

Method one

The business and financial plans are reviewed and modified periodically, as changes in expectations of key operating variables are incorporated into the model. The frequency of revisions are to be determined by management decision, but should be a function of industry business cycles or volatility characteristics of industry variables.

The continuous process of updating the financial planning model with anticipated changes in key variables is a necessary part of financial optimization. This can be compared to the optimization of investment portfolios in investment management, where periodic rebalancing is undertaken to dynamically optimize the risk-return profile.

Of course, a bricks-and-mortar business cannot be optimized by rapid rebalancing of past decisions, as can be done in the case of purely financial asset management. Stability is necessary in the planning process. It is management's judgment here that should determine how proactive it should be in recognizing change and how it should adapt to it optimally and dynamically.

Method two

An additional technique used to incorporate dynamic changes in operating conditions is to make the business plan stochastic as opposed to deterministic. In other words, incorporate appropriate probability distributions to each financial variable in the balance sheet, income statement, and cash flow statement to account for their uncertainty. In practice, the actual past behaviour of each financial variable determines its empirical probability distribution. Once these probability distributions are assigned, financial statement simulations are undertaken to determine highest probability scenarios of future business plan outcomes.

Applying advanced quantitative techniques on the financial plan thus provides management with superior insights on which financial variables are most sensitive, and how to manage corporate performance results by managing these key variables and performance drivers. Clearly, the dynamism of the business lends itself to continuous change monitoring and management.

NOTES

1 Exxon-Mobil Annual Report (2002).

2 Deloitte & Touche (2003).

3 PricewaterhouseCoopers (2003e).

4 Freswick, K (2003).

5 Zsolt, T (2003).

6 Emmott, B (2003).

7 Roehl-Anderson and Bragg (2002).

8 Tufano (1996).

9 Roehl-Anderson and Bragg (2002).

10 The classic references of simultaneous equation corporate financial planning models are Willard (1970), Warren and Shelton (1971), and Francis and Rowell (1978). But their models are not detailed enough for GAAP accounting treatment.

11 Coveney *et al*. (2002).

12 PricewaterhouseCoopers (2003d).

13 PriceWaterhouseCoopers (1997).

14 Sammer, J (2001)

15 *Corporate Finance Magazine* (2002 July).

16 Ramos, A (2002)

17 Hazou and Cheung (2002)

18 Corporate Finance (2002)

19 Foote (2003).

20 Bragg, S M (2002).

21 Ibid.

22 Corporate Finance (2003).

23 Blue Book of Bank Prices (2003) is a survey of prices paid for cash management services published by Phoenix-Hecht.

24 Gamble, R H (2003).

25 Gamble, R (2003b).

26 Ibid.

27 HSBC Annual Report (2002).

28 Citigroup Annual Report (2002).

29 General Electric Annual Report (2002).

30 Merrill Lynch Annual Report (2002).

31 Ericsson Annual Report (2002).

32 *Corporate Finance Magazine* (2002, June).

33 Ibid.

34 Marks & Spencer Annual Report (2002).

35 Toyota Annual Report (2002).

36 Shell Annual Report (2002).

37 Nestlé Annual Report (2002).

38 *Corporate Finance Magazine* (2002, June).

39 DuPont Annual Report (2002).

40 GlaxoSmithKline Annual Report (2002).

41 Gamble, R (2003).

42 Roehl-Anderson and Bragg (2000).

43 Citigroup Annual Report (2002).

44 Marks & Spencer Annual Report (2002).

45 Royal-Dutch/Shell Annual Report (2002).

46 Exxon-Mobil Annual Report (2002).

CHAPTER 6

Corporate performance management: the balancing act?

Introduction

Performance measurements at most companies are out of step with the business environment. Traditional performance measurements focus more on internal goals of cost and efficiency than on external realities of customer satisfaction and competitive capabilities.[1]

Every business is different, so each should have its own set of performance measurements. But there are some common rules to follow in designing effective measurements. For example, in addition to the standard set of accounting-based and economic value based (EVB) financial metrics, the set of measures should include non-financial metrics that view the company from outside-in.

Customer satisfaction measures and its trends over time ought to be a primary non-financial measure. Other measures should include customer value proposition, process efficiency, product quality, employee satisfaction, competitive position, effectiveness in strategy execution, social and environmental consciousness, and leadership quality.

The purpose of performance measurements is to focus the energy of the organization on its strategic goals, to track progress toward the goals, and to provide feedback. If performance measurements have not been realigned with the new priorities of the business, they will keep the organization from achieving a competitive advantage.

In just the past few years, executives have been exposed to value based management (VBM), economic value added (EVA), balanced scorecard, cash flow return on investment, and a flurry of other performance measures. Although these are sophisticated measures, if they are not adapted to your company's specific situation, they will fail. Externally focused, process-oriented, and system-wide performance measurements are essential for encouraging the actions that create competitive advantage today. In addition, the timeliness of these measures is critical, as the value of information falls quickly if it is late. Real-time corporate performance management (CPM) systems offer the most promising solution thus far, and many companies have demonstrated the improvement in quality of operational and financial effectiveness using these systems. CPM systems are similar to the balanced scorecard which measures financial and non-financial metrics. The difference is that CPM measures those items in the context of business strategy execution and management.

A driving force behind the CPM concept is the quest for alignment and transparency – two inescapable corporate buzz-words that can prove difficult to achieve – largely because there is often no vantage point from which the entire organization can be clearly viewed.

Some manufacturing entities, for example, make sub-optimal procurement decisions because sales, manufacturing, and procurement departments are not aligned in a way that optimizes material requisitions.

CPM is not brand new, but it represents an evolutionary advance over earlier budgeting, planning, forecasting, analytics, and related functions. Companies that pioneered those functions are now leading the CPM charge, seeing value for both customers and themselves in uniting a group of disparate financial applications into a suite of products that can serve as a sort of small-scale implementation of an enterprise resource planning (ERP) system for finance.[2]

"Until now, the general ledger had no understanding of the purchasing system," says Nazhin Zarhamee, chief marketing officer of Hyperion Solutions Corp. "The notion of an integrated flow of information across the organization did not exist. Goal setting, planning, budgeting, performance monitoring, and other activities often took place in a near vacuum. CPM unites these related methods and metrics in order to consolidate and analyse financial and operational data, thus providing insight into key business drivers."[3]

Each enterprise, given its particular market, customer base, vendor relationships, and so on, requires different types of data and metrics. But it all boils down to the same thing – turning data into information for decision-making purposes.

Do current planning, budgeting, forecasting, and reporting processes provide the detail necessary to understand the drivers of corporate results?

Chief finance officers (CFOs) are pressed by regulators and investors to produce timely, reliable, and more transparent financial reports. But many are unable to create better reports and forecasts because of inadequate systems and processes for gathering data about corporate performance. For example, finance staffs at many companies still manage financial performance using spreadsheets, making the process slow, rigid, and more geared to reporting accounting results than providing the insight needed to guide the business.

Survey results

According to a survey of 245 CFOs of global multinationals conducted by CFO Research Services, few senior financial executives are satisfied with their performance management capabilities – their ability to plan, budget, and forecast.[4]

Most CFOs indicated that their firms continue to struggle with creating a finance function that can act as a true partner to the business units. Some have made meaningful progress toward this goal, however, by embracing state-of-the-art technology solutions and adopting best practice processes and procedures.

Notable findings from the survey include those shown below:

- Performance management processes are broken: while 63 percent of finance executives polled said they are satisfied with the speed and accuracy of their monthly financial reports, only 48 percent are satisfied with the speed and accuracy of plan reforecasts during the fiscal year. Just 31 percent are satisfied with their ability to model and test the impact of proposed changes.

- Most CFOs plan changes to their performance management systems and capabilities: 61 percent of survey respondents plan changes to their performance management systems in the next 18 months.

- Major reasons for seeking change are to improve visibility into current results and to better understand future performance trends.

- There are obstacles to improving performance management: the two main barriers are a lack of integrated IT systems and competing priorities. Other obstacles included change management fatigue, lack of funds for process or systems change, concern about the difficulty of implementing a new system, inadequate senior management support, and resistance from the business units.

- There is pressure to abandon spreadsheet-based planning and budgeting: only 11 percent respondents are confident that a spreadsheet-based process ensures the accuracy required.

- Companies are migrating toward single-solution software: about half of the companies surveyed use a disparate mix of performance management software across their organizations. In three years, most plan to standardize – either using a single solution across the company or using an integrated set of best-of-breed software.

That more than half of the CFOs surveyed plan changes in these areas speaks of a high level of dissatisfaction with the current state of CPM – the planning, budgeting, forecasting, financial consolidation, management reporting, and analytical activities that help to shape a company's long-term success. CFOs are not the only ones dissatisfied with the current state of performance management. At many companies, finance is not providing the level of decision-support demanded by the chief executive officer (CEO).

Key drivers for companies that plan to adopt CPM are as follows:[5]

- need for better visibility of current results;
- need for better understanding of future performance trends;
- poor economic conditions: need for tighter cash-flow control;
- accelerating rate of change within industry;
- regulatory changes (e.g. Sarbanes-Oxley);
- pressure from shareholders/board of directors.

According to the CFO Research Services report, while 92 percent of companies say their CEOs want finance to be involved in corporate strategy, only 77 percent say they are able to do so. While 77 percent of the CEOs want finance to provide business performance analysis on demand, only 57 percent of finance departments are up to the task. On top of the pressures from investors and regulators, corporations are being pushed by their own boards of directors to improve the quality, detail, and timeliness of financial performance reports.

The problem extends beyond finance's ability to provide advice to the business on strategy execution – CFOs also confront difficulties in providing accurate forecasts.[6] Forecasts can be dicey if finance does not have easy access to current financial and operational data – a common problem at companies relying on antiquated spreadsheet-based technology. For example, only 11 percent of the CFOs of multinationals are confident that spreadsheet-based processes provide adequate control.

During times of economic uncertainty and market volatility, visibility into the future gets blurred, and it becomes hazardous to forecast anything beyond two years. Without a good basis of actuals, it is impossible to produce accurate forecasts. Therefore, it is imperative to have a strong link between the accounting side and the forecasting and planning side of the business.

Apart from finding a way to gather and process data more efficiently, many companies face the challenge of figuring out what to measure and report. Unless they are tracking the key drivers of sales and costs, both financial and non-financial, all the budgeting and forecasting in the

EXAMPLE

Until two years ago, Computer Associates (CA) employed a static, top-down, budgeting process that consumed four months each year. "By the time we were done, it was dated," says finance director Carl Caputo. Today, CA uses a web-based financial performance management system to create its budget in less than half that time. The company also uses the power of that system to update its budget on a monthly basis, and has begun to develop a rolling rather than static forecasting process to bring further finesse to its planning activities.[7]

world will not boost the bottom-line. Accountants and finance professionals in general, have accurate historical measures, but usually lack comprehensive leading indicator dashboards.

Even with companies that do have the right metrics, it can be difficult to apply them in a meaningful way to the company's planning and budgeting processes, in part because many of those metrics reside in far-flung corners of the enterprise, and getting access to them can be a challenge. Nearly half of the CFOs surveyed in the CFO Research Services report said their CPM systems cannot handle non-financial metrics at all. Those that do report non-financial metrics focus on customer and employee measures.

Nearly half of the CFOs surveyed said their CPM systems cannot handle non-financial metrics at all.

One consequence of data collection difficulties is that it may be hard to create and manage a budget that focuses on measures beyond traditional line items, and includes additional operating drivers. Furthermore, because of a lack of integrated performance management systems, many companies have budgets that tend to be static documents, reflecting management's thinking at a single point in time. Though not wholly useless, they tend to be backward-looking, so-called "rear-view mirror" approaches.

A far better approach for most companies, and already standard at best-practice organizations, is to implement a system of rolling budgets in which actual results are combined with the best possible intelligence from every facet of the organization to create an up-to-the-minute budget on a monthly or quarterly basis.

That can only happen with an integrated performance management system that will allow the organization to pull the necessary data together quickly. The larger and more complex the organization, the more critical a tool the performance management system becomes.

Like budgeting, financial forecasting is in poor shape at many companies.[8] Forecasts need to be dynamic and conditional on events that are likely to have a tangible impact on future performance. Financial forecasting should be based on run rates, current economic and industry conditions, competitor activities, etc. It is not about simply extrapolating current trends or managing from the rear-view mirror. The less accurate the forecast, the less confidence a company will have in its strategy. Accurate forecasts lead to more accurate budgeting, better decision making, and a reduced likelihood of earnings surprises.

Ideally, most CFOs would like to move to rolling forecasts. In the CFO Research, only 36 percent of CFOs said that they have a system of rolling forecasts in place today, although 84 percent expect to adopt it in the next three years.

CPM is not only for internal consumption. Investors and creditors eagerly await quarterly financial and operating results, and are often ruthless to react to negative surprises. Blue chip corporations openly acknowledge that they have little choice but to smooth their earnings, given Wall Street's allergy to surprises.[9] The "big bath hypotheses" are corroborated by the fact that big earnings declines have been shown to be more common than large increases.[10] However, overstating earnings would appear to be a self-defeating strategy in the long term, since it has a tendency to catch up with the perpetrator.

Key performance measures in active use

CPM has been under the focus of much academic and management discussion and debate. Some of the key performance measures in active use are accounting based performance measures such as earnings per share, earnings before interest, taxes, depreciation, and amortization (EBITDA) margins, operating margins, return on equity, return on assets, return on invested capital, and interest coverage; economic profit measures such as EVA, cash flow return on investment, and economic margin; and operating efficiency measures such as asset turnover, acid-test ratio, revenue per employee, sales, general and administrative (SG&A) expenses as a percent of operating revenues, etc.

However, no single measure encapsulates all of a company's pertinent financial traits. Operating earnings tend to be more stable than reported earnings, earnings before interest and tax (EBIT) tends to be more stable than operating earnings, and EBITDA tends to be more stable than EBIT. Companies welcome analytical migration toward less variable measures of performance, because investors reward stability with high price-earnings multiples. Although accounting measures are well understood by the financial and business communities, increased use of economic measures attests to the fact that there has been a welcome acceptance of economic measures.

Each category of performance measure indicates a different aspect of performance, and is therefore useful in its own right. The many different categories of measurement include financial profitability, economic profitability, operational effectiveness, liquidity, financial leverage, and operating leverage. And even these categories are not exhaustive, since they do not include important business considerations such as customer satisfaction, employee satisfaction, and comparative industry performance.

An integrated performance measurement apparatus is necessary which not only focuses on financial or economic-based measures, but views corporate performance more holistically. It should allow management to understand, monitor, and manage corporate performance effectively. The balanced scorecard is an integrated performance measurement apparatus that is being used by leading companies such as Exxon-Mobil, CIGNA, and Nova Scotia Power.[11]

Software in use

State-of-the-art software systems can help the finance function become a more efficient collector and analyst of data, well-equipped to model and test the impact of changes both within and external to the organization. These systems allow budgets and forecasts to be created and updated on a real-time basis, based on a continuous inflow of both financial and non-financial data. Because such a system allows business units to feed in much of the raw data and market intelligence directly, it makes operations managers part of the planning and forecasting process. In addition, it frees finance to spend more time on data analysis than on data collection. The best systems offer capabilities for analyzing data and modeling 'what-if' scenarios. Many financial executives stress the value of a web-based product, where the goal is to eliminate the hassles and pitfalls of trying to ensure that all users have the same current version of the software on their desktop, along with the latest version of the data that they want to use.

In addition to web-based analytical tools, many companies are planning to have technology that provides them with the ability to automate the generation and distribution of reports, create an 'executive dashboard' of key performance indicators (KPI), offer an enterprise-wide portal where mangers can drill down in greater detail on the company's performance data, and automatically alert users to potential budgeting or performance problems using exception analysis techniques.

While many companies have sought to enhance their performance capabilities by adding additional software to their arsenal of tools, they typically have used those systems only for discrete portions of the process, and with varying degrees of success. Whether to take a best-of-breed or a single-solution approach is less important than whether the applications are integrated across the organization.[12]

Information becomes obsolete quickly if you do not have a way to embed it into the fabric of the company. Although CPM sounds like the answer to any number of corporate headaches, to date few companies have deployed it. According to technology consulting firm Gartner, fewer than 10 percent of the global 2000 multinationals have implemented CPM, although Gartner believes that this will skyrocket to 40 percent by 2005.

A recent McKinsey report recommends four principles to follow in order to keep performance on track:[13]

■ understand how your company creates value;

■ integrate financial and operational measures;

■ keep the measurement system transparent and uniform;

■ focus on effective dialog within the management team.

The execution problem

To consistently attain the business profitability and value creation objectives, execution is more important than good vision. Corporate business and financial planning is an integral precursor to implementation as it sits between corporate strategy on the one side and operations management on the other. In fact, financial planning brings together the strategy and operations sides of the business on a common platform. However, even leading corporations have demonstrated the practical difficulties in implementing strategy through a well-crafted business and financial plan. Flawless execution has been a rarity.

According to Ernst & Young, a study of 275 senior business managers reported that the ability to execute strategy was more important than the quality of the strategy itself.[14] These managers cited strategy implementation as the most important factor shaping management and corporate valuations.

In the early 1980s, a survey of management consultants reported that fewer than 10 percent of effectively formulated strategies were successfully implemented.[15]

More recently, a 1999 Fortune cover story of prominent CEO failures concluded that the emphasis placed on strategy and vision created a mistaken belief that the right strategy was all that was needed to succeed. "In the majority of the cases – we estimate 70 percent – the real problem isn't bad strategy but bad execution".[16]

Market leaders create a competitive advantage and sustain it through intelligent, nimble execution. How do best-in-class companies achieve excellence in executing the daily processes that ultimately comprise business strategy? They do so by being able to model, monitor, and adjust processes automatically. These capabilities give market leaders the agility to change direction quickly, and take advantage of shifting market conditions.

Of course, this is easier said than done. Achieving flawless execution is difficult in today's extended, virtual enterprise in which companies no longer directly control their products. With many core functions being outsourced to business partners – from design and manufacturing to logistics and inventory – good execution is hard to achieve in an environment characterized by all accountability and little control.

Despite the billions invested in technology over the last decade, most current global 1000 systems do not support the requirements of flawless execution. These legacy systems cannot manage collaborative, real-time processes; rather, they operate in a transaction-based batch mode that does not easily accommodate processes extending outside company boundaries.[17]

Over the past decade, corporations have made large investments in packaged software and technology. First there was the enterprise resource planning (ERP) boom, which automated and integrated key back-office internal functions within a company.

Next, companies started to make similar investments in customer relationship management (CRM), which automates and integrates key front-office, customer-facing functions within a company. Now companies are automating and integrating key externally focused applications with internal ones. Highly regarded companies deliver, without fail, goods and services at the expected time with the expected terms and conditions. And the best ones are often highly profitable.

Detecting and resolving exceptions within a business process is not a new best practice. However, the increased velocity and visibility afforded to individuals and companies over the web has forced all enterprises to become more fleet of foot when dealing with problems, and closing the loop in business exceptions.

The balanced scorecard

Every company will have its own key measures and distinctive process for implementing change. The leading indicators of business performance cannot be found in financial data alone. Product quality, customer satisfaction, innovation, market share, employee retention – metrics like these often reflect a company's economic condition and growth prospects better than its reported accounting earnings do.

According to a seminal article in the *Harvard Business Review*, more and more leading global companies are changing their company's performance measurement systems to track non-financial measures to supplement traditional financial measures, thus reinforcing new competitive strategies.[18]

The idea of looking at a business in terms of a "scorecard" has aroused considerable interest since 1992 when it was introduced. We usually measure corporate performance results in monetary terms. The income statements or profit and loss (P&L) for particular business units or divisions are modeled on the income statement of the company.

But adding non-financial measures within the scope of management reporting has provided senior management with additional clarity of the operating results and drivers of the business. New technologies and more sophisticated databases have made the change to non-financial performance measurement systems possible and economically feasible.

Dissatisfaction with using financial measures to evaluate business performance is nothing new. As far back as 1951, Ralph Cordiner, the CEO of General Electric, commissioned a high-level task force to identify key non-financial corporate performance measures. One important difference between then and now is the intensity and nature of the criticism directed at traditional accounting systems. During the past few years, academics and practitioners have begun to demonstrate that accrual-based performance measures are at best obsolete – and more often harmful.[19]

More importantly, Generally Accepted Accounting Principles (GAAP) and International Accounting Standards (IAS) based systems generate numbers that often fail to support investments in new technologies and markets that are essential for successful performance in global markets. In addition, for publicly listed companies, corporate managers' willingness to play the earnings game calls into question the very measures the market focuses on. The investor community often focus on top-line revenues and accounting earnings per share as key performance metrics supporting shareholder value

In order to meet quarterly guidance, corporate management becomes short-term focused.

creation. In order to meet quarterly guidance, corporate management becomes short-term focused. Moreover, to the extent that managers do focus on reported quarterly earnings – and thereby reinforce the investment community's short-term perspective and expectations – they have a strong incentive to manipulate the figures they report.[20]

For longer-term performance management, many leading companies have adopted a balance of cash-flow based economic performance measures supplemented by non-financial operating measures into a scorecard that represents a balanced view of the firm's actual performance during a stated period.

The balanced scorecard is a method for reaching agreement on where an operation should be heading, and for making sure it stays on course. As the term implies, the balanced scorecard is an aid in creating a "balance" among various financial and non-financial factors to be considered. The balance adopted reflects the strategic choices of the business.

The measures selected for the balanced scorecard complement purely financial metrics with operational, customer, and market-driven perspectives. Although financial metrics form the ultimate yardstick for senior management, the execution of the business plan happens lower in the organization – at the grass-roots levels – where nebulous shareholder value metrics and economic profit objectives need to be supplemented with real operational metrics and performance targets, so that they resonate at the individual level.

Moreover, financial controls tend to be short-sighted as a result of the quarterly pressure to meet financial guidance to the capital market. Management control therefore focuses on short-term profit, and fails to present a large part of the fuller picture of an operation. Profit is a good bottom-line metric, but does not tell us enough about how an operation is managed. The balanced scorecard combines outcome measures, of which profit is only one, along with other performance drivers.

Profit is a good bottom-line metric, but does not tell us enough about how an operation is managed.

We live in an era of change. Markets become fragmented as a result of the dynamics of the business. This development poses a challenge to the adaptive capacity of the business. This applies not only to companies that sell to other companies, but also to the so-called mass consumer or end-user market. Traditional financial control is ill-adapted to such an environment because the information it provides is backward looking and lacks sufficient operational content.

In the last decade, there has been growing criticism of traditional management control as being too narrowly focused on financial measures.[21] Sophisticated technologies and production processes have led to new demands on company systems of management control. Purely financial measures show the effects of decisions already taken, but fail to provide adequate guidance for long-term strategic development.

Traditional accounting-based financial measures of corporate performance ignore less tangible non-financial measures such as product quality, customer satisfaction, industry competitive dynamics, product delivery time, factory flexibility, new-product lead-time, and employee knowledge base and know-how. It encourages short-term thinking and sub-optimization. The critical challenge is to achieve balance between the short and long run. Financial measures do not provide a true and fair view of how a business is developing.[22]

New corporate strategic directions call for new information for planning, decision making, and control. Management control must take account of external factors and be broadened to include assessment of future competitive position. As a model of corporate performance measurement that provides a "balanced" perspective of both financial and operational aspects of business results, the balanced scorecard helps execution effectiveness.

Strategy-focused organizations are utilizing this model for effectively managing their businesses. Examples include Exxon-Mobil, CIGNA, Nova Scotia Power, and many others. Since each business has its unique characteristics, the balanced scorecard is unique to each individual business organization. It basically includes four areas of performance measurement (see Figure 6.1):

■ *financial* perspective,

■ *customer* perspective,

■ *internal/process* perspective,

■ *learning and growth* perspective.

The *financial* perspective includes traditional financial and economic performance measures as earnings per share, return on capital, EVA, and others based on management priorities and judgment. The balanced scorecard is intended to link short-term operational control to the long-term vision and strategy of the business. In each of the four areas, management formulates statements of objective, targets, and initiatives to attain predetermined

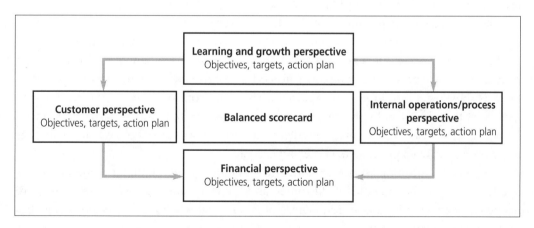

FIGURE 6.1 ■ Four areas of performance measurement

targets. Measures include return on capital employed, cash flow, EVA, sales growth, and profit forecast reliability.

The financial perspective should show the results of the strategic choices made in the other perspectives, while at the same time establishing several of the long-term goals and thus a large part of the general ground rules and premises for the other perspectives. Here we find a description of what the owners expect of the company in terms of profitability and growth, acceptable financial risks, cost and investment strategies, product revenue growth, market share, product mix, productivity, etc.

The *customer* perspective describes the ways in which value is to be created for customers, and how to increase and ensure customer loyalty. Here we find pricing strategies, product quality and functionality, delivery time, brand image, customer satisfaction and changes in preferences, customer relationships, etc. This includes measures such as customer satisfaction, response time, delivery reliability, and quality.

The *learning and growth* perspective includes a focus on internal human capital and the quality of improvement that is taking place. Are employees being trained to remain at the cutting edge of new ideas, tools, innovations, and skills that are needed to perform their jobs most efficiently? Are they learning everyday how to do what they do, better? Are employees happy? What is your score? The learning and growth perspective may include measures such as the percentage of revenues derived from new products or services, number of employee-generated new ideas, progress on process changes, and improvement programs.

The *internal operations and process* perspective includes metrics that show how well the business operations is working. What is the rate of error in production? Benchmark your performance in capacity utilization against your principal competitors. Has continuous process improvement been adopted as a principle? How much more efficient could you be with a more efficient process flow? This may include measures such as process reliability, rework, inventory level, capacity utilization, and employee turnover.

The balanced scorecard is not an off-the-shelf measure but needs to be modified according to the unique needs of each organization. Details of its components are shown in Figure 6.2.

With the balanced scorecard, the company focuses on a few key ratios or metrics in meaningful target areas. The company is forced to control and monitor day-to-day operations as they affect developments tomorrow. Thus, the company's focus is broadened to include both financial and non-financial ratios.[23] Companies therefore, utilize the balanced scorecard to describe the essential ingredients of business success, all the way from strategy to planning, and from planning to successful execution.

Although financial measures are ultimately paramount in a company operating in a market economy, the operational, customer, and the leaning and growth perspectives are needed as leading indicators – early signals of factors that will not be reflected in financial performance until much later.

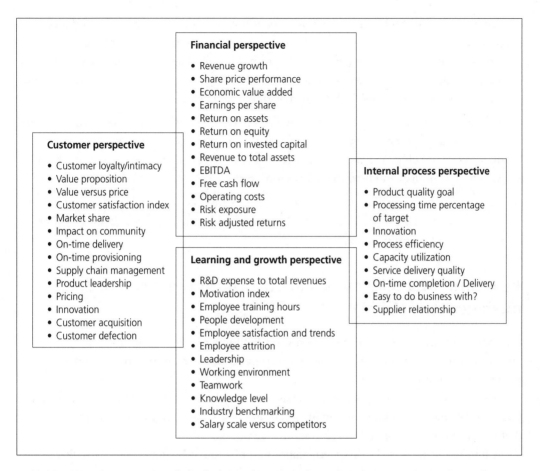

Financial perspective

- Revenue growth
- Share price performance
- Economic value added
- Earnings per share
- Return on assets
- Return on equity
- Return on invested capital
- Revenue to total assets
- EBITDA
- Free cash flow
- Operating costs
- Risk exposure
- Risk adjusted returns

Customer perspective

- Customer loyalty/intimacy
- Value proposition
- Value versus price
- Customer satisfaction index
- Market share
- Impact on community
- On-time delivery
- On-time provisioning
- Supply chain management
- Product leadership
- Pricing
- Innovation
- Customer acquisition
- Customer defection

Internal process perspective

- Product quality goal
- Processing time percentage of target
- Innovation
- Process efficiency
- Capacity utilization
- Service delivery quality
- On-time completion / Delivery
- Easy to do business with?
- Supplier relationship

Learning and growth perspective

- R&D expense to total revenues
- Motivation index
- Employee training hours
- People development
- Employee satisfaction and trends
- Employee attrition
- Leadership
- Working environment
- Teamwork
- Knowledge level
- Industry benchmarking
- Salary scale versus competitors

FIGURE 6.2 ■ Components of the balanced scorecard

Some authors have referred to the corporation as "The Intelligent Enterprise" and emphasized the importance of cultivating a "core competency"[24] Companies that have successfully employed the balanced scorecard in Europe include ABB, Coca Cola, Electrolux, British Telecom, Nat West Bank, Skandia, and Volvo.[25]

At first glance, the balanced scorecard seems to be just a variation of management by objectives. However, a closer look at how it is used shows that it is more than identification of multiple objectives and measurements. It is really a system for managing strategy. Successful use in a number of companies shows the following:[26]

■ The process of identifying the measures is often more important than the scorecard data. At Apple Computers, it is a planning device. If that planning process involves managers from a variety of functions, the scorecard provides a basis for examining the inter-dependence of the functions.

■ Key objectives in each perspective must be identified, and their inter-dependence with other perspectives put on the table for discussion. A target for improved customer response, for example, will have an impact on internal objectives. Innovation and learning will require management attention, time, and costs. The scorecard provides a useful template for choosing and building management initiatives.

■ The balanced scorecard helps clarify the links between strategy and action. For example, if the strategy is to enter new markets or design new products, each of the four perspectives will be affected. The scorecard encourages managers to be specific about what they want to accomplish and how to measure progress.

■ The impact of using the balanced scorecard seems to be strongest if it is part of a process of change. It provides a discipline to help managers coordinate elements to bring about the desired change.

Real-time financial systems: corporate performance management (CPM)

Corporate performance reporting is a critical CFO function. Real-time performance reporting allows top management to understand the pulse of the business from its financial and operational metrics.

Real time financial and operational management seeks to reduce lag time or 'information float' out of core operational and managerial processes. Businesses have long understood that time is money, and speed is a competitive advantage.

Real-time business is about speed, agility, and efficiency. Businesses get visibility across the extended enterprise to be able to anticipate and capitalize on opportunities before others. This requires strategic alignment of business processes to make up-to-date information available to everyone who needs it, whenever they need it. This applies internally as well as externally to customers.

In today's rapidly changing business environment, decision-makers cannot afford to wait for batch reports to tell them how their business is performing. Instead, managers require instantly up-to-date information to judge their business and to react to issues and conditions as they occur. The lack of visibility to changing business conditions is a big reason for lack of profitability for major corporations.[27]

Consider the automobile manufacturer that wrote-off $1bn in inventory on precious metals because its purchasing department continued buying when it had no visibility into demand. Or the network and telecom companies that wrote off $2.5bn and $19.5bn respectively for excess inventory because they did not identify a lack of product demand during a market downturn.

Similarly, financial institutions lose millions each year to fraud when they are not able to recognize quickly exceptional transactions. And many companies disenfranchise loyal and key customers when they do not respond in a timely manner to customer complaints. Companies therefore need the ability to get a real-time, event-driven analysis of business metrics by monitoring and evaluating business activities as they happen. This provides enhanced levels of predictability, agility, and exactness to business, and helps execution effectiveness.

According to Gartner Inc., a US-based IT consulting firm:

> "The real-time enterprise is an enterprise that competes by using up-to-date information to progressively remove delays to the management and execution of its critical business process."[28]

To approach the real-time enterprise where managers make decisions based on up-to-date information, you need a solution with an adaptive architecture that provides:[29]

■ a *streaming cache* of events tapped from the message streams and the event generation and transport mechanisms, and combined with the contextual information stored in the data warehouse, to report events in the business;

■ *dynamic modeling* of business activities such that the models can quickly be created and changed by business managers, not programers;

■ *temporal processing* of events and activities to identify and understand trends, not just spot threshold crossings;

■ *business rules engine* that uses familiar business formulae to quickly process events, put them into context, and identify exceptional conditions;

■ *exception-driven processes* that immediately send alerts to key business users by providing them with the metrics necessary to address critical business issues.

Powerful web-based executive information systems provide a consolidated real-time view of an organization's performance, making it easy to take advantage of a balanced scorecard approach to management, and measure and understand an organization's key performance indicators and performance metrics.

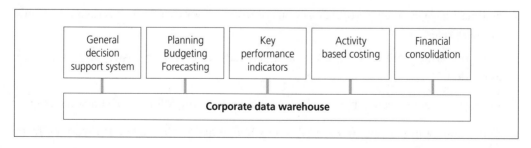

FIGURE 6.3 ■ Real-time financial systems

CPM systems provide management tools for setting expectations for every organization at every level, with easy-to-understand reporting of the status of progress throughout the year. The executive software measurements set at each level roll up to higher indicators, creating a means for gauging the status of your organizational progress.

Areas such as sales, production, efficiency, effectiveness, and product quality all affect an organization's financial performance. However, few companies are able to capture and report their many data points, real-time, on all levels. Reasons include:

- tardy and inaccurate access to key performance indicators;
- inability to spot negative trends early;
- human errors and eliminating duplicate data entry;
- inability to generate detailed reports to show emerging trends;
- inability to pin-point operational inefficiency root-causes;
- inability to identify and proactively apply preventive measures;
- lack of specific performance goals at each level.

In fact, the move to real-time business and to real-time business analysis demands more than evolutionary improvements in older-generation systems. It demands a new level of sophistication, and new technology that can solve the dilemma of real-time visibility combined with in-depth, contextual insight.

What best performers have done is move from solely relying on periodic performance or operational reports to combining them with real-time monitoring or business intelligence systems that:[30]

- listen to the transactions in real time, as they occur (or do not occur) across multiple business systems;
- automatically detect any user-defined exceptions, issues, or opportunities requiring immediate action;
- notify all the appropriate parties simultaneously about the issue – with real-time alerts;
- automatically take the appropriate actions or response for that issue – as defined by your business rules;
- track the issue until it is resolved on a centrally accessible website, and escalate it as needed.

According to recent research, best-in-class companies have the following characteristics:[31]

- These companies know in near-real-time when actual performance is diverging from plan.

■ These companies not only send out formal monthly or weekly plans to suppliers but also notify them, by exception, of key changes in the plan, and potentially even postpone or cancel purchase orders automatically.

■ These companies know the key metrics on which their customers rate them – those that impact their customers' costs, customer service, responsiveness – and provide early warning to them on impending violations or problems, along with collaborative capabilities to ensure rapid dialog and resolution.

■ These companies agree on two-way communication with customers and suppliers – to turn uncertainty into known conditions.

■ Best-in-class company execution systems support real-time enforcement of a range of business rules that work across systems, databases and enterprises – ensuring prevention of violations rather than having to rework after the fact.

■ Best-in-class companies automate all routine tasks to minimize labor cost, reduce time lags, and eliminate human errors.

■ Best-in-class companies track internal and external facing metrics to drive objective and target setting, and to drive behaviour.

■ Best-in-class companies continually monitor performance, and flag when key metrics are trending down or below key target levels. They know of performance problems while there is still time to respond to the situation.

■ These companies not only measure performance in near-real-time, they proactively monitor the business process for early warning or predictive problems. They detect and respond to problems as they arise and before they adversely impact performance.

■ Best-in-class companies keep track of exceptions or problems and periodically try to eliminate the most common ones that disrupt their supply chain, with a continuous improvement program.

EXAMPLE

Examples of companies that have invested in and have transformed to real-time enterprises are Hewlett-Packard, Avnet, BP Castrol, Seagate, Dresser, Pirelli, Royal Dutch/Shell, Telecom Italia, NASDAQ, Delta Airlines, and EBAY among thousands of others.

How do leading companies identify and manage risk exposures and treasury functions in real time? They use various financial systems that capture the data at the point of transaction, and perform real-time data compilation and analysis, and provide management output. Corporate treasurers look for a single system to manage risk and handle the varied needs of

"Forget budgeting and planning software. What companies need to see is performance".[33]

the treasury. The treasury management system suppliers are edging in on the risk system market.[32]

Over the past few years, the unique risk management needs of corporates have increasingly been recognized by risk system providers, who have customized offerings aimed specifically at clients. But lately, the boundaries have blurred between corporate risk management and treasury management systems.

Treasury management systems suppliers are now going head-to-head with the risk management system suppliers by incorporating increasingly sophisticated risk analysis in their systems. These treasury management systems have the following capabilities:

- pricing, valuation and processing of almost any financial instrument;

- combining powerful analytical and transactional tools;

- process, monitor and rebalance holdings;

- streamline administrative and reporting functions;

- incorporate real-time valuations into multiple portfolios across the globe and in widely differing banking systems.

Such efficiencies can both cut costs and increase income through more effective investment and management of cash resources. Many of the traditional risk management systems were originally designed for financial institutions and later adjusted for corporate clients. However, the risk management needs of corporates are on the whole very different from those of financial institutions, and some of the metrics incorporated into traditional systems do not meet corporate needs.

For the majority of corporates, *cash is used* to support the running of the primary business, but for financial institutions, *cash is the primary business*. And as corporates have become more sophisticated in their risk management strategies over the past few years, they are demanding more from system suppliers.

EXAMPLE

RiskMetrics is one of the few major traditional risk management systems suppliers to specifically gear an offering – *RiskManager* – to corporates. Formerly a division of JP Morgan, *RiskMetrics* was spun-off as an independent company in 1998. *RiskManager* is a ready-built total risk management system with a front-end interface that offers real-time interactive ports and graphs, what-if scenario generation and interactive drill-down analysis. The system is designed to have an open architecture, with drop-in importing, reporting and price modules.

Typically, non-financial corporates look at a longer time horizon for purposes of risk exposure estimation and management than financial institutions. Where financial institutions look at one to ten days, manufacturing companies or utility companies will look at one month to one year. ABB and DaimlerChrysler, for example, check whether the company is within Bank for International Settlements (BIS) regulatory capital requirements. Even though the company is not a financial institution and therefore is not required to do this, they benchmark themselves against this standard.

Risk managers want to be able to look at the risk of the derivative contracts they are holding globally which need to be re-marked monthly or quarterly. The new breed of highly sophisticated treasury systems that are coming to market are aimed at multinational corporates with global subsidiaries. By incorporating risk and treasury functions, the systems help the user to effectively manage investment instruments, multi-currency cash flows and provide straight through processing (STP). In addition, they have the advantage of being a completely integrated, single treasury and risk system.

EXAMPLE

Swedish group Electrolux uses Trema's *Finance KIT*, which is one such treasury system, combining a web-enabled offering with risk management solutions. From the outset, *Finance KIT* was designed with real-time risk management capabilities. The risk offering consists of three main parts. The first involves traditional single parameter risk measures, basis points risk measures, and sensitivity measurement against single market parameters. The second offers what-if scenario analysis – which extends single parameters to measure various scenarios that could arise. And finally, the system includes statistical measures, including VAR, that are also integrated into the real-time engine.

Corporates want a higher level of control over the underlying liquidity of their organization and having a centralized system allows them to get the whole picture across their business. Once integrated, the systems allow users to see online what their total exposure is in each of the currencies they hold positions in. From that they can work out their net liquidity globally, allowing the traders and risk managers to act on that information.

EXAMPLE

Shell, Pirelli, NASDAQ, Telecom Italia, Delta Airlines, and EBAY, for example, use *TIBCO* software for their real-time corporate reporting.

The new-generation systems

Many of these risk systems can input scenarios – such as interest rate movements – to see the worst case scenario. The user can monitor financial risks and limit exposures, as settlement or default risk may be monitored as needed, by deal type, portfolio, dealing entity, dealer, counterparty issuer and counterparty sector. Mark-to-market and other key figures such as duration, convexity and options may be viewed for individual deals, trial deals and hedge strategies.

Benchmarking, cost-of-funds, liquidity forecasts, and maturity and interest refixing gap reports can also be generated by these systems. Different modules offer analyses of currency risk, interest rate risk, position risk, and operational risk in terms VAR. The system will give warning signals when preset risk tolerance limits are breached.

Non-financial corporates can be more flexible than a bank, in terms of time horizon for risk exposure estimation and hedging. Typically, financial institutions tend to go for best-of-breed technology for each of their sectors, taking a product from each and bolting them together to try and create a real-time system. Any corporate treasury has to fit into its corporate environment, and therefore financial systems can vary in large proportion depending on the scale and complexity of business needs.

Many CFOs want a system that can give their executives a so-called real-time snapshot of how the company was performing. That means using the web to make the system and its information accessible to all offices. It requires linking the software with other company data, and not necessarily financial data. Although a surprisingly large number of companies are still using spreadsheets, the trend toward real-time financial reporting is a sustained one, especially in the more advanced economies, and leading multinationals.

Developing a system that actually tells executives how well the company is meeting its performance goals allows on-time optimal decision making regarding both operational and financial variables.

Multi-dimensional analysis is powerful, as it allows one to slice and dice data, understand performance and get a graphical representation of performance. You can thus pin-point the problem, and remedy the root-cause issue quickly. In recent years, planning, budgeting, and reporting software has been developing into something more comprehensive, as is evident from the new monikers that such systems are sporting, like business performance management or enterprise performance management solutions. Comshare Inc., for example, describes its system as a "corporate performance management application."

It is necessary to understand how this new generation of integrated softwares differ from the old planning and budgeting software: the new systems have the ability to access operational and financial data like production numbers, web-enabled to get input on budgets from many employees and alert systems that warn the right executives when the company is falling behind budget.

The concept of tying together financial and non-financial data is not that new. In the early 1990s, the "balanced scorecard" approach was advocated by Robert Kaplan and David Norton. But without the web, it was difficult for companies to get a picture across the organization. Now that many companies have in place back-end applications, such as customer relationship management systems and supply chain management systems, capturing that information and analyzing what it says about the company is finally possible.

With the tighter reporting deadlines mandated by Sarbanes-Oxley in the US and its requirement that CEOs and CFOs sign off on their companies' financial reports, and higher accountability standards for auditors, most believe the pressures are mounting to give up spreadsheets. Add to that the intolerance the equity and credit markets show these days toward errors in financial data, even honest ones, and one can easily sketch out a scenario in which spreadsheets become as outmoded as adding machines within the next couple of years.

Software systems make the process of consolidating data faster and more reliable, and dramatically slash the amount of staff time it takes to budget and report. They thus allow a remarkable improvement in organizational effectiveness and productivity. These systems also allow executives to drill down and give them, as Mark Stimpson, director of product management for Cognos Inc., puts it, "a greater degree of comfort about how the numbers have been made up."

Financial discipline is key to corporate financial management in an increasingly information intensive new economy. CFOs of leading companies pay particular attention to advanced and sophisticated financial information systems that can provide operational and financial status in real time. JP Morgan, for example, uses its risk management system *RiskMetrics™* to calculate daily earnings at risk (DEAR) at the close of business every day.[34]

EXAMPLES

Matáv is Hungary's largest telecommunications company with revenues over $1.6bn. Since adoption of real-time corporate performance management (CPM) system, it tracks financial and non-financial performance metrics with powerful functionality for tasks such as business modeling and "what-if" analysis. The system follows a rolling three-year methodology. Zita Imrene Kartyik, head of business planning at Matáv says, "We can now quickly pinpoint deviations from strategy because actual and budget data are stored in one database. Management can therefore manage corporate performance more effectively."

ICI Paints, one of the world's largest manufacturers of paints and industrial coatings employs CPM systems to solve two problems: manage the multi-dimensional nature of the business and streamline the growing budgeting process. Martin Harrison, finance director at ICI Paints, UK, says, "We were looking for a single system that provided one common version of the truth insofar as actual performance results are concerned."[35]

> Brisbane City Council in Australia uses an integrated CPM system as well as the balanced scorecard for performance assessment and to improve strategic execution and organizational accountability. Similarly, Dutton-Forshaw, a leading European automotive and machinery group operating a fiercely competitive and low margin market with a annual turnover of over €450m simplified data analysis by integrating operating and financial data collection in one database for consolidated reporting. Its financial planning and forecasting processes became more efficient as a result of adopting real-time CPM systems.

Every company has some sort of financial analysis tool that it uses to conduct business and financial planning. Excel spreadsheets are typically used for financial planning, since powerful financial analysis software add-ins use Excel as the interface. Examples of financial add-ins include *RiskOptimizer, OptQuest, Crystal Ball*, etc. But real-time financial systems need much more analytical capability than all-purpose spreadsheet packages.

Hyperion, SAP, and *PeopleSoft*, for example, specialize in customized financial applications, and are essentially very large and detailed financial databases linking real-time to corporate transaction data, and assimilated to deliver financial data for decision making. These financial systems include integrated risk management systems, the balanced scorecard performance measurement systems, as well as ERP and CRM systems. The systems are necessary for dynamic business and financial planning and execution.

Based on exception-reporting from these systems, top management can identify outlying events and adapt to changing business circumstances almost on a real-time basis. It is a source of comparative advantage for those that have these tools at their finger-tips. Without these tools, the information delivery and analysis infrastructure and business planning will be sub-optimal and unable to maximize profitability.

Fragmented IT application architectures not only greatly complicate the CRM process, but also interferes with a company's core business operations. Operational risk is the main potential problem arising for firms whose IT infrastructures are either inadequate to support the analytical requirements of a sound financial and operational management process, or whose applications architectures are too fragmented to facilitate appropriate risk measurement, reporting, and oversight.

For treasury cash management, a complete, end-to-end, financial flow management solution can be utilized. Such solutions include integrated, on-line, real-time tools for e-banking, e-payments, security, in-house banking, netting, and front-to-back office dealing and risk management, all within one multi-company, multinational, multi-currency, multi-bank environment.

Streamlined communication management facilitates the exchange of financial flows between the corporation's banks for continuous electronic banking and financial processing. By centralizing financial activity, companies have the ability to make bank balance and transaction information available to subsidiaries using all data exchange supports, file transfer formats, electronic mail and internet/intranet online web services.

Compliance and other global features

CFO departments with global functions need to handle a wide range of foreign exchange, money market and capital market instruments, both cash and derivative, tradable and over-the-counter, to manage positions and financial risks effectively. Transactions are securely booked to the enterprise accounting system, from transaction input to accruals, valuation, and revaluation. Market data is interfaced with the real-time corporate performance management system for direct calculation of mark-to-market and pricing information so that data are FAS133/IAS39 compliant, while an audit trail monitors all changes made to the database.

Other systems are designed to cover the complex requirements of global corporations and financial institutions for in-house banking and intercompany dealing. By setting up internal or inter-company accounts, group cash requirements can be met on a global basis. The central treasury department is able to share or distribute cash resources as required.

Risk management systems enable corporate treasury to measure and assess enterprise-wide financial risk and to act according to its enterprise policy to ensure that financial risks are maintained at an appropriate level. These systems provide real-time analytical tools to help identify, quantify, and report financial risks, apply effective hedging strategies, and monitor the effectiveness of the risk management programs. The operative term here is *flexibility*.

The operative term here is flexibility.

CPM systems integrate key management processes, such as strategic planning, risk management, balanced scorecard, and budgeting. These systems help create a clear understanding of corporate strategy and establish accountability, while enabling managers to proactively monitor actions and performance against company targets.

Real-time performance systems support the quality of strategy execution. Latest innovations in scorecard automation empower users to align valuable resources with strategy more effectively, thus resulting in the greatest impact on performance. Benefits include:

■ alignment of organizational activities with business objectives, resulting in better strategy execution;

■ no client/server administrative connections or additional systems software are required;

■ complete browser-based solutions enable management of strategy for the enterprise to be conducted entirely over the web.

Executives manage risks that may prevent the effective execution of strategy. They get a strategic view of risk management while facilitating risk methodology deployment throughout all levels of the organization. Real-time information enables organizations to collaborate, integrate, and share the responsibility for risk management.

Real-time corporate performance systems support the rolling forecast beyond budgeting methodology, but provide a comprehensive financial management solution to support any business model. These systems leverage the value of data in general ledger and spreadsheet applications.

Business management is a complex task, which benefits from accurate and timely information that is useful in decision making. However, turning a profit now requires careful attention to detail that can hide beneath the business surface, often at the intersection between various departments and functions, and between distinctly different systems and applications.

BPM in detail

In the quest to increase earnings, organizational efficiencies, and financial accountability, and to address regulatory and investor demands for financial transparency, many enterprises are now examining business performance management (BPM). BPM is a process and technical solution that enables both executives and line managers to assess the performance of their business and respond quickly to market opportunities or problems. It requires a cross-enterprise platform – not only to extract, integrate, and store business data, but also to promote collaboration among decision makers. By empowering the decision makers with relevant, timely, and accurate information, and enhancing the interchange of information across departments, BPM has proved that it can drive corporate accountability and help maximize profits.

As information technology in all its forms becomes an integral part of business, companies continue to sharpen their management processes with new tools and capabilities. Business intelligence capabilities are increasingly being built into the applications used to automate processes used to develop products and services, manage the interaction with customers, and support processes such as accounting and human resources.

Real-time business intelligence is used to monitor business processes and generate alerts or event notifications when there is a departure from expected behavior. These alerts can relate to an individual occurrence – for example, a supply chain event management application that generates an alert if a supplier fails to deliver a parts shipment on time – or to the results of numerous transactions, such as inventory levels falling below predefined thresholds.

To be useful, these alerts need to be generated and delivered quickly enough for corrective action to be taken before a problem results – often in a matter of minutes or hours. At still higher levels, business activity monitoring tracks the overall state of one or more interrelated processes, potentially with a higher degree of latency in the data. For example, key performance indicators can be displayed on a digital dashboard; the scope can range from overall enterprise financial and operational performance indicators in a balanced scorecard down to details on process-specific indicators, such as on-time delivery performance of key suppliers, or to key customers.

For this purpose, it may be acceptable if data is refreshed only daily, unless intra-day refresh is necessary. Historical financial and operational data are used to provide a context for the current data – to see whether similar patterns have occurred in the past, for example. In addition to their use in monitoring, analytics are also used in planning the execution of tasks associated with specific business processes – for example, selecting customers to be called as part of a telemarketing campaign. This type of planning is one step removed from the execution of a business process, and uses business intelligence to plan and optimize how the execution occurs. However, it is still relatively tactical: it takes place within the framework of a predetermined set of business processes and a predetermined business strategy.

Business intelligence using the highest degree of aggregation and covering the longest period of time corresponds to traditional data warehousing applications. In addition to being used for tactical decision making, these are often used to make strategic decisions, such as whether a company should develop a new set of products or services, enter a new geographic or demographic market, or redesign core business processes.

Real-time capabilities

Real-time capabilities are now an important part of business intelligence systems. These capabilities range from the application of analytic techniques through to individual transactions that are in process to the use of alerts, event notification, and digital dashboards. This is particularly necessary for automated treasury management systems. Beyond business intelligence, real-time functionality is being incorporated into a range of other applications, such as:

■ supply chain event management,

■ accounting, finance, and customer relationship management,

■ real-time business integration.

Real-time capabilities are being added to enterprise resource planning (ERP) and supply chain management (SCM) applications in a variety of ways. For example, SCM applications provide real-time information about order status and inventory levels as well as other supply chain events such as deliveries, shipments, and production. They also provide both real-time notification of exceptions or problems, and the ability to respond in real-time by changing production plans or diverting shipments.

Real-time capabilities in the supply chain will increase as a result of the growing use of radio frequency identification (RFID) technology, which allows pallets, cartons, and individual units of inventory to be labeled with tags that can be read electronically. Service based firms may also adopt RFID technology to track provisioning status.

These systems greatly improve a manufacturing organization's ability to know where products, parts, and shipping containers are at any given time, and they provide an unprecedented view of a product throughout its life-cycle.

Businesses are also increasing the speed with which their systems process information in the area of finance and accounting. For example, the virtual close is a set of techniques that allow a company to simulate the monthly or quarterly accounting period close on a more frequent basis – often daily.

Like business activity monitoring, the virtual close lets companies monitor critical business information in near real-time. It also speeds the process of completing the actual end-of-period close. This benefits US listed companies facing an accelerated schedule for financial reporting under the provisions of the Sarbanes-Oxley Act.[36]

Additional real-time capabilities are being incorporated into CRM systems. Online marketing, merchandising, and personalization systems have been doing real-time tailoring of content presented to website visitors since the early days of web-based e-commerce. New real-time marketing applications, for example, predict customer actions by using behavioral models that analyse data obtained from the customer during the sales transaction in addition to stored data about the customer's demographic characteristics and past purchases.

Business integration technologies are the foundation for many of the real-time capabilities we have discussed. For a business intelligence application to provide business activity monitoring, it must have access to data from a variety of enterprise systems. Similarly, one of the key requirements for a virtual close is achieving automatic consolidation of financial information from multiple systems.

In addition, real-time business integration enables end-to-end automation of business processes, thereby allowing the company to react more quickly to changes to business conditions. The stage beyond process integration is closed-loop integration, in which a company automatically uses information about business events and business performance to modify its operations – ideally within minutes rather than in days or weeks.[37]

Business integration is also being enabled by developments in enterprise application suites. The leading ERP suite vendors have introduced technologies for creating composite applications, which encapsulate the functionality of parts of their suites and allow them to be integrated to create an automated business process.

However, most companies' ERP systems cannot aggregate the wide range of information from disparate operational systems and external sources that is needed for financial reporting. Therefore, companies cannot increase reporting transparency without either significantly enhancing largely manual processes or reengineering reporting processes through the use of IT.

Many of the technologies that are relevant to financial reporting are also useful in meeting other regulatory compliance requirements. For example, financial institutions – particularly those having several back-office systems as a result of mergers or acquisitions – need business integration and business intelligence technologies to collect and analyse the data required for ensuring compliance with capital adequacy requirements such as those specified by the New Basel Capital Accords (Basel II). These technologies provide companies with instant and deep visibility into enterprise operations, and allow them to be adaptive, responsive, and operate in real-time – characteristics needed in order to compete in today's ever more difficult and dynamic markets.

Business intelligence has come a long way in the last several decades. During this time, business enterprises have continually sought newer and better ways to put financial and operating performance information to use to aid decision making.

Today, real-time business intelligence is more than a vision of the world's largest enterprises – it is a fundamental, and mission-critical strategic resource. Businesses succeed or fail on their financial and operational performance. No longer can businesses, large or small, ignore the need for capturing and analysing information in real time. It is therefore imperative that managers take advantage of real-time data to optimize decision making.

In February 2003, *InformationWeek* research conducted an editorial study to examine the strategies that companies are using to improve the speed and efficiency of placing operational performance data in the hands of key decision makers and managers.[38] The study interviewed 261 chief technology officers and chief strategists in global multinational companies.

According to the research, the following reasons lead companies to adopt real-time operations:

■ improved business agility,

■ cost savings,

■ improved customer service and retention,

■ enhanced financial reporting,

■ improved risk management,

■ supply-chain efficiencies.

However, few companies have achieved an acceptable level of effectiveness in monitoring real-time business operations. Despite potential payoffs of lower costs, improved business agility, and better customer retention, real-time business operations are not easy to accomplish. Difficulties pertain to data-source integration, the cost of collecting and monitoring information, cost and resource constraints. Forty percent of real-time adopters report that a combination of corporate culture and technology issues are serious obstacles in making real-time business a reality.

Integrated financial management

Corporate financial planning supports corporate strategy development and execution within a disciplined approach to financial and operating resource optimization, corporate risk management, and balanced performance assessment, thus maximizing enterprise and shareholder value.

In an increasingly competitive and global business environment, businesses need insightful and focused business strategies, supported by strong execution, performance assessment, and dynamic risk management. Enterprise-wide risk management (EWRM) is a powerful approach to assessing and optimally managing business and financial risks to enhance shareholder value through minimizing earnings and cash flow volatility.

The balanced scorecard includes both financial and non-financial metrics to assess corporate performance, allowing management to align performance with strategic objectives.

Financial resource optimization forms the basic foundation upon which enterprise value maximization can be pursued, where economic value creation becomes the primary goal through generating returns in excess of the total cost of the firm's debt and equity capital. Optimizing cash management, dividend policy, leverage ratios, customer satisfaction, and target market focus, and investing in growth, managing people, processes, and execution, all form pieces of the total corporate performance view.

Given the limitations of the accrual-based accounting system, economic value measures such as EVA have gained prominence. In order to gain competitive edge, advanced financial analytics should be used in the business and financial planning process, while real-time integrated financial, treasury, and risk management systems provide essential tools and information for superior and timely decision making.

In order to help the company improve execution performance, the business strategy, planning, and operations functions need to be integrated and streamlined, so that decision making can be optimized with hard facts real-time.

A deep understanding of the financial markets, external business, and economic and competitive environment is necessary to identify where competitive advantages can be enhanced. Risks need to be managed proactively and optimally, while internal financial controls and audit functions are routinely optimized.

NOTES

1 Malchione, R (1998).

2 Banham, R (2003).

3 Ibid.

4 CFO Research Services (2003).

5 Ibid.

6 Ibid.

7 Ibid.

8 Ibid.

9 Fridson and Alvarez (2002).

10 Zeckhauser *et al.*, (1994).

11 Kaplan and Norton (1996).

12 CFO Research Services (2003).

13 Koller and Peacock (2002).

14 Ernst & Young (1998).

15 Keichel (1982).

16 Charan and Colvin (1999).

17 Vigilance (2003).

18 Eccles (1991).

19 Curtis (1985) and Johnson and Kaplan (1987).

20 Eccles (1991).

21 Hally, (1994).

22 Johnson and Kaplan (1987).

23 Olve *et al.* (1999).

24 Quinn (1992).

25 Olve *et al.* (1999).

26 Rotch, W (1997).

27 Celequest (2003).

28 Ibid.

29 Ibid.

30 Golovin, J (2003).

31 Golovin, J (2003b).

32 Osborne, C (2002).

33 Kelly, S (2002).

34 JP Morgan (1996).

35 Coveney *et al.* (2002).

36 PricewaterhouseCoopers (2003)

37 Coveney *et al.* (2002)

38 *InformationWeek* (2003).

Applied financial optimization modeling

Value maximization: analytical techniques

Estimating the value of a company is a necessary part of business planning, since it provides guidance on alternative valuations that result from different courses of action taken by management. In theory, corporations should choose positive net present value projects to generate incremental shareholder value. However, in practice, corporate value maximization is not simply an analytical exercise, but results from identifying and capturing growth opportunities through prudent strategic investments, and executing the business plan in the backdrop of sound financial and operational risk management. Notwithstanding this caveat, advanced analytical techniques can still support superior decision making.

There are many environmental variables that are beyond the control of the company, such as general macro-economic trends, but aspects that can be optimized by management include some financial and operational variables within the sphere of management influence. Think about the business as comprised of a set of strategic, operational, financing, and investing activities.

The financial plan captures current and future expectations of revenues, expenses, investments, assets, liabilities, and cash flow consequences on the balance sheet, income statement, and cash flow statement. It provides a detailed quantitative model of the company's financial position and future expectations. It allows assessment of the impact on value, of courses of action, through counterfactual simulations.

Since the present value of the future cash flows is the value of the company, in theory, the maximization of this value can be analytically assessed by applying various dynamic stochastic financial optimization and simulation techniques. This often provides superior insights into which of the many alternative options will provide the maximum profits.

Basically the process involves taking the corporate financial planning model and turning it into a stochastic dynamic simulation model. The optimization model tells us what levels of the choice variables, such as accounts receivable, dividend payout, cash balances, debt-to-equity ratios, inventory balances, operational leverage, etc. are optimal to maximize shareholder value.

Similarly, it can provide guidance regarding risk exposure management, so that optimal hedges can be undertaken to minimize cash flow and earnings volatility. However, in practice, these modeling techniques do not enjoy wide application, except in a select few cases where the analytical capability exists to apply these techniques to derive superior insights into the complex interrelationships in a corporate financial model. Since the statutory tax rate is a convex schedule, minimizing earnings volatility through risk management can protect and enhance shareholder value through higher after-tax returns.

Company size, asset utilization, and financial leverage

Company		2002 annual reports (full-year data) (Currency units in billions)				
		Revenue	Total assets	Total debt	Revenue to total assets	Total debt to total assets
Royal Dutch/Shell	USD	235.6	152.7	19.7	154%	13%
Exxon-Mobil	USD	204.5	152.6	6.7	134%	4%
Daimler-Chrysler	USD	156.8	196.4	55.2	80%	28%
General Electric	USD	131.7	575.2	279.4	23%	49%
Toyota	USD	123.1	167.7	60.4	73%	36%
Citigroup	USD	92.6	1097.2	157.6	8%	14%
IBM	USD	81.2	96.5	26.0	84%	27%
Siemens	USD	79.3	81.5	12.9	97%	16%
	EUR	84.0	77.9	12.3	108%	16%
Nestlé	USD	63.3	62.6	0.2	101%	0%
	CHF	89.2	87.4	0.3	102%	0%
Hewlett-Packard	USD	56.6	70.7	7.8	80%	11%
Procter & Gamble	USD	43.4	43.7	13.6	99%	31%
AT&T	USD	37.8	55.3	22.6	68%	41%

▶

Company		2002 annual reports (full-year data) (Currency units in billions)				
		Revenue	Total assets	Total debt	Revenue to total assets	Total debt to total assets
GlaxoSmithKline	USD	31.8	35.9	19.5	89%	54%
	GBP	21.2	22.3	12.1	95%	54%
Microsoft	USD	28.4	67.6	0.0	42%	0%
Merrill Lynch	USD	28.3	447.9	258.7	6%	58%
Intel	USD	26.8	44.2	1.4	61%	3%
HSBC	USD	26.6	759.2	35.0	4%	5%
DuPont	USD	24.0	34.6	6.8	69%	20%
Coca-Cola	USD	19.6	24.5	5.4	80%	22%
Cisco	USD	18.9	37.3	0.0	51%	0%
ABB	USD	18.3	29.5	8.0	62%	27%
Ericsson	USD	17.5	25.6	5.4	68%	21%
	SEK	145.8	208.3	44.2	70%	21%
Marks & Spencer	USD	12.2	11.6	3.6	105%	31%
	GBP	8.1	7.2	2.2	113%	31%
Gillette	USD	8.5	9.9	3.0	86%	30%
Total	**USD**	**1,566.5**	**4,280.2**	**1,008.8**	**37%**	**24%**

Exchange rates:	2002 average	2002 year-end
USD/GBP	1.500	1.610
EUR/USD	1.060	0.957
USD/SEK	0.120	0.123
USD/CHF	0.710	0.717
USD/EUR	0.943	1.045
EUR/GBP	1.590	1.540

Acronyms

ABS	Asset backed securities
ADR	American Depository Receipts
AFP	Association of Financial Professionals
ALCO	Asset and Liability Committee
AMPS	Auction market preferred stock
ARFIMA	Autoregressive Fractionally Integrated Moving Average
ART	Alternative risk transfer
BA	Banker's acceptance
BPM	Business performance management
CAPM	Capital asset pricing model
CAR	Capital at risk
CAT	Catastrophe bonds
CDS	Credit Default Swaps
CEO	Chief executive officer
CER	Constant exchange rate
CFAR	Cash flow at risk
CFC	Controlled foreign corporation
CFO	Chief financial officer
CFROI	Cash flow return on investment
CP	Commercial paper
CPC	Commercial paper conduits
CPM	Corporate performance management
CRM	Corporate risk management
CRM	Customer relationship management
CTB	Check the box
DEAR	Daily earnings at risk
DFI	Derivative financial instrument
EAR	Earnings at risk
EBIT	Earnings before interest and taxes
EBR	Effective Borrowing Rate
EBITDA	Earnings before interest, taxes, depreciation, and amortization
EBOR	Equity buyback obligation rights
ECR	Earnings credit rate
EM	Economic margin
EMU	European Monetary Union
ENPV	Expanded net present value

EPS	Earnings per share
ERP	Enterprise resource planning
ESOT	Employee share ownership trust
EV	Enterprise value
EVA	Economic value added
EVAR	Excess Value at Risk
EVP	Executive vice president
EVT	Extreme value theory
EWRM	Enterprise wide risk management
FAS	Financial Accounting Standards
FASB	Financial Accounting Standards Board
FCFE	Free cash flow to equity
FCFF	Free cash flow to the firm
FEI	Financial Executives' Institute
FGIC	Financial Guaranty Insurance Company
FIFO	First in, first out
FRA	Forward rate agreement
FX	Foreign exchange
G-7	Group of seven countries
GA	Genetic algorithm
GAAP	Generally Accepted Accounting Principles
GAMS	General algebraic modeling system
GARCH	Generalized Autoregressive Conditional Heteroskedasticity
GECS	General Electric Commercial Services
GLOBE	Global business excellence
GMM	Generalized method of moments
GPD	Generalized Pareto Distribution
HP	Hodrick-Prescott filter
HSE	Health and safety environment
IAS	International Accounting Standards
IASB	International Accounting Standards Board
IFC	International Finance Corporation
IFRIC	International Financial Reporting Interpretations Committee
IFRS	International Financial Reporting Standards
IMF	International Monetary Fund
IRR	Internal rate of return
IRS	Internal Revenue Service
ISDA	International Swaps and Derivatives Association
IT	Information technology
JIT	Just in time
KPI	Key performance indicators
LAN	Local area network
LIBOR	London Inter-Bank Offered Rate
LIFO	Last in, first out
M&A	Merger and acquisition

MD&A	Management's discussion and analysis
MF	Mezzanine financing
MIGA	Multilateral Investment Guarantee Agency
MM	Modigliani and Miller
MVA	Market value added
NOL	Net operating loss
NOPAT	Net operating profit after taxes
NPV	Net present value
OBS	Off balance sheet
OCF	Operating cash flow
OECD	Organization for Economic Cooperation and Development
OLS	Ordinary least squares
P/E	Price-earnings ratio
PV	Present value
QSPE	Qualifying special purpose entity
R&D	Research and development
RAPM	Risk adjusted performance measurement
RAROC	Risk adjusted return on capital
RARORAC	Risk adjusted return on risk adjusted capital
RCA	Revolving credit agreement
RFID	Radio frequency identification
ROA	Return on assets
ROC	Risk oversight committee
ROE	Return on equity
ROIC	Return on invested capital
RONA	Return on net assets
RRA	Reverse repurchase agreements
S&P	Standard & Poors
SAVANT	Strategy, anticipation, value-adding, negotiating, transforming
SCM	Supply chain management
SEC	Securities and Exchange Commission
SEK	Swedish kroner
SFAS	Statement of Financial Accounting Standards
SG&A	Sales, general, and administrative expenses
SGR	Sustainable growth rate
SPE	Special purpose entity
SPV	Special purpose vehicle
STP	Straight through processing
TFS	Treasury and Financing Services
TQM	Total quality management
TSR	Total shareholder return
VAR	Value at risk
VBM	Value based management
VIE	Variable interest entity
WACC	Weighted average cost of capital

Bibliography

Agate, Robert M (1997), 'The role of finance in increasing shareholder value', *The CFO Handbook*, Maidenhead: McGraw-Hill.

Allen, Larry (2001), *The Global Financial System 1750 – 2000*, Trowbridge: Cromwell Press.

Allen, Steven (2003), *Financial Risk Management: A practitioner's guide to managing market and credit risk*, Chichester: John Wiley & Sons.

Asaf, Samir (1997), 'Maximizing corporate shareholder value using risk profile dynamics', Templeton College, University of Oxford.

Asaf, Samir and Marc L Bertoneche (1998), 'Protecting corporate shareholder value using risk profile dynamics', Harvard Business School, Research paper.

Bakane, John L (1997), 'The high-performance CFO role or "Zen and the art of Bean Counting"', *The CFO Handbook*, Maidenhead: McGraw-Hill.

Banham, Russ, 'Quantum Loop', *CFO Magazine*, March (2003).

Bank for International Settlements (2003), *Basel Committee on Banking Supervision: The new Basel capital accord*, Consultative Document, April.

Barberis, N and Thaler, R (2002), *A Survey in Behavioural Finance*, NBER Working Paper Series 9222.

Barton, L Thomas, William G Shenkir, Paul L Walker (2002), *Making Enterprise Risk Management Pay Off: How leading companies implement risk management*, Harlow: Financial Times Prentice Hall.

Batchelor, Charles (2004) Credit Default Swaps Join Booming Derivatives Line-Up, *Financial Times*.

Beck, Douglas J and Roger E Brinner (1997), 'Understanding the business and economic environment', *The CFO Handbook*, Maidenhead: McGraw-Hill.

Bender, Ruth and Keith Ward (2002), *Corporate Financial Strategy*, Second Edition, Saint Louis, MO: Butterworth Heinemann.

Bernard, Bailey S (2002), *Mezzanine Financing Demystified*, Caltius Capital Management.

Bertoneche, Marc L and Rory Knight (2001), *Financial Performance*, Saint Louis, MO: Butterworth Heinemann.

Blue Book of Bank Prices (2003), Phoenix-Hecht.

Booth, Laurence, Vaouj Aivazian, et al., 'Capital structures in developing countries', *The Journal of Finance*, **61**, 1 (2001).

Boquist, John A, *et al.* (2000), *The Value Sphere: Secrets of creating and retaining shareholder wealth*, Bloomington, IN: Value Integration Associates.

Bragg, Steven M (2001), *Accounting Best Practices*, Second edition, Chichester: John Wiley & Sons.

Brancato, Carolyn (1995), *New Corporate Performance Measures: A research report*, Conference Board.

Brenner, Reuven (2002), *The Force of Finance: Triumph of the capital markets*, New York, NY and London: Texere.

Butler, Cormac (1999), *Mastering Value at Risk: A step-by-step guide to understanding and applying VAR*, Harlow: Financial Times Prentice Hall.

Buzzell, R, B Gale and R Sultan, 'Market Share: A key to profitability', *Harvard Business Review*, Jan-Feb (1975).

Campbell, TS and W A Kracaw (1993), *Financial Risk Management: Fixed income and foreign exchange*, Glenview, IL: HarperCollins College Publishers.

Carleton, Willard T, 'Analytical model for long range financial planning', *The Journal of Finance*, **25** (1970).

Celequest Activity Suite 2.0 (2003), 'Business activity monitoring with Celequest Activity Suite', Technical Document.

CFO 2000 Survey (1997), *Worldwide Survey of 300 CFOs*, PricewaterhouseCoopers.

CFO Research Services (2002), *The Future of Business Risk Management*, CFO Publishing Corp.

CFO Research Services (2003), *How Viable is Alternative Risk Financing?*, CFO Publishing Corp.

CFO Research Services (2003), *What CFOs Want from Performance Management*, CFO Publishing Corp.

CFO (1995), 'Fast times at General Electric', *CFO Magazine*.

Chew, Donald H Jr (ed.) (1999), *The New Corporate Finance: Where theory meets practice*, Second Edition, Maidenhead: McGraw-Hill.

Colvin, G and R Charan, 'Why CEOs Fail', in *Fortune*, **21** (1999).

Corporate Finance, 'Outsourcing offers new models for treasury', *Corporate Finance Magazine*, June (2003).

Coveney, Michael, et al. (2002), *The Strategy Gap: Leveraging technology to execute winning strategies*, Chichester: John Wiley & Sons.

Cruz, Marcelo G (2002), *Modelling, Measuring, and Hedging Operational Risk*, Chichester: John Wiley & Sons.

Culp, Christopher L (2001), *The Risk Management Process: Business strategy and tactics*, Chichester: John Wiley & Sons.

Culp, Christopher L, MH Miller, and AMP Neves, 'Value at Risk: Uses and abuses', *Journal of Applied Corporate Finance*, **10**, 4 (1998).

Curtis, Donald A, 'The modern accounting system', *Financial Executive*, Jan-Feb (1985).

Damodaran, Aswath (1994), *Damodaran on Valuation: Security analysis for investment and corporate finance*, Chichester: John Wiley & Sons.

Damodaran, Aswath (1999), *Applied Corporate Finance*, Chichester: John Wiley & Sons.

Dann, LY and H DeAngelo, 'Corporate financial policy and corporate control: A study of defensive adjustments in asset and ownership structure', *Journal of Financial Economics*, **20** (1988).

Dauphinais, William G, Grady Means, and Colin Price (2000), *Wisdom of the CEO: 29 global leaders tackle today's most pressing business challenges*, Chichester: John Wiley & Sons.

Dell, Michael S (2000), 'Creating and Managing Hypergrowth', in Dauphinais *et al*.

DeLoach, JW (2000), *Enterprise Wide Risk Management*, Harlow: Financial Times Prentice Hall.

Deloitte & Touche (2003a), *Convergence to International Reporting Standards*, Deloitte Touche Tohmatsu.

Deloitte & Touche (2003b), *Restoring Trust: Empowering the CFO*, Deloitte Research.

Deloitte & Touche (2003c), *GAAP Differences in Your Pocket: IAS and US GAAP*, Deloitte Touche Tohmatsu.

Denis, David J and Diane K Denis, 'Leveraged recaps in the curbing of corporate overinvestment, *Journal of Applied Corporate Finance*, 6, 1 (1993).

Deutsche Bank AG and Ernst & Young AG (2002), *Tax Implications of International Liquidity Management Structures*.

Dolan, Robert J and Hermann Simon (1996), *Power Pricing: How managing price transforms the bottom line*, London: The Free Press.

Doorley, Thomas L, 'What the winners can teach us', *WorldLink*, Jan-Feb (2000).

Dowd, Kevin (1998), *Beyond Value at Risk: The new science of risk management*, Chichester: John Wiley & Sons

Eccles, Robert G, 'The performance measurement manifesto', *Harvard Business Review*, Jan-Feb (1991).

Economist Intelligence Unit (1995), *Managing Business Risks: An integrated approach*.

Edwards, Chris (2003), *Nearly All Major Countries Provide Dividend Tax Relief*, Washington, DC: Cato Institute.

Edwards, William J (1994), 'Planning Models for M&A Analysis', *The M&A Handbook*, Maidenhead: McGraw-Hill.

Emmott, Bill (2003), 20:21 *Vision: Twentieth century lessons for the twenty-first century*, Gordonsville, VA: Farrar, Straus and Giroux.

Ernst & Young (1998), *Measures That Matter*.

Fabozzi, Frank J and James L Grant (eds) (2000), *Value Based Metrics: Foundations and practice*, Chichester: John Wiley & Sons.

Final, Colin, 'Testing the waters of US ABS', *Corporate Finance Magazine*, November (2002).

Financial Times (1998), *Mastering Finance: The definitive guide to the foundations and frontiers of finance*, London: Financial Times Pitman Publishing.

Fink, Ronald, 'New math: Synthetic lease plus recession equals double whammy', *CFO Magazine*, January (2002).

Fink, Ronald, 'Natural performers', *CFO Magazine*, July (2003).

Foote, Angus, 'Treasury takes the lead', *Corporate Finance Magazine*, June (2003).

Francis, J Clark and Dexter R Rowell, 'A simultaneous equation model of the firm for financial analysis and planning', *Financial Management*, Spring (1978).

Freswick, Kris (2003), 'The five year itch', *CFO Magazine*, Feb (2003).

Fridson, Martin and Fernando Alvarez (2002), *Financial Statement Analysis: A practitioner's guide*, Third Edition, Chichester: John Wiley & Sons.

Frost, Chris, David Allen, James Porter and Philip Bloodworth (2001), *Operational Risk and Resilience: Understanding and minimizing operational risk to secure shareholder value*, PricewaterhouseCoopers, Saint Louis, MO: Butterworth-Heinemann.

Galitz, Lawrence (1994), *Financial Engineering: Tools and techniques to manage financial risk*, London: Financial Times Pitman Publishing.

Gamble, Richard H, 'The Global Treasury Squeeze', *Business Finance Magazine*, May (2003a).

Gamble, Richard H, 'Watertight Cash Management', in *Business Finance Magazine*, July (2003b).

George, Abraham M (1996), *Protecting Shareholder Value: A guide to managing financial market risk*, Maidenhead: Irwin

Gilson, Stuart C (2001), *Creating Value through Corporate Restructuring: Case studies in bankruptcies, buyouts, and breakups*, John Wiley & Sons.

Glantz, Morton (2000), *Scientific Financial Management: Advances in financial intelligence capabilities for corporate valuation and risk assessment*, New York, NY: Amacom.

Goldman Sachs and UBS (1998), *The Practice of Risk Management: Implementing processes for managing firm-wide market risk*. London: Euromoney Books.

Golovin, Jonathan (2003a), *Real Time Alerts/Event Management: The next wave of business intelligence for the real time enterprise*, Vigilance Inc.

Golovin, Jonathan (2003b), *Ten Symptoms of Poor Supply Chain Execution: A best practices scorecard*, Vigilance Inc.

Graham, JR and CR Harvey (2001), 'Theory and practice of corporate finance: Evidence from the field', *Journal of Financial Economics*, **61** (2001).

Greenwood, Robert (2002), *Handbook of Financial Planning and Control*, Third Edition, Aldershot: Gower.

Group of 30 (1993), *Global Derivatives and Principles*, The Group of 30.

Hally, DL (1994), 'Cost accounting for the 1990s', *Finance*, December (1994).

Harris, Milton and Artur Raviv, 'The Theory of Capital Structure', *The Journal of Finance*, **44**, 1 (1991).

Harvard Business Review (1998), *Measuring Corporate Performance*, Jackson, TN: Harvard Business School Press.

Haskins, Mark E and Benjamin R Makela (eds) (1997), *The CFO Handbook*, Maidenhead: Irwin.

Haspeslagh, Boda & Boulos (2001), 'Managing For Value', *Harvard Business Review*.

Hatfield, Gay B, Louis TW Cheng and Wallace N Davidson, 'The determination of Optimal Capital Structure: The effect of firm value and industry debt ratios on market value', *Journal of Financial and Strategic Decisions*, **7**, 3 (1994).

Have, Steven T, Wouter T Have and Frans Stevens (2003), *Key Management Models: The management tools and practices that will improve your business*, Harlow: Financial Times Prentice Hall.

Hazou, Peter and Shannon Cheung (2002), *Technical Document*, The Hong Kong and Shanghai Banking Corporation Ltd.

Helfert, Erich (2003), *Techniques of Financial Analysis: A guide to value creation*, Eleventh Edition, Maidenhead: McGraw-Hill.

Henry, David, 'The latest magic in corporate finance', *BusinessWeek*, Sept (2003).

Higgins, Robert C (2001), *Analysis for Financial Management*, Sixth Edition, Maidenhead: McGraw-Hill.

Hoffman, Douglas G (2002), *Managing Operational Risk: 20 firm-wide best practice strategies*, Chichester: John Wiley & Sons.

Hyperion Financial Management (2003), *Business Modelling: Ready for prime time*, Technical Document.

IMF (2003), *World Economic and Financial Surveys: Global financial stability report*, International Monetary Fund.

InformationWeek (2003), *Real-Time Business: Research brief*.

James, George B and Katherine Ann Woodall (1997), 'Making ethical values a tangible part of the enterprise's financial function', *The CFO Handbook*, Maidenhead: McGraw-Hill.

Johnson, Mark B, '1st Silicon deal raises hopes in Asia', in *Corporate Finance Magazine*, November (2001).

Johnson, TH and RS Kaplan (1987), *Relevance Lost: The rise and fall of management accounting*, Jackson, TN: Harvard Business School Press.

Jorion, Philippe (1997), *Value at Risk: The new benchmark for controlling derivatives risk*, Maidenhead: McGraw-Hill.

Jorion, Philippe (2003), *Financial Risk Manager Handbook*, Second Edition, Chichester: John Wiley & Sons.

JP Morgan (1996), *Riskmetrics™ Technical Document*, Fourth Edition.

Kalotay, Andrew J, Dennis E Logue and Howard L Hiller (1990), 'Managing the capital structure', *Handbook of Modern Finance*, Carol Stream, IL: Warren Gorham & Lamont.

Kaplan, Robert P and David P Norton (1996), *The Balanced Scorecard: Translating strategy into action*, Jackson, TN: Harvard Business School Press.

Kaplan, Robert P and David P Norton (2001), *The Strategy Focused Organization: How balanced scorecard companies thrive in the new business environment*, Jackson, TN: Harvard Business School Press.

Karayan, John E, Charles W Swenson and Joseph H Neff (2002), *Strategic Corporate Tax Planning*, Chichester: John Wiley & Sons.

Kaye, Roland G (1994), *Financial Planning Models: Construction and use*, London: Thomson Business Press.

Kelly, Susan, 'Make it Count', *Treasury & Risk Management*, April (2003).

Kester, W Carl (1997), *Case Problems in Finance*, Maidenhead: Irwin.

Kiechel, Walter, 'Corporate strategists under fire', *Fortune*, December(1982).

Kiewell, Dieter and Eric V Roegner, 'The CFO guide to better pricing', *McKinsey on Finance*, Autumn (2002).

Kim, Chan W and Renée Mauborgne, 'Value Innovation: The strategic logic of high growth', *Harvard Business Review*, Jan-Feb (1997).

King, Jack L (2001), *Operational Risk: Measurement and modelling*, Chichester: John Wiley& Sons.

Knight, Rory and D Pretty, 'Managing the risks behind sudden shifts in value', *European Business Forum*, **12** (2002).

Kohli, Ajay and Arvind Sahay, 'Market-driven versus driving markets', *Journal of the Academy of Marketing Science*, **28**, 1 (2000).

Kolb, Robert W (1993), *Financial Derivatives: Futures, options, options on futures, swaps*, New York, NY: New York Institute of Finance.

Kolb, Robert W (2000), *Futures Options, & Swaps*, Oxford: Blackwell Publishers.

Koller, Timothy M and Jonathan Peacock, 'Time for CFOs to step up', *McKinsey on Finance*, Winter (2002).

KPMG (2003), *Basel II: A worldwide challenge for the banking business*, KPMG International.

Krallinger, Joseph (1997), *Mergers & Acquisitions: Managing the transition*, Maidenhead: McGraw-Hill.

Lambert, Tom (2003), *Key Management Questions: Smart questions for every management situation*, London: Financial Times Prentice Hall.

Lambin, J (1976), *Advertising, Competition, and Market Conduct in Oligopoly over Time*, Amsterdam: Elsevier.

Leland, Hayne E, 'Corporate debt value, bond covenants, and optimal capital structure', *The Journal of Finance*, 159, 4 (1994).

Linsmeier, TJ and ND Pearson (1996), *Risk Measurement: An introduction to value at risk*, University of Illinois at Urbana-Champaign, (http://www.gloriamundi.org/picsresources/LandP.pdf)

Logue, Dennis E (ed.) (1984), *Handbook of Modern Finance*, Carol Stream, IL: Warren Gorham & Lamont.

Lorange, Peter, Eugene Kotlarchuk, and Harbir Singh (1994), 'Corporate acquisitions: A strategic perspective', *The M&A Handbook*, Milton R Rock (ed.), Maidenhead: McGraw-Hill.

Malchione, Robert (1998), 'Making performance measurements perform', *The Practice of Business Strategy*, Carl W Stern and George Stalk Jr. (eds), Chichester: John Wiley & Sons.

Merrill Lynch (1998), *EVA and share price performance*, Technical document.

Mulvey, John M and Koray D Simsek (2002), 'Rebalancing strategies for long-term investors: Computational methods in decision-making', *Economics and Finance*, Dordrecht: Kluwer.

Mun, Jonathan (2002), *Real Options Analysis: Tools and techniques for valuing strategic investments and decisions*, Chichester: John Wiley & Sons.

Mun, Jonathan (2003), *Real Options Analysis Course: Business cases and software applications*, Chichester: John Wiley & Sons.

Nagle, Thomas T and Reed K Holden (2002), *The Strategy and Tactics of Pricing: A guide to profitable decision making*, Harlow: Prentice Hall.

Nash, John F and Robert Bartell Jr (2000), *Cases in Corporate Financial Planning and Control*, Dame Thomson Learning.

Nissim, Doron and Amir, Ziv, 'Dividend changes and future profitability', *The Journal of Finance*, **56**, 6 (2001).

Nolan, Richard L (1996), *Sense and Respond*, Jackson, TN: Harvard Business School Press.

Obrycki, Daniel J and Rafael Resendes, 'Economic margin: The link between EVA and CFROI', in Fabozzi and Grant (eds) 2000.

OECD (2002), *Financial Statistics: Non-financial enterprises financial statements*.

Ogden, Joseph P, Frank C Jen, Phillip F O'Connor (2003), *Advanced Corporate Finance: Policies and strategies*, Harlow: Prentice Hall.

Olivier, Charles, 'Tough times: Look to securitization', *Corporate Finance Magazine*, Sept-Nov (2001).

Olsen, Eric E (1998), 'Economic Value Added', *The Practice of Business Strategy*, Carl W. Stern and George Stalk Jr (eds), Chichester: John Wiley & Sons.

Olve Nils-Göran, Jan Roy, and Magnus Wetter (1999), *Performance Drivers: A practical guide to using the balanced scorecard*, Chichester: John Wiley & Sons.

Osborne, Charlotte, 'Searching for a single system', *Corporate Finance Magazine*, May (2002).

Osterland, Andrew, 'M&A: Back to basics', *CFO Magazine*, Oct (2002).

Palepu, Krishna G, 'Predicting takeover targets: A methodological and empirical analysis', *Journal of Accounting and Economics*, **8**, no.1 (1986).

Paul-Choudhury, S, '"This year's model"', *Risk Magazine*, **10** (1997).

Peterson, Pamela P and David R Peterson (1996), *Company Performance and Measures of Value Added*, The Research Foundation of AIMR.

Pinegar J Michael and Lisa Wilbright, 'What managers think of capital structure theory: A survey', in *Financial Management*, Winter (1989).

Pratt, P Shannon, Robert F Reilly and Robert P Schweihs (2000), *Valuing a Business: The analysis and appraisal of closely held companies*, Fourth Edition, Maidenhead: McGraw-Hill.

Price Waterhouse (1997), *CFO: Architect of the corporation's future*, Price Waterhouse Financial & Cost Management Team, John Wiley & Sons.

PricewaterhouseCoopers (2002), 'International Tax Planning', Technical document, Tax and Legal Services, PricewaterhouseCoopers.

PricewaterhouseCoopers (2003a), *6th Annual Global CEO Survey: Leadership, responsibility, and growth in uncertain times*, PricewaterhouseCoopers.

PricewaterhouseCoopers (2003b), *Taxation of Derivative Financial Instruments in Asia*, PricewaterhouseCoopers.

PricewaterhouseCooper (2003c), *Technology Forecast 2003-2005: The intelligent real time enterprise*, PricewaterhouseCoopers.

PricewaterhouseCoopers (2003d), *Finance and Treasury*, PricewaterhouseCoopers.

PricewaterhouseCooper (2003e), *European and U.S. Multinationals Place Different Emphasis on Corporate Sustainability*, PricewaterhouseCoopers.

Prowse, Stephen D, 'The Economics of the Private Equity Market,' *Economic Review*, Third Qtr 1998.

Quinn, JB (1992), *Intelligent Enterprise*, London: The Free Press.

Ramezani, Cyrus A, Luc Soenen and Alan Jung, 'Growth, corporate profitability, and value creation', *Financial Analysts Journal*, **58**, 6 (2002).

Ramos, Abe De, 'The perfect treasury: Backed by the latest IT advances, treasurers of multinationals in Asia leave nothing to chance', *CFO Asia*, April (2002).

Reason, Tim, 'Reporting: See-through finance?', *CFO Magazine*, Oct (2002).

Reilly, Robert F and Robert P Schweihs (1999), *Valuing Intangible Assets: A comprehensive guide*, Maidenhead: Irwin.

Rigby, D, 'Management tools and techniques: A survey', *California Management Review*, **43** (2001).

Rock, Milton L, Robert H Rock, and Martin Sikora (1994), *The Mergers and Acquisitions Handbook*, Maidenhead: McGraw-Hill.

Rock, Robert H (1994), 'Economic Drivers of M&A', *The M&A Handbook*, Maidenhead: McGraw-Hill.

Roehl-Anderson, Janice M, and Steven M Bragg (2000), *The Controller's Function: The work of the managerial accountant*, Chichester: John Wiley & Sons.

Roeloffs, Pieter, Miguel Rosellón and Brett Savill, 'How to improve shareholder returns in the long-term', *Corporate Finance* (2003).

Sammer, Joanne, 'What CFOs want from treasurers', *Treasury & Risk Management*, July-Aug (2001).

Savarese, Craig, 'Economic value added: The practitioner's guide to a measurement and management framework', *Business and Professional Publishing* (2000).

Schwartz Robert J and Clifford W Smith Jr (eds) (1994), *Advanced Strategies in Financial Risk Management*, New York, NY: New York Institute of Finance.

Scovanner, Douglas A (1997), 'Financing with debt', *The CFO Handbook*, Maidenhead: McGraw-Hill.

Simon, H (1992), *Preismanagement: Analyse-Strategie-Umsetzung*, Weisbaden: Gaber.

Smithson, Charles W and Donald H Chew, *Journal of Applied Corporate Finance*, 4, 4 (1992).

Starr, Samuel P and Steven M Woolf (1997), 'Income Tax planning for the CFO', *The CFO Handbook*, Maidenhead: McGraw-Hill.

Steiner, George A and Warren M Cannon (1946), *Multinational Corporate Planning*, New York, NY: Macmillan.

Stern, Carl W and George Stalk Jr (eds) (1998), *Perspectives on Strategy: From the Boston Consulting Group*, Chichester: John Wiley & Sons.

Stonich, Timothy W (1997), 'Challenges for CFOs in privately held companies', *The CFO Handbook*, Maidenhead: McGraw-Hill.

Stowe, John D, Thomas R Robinson, Jerald E Pinto and Dennis W McLeavey (2003), *Analysis of Equity Investments: valuation*, The Research Foundation of AIMR.

Talmor, Eli and Sheridan Titman, 'Taxes and dividend policy', *Financial Management*, Summer (1990).

Tellis, G, 'The price elasticity of selective demand: A meta-analysis of econometric models of sales', *Journal of Marketing Research*, **25** (1988).

Thortveit, Eric and Ulrich Schaefer (2002), *A Taxing Equation*, Deutsche Bank AG and Ernst & Young AG.

TIBCO (2003), *Enterprise Application Integration Solutions*, Technical Document.

Titman, Grinblatt and Sheridan Titman (2002), *Financial Markets and Corporate Strategy*, Second Edition, Maidenhead: McGraw-Hill.

Tregorgis, Lenos (1998), *Real Options*, London: MIT Press.

Tufano, Peter, 'How financial engineering can advance corporate strategy', *Harvard Business Review*, Jan-Feb (1996)

Vermaelen, Theo, 'Common stock repurchases and market signalling: An empirical study', *Journal of Financial Economics*, **9**, 2 (1981).

Vigilance (2003), *Bridging the Gap Between Strategy and Execution: Achieving new levels of performance and profitability through business process management*, Vigilance Inc.

Warren, James M and John P Shelton, 'A simultaneous equation approach to financial planning', *The Journal of Finance*, **26** (1971).

White, Gerald I (2003), *The Analysis and Use of Financial Statements*, John Wiley & Sons.

Williams, D, *Not-so-simple solutions. Firm-wide risk management: A Risk Special supplement*, July (1996).

William, Rotch (1997), 'Measuring and rewarding performance', *The CFO Handbook*, Maidenhead: McGraw-Hill.

Wilson, Thomas, 'Value at Risk', *Risk Management and Analysis*, **1** (1998).

Winston, Wayne (2000a), *Decision Making Under Uncertainty with RiskOptimizer*, Palisade Corporation.

Winston, Wayne (2000b), *Financial Models Using Simulation and Optimisation*, Palisade Corporation.

Winston, Wayne (2001), *Financial Models Using Simulation and Optimisation II: Investment valuation, options pricing, real options & product pricing models*, Palisade Corporation.

Ylä-Liedenpohja, Jouko, 'On optimal financing, dividends, and investment of the firm', *Acta Academiae Oeconomicae Helsingiensis*, Series A, **18** (1976).

Young, David S *Value Based Management and EVA: A Global Perspective*, in Fabozzi and Grant (eds) (2000).

Zeckhauser, Richard, Jayendu Patel, Francois Degeorge and John Pratt (1994), 'Reported and predicted earnings: an empirical investigation using prospect theory', project for David Dreman Foundation.

Zsolt, Thomas (2003), 'Business modelling: Ready for prime time', Hyperion Technical Document.

Index

abandon options 102
ABB 276, 293, 329, 342
ABS (asset backed securities) 139–40
ABSA bank 40
absolute price or rate change 148
absorption cost pricing 82
accelerated depreciation 91
Accor 16
accounting 8
  accrual-based 338
  compliance risks 22
  for derivatives 222
  internal controls 302
accounting-based financial measures 320–1
accounting-based performance measures 316
accrual-based accounting 338
accrual-based performance measures 319
ACE 281
acid-test ratios 316
acquisitions see mergers and acquisitions
action and strategy, links between 324
activity-based analysis 26
actuarial model risks 22
ADR (American Depository Receipts) 78
AFP (Association of Finance Professionals) 232
Agilent 281
alerts 334
alignment 312
alliances 19
alternative channels 83
alternative cost strategies 15
alternative risk financing 232
alternative risk management 228–30
alternative risk transfer (ART) 194, 230, 231
American Depository Receipts (ADR) 78
amortization 44
analysis financial leverage optimality 70
analytical techniques 340
Anderson-Darling distribution 212, 216, 219
anticipation of tax changes 88
ANZ Bank 41
AOL Time Warner 44
Apple Computers 323
applied financial optimization modeling 340–2

arbitrage 14, 62, 88, 221
arbitrage pricing theory 36
ART see alternative risk transfer
Asia-Pacific financial crisis 276
asset accumulation method of corporate valuation 30–31
asset approach to calculation of capital 42
asset backed securities (ABS) 139–40
asset-backed securitization 145
asset-based approach to corporate valuation 30–31
asset-liability management 62, 118–20
asset-linked debt structures 63
assets
  balance sheets 12
  contingent 30
  mismatches with liabilities 64
  off-balance-sheet 8
  returns on 47, 316
  risk exposures as 225
  turnover 316
  utilization optimization 46
Association of Finance Professionals (AFP) 232
AT&T 103, 156–8, 341
attritional losses 132
audits 22, 301–7
Australia 77
Austria 77

balance sheets 12, 118–20, 222, 224
balanced scorecard 3, 7, 8, 311, 319–24, 331, 332, 338
Banc One 40
Bang & Olufsen 81
Bank for International Settlements (BIS) 329
Bank of Credit and Commerce International 168
bank-oriented economies 13
Bankers Trust 179
banks 195–6, 231, 277, 285
Barings 127, 128, 167, 168
barrier options 102
Basel II Capital Accord 51, 195–6, 336
BASF 282
basic EVA 43
basis correlation 148

basis swaps 63
basket policies 194
Bearing Point 93
Belgium 77
benchmarking 22, 330
Bert Claeys 16
beta-general distribution 217
big bath hypotheses 315
BIS (Bank for International Settlements) 329
Black-Scholes 158
blended layering 194
Blue Book of Bank Prices 285
BMW 81
boards of directors 4, 5
Boeing 103
bondholders 74–5, 76
bonds
 catastrophe 229
 covenants 63, 74
 markets 12, 13, 14
 prices, dividends effects on 74–6
 refunding provisions 63
 special purpose vehicles 139
 tax-free 90
book values 12
Booth, Laurence *et al* 55
Boston Consulting Group 46
bottom-up approach to NOPAT 41
Box Jenkins Autoregressive 268
BP 281
BPM (business performance management) 334–5
brands 18, 82
break-even analyses 85
break-even points 82
Brisbane City Council 332
Britain *see* United Kingdom
budgets 3, 100–7, 261, 265–7
Buffett, Warren 222
bundling 83
Burry, Roy 20
business activity monitoring 336
business and financial planning 3, 6, 69, 253–69,
  302, 308, 317–18
 see also financial planning
business environments 10–15
business integration technologies 336
business intelligence 326, 334–5, 336–7
business life-cycles 54–7, 74
business management 15
business modeling 254, 255–8
business partners 6
 business performance management (BPM) 334–5
business planning *see* business and financial planning
business process approaches 8
business rules engines 325

business strategies 3
BusinessWeek 4

call options 63
Canada 77
Cap Gemini Ernst & Young 93
capital
 adequacy 51
 calculation of 42
 contingent 229
 cost of *see* costs: of capital; weighted average
  cost of capital
 minimum requirements 196
 return on capital investment (ROIC) 26–7, 316
capital asset pricing model (CAPM) 32, 33, 36
capital at risk (CAR) 193
capital budgeting 100–7
capital charges 45
capital gains 77
capital investments 44, 100, 265
capital leases 56–7
capital markets 10, 11, 12–13
capital structure 51–70, 73
CAPM (capital asset pricing model) 32, 33, 36
caps 63
Caputo, Carl 314
CAR (capital at risk) 193
Cargolux 282
Cartier Jewelry 81
cash concentration 93–4, 95
cash cows 79
cash dividends 72
cash-flow at risk (CFAR) 126, 133–4, 194–5, 209
cash-flow based approach to corporate valuation 29
cash-flow based economic performance measures
  320
cash flow return on investment (CFROI) 44–5,
  257, 311, 316
cash flow timeline 273–4
cash flows 58
 excess 72
 financial contracts 221
 GlaxoSmithKline 164
 hedges 236, 241
 multi-currency 329
 projections 36
 statements 55, 259
 variance 126
 volatility 126
 see also discounted cash flows
cash management 55, 92, 279, 282, 292, 298, 328, 332
catastrophe (CAT) bonds 229
catastrophe risks 187
catastrophic losses 131
Cemex 260

Centura Bank 40
CEO *see* chief executive officers
CER (constant exchange rate) 47
CFAR *see* cash-flow at risk
CFC *see* controlled foreign companies/corporations
CFO *see* chief financial officers
CFO 100 Survey 110
CFO 2000 225
CFO Research Services
CFROI *see* cash flow return on investment 232, 312–15
chairman roles 4
Chanel 81
change management 113
Chase Manhattan 191
check-the-box (CTB) 277
chi-squared distribution 212, 215, 218
chief executive officers (CEO) 1, 4, 5, 257
chief financial officers (CFO) 1, 4, 5, 6, 11, 312–15
China 278–9
chooser options 102
Cisco 281, 298, 342
Citibank 40
Citigroup 140–1, 151, 182–4, 199–201, 287–9, 303, 342
clientele effect 75
closely held company valuation models 33–7
Coca-Cola 20, 40, 283, 286, 342
Cognos 331
collars 157–8
commercial paper conduits (CPC) 137
commercial risks 127
commitment fees 59
commodity price risks 234, 235, 241
commodity swaps, options and futures 297
communication 113
communication management 332
comparative advantages 13
competition 6, 13
competitive advantages 6, 82
competitive analyses 257
competitive differentiation 17
competitive dynamics 10, 13, 15
competitive positions 311
compliance 333–4
compound options 102
Computer Associates 314
Comshare 330
conduit programs 138
Conference Board 38
consolidation 55
    see also mergers and acquisitions
constant exchange rate (CER) 47
consumer credit risks 200
contingency funding plans 289

contingent assets 30
contingent capital 229
contingent convertibles 59
continuous change 308
contraction options 102
control
    financial planning 59
    premiums 34
    systems 303
    values 36–7
controlled foreign companies/corporations (CFC) 94, 277
controlling interests 34
controlling shareholders 34
conversion options 63
conversion, tax savings strategies 88
convertible debt 52, 61
convertibles, contingent 59
convexity 130, 148, 330
Cordiner, Ralph 319
core businesses 256
core competencies 323
corporate bond markets 13, 14
corporate credit risks 200
Corporate Finance Magazine 222, 280
corporate financial strategies 10–15
corporate governance 4–5, 124, 169, 170, 171
corporate income tax 77–8
corporate loan markets 14
corporate performance management (CPM) 15, 311–38
corporate performance measurement 37–8
corporate planning *see* planning
corporate strategies 2, 3, 5, 13, 27
corporate sustainability 252
corporate valuations 26, 28–38
corporate values 3
cost-based pricing 82
cost-plus pricing 80, 86
costs
    alternative strategies 15
    of capital 11, 16, 39, 96, 256
        weighted average *see* weighted average cost of capital
    containment 260
    of debt 52, 57
    of equity 33, 47, 52
    fixed 84
    of funds 330
    of growth 17
    risks and, trade-off between 62
    semi-variable 82
    structures 84
    variable 85
counterparty risks 200, 208, 295

covenants, bonds 63, 74
CPC (commercial paper conduits) 137
CPM (corporate performance management) 15, 311–38
creation, tax savings strategies 88
credit default swaps 223
credit derivatives 14
credit lines 59
credit risks 22, 130
    Citigroup 182–3, 200
    HSBC 179–81, 207
    Intel 186–7
    Merrill Lynch 185, 203
    Nestlé 162–3
    Procter & Gamble 208
    Toyota 186
credit standards 21
Credit Suisse First Boston 40, 43
CRM (customer relationship management) 318, 336
cross-market arbitrage 14
Crystal Ball 270, 332
CTB (check-the-box) 277
cultural issues 109, 113
customer management 124
customer perspective, performance measurement 322, 323
customer relationship management (CRM) 318, 336
customer satisfaction measures 311
customer segmentation 17–18
customer value propositions 311
Czech Republic 77

daily earnings at risk (DEAR) 331
DaimlerChrysler
  annual report details 341
  capital adequacy 51
  corporate performance management 329
  earnings at risk 212–13
  economic value added 40, 44, 47–8
  enterprise-wide risk management 206–7
  financial risk management 159–60
  operational risk management 185
  straight through processing 280
  tax planning 97
Dammerman, Dennis 39
Daniels, John 253
data collection 315
data warehouses 325
Dauphinais, William G *et al* 17
DCF *see* discounted cash flows
deal fatigue 113
DEAR (daily earnings at risk) 331
debt
  convertible 52, 61
  cost of 52, 58

currency composition 54
and equity mix 61
external 61
financing 53–4, 56, 61
floatation of 62
holders 25
hybrid 56
instruments 52
leverage 52
long-term 57
maturities 60
ratings 59
ratios 54
reduction 56
securities 161–2, 186–7
straight 61
structures 63
zero-interest cost 59
debt-to-capital ratios 62
decisions 2, 6, 10, 13, 24–5, 255, 267
decline stage of corporate life-cycles 56
deemed dividends 277
default rates 12
defensive risk management 174
deferral of taxes 90, 91
defined-benefit pensions 11
deleveraged floating rate notes 63
deleveraging 56
Dell 18, 282
Dell, Michael 19
Deloitte & Touche 46, 93
Deloitte Consulting 4
Delta-EVT 149, 177–9
delta method 177
demand-oriented penetration strategy 83
Denmark 77
depreciation 44, 91, 259
derivatives 14, 135, 220–3, 232, 329
  accounting for 222
  AT&T 156–8
  Citigroup 183–4
  embedded 243
  equity 238
  Ericsson 239
  Exxon-Mobil 243–5
  General Electric 158
  GlaxoSmithKline 242–3, 299–300
  IAS 39: 223–4
  IBM 237–8
  Intel 186–7
  Marks & Spencer 295
  Nestlé 235–6
  Procter & Gamble 208, 245–6
  Royal Dutch/Shell 241

derivatives *continued*
  Shell 297
  Siemens 153, 222
  Toyota 233–5
  trading 236
Deutsche Bank 92–3
developing countries 55
differential swaps 63
differentiation 17, 82
directors, boards of 4, 5
disabling events 132
disciplined risk taking 226–8
disclosed EVA 43
discount rates 36, 148
discounted cash flows (DCF) 32, 37, 45, 102–3
discounted expected future income streams 109
discounting 83
disintermediation 13–14
distribution 18
diversification 115
divestitures 19
dividends 13, 94
  alternatives to 76–8
  cash 72
  deemed 277
  double taxation of 77
  payout ratios 12
  policies 51, 72–8
  smoothing 73
  tax policies 77–8
  valuation models 32, 45
  yields 12, 75
Dolan, Robert 78, 85
double taxation of dividends 77
double-taxation treaties 94
downside cases 261
downside risks 174
Drexel Burnham Lambert 129, 168
dual income tax systems 77
due diligence 112–13
DuPont 126, 191, 196–8, 210, 298, 342
duration 62, 130, 330
Dutton-Forshaw 332
dynamic modeling 266–7, 325
dynamic value management 22–3

e-business 95
EAR *see* earnings at risk
earnings
  growth 20, 21–2
  management 20, 260
  operating 316
  pre-tax 91
  reported 316
  retained 61, 72
  volatility 149, 167
earnings at risk (EAR) 126, 177, 179, 209–10
  Citigroup 200–1
  daily (DEAR) 331
  DuPont 197–8
  examples 210–19
earnings before interest and tax (EBIT) 316
earnings before interest, taxes, depreciation and
  amortization *see* EBITDA
earnings credit rates (ECR) 285
earnings per share (EPS) 59, 316
EBIT (earnings before interest and tax) 316
EBITDA 31–2, 259, 316
EBOR (Equity Buyback Obligation Rights) 260
econometric forecasting techniques 268
Economic and Monetary Union (EMU), EU 92
economic margins (EM) 45, 316
economic performance measures 320
economic profits 39, 40, 43, 193, 316
economic recovery 13
economic trends 13
economic valuations 26
economic value added (EVA) 37–8, 51, 193, 257,
  311, 316, 338
Economist Intelligence Unit 126
ECR (earnings credit rates) 285
effective convexity 130
effective duration 130
effective tax rates 90
efficiency 15, 16, 61, 311, 316
Electrolux 329
EM (economic margins) 45, 316
embedded derivatives 243
employee satisfaction 311
employee share and option plans 112
employee share ownership trusts (ESOT) 165
EMU (Economic and Monetary Union), EU 92
ENPV (Expanded Net Present Values) 105–7
Enron 58, 277
enterprise market values 31
enterprise resource planning (ERP) 15, 277, 312,
  318, 335, 336
enterprise values 25, 28, 31, 33, 135–7
enterprise-wide risk management (EWRM) 22, 51,
  125, 169, 187–209, 338
entry to markets 18
environmental consciousness 311
environmental liabilities 231
EPS (earnings per share) 59, 316
equity
  cost of 33, 47, 52
  currency composition 54
  and debt mix 61
  derivatives 238

equity *continued*
  external 54, 62
  hedges 158
  instruments 52
  investments 164
  issuance 62
  market capitalization 33
  markets 12, 146
  price risks 204, 234
  repurchases 76–7
  return on *see* return on equity
  values, residual income models 39, 45
Equity Buyback Obligation Rights (EBOR) 260
Ericsson 1, 144, 184, 205–6, 239–40, 292, 342
Ernst & Young 77, 318
ERP *see* enterprise resource planning
ESOT (employee share ownership trusts) 165
Eurika Securitization plc 144
euro 92
EVA *see* economic value added
EVAR (excess value at risk) 178
EVP (executive vice presidents) 4
EVT (extreme value theory) 177–8
EWRM *see* enterprise-wide risk management
Excel 332
exception-driven processes 325
exception-reporting 332
excess cash flows 73
excess value at risk (EVAR) 178
exchange rates *see* foreign currencies
execution 169, 170, 257, 317–19
executive information systems 325
executive vice presidents (EVP) 4
Expanded Net Present Values (ENPV) 105–7
expansion options 102
external business environments 10–15
external debt 62
external economic trends 13
external environments 3, 10–15
external equity 54, 62
external financial market conditions 13
external funding requirements 259
external growth 6–7, 15
extreme value distribution 218–19
extreme value theory (EVT) 177–8
Exxon-Mobil 117, 243–5, 251, 307, 341

failure, avoiding 173
fair market values 28
fair value hedges 236, 237, 241
fair values 224, 243, 244
FASB (Financial Accounting Standards Board) 137, 141
FCFE (free cash flow to equity) 33

FCFF (free cash flow to the firm) 29, 32
FEI (Financial Executives Institute) 188, 191
Feldstein, Andrew 138
finance functions 4, 5–6, 8
finance receivables 235
Finance KIT 329
Financial Accounting Standards Board (FASB) 137, 141
financial analysis 28
financial comparative advantages 13
financial controls 301–7, 320
financial decisions 10, 13, 287
financial discipline 331
Financial Executives Institute (FEI) 188, 191
financial flexibility 61–3, 73–4
financial forecasting 315
financial functions 2–3
Financial Guaranty Insurance Company 143
financial institutions 51, 62, 83, 328–9, 330
financial instruments 13, 184, 186–7, 239
  see also derivatives; options; swaps; swaptions
financial leverage 12, 53, 55, 58, 66–70
financial management 2, 6, 19–20, 46, 337–8
financial markets 13, 14, 75, 134, 147
financial modeling 70–1, 266–9
financial operations 3
financial optimization 8, 340–2
financial performance 38, 321–2, 323, 326
financial planning 1–2, 3, 5, 6, 7, 10, 73, 340
  see also business and financial planning
financial policies 2, 4–5, 50–120
financial positions 59
financial projections 70
financial prudence 80
financial reporting 250–3, 336–7
financial resource optimization 338
financial risks 125, 127, 128
  management 22, 146–65, 188, 196–8, 276, 277
  Marks & Spencer 295
  on-balance-sheet 135
financial statements 8, 29, 261, 264, 265
financial strategies 3, 10–15
financial systems, real time 324–37
financing decisions 2, 25, 83
finite risk 229, 231
Finland 77
fiscal policies 11
fixed costs 84
fixed interest rates 60–1
fixed-rate debt 63
flat-rate pricing 83
flexibility 61–3, 73–4, 333
floatation of debt 62
floating interest rates 60–1

floating-rate debt and notes 63
floors 63
forecasting 253–4, 261, 268–9, 315
foreign currencies
  borrowings 164
  contracts 183–4
  debt and equity composition 54
  exchange rates 12, 146, 147, 299
    risks *see* risks *below*
  forward contracts 161, 224, 233, 238, 242, 297
  hedging 132, 209, 241
  internet transactions 276
  options 161, 238, 246
  risks 129, 131, 221, 330
    AT&T 157
    DaimlerChrysler 160
    Ericsson 239–40
    Exxon-Mobil 244
    IBM 238
    Marks & Spencer 295
    Microsoft 204
    Nestlé 235
    Royal Dutch/Shell 241
    Shell 294
    Siemens 153–4
    Toyota 234
    transaction *see* transaction risks *below*
    translation *see* translation risks *below*
  swaps 164, 223, 224, 237, 238, 242, 246
  transaction risks 160, 162, 225, 233
  translation risks 154, 159, 160, 162, 233, 240, 245
foreign investments 91
foreign subsidiaries 54, 224
foreign taxes 91
forward contracts *see* foreign currencies
fragmented application architectures 332
France 77
free cash flow 29
free cash flow to equity (FCFE) 33
free cash flow to the firm (FCFF) 29, 32
Frost, Chris 172
fund exposure management 5
fund sourcing 12
funding requirements, external 59
funding risks 299
funds, cost of 330
futures, commodities 297

GA (genetic algorithm) technology 65
GAAP *see* Generally Accepted Accounting Principles
Gartner 317, 325
General Electric 142–4, 158–9, 282, 289–90, 341
General Motors 39, 103, 168

generalized pareto distribution (GPD) 178
Generally Accepted Accounting Principles
    (GAAP) 8, 39, 43, 138, 251–3, 319
genetic algorithm (GA) technology 68
Georgio Armani 81
Germany 13, 75, 77
Gillette 83, 233, 342
GlaxoSmithKline 47, 99–100, 117–118, 164–5,
    242–3, 299–300, 342
global business environment 10
global competition 13
global contexts 10
global perspective on taxes 91–100
globalization 13, 95
GM *see* General Motors
Godiva Chocolates 81
Goldman Sachs 40
Gordon dividend discount model 32
Gordon equity valuation model 32
governance
    corporate *see* corporate governance
    risk governance 203
GPD (generalized pareto distribution) 178
Great Britain *see* United Kingdom
Greece 77
growth
    approaches to 17
    corporate life-cycles 55
    costs of 17
    earnings 20, 21–2
    external 6–7, 15
    high 15–23
    hypergrowth 18–20
    internal 6–7
    managing 18
    organic 15, 19
    profitability 15
    revenues *see* revenues
    sales 21–2
    sustainable 19, 21, 73
growth and learning perspective, performance
    measurement 322, 323

Hackett Group 282
hard risks 126
Harley Davidson 281
Harrison, Martin 331
Harvard Business Review 79, 101, 319
Hashagen, Jörg 195
hazards, risks as 174
hedging 11, 63, 130, 134, 220–3
    alternative risk management 228–30
    case studies 233–46
    DaimlerChrysler 160

disciplined risk taking 226–8
foreign currencies 132, 209, 241
GlaxoSmithKline 164
IAS 39: 223–4
insurance as strategy for 230–2
Intel 161
Microsoft 204
Nestlé 163
Procter & Gamble 208–9
ratio 129
risk classes 226, 227
risk management as integral to business 224–6
Hewlett Packard 103, 282, 301, 341
high growth 15–23
high-priced brands 82
high-severity low-frequency risks 230
higher margins 46
historical cost accounting 253
Hodrick-Prescott filters 268
HSBC 154–6, 179–81, 207, 286–7, 342
human factor losses 133
human resources 112
Hutchison-Whampoa 281
hybrid debt 56
hypergrowth 18–20
hyperinflation 14
Hyperion 268, 332
Hyperion Solutions 312

IAS (International Accounting Standards) 319
IBM 97, 115–16, 142, 237–8, 341
Iceland 77
ICI Paints 331
IFRS see International Financial Reporting
        Standards
in-house banking 293, 333
income
    approach to corporate valuation 29, 32, 33–4
    passive 95
    shifting 91
    statements 39
    transforming into gains 89
incremental-use pricing 83
index amortization swaps 65
individual income tax 77–8
industrial firms 62
industry competitive dynamics 10, 13, 15
inflation 14
information technology (IT)
    business intelligence 334–5
    fragmented application architectures 332
    see also software
Information Week 337
innovation, products 16, 17

institutional shareholders 72, 74
insurance 130, 194, 228–32
integrated financial management 337–8
integrated performance measurement 316
integrated risk management systems 332
integrated simple pricing 83
integration teams 113
Intel 18, 161–2, 186–7, 342
intellectual property 95
intellectual risks 169
'The Intelligent Enterprise' 323
inter-company dealing 333
inter-company lending 93–4, 278, 279–80
interest
    coverage 316
    cash flow risks 162
    payments 52, 94
    price risks 162
    rates see interest rates
    tax shields 53
interest rates 59, 60
    changes 11, 12, 147
    risks 11, 60–1, 129, 130, 221, 330
        Ericsson 240
        Exxon-Mobil 244
        GlaxoSmithKline 164, 299
        Marks & Spencer 295
        Microsoft 204
        Nestlé 162, 235
        Royal Dutch/Shell 241
        Shell 296
        Siemens 154
        Toyota 234–5
    swaps 63, 224
        AT&T 157
        GlaxoSmithKline 242
        IBM 237
        Procter & Gamble 208, 246
internal accounting controls 302
internal audits 22, 302
internal capital structure drivers 52
internal financing 54
internal growth 6–7
internal operations and process perspective,
        performance measurement 322, 323
internal rate of return (IRR) 100
Internal Revenue Service (IRS) 89
International Accounting Standards (IAS) 319
international financial markets 147
International Financial Reporting Standards (IFRS)
        195, 223–4, 252
intrinsic valuations 34–5
introductory phase of corporate life-cycles 55
inventories 265

inverse Gaussian distribution 215
investments
    capital *see* capital investments
    decisions 2, 10, 24–5
    foreign 91
    instruments 329
    management 3
Ireland 77
IRR (internal rate of return) 100
IRS (Internal Revenue Service) 89
IT *see* information technology
Italy 77

Japan 13, 74, 85, 257
Jen, Frank C (Ogden, Joseph P *et al*) 12
JIT (just in time) 169
job creation 16
Jobs and Growth Tax Relief Reconciliation Act 78
JP Morgan 222, 331
JP Morgan Chase 138
just in time (JIT) 169

Kaplan, Robert 331
Kartyik, Zita Imrene 331
keiretsu 257
key performance indicators (KPI) 267, 271, 317, 334
key performance measures in active use 316
Kidder Peabody 167
Kim, W Chan 15–16
knowledge management 124
Kolmogorov-Smirnov distribution 212, 217, 219
KPI *see* key performance indicators
KPMG 46, 195

Lambin, J 87
latent business risks 131
Latin hypercube simulation 65, 262, 269
leadership 257, 311
learning and growth perspective, performance
        measurement 322, 323
leases and leasing 52, 56–7, 138
Leeson, Nick 127
legal risks 169
lending, inter-company *see* inter-company lending
less-developed countries 13
leverage
    debt 52
    financial *see* financial leverage
    increases in 60
    operating *see* operating leverage
    optimization 57, 62
leveraged recapitalizations 56, 61
liabilities
    mismatches with assets 62

off-balance-sheet 8
    risk exposures as 224–5
LIBOR (London Interbank Offer Rate) 60–1
life-cycles
    businesses 54–7, 74
    products 15
Lindquist, Lars 1
lines of credit 59
liquidity 59–61, 118
    forecasts 330
    management 92–3, 277, 277–80
        Cisco Systems 298
        Citigroup 287–8
        Ericsson 292
        General Electric 289–90
        GlaxoSmithKline 299
        HSBC 286–7
        Merrill Lynch 290
    risks 22, 129, 163, 200, 207
loans, inter-company *see* inter-company lending
Lockbox 280
log-normal distribution 216
logic of value motivation 15–16
logical decision functions 267
logistic distribution 213
London Interbank Offer Rate (LIBOR) 60–1
long-range financial plans 265
long-term business plans 254
Long Term Capital Management 168
long-term debt 57
losses
    attritional 132
    catastrophic 131
    maximum possible 149
    net operating losses (NOL) 88, 90
    operational 168
    probable, estimation 177
    significant 131–2
low-severity high-frequency risks 230
Luxembourg 77

M&A *see* mergers and acquisitions
macro-economic competitive dynamics 10
macro-economic conditions 15
macro-financial competitive dynamics 10
macro-financial conditions 10–11
management by exception 262
management by objectives 323
management controls 320
managing growth 18
manufacturing companies 57, 84
margins 17, 46, 316
mark-to-market 330

market approach to corporate valuation 29, 31, 34
market-oriented economies 13
market revenue shares 79
market risks 22, 130
　AT&T 156–8
　DaimlerChrysler 159–60
　Citigroup 151
　General Electric 158–9
　HSBC 154–6, 207
　Intel 161–2
　measurement 148–50
　Merrill Lynch 203
　Siemens 151–4
　Toyota 234–5
market shares 81
market surpluses 80
market valuation 245
market value added (MVA) 42–3
market values 12, 28, 58–9
market VAR 178
marketing 82
markets
　development 18
　entries 18
　fragmentation 320
　globalization 13
　niches 11
　segmentation 11, 14
　volatility 14
　see also bonds: markets; capital markets;
　　financial markets and entries beginning
　　with market
Marks & Spencer 294–5, 304–5, 342
Matáv 331
materiality, risks 131–2
maturity analyses 60
maturity and interest refixing gap reports 330
maturity-matching principle 119
maturity stage of corporate life-cycles 55–6
Mauborgne, Renée 15–16
maximum possible loss 149
McGraw-Hill 282
McKinsey 46, 80, 87, 317
Means, Grady (Dauphinais, William G et al) 17
Measurisk.com 197
mergers and acquisitions (M&A) 15, 19, 34, 90,
　108–18, 222
Merrill Lynch 119–20, 185, 202–3, 290–2, 342
Metallgesellschaft 168
Mexico 77
Microsoft 18, 54, 57, 191–2, 204–5, 214–17, 342
minimum capital requirements 196
minority interests 34
minority values 36–7

Mobil see Exxon-Mobil
Modigliani–Miller (MM) irrelevance proposition
　53, 190
monetary policies 11
monetization 222
monitoring systems 326
Monte Carlo simulations 103, 198, 245, 262, 269
multi-channel sales distribution 18
multi-currency cash flows 329
multi-dimensional analyses 330
multi-disciplinary acquisition teams 112
multi-period stochastic programing 267
multi-year, multi-line insurance products 231
MVA (market value added) 42–3

negative arbitrage 64
negative economic profits 43
negative EVA 43
negotiating tax benefits 88
Nestlé 98, 162–3, 235–6, 297, 341
net debt 31
net operating losses (NOL) 88, 90
net operating profit after taxes (NOPAT) 40–2, 43, 44
net present values (NPV) 100–5
Netherlands 77
new technology 277–80
New Zealand 77
Nokia 294
NOL (net operating losses) 88, 90
non-financial metrics 28
non-financial operating measures 320
non-financial performance measures 38–9
non-marketability discounts 34
non-recoverers 133
NOPAT see net operating profit after taxes
Norton, David 331
Norway 77
notional pooling 93–4, 95
NPV (net present values) 100, 105

OBS see off balance sheet
Occidental 133
OCF (operating cash flows) 45
O'Connor, Phillip F (Ogden, Joseph P et al) 12
OECD (Organization for Economic Co-operation
　and Development) 77, 95
off balance sheet (OBS)
　assets 8
　contingent assets 30
　fixed obligations 52
　liabilities 8
　risks 134–46
　transactions 256, 277
offensive risk management strategies 174

Ogden, Joseph P *et al* 12
on-balance-sheet financial risks 135
on-balance-sheet production risks 135
one-time events 20–2
open market repurchases 76
operating cash flows (OCF) 45
operating conditions 308
operating cycle 273–4
operating decisions 2, 25
operating earnings 316
operating efficiencies 62, 316
operating flexibility 73
operating leases 52, 57
operating leverage 71–2, 84, 169
operating loss distribution 167
operating margins 316
operational controls 169, 170, 303
operational decisions 10
operational effectiveness 22, 169
operational losses 168
operational results 28
operational risks 125, 127, 332
    estimation 167, 168
    financing 231
    management 165–87, 188, 207
    unaffected 129
operational strategies 10
operational VAR 178
opportunities 15, 173
optimal capital budgeting with real options 100–7
optimal capital structure 51–2, 53–4, 59, 63
optimal cash management 55
optimal financial leverage ratios 66–70
optimal portfolio selection 190
optimal price determination 78–9
optimal risk tolerance 192
optimization
    analyses 267, 269
    applied financial optimization modeling 340–2
    changing operating conditions and 308
    corporate finance functions 1–23
    financial resources 338
    modeling 68
    of resources 20
options 330
    call 63
    for capital budgeting 101–2
    commodities 297
    foreign currencies 161, 238, 246
    Microsoft 204
    put 63
    real 100–7
OptQuest 332
organic growth 15, 19

Organization for Economic Co-operation and
    Development (OECD) 76, 95
outsourcing 169, 283

P/E (price-earnings) ratios 12, 13
Palepu, Krishna G 61
Palisades' BestFit analytical software 210
Palisades' RiskOptimizer 68, 269, 332
Pan Am 133
partnerships 19
pay-fixed swaps 63
pecking order hypothesis 54, 58, 63
penetration strategy 83
pensions, defined-benefit 11
PeopleSoft 267, 332
percent of sales forecasting method 268
performance
    assessments 8
    key indicators *see* key performance indicators
    management 3, 15, 255–6, 311–38
    measurement 38–48, 316, 321–2, 323
Phillip Morris 18
Pinegar, J Michael 63
planning 13, 15
    balanced scorecard as device for 323
    horizons 258–60
    taxes 3, 87–100, 277–8
    see also business and financial planning
Poland 77
political risks 14
Polverino, Antonio 222
pooling, notional 93–4, 95
portfolio optimization 103, 190
position risks 330
positioning 6, 82
post-acquisition problems 109
pre-paid pricing 83
pre-tax earnings 91
preferred stock 52
premature recognition of sales 20
price changes 84, 86–7
Price, Colin (Dauphinais, William G *et al*) 17
price-cutting 81
price discrimination 83
price-earnings (P/E) ratios 12, 13
price elasticities 85, 87
price–response estimation 85, 86–7
price risks 200
price setting 79
price skimming 82
price-to-book multiples 29
price-to-income multiples 29
PricewaterhouseCoopers 46

CEO survey 1
  dynamic value management 22
  global perspective 91, 93
  mergers and acquisitions 111, 115–16
  risk management 123, 127, 172, 173, 230
  treasury management 270, 271, 273
  ValueReporting 252, 253
pricing 14, 15, 78–87, 169
  see also transfer pricing
privacy risks 22
private companies 21, 33
privately negotiated repurchases 76
pro forma business plans 264
pro forma financial models 70–1
pro forma financial statements 261, 262, 268
pro forma financial plans 71
probable losses, estimation 177
process effectiveness 170
process efficiency 311
process execution 169, 170
process inefficiencies 169
process-led changes 8–10
Procter & Gamble 18, 98–9, 127, 128, 167, 208–9,
  245–6, 342
product management 124
production risks 134
products
  differentiation 82
  innovation 16, 17
  life-cycles 15
  quality 311
profitability 6, 11–12, 15, 84, 147, 255
profits 83, 85, 86–7
  see also economic profits
progressive segmentation 83
project appraisal techniques 100
project financing 62
prudence 80
Prudential 167
prudential risk-taking 173
public company valuation models 31–4
put options 63

Q-Risk 293
QSPE (qualifying special purpose entities) 140–2
qualified foreign corporations 78
qualifying special purpose entities (QSPE) 140–2
quality 169, 311
quantitative optimality numbers 8

radio frequency identification (RFID) 335
RAPM (risk adjusted performance measurement)
  179
RAROC *see* risk-adjusted return on capital
real options 100–7

real-time business intelligence 334, 337
real-time financial performance reporting 251
real time financial systems 324–37
real-time performance systems 333–4
recapitalizations 56, 61
receivables 265
receive-fixed swaps 63
receivers' swaptions 63
recoverers 133
reduction of taxes 91
reengineering processes 16
refunding provisions, bonds 63
reinsurance 231
reported earnings 316
reporting, financial 250–3
repurchase tender offers 76
residual income models of equity values 39, 45
resources
  optimization 20
  planning *see* enterprise resource planning
results based leadership 257
retained earnings 61, 73
retention ratios 21
return on assets 316
return on capital investment (ROIC) 26–7, 316
return on equity (ROE) 12, 21, 48, 316
return on net assets (RONA) 47
return-to-risk ratios 193
revenues
  growth 6, 15–17, 21, 46
  maximization 85
  objectives 255
  opportunities 15
  per employee 316
  price change impacts on 84
  recognition 20
RFID (radio frequency identification) 335
Rhone-Poulenc 260
risk adjusted performance measurement (RAPM) 179
risk-adjusted return on capital (RAROC) 133, 179,
  193
risk exposures 3, 5, 60–1, 126–34, 224–5, 329, 330
risk management 3, 123–6
  budgeting 129
  cash flow at risk estimation 209
  cycles 227–8
  defensive 174
  earnings at risk estimation 209–20
  enterprise-wide *see* enterprise-wide risk
    management
  financial *see* financial risks: management
  hedging strategies 220–46
  identifying and estimating risk exposure 126–34
  as integral to business 224–6
  integrated systems 332

risk management *continued*
  off-balance-sheet (OBS) risks 134–46
  offensive strategies 174
  operational *see* operational risks
  systems 328, 333
  technologies 277
  value adding 53–4
risk taking 173, 174, 202, 226–8
RiskMetrics 245, 328, 331
RiskOptimizer 65–9, 269, 332
risks
  appetites 224, 225
  assessments 15, 166
  aversion 224
  classes 226, 227
  commercial 127
  comparability 149
  control 125
  costs and, trade-off between 62
  credit *see* credit risks
  debt financing 61
  downside 174
  estimation 167, 169, 170
  evaluation 125
  exposures *see* risk exposures
  financial *see* financial risks
  financing 166, 229, 231, 232
  foreign currency *see* foreign currencies: risks
  governance 203
  hard 126
  as hazards 174
  identification 166
  integration 175
  interest rate *see* interest rates: risks
  liquidity *see* liquidity: risks
  management *see* risk management
  market *see* market risks
  materiality 131–2
  mitigation 167
  operational *see* operational risks
  as opportunities 173
  portfolios 231
  pro forma financial plans, incorporating into 70
  production 135
  reduction 167–9
  responses 166
  retention 197, 229, 230
  roll-over 64
  soft 126
  strategic 127
  taking *see* risk taking
  technical 128
  tolerance 192
  transfer 229, 230

  as uncertainties 173
  upside 174
  see also entries beginning with risk
ROE *see* return on equity
ROIC (return on capital investment) 26–7, 316
roll-over risks 62
rolling forecasts 269, 315
RONA (return on net assets) 47
Royal Dutch/Shell 187, 218–20, 241, 306–7, 341
  see also Shell

sales 20, 21–2, 261
sales, general and administrative (SG&A) expenses 316
Salomon Smith Barney 40
SAP 267, 332
Sarbanes-Oxley Act 20, 331, 336
SAVANT tax planning framework 88
scenario analyses 71, 262
scenarios 330
SCM (supply chain management) 335
Securities and Exchange Commission (SEC) 89, 135–7
securitization 97, 138–46, 256
security risks 22
Sedgwick Group 133
segmentation 11, 14, 17–18, 83
self-insurance 230
semi-variable costs 82
sensitivity analyses 71
  AT&T 157
  business and financial planning 262–5
  General Electric 158
  GlaxoSmithKline 164
  Intel 161
  Procter & Gamble 245
  Siemens 152
  Toyota 235
sequential compound options 102
service firms 84
settlement risks 163
SG&A (sales, general and administrative) expenses 316
SGR (sustainable growth rates) 73
share buybacks *see* stock repurchases
share value performance 133
shareholder value
  cost of capital 96
  creation 58, 252, 255
  drivers of 176
  maximization 2, 24–48
  revenue growth and 16
  risk management and 125, 146
shareholders
  bondholders and, conflicts between 74

controlling 34
influence on boardrooms 149
institutional 72–4
mergers and acquisitions concerns 111–14
total shareholder returns (TSR) 17, 28
see also shareholder value 193
Sharpe ratios 282, 296–7
Shell
see also Royal Dutch/Shell
shifting, tax savings strategies 88
shock tests 158
short-termism 147
Siberg, Johan 1
Siemens 51, 151–4, 201–2, 222, 341
significant losses 131–2
simulations 68, 70, 104–5, 257, 262, 268–9, 340
see also Monte Carlo simulations
social consciousness 311
soft risks 126
software
corporate performance management 316–17
real time financial systems 324–37
simulation 68, 269
Sortino ratios 193
source of financing approach to calculation of
capital 42
special purpose entities (SPE) 137, 140–4
special purpose vehicles (SPV) 139
speculation 221
splitting, tax savings strategies 88
spreadsheets 313, 330, 331, 332
Sprint 103
SPV (special purpose vehicles) 139
Stalnecker, Susan 197
Standard and Poor's 138
Stern Stewart 40
Stimpson, Mark 331
stochastic business planning 308
stochastic dynamic simulation models 340
stochastic programing 267
stock intensive-related structured products 222
stock markets 133
stock prices 73
stock repurchases 13, 54, 72–3, 74, 75
stockholders *see* shareholders
stop loss limits, foreign currency transactions 225
STP *see* straight through processing
straight debt 61
straight through processing (STP) 277, 280–4, 329
strategic analysis 28
strategic controls 303
strategic financial planning 1–2
strategic logic of high growth 15–23
strategic planning 15

strategic pricing 80
strategic risks 127
strategy and action, links between 324
strategy execution effectiveness 311
strategy implementation 318
streaming caches 325
stress testing 148–9, 156, 192–3, 262, 288–7
structured finance 138
structured financial vehicles 63
subsidiaries, foreign 54, 224
subsidiary budgets 266
Sumitomo Corporation 168
supply chains 95–6
management (SCM) 335
risks 169
sustainability, corporate 252
sustainable growth 19, 21
sustainable growth rates (SGR) 73
swap-linked notes 63
swaps
credit default 223
commodities 298
foreign currencies *see* foreign currencies
interest rates *see* interest rates
swaptions 63, 224
Sweden 77
switching options 102
Switzerland 77
synergies 108–9, 111, 115
synergistic acquisitions 19
synthetic asset exposures 221
synthetic leases 138

tactical controls 303
tax-free bonds 90
taxes 11
deferral 90, 91
dividends, policies 77–8
foreign 91
global perspective 91–100
planning 3, 87–100, 277–8
reduction 91
reviewing implications for each jurisdiction 94
savings strategies 88
shields 52–3
technical risks 128
technology 277–81, 318
temporal processing 325
Texaco 168
thin capitalization 94
TIBCO 329
time value of money 88
timing differences 91
top-down approach to NOPAT 41–2

total quality management (TQM) 169
total shareholder returns (TSR) 17, 27
Toyota 98, 145–6, 160–1, 186, 233–5, 296, 341
TQM (total quality management) 169
trade receivables 186–7
trading derivatives 236
transaction risks *see* foreign currencies
transfer pricing 83, 94, 95
transforming income into gains 89
translation risks *see* foreign currencies
transparency 251, 312
treasuries 5
  management 92–3, 96, 269–301, 328, 332
  operations 3, 232
Treasury and Risk Management 273
Trema 329
triangular distribution 211
true EVA 43
TSR (total shareholder returns) 17, 27
Tufano, Peter 260
'tyranny of the executive' 4

UK *see* United Kingdom
uncertainties 6, 173
Union Carbide 133
United Grain Growers 191–2
United Kingdom
  dividend tax policies 77
  market-oriented economy 13
United States
  capital markets 12–13
  dividends, double taxation of 75
  Jobs and Growth Tax Relief Reconciliation Act
    78
  market-oriented economy 13
  Sarbanes-Oxley Act 20, 331, 336
Unocal Corp 191
upside cases 261
upside risks 174

valuations
  corporate 26, 28–37
  economic 26
  intrinsic 34–5
  mergers and acquisitions 109
value-adding 53–4, 88, 176, 257
value at risk (VAR) 126, 128–9, 132, 192–3
  DaimlerChrysler 159, 185
  delta method 177
  excess (EVAR) 178
  HSBC 156
  market risk measurement 148–50
  Microsoft 204–5
  Nokia 294

operational risks 167
Procter & Gamble 245
Siemens 152
Toyota 234
value based management (VBM) 26–7, 311
value based metrics 40
value-based pricing 80–81
value centers 28
value chains 96
value creation 6, 26
value drivers 46
value loss 113
value management 22–3, 26
value maximization 8, 21, 24–48, 340
value measures 28
value motivation, logic of 15–16
value protection and enhancement 114–18
ValueReporting 252, 253
VAR *see* value at risk (VAR)
variable cost pricing 82
variable costs 84
variable interest entities (VIE) 137–8, 144
variance, cash flows 126
VBM (value based management) 26–7, 311
VIE (variable interest entities) 137–8, 144
Virgin Atlantic 16
virtual close 226
volatility 148
  cash flows 126
  earnings 149, 167
  financial markets 134
  management 208
  markets 14
volume goals 85
WACC *see* weighted average cost of capital
warrants 238
Weibull distribution 219–20
weighted average cost of capital (WACC) 26–7, 29,
    32, 40, 43, 53
White Plains 267
Wilbright, Lisa 63
Wilson, Thomas 149
'winner's curse' 111
working capital 59, 256, 259, 265, 278
World Economic Forum 16
worst case scenarios 330

yields, dividends 12, 75

Zarhamee, Nazhin 312
zero balancing 93
zero-interest cost debt 59